The Origins of the Modern
Japanese Bureaucracy

Published:
Women and Democracy in Cold War Japan, Jan Bardsley
Christianity and Imperialism in Modern Japan, Emily Anderson
The China Problem in Postwar Japan, Robert Hoppens
Media, Propaganda and Politics in 20th-Century Japan, The Asahi Shimbun Company (translated by Barak Kushner)
Contemporary Sino-Japanese Relations on Screen, Griseldis Kirsch
Debating Otaku in Contemporary Japan,
edited by Patrick W. Galbraith, Thiam Huat Kam and Björn-Ole Kamm
Politics and Power in 20th-Century Japan, Mikuriya Takashi and Nakamura Takafusa (translated by Timothy S. George)
Japanese Taiwan, edited by Andrew D. Morris
Japan's Postwar Military and Civil Society, Tomoyuki Sasaki
The History of Japanese Psychology, Brian J. McVeigh
Postwar Emigration to South America from Japan and the Ryukyu Islands,
Pedro Iacobelli

The Origins of the Modern Japanese Bureaucracy

Yuichiro Shimizu, Keio University, Japan
Translated by Amin Ghadimi, Utsunomiya University, Japan

BLOOMSBURY ACADEMIC
LONDON • NEW YORK • OXFORD • NEW DELHI • SYDNEY

BLOOMSBURY ACADEMIC
Bloomsbury Publishing Plc
50 Bedford Square, London, WC1B 3DP, UK
1385 Broadway, New York, NY 10018, USA

BLOOMSBURY, BLOOMSBURY ACADEMIC and the Diana logo
are trademarks of Bloomsbury Publishing Plc

First published in Great Britain 2020

Cover image: Exams for higher civil service held in a classroom in the Hongo
campus of Tokyo Imperial University. 1946/11. © Shigeo Hayashi/The Center of
the Tokyo Raids and War Damage.

A catalogue record for this book is available from the British Library.

A catalog record for this book is available from the Library of Congress.

ISBN: HB: 978-1-3500-7955-7
         ePDF: 978-1-3500-7956-4
      eBook: 978-1-3500-7957-1

Typeset by Integra Software Services Pvt. Ltd.
Printed and bound in Great Britain

To find out more about our authors and books visit www.bloomsbury.com
and sign up for our newsletters.

Contents

Figures

Acknowledgements

Five years after the Japanese-language edition appeared, *The Origins of the Modern Japanese Bureaucracy* now faces the scrutiny of the English-reading world. The intervening half-decade has offered me a chance to encounter anew and deepen my interaction with the global community of Japanese studies – and thereby to re-evaluate the significance of my own research.

Accompanied by my family, I arrived in Boston in the spring of 2014 to begin a stint as a visiting researcher at the Reischauer Institute of Japanese Studies at Harvard University. As if in a dream, I was immersed in an environment where Japan scholars from around the world gathered together. I came to understand, through forums organized twice a week, how Japan studies in the United Studies, Japan studies in Europe, and Japan studies in Japan each bears its own dynamic historiography and operates under that heritage.

Many scholars from Japan use their time abroad to discover new sources and write new articles; I invested my energies in presenting my research in English. As I bustled about with imperfect English, Professor Andrew Gordon, my host professor, looked after me with smiling solicitude, and Ted Gilman, director of the Reischauer Institute, introduced various conferences to me. Benefiting from their aid, I had the chance to present at various places: I gave reports at the conference of Asian Studies on the Pacific Coast (ASPAC), the New York Conference on Asian Studies (NYCAS) and the Australian Political Studies Association (APSA), as well as at the research forum on the First World War at Ruhr-Universität Bochum and the Modern Japan Workshop at the University of Pennsylvania; I delivered lectures, moreover, at the University of Edinburgh, the University of Nottingham, Ruhr-Universität Bochum, Freie Universität Berlin and the University of Oxford.

At each of these venues, I discussed part of the content of this book; I spoke on the birth and development of the bureaucracy of modern Japan. These experiences provided me with diverse new perspectives different from those I had gained through discussions in Japan. As my conversations continued, I began to wish I could share the content of this book with even more people.

Conversations at Harvard with Amin Ghadimi had broadened my perspectives, and indeed it was he who was able to help me realize my vision. Amin responded to my wish, drawing from the depth of his education and from a sense of love to produce an elegantly and carefully rendered draft. If there are any shortcomings in this book, they are the fault of its original author; if there are moments where it shines, they are because of the warm thought and deep understanding of Amin. Professor Gordon, one of Amin's advisors, offered abundant advice on the publication of this book. My admiration of and gratitude for his generosity are boundless.

Through my unfamiliarity with the English-language publication process, I was patiently guided by Dr Christopher Gerteis, the editor of the series to which this book belongs, and by Rhodri Mogford, Beatriz Lopez and Laura Reeves, members of the staff at Bloomsbury. I would also like to acknowledge my gratitude to Keio University, my place of employment, for the financial support it provided for the translation of this book.

This book has forged new bonds for me with truly a great many people. Just as the bureaucrats of the Meiji era spurred one another on to make modern Japan, I hope this book will build further bonds that will help open new horizons for the study of Japan. And as I thank the many people who made this book possible, most of all I dedicate this book to my family, who let me spend so much of my time off jetting about the world.

Yuichiro Shimizu
2 December 2018
En route home from Berlin

Translator's Preface

It must be regarded as among the most extraordinary and important documents in history. In the Charter Oath of 1868, the fledgling Meiji regime promised its people deliberative councils and public discussion. It pledged to unite all classes. It hailed the pursuit of knowledge throughout the world. Perhaps the Oath was a vague, deliberately tergiversating document aimed primarily at placating restive powers, concerned with securing legitimacy for a regime with almost none to its name. But the principles it proclaimed marked an unmistakable revolution into modernity.

In this astonishing, at times exhilarating book, fastidious in its documentation of the twists and turns of pre-war politics yet endearing in the tales it tells of the builders of Japanese modernity, Professor Yuichirō Shimizu makes a brazen, intensely controvertible, but vigorously and bracingly argued claim: the Meiji regime fulfilled the spirit of the Charter Oath, especially that of its third clause, which promised that every man 'be allowed to pursue his calling so that there may be no discontent'. With little other choice once Tokugawa autocracy came crashing down, the Meiji regime built up a bureaucracy and thereby an entire nation founded on the fundamental belief that the individual Japanese citizen must learn for himself, know for himself and run after his own ambitions. And if only he worked and studied hard enough, that citizen could rise to the helm of his entire nation.

By announcing and fulfilling the promises of the Charter Oath, the Meiji government led an upheaval in politics and society without precedent in the Japanese past. It tore down centuries of a hereditary tradition that had barred all but a privileged few from governmental affairs. It obliterated a status system that had pervaded an early modern federalist state and had harshly curtailed access to knowledge and power. It established a sophisticated network of educational institutions to train men in the cutting edge of learning. It flung the doors of education and government open to human talent irrespective of social or geographic origin. It recruited these living resources to help in ruling over the people. And because the Meiji regime succeeded in gathering talented men, in training and educating them, in using them to build a meritocratic system of bureaucracy, it made modern Japan.

Professor Shimizu writes that these changes were 'epochal', that things 'transformed', that 'new eras were made'. We might call these transformations revolutionary. The upheavals he brings to life entailed the cultivation of a new form of common sense in which public debate and deliberation supported rather than vitiated the power of the state. They made a world in which practical, applied education, and the knowledge and power that that education endowed in the individual, became the bedrock of civilization and government. The Meiji regime built a new nation on a new belief in the benefits of knowing and being for oneself.

The image of the Meiji state that emerges in Professor Shimizu's account is of benevolent authoritarianism, of a regime that did not entirely intend to cede the clutches of power even as it opened up unprecedented possibilities for men to join it and support it. Perhaps ironically, the generality of people did not have much of a say in changes that targeted them. Everyday men – and often they were descendants of samurai, not really everyday men – studied, strove and functioned well within a system largely ordained for them by the state. If they did what they were told, they could join the authorities. Join they did. Upstarts born in the bakumatsu and Meiji eras streamed into new schools and universities, marched into the state and toppled the oligarchic bureaucracy. They formed new cliques of the *haut monde*, displacing factionalist oligarchy with academic elitism, replacing one form of snobbish exclusivity with another. In Professor Shimizu's account, this system worked. His is a story of elites working on behalf of the people, of generally rather good elites, of elites with the usual foibles and flaws but with unusual vision and ambition.

We might find ample evidence within the study to undermine the general success story it conjures up. Corruption appears but is often brushed aside. Women remain invisible. The empire exists, seemingly inertly, as an empty stage on which Gotō Shinpei flashes his executive panache. Professor Shimizu does not downplay these important elements of Japanese history because he is callous or blasé. They matter to him. But they do not, in his reading, change the fundamental point that men could pursue their political calling for the first time in Japanese history; that government became based on male talent not on male pedigree; that it was these changes that engendered modernity. We might disagree. But we must admire the cogency and audacity with which Professor Shimizu sets forth his argument and push back with equal and opposite cogency and audacity. And that will be no easy task.

This might not be a breezy book to read. And that is the whole point. In some places, Professor Shimizu argues through personal story, his human narratives bringing to scintillating life a revolutionary spirit of ambition and achievement. But elsewhere, Professor Shimizu argues through the byzantine bureaucratic itself, untiringly tracking the shifting policies and practices of a mercurial regime. It is a brilliant intellectual strategy, part and parcel of his audacious argument. Our English-language historiography has largely abjured high-end political histories of Japan in favour of more socially and culturally oriented studies. The turn has helped to correct for history-writing in which everyday people hardly mattered, in which the state had seeming omnipotence in directing the nation. But the turn has come with an unfortunate cost: where once the historiography might have exaggerated the power of the pre-war Japanese state, perhaps it now fails to give it due justice. In unapologetically describing the endless, excruciating configuration and dissolution and reconfiguration of ministries and departments and political posts and administrative titles, Professor Shimizu makes an important stand for the central importance of these seemingly recondite details to understanding Japanese history. These were not mere cosmetic changes. They cannot be separated from the personal narratives of the characters punctuating the book, the men and women populating the Japanese past. The political details were at the very heart of the development of a government by meritocracy, of a world in which individual striving could lead to power, of a past in which the destiny of an entire nation rested on the knowing and learning of its constituent members.

It is a thrill to make this sterling book available to readers of English. I hope they enjoy it as much as I have.

Amin Ghadimi
Kobe, Japan

Introduction

What is a bureaucracy? Whence does it come? Whither does it go?

Japanese have long described their politics as a 'kingdom of bureaucrats', as a world of 'executive supremacy', as a realm 'forlorn of politicians'. True, the bureaucracy is a faceless behemoth wielding formidable power, but it is a behemoth that gets things done – such has been the image that 'bureaucracy' has long evoked.[1]

Things changed when the economic bubble burst at the end of the twentieth century. Bureaucrats responded fecklessly to the crisis. Japan tumbled into befuddlement. Botched responses to healthcare scandals, a spate of corruption incidents – as controversies piled up, trust in the national bureaucracy, built up over so many years, came crashing down. Blame for the stagnation of a nation, for what was scorned as 'two lost decades', was heaped onto the bureaucratic governance of the Liberal Democratic Party. In 2009, the Democratic Party of Japan (DPJ) swept into power and shoved the government by bureaucrats aside. In the first genuine transfer of administrative authority since the Second World War, the DPJ claimed to form a government by politicians.[2]

The rise of a government by politicians transformed the nature of rule. In itself it resolved problems that had accumulated over time. But the state floundered as bureaucratic talent went unexploited.[3] As the DPJ administration entered its latter years, people began to murmur. Had the broadsides hurled at the bureaucracy gone too far?[4]

The Cabinet of Shinzo Abe elevated the decision-making functions of the office of the prime minister to a point that some see as a new threshold in governance by politicians.[5] Supporting the work of the office are seven politicians accompanied by three hundred bureaucrats; before reform, there were three politicians and twenty bureaucrats.[6] It is true that there are more politicians. But the bureaucracy, even more, has burgeoned. Do we find here a government by politics or a government by bureaucracy? Fundamental questions have emerged anew. How should a government be? How should politicians be? How should a bureaucracy be?

--

When we trace it through time, we find the origins of the modern Japanese bureaucracy in the Meiji Restoration.

Born in the Meiji era as the load-bearing pillars of the executive state, bureaucrats accumulated experience in governance, applied themselves to government management and transformed into politicians. Their path from bureaucrat to politician was the path of *risshin shusse*, that ideal of rising through the world by autonomous will. It was a path carved out as modern Japan itself took form. Scores of young men in the Meiji era began marching down this path.[7]

There is no shortage of studies that tell the history of Japan through political figures. Saigō Takamori, Ōkubo Toshimichi, Kido Kōin – shelves and shelves tell the story of the Meiji Restoration as the story of the accomplishments of these and other 'men of spirit'.[8] Then more bookcases tell the history of party politics as the history of Hara Kei and Hamaguchi Osachi and their infighting.[9] But there is something that comes prior to these men, something that made them and their lives possible: a bureaucracy of men with professional, specialized knowledge. It was only after these bureaucrats had built a stage that politicians could step onto it.

It is especially significant that a path opened in Japan for bureaucrats who gained government experience to turn into politicians.[10] The bureaucrats who made the Meiji regime transformed into oligarch-politicians and dedicated themselves to building a constitutional system. The bureaucrats who then built that national constitutional system became bureaucrat-politicians who led the First Sino-Japanese and the Russo-Japanese wars. They then entered political parties and drove Japanese party politics. Institutions made men, and men made institutions.

Hara Kei, Takahashi Korekiyo, Katō Kōmei, Wakatsuki Reijirō, Tanaka Giichi, Hamaguchi Osachi – these and most of the other outstanding politicians of the early era of party politics began their years as bureaucrats. In the post-war era, prime ministers from Yoshida Shigeru to Miyazawa Kiichi started their careers in the bureaucracy. Even today, in the twenty-first century, the bureaucracy remains the primary launching pad for politicians. This is strange. Japan took Britain, Germany and the United States as its models for modernization, but in none of these nations do we find a pattern of bureaucrats turning into politicians.[11] Examples of men who made it all the way from the bureaucracy to the presidency or the prime ministership are scanty.

Post-war Japanese politics has of course operated under a parliamentary cabinet system, one that extends from the pre-war era.[12] It is well understood that policy in this Japanese political system is born from the collaborative relationship between politicians and bureaucrats.[13] But what is the basis of that relationship? The two are intimately linked by a path on which bureaucrats transformed into politicians.

--

It was because human talent was so concentrated in the bureaucracy that this system of close links between bureaucracy and politics emerged. The Meiji regime opened the path to bureaucracy to youths across the country. It brought talented young men into its fold through its nationwide school system. That the future of modern Japan was made through learning, that the vitality of the entire nation was built through the realization of the ideal of rising in the world by autonomous will (*risshin shusse*) – these realities are well known.[14] But where did individual ambition lead? Boys studied hard to reach the road to the bureaucracy, where they could go on to take charge of the executive state. It was a road that was already paved for them.

It would have been possible, of course, for Satsuma, Chōshū and other winners of the Boshin War to consolidate the world of officialdom on their own. And yet they opened the path to the bureaucracy to men across the nation. Here we can discern the grand plan of the Meiji government: to build up a prosperous nation through the individual will and calling (*kokorozashi*) of each of its constituent members.

Men could partake in politics through elections, and they could the join the executive government by becoming bureaucrats – developing these dual forms of government participation endowed the Meiji government with thoroughgoing legitimacy as a national administration both in name and in practice. As the legitimated state began attracting talented young men to serve as its supporting human resources, modern Japan itself began its process of progress.

--

To tell the history of the Japanese bureaucracy is to tell the history of the making of modern Japanese politics itself. And yet no one, until now, has undertaken this endeavour. Political history has told the past by depicting individual politicians or their circumstances. Historians of different eras have each focused on their particular periods of expertise and resisted extending beyond their specializations. The result is a dearth of work that examines a particular theme over a long span of time. Because trees are so intricately studied, the forest is hard to see.

--

A broader vista on the bureaucracy brings new insights not only to the study of history but also to that of politics and of society. Japan has long been taken as a prototype of the administrative state, of a nation dominated by the executive branch (*gyōsei kokka*).[15] Japanese bureaucrats have been seen as both extraordinarily talented and formidably powerful.[16] Why did a quintessential administrative state emerge in Japan? Through this book, we can arrive at an understanding of the historical structures of that state.

Scholarship today continues to speak of the deep professionalization and specialized abilities of Japanese bureaucrats.[17] These features developed because Japan established institutions for professional education, most notably universities, from the very beginning of its modernity and set up a system to assemble into the executive state the human resources that those institutions nurtured. If we think by means of theories of historical institutionalism, then we might say that a system of concentrating human resources in the state administration became locked in during the mid-Meiji era.[18] By path dependency, the system persisted to this very day, continually propping up the executive branch.

Of course, these developments were not purely good. From the perspective of political science, we might see that the system produced over-reliance on a government some call a 'dominating overlord', an *okami*. This over-reliance obstructed the development of autonomy among the general population. Throughout the arguments of this book appears what is often taken as a problem of Japanese politics: low political consciousness among citizens in a representative democratic system.[19]

Another negative by-product of the administrative state was that the great acclaim heaped onto the bureaucracy forced bureaucrats to overwork under its weight. In a case of telling irony, none other than the Ministry of Health, Labour, and Welfare (*kōsei rōdō shō*), which is supposed to oversee labour administration, is often taken as a token site of bureaucratic overwork.[20] It has become clear that the reason for this overwork lies in the dearth of career-track national public servants in Japan.[21] These conditions did not arise in the post-war era. They arose from a political culture, a social culture and a bureaucratic culture that developed before the Second World War – developments this book elucidates.

This book ventures to tell the story of the birth and growth of Japanese bureaucracy over the half-century between the Meiji Restoration and the era of Taishō democracy. From where did the men in the bureaucracy come, and where did they go? By tracing their footsteps, I seek to answer a basic question: what is a bureaucracy?

How did the bureaucrats born in the era of the Meiji Restoration learn of the executive systems of the West and establish them in Japan? As a cabinet system was built, the Meiji Constitution applied and the modern nation-state itself reared, how was the human talent that became the bureaucracy assembled, cultivated and organized into an institution? How did bureaucrats navigate the movement towards party politics? In all of these processes we find young men who dreamed of rising in the world by their own will, who dedicated themselves to academic endeavour and who strove after their own success.

By examining the systems that gave rise to the bureaucracy, and by casting a light on the thoughts of the youth who became its officers, we can draw nearer to an understanding of the reality of bureaucracy. I hope we can, as a result, transcend mere superficial chatter based on outward appearances and think about the nature of bureaucracy, and the nature of Japanese government itself, with a more constructive vision.

1

The Making of Restoration Bureaucrats

The birth of the Meiji state: Establishing executive structures

The restoration of imperial rule (ōsei fukko) and a new administration

In the early spring of 1867, the third year of the Keiō era, the Tokugawa bakufu began a rapid descent into demise. At the end of the previous reign year, the Kōmei emperor, who had dedicated himself to the policy of unifying the imperial court and the Tokugawa bakufu (kōbu gattai), perished abruptly. The new year opened with Imperial Prince Mutsuhito ascending the throne. He was just 15 years old.[1] The Meiji era began. Suppressed up to this point, anti-bakufu agitation was ignited into a full-fledged movement. Satsuma and other domains marched troops to the imperial capital of Kyoto in the tenth month to demand the abdication of the shogun. Tensions flared.

The bakufu responded forthwith. To forestall his adversaries, Shogun Tokugawa Yoshinobu resolved to return political power to the imperial court (taisei hōkan). The designs of the anti-bakufu faction, which had banked on violence to settle scores, were confounded. The decision kept the expansive territory and military might of the now-defunct bakufu intact. The prospect that the disbanded bakufu would retain political influence even in a remodelled political infrastructure seemed favourable.[2]

The idea of 'public opinion' or 'public debate' (kōgi) came to form the foundation of a new political structure. Visions emerged of a disavowal of shogun-centred autocracy: in a new political authority based on deliberative organs, men of power would consult on and determine the course of governance. All had plainly seen, in the wake of the Black Ships over a decade earlier, that the political machinery of the Tokugawa state had been malfunctioning. As autocratic rule came undone, a participatory political model centred on public discussion became a means of securing political legitimacy. Many influential power-holders, including those from the bakufu, rallied behind the inauguration of this new system of public debate. But a question remained: who would actually implement it? Who would make the system work?

On the ninth day of the twelfth month (= 3 January 1868), the imperial court proclaimed the Restoration of Imperial Rule (ōsei fukko), taking advantage of the power handed to it by the bakufu to declare a new government based on public opinion. With this decree, a range of administrative posts that had been responsible for substantive governance in the bakuhan system were dissolved: the shogunate, the regency (sesshō) and the chancellorship (kanpaku) were all eliminated, as were the posts of the second to the chancellor (*nairan*); the commissioners of state affairs (*kokuji goyō gakari*); the aides to the imperial court (*gisō*); the liaisons between the imperial court and the bakufu (*buke tensō*); the guardians in the imperial capital (*shugoshoku*); and the military governor of the imperial capital (*shoshidai*).[3,4]

This change in government was not brought about by the anti-bakufu faction alone. The Satsuma domain, present-day Kagoshima, had of course acted as its prime mover, but the Geishū domain, or Hiroshima, which had mobilized behind the return of power to the court; the Echizen domain, or Fukui, which was close to the bakufu; and the Tosa domain, or Kōchi, all fully supported the change – a change that was carried out only after it was communicated to Tokugawa Yoshinobu himself.[5] At this stage, then, the 'public debate' envisioned in the new government still included the voice of the shogunal household.

What was carried out at this point was the elimination of old forces that would impede the peaceful inauguration of a government by public debate. Such a peaceful transition entailed two processes: the replacement of one centre of authority with another, and the development of a system that would support this new authority. In the first process, the upper nobility (*jōkyū kuge*) represented by the five regent houses (*gosekke*) was ejected from power and replaced by mid- and lower nobles from anti-bakufu forces. A hereditary order of noble society (*kuge shakai*) that had endured for over a thousand years collapsed, and in its place emerged a system of rewards and merits (*ronkō no taikei*) based on the degree of contribution one had made to regime change.

Change overcame samurai society in the second process. *Shinpan* and *fudai* daimyo found their power eroded. These had been daimyo closest to the bakufu, represented by the guardian of the imperial capital (*Kyōto shugoshoku*), a position held by Aizu domain head Matsudaira Katamori, and by the imperial capital military governor (*shoshidai*), a post held by Kuwana domain head Matsudaira Sadaaki. Into their void stepped the *yūhan*, powerful daimyo of relatively distant, large domains. Thus crumbled a feudal order based on relative propinquity to the authority of the shogunal household, an order that had persisted for over seven hundred years since the rise of the Kamakura bakufu. Its limits had been fatally exposed during the political upheavals of the end of the Tokugawa era.[6]

These were epochal transformations. A system of dual authority splitting power between the court and the bakufu had been firmly established for so long that it seemed entirely natural, so natural as to defy questioning or doubt. Now, in a single instant, leaders sought to transform both sides in the balance of power. It was only a matter of course that dissent would erupt. The only common objective uniting the powers behind the political upheaval was a commitment to reforming the structure of rule. They shared no consensus on the content of reform. In the common bed of regime change, they dreamed different dreams. Right from the outset, the treatment of the household of Tokugawa Yoshinobu, the largest domain-holder, led to deep conflict.

To carry the political transformation to its completion, the new regime had to build legitimacy and open chances for political engagement to a vast number of power-holders. It attenuated the persistent influence of regents and chancellors (*sekkan*) as well as of *shinpan* and *fudai* daimyo; abjured the bakuhan system; and created an open government built on new political forces. It cemented its authority by upholding the restoration of imperial rule (*ōsei fukko*) and opened up new possibilities for political participation through the ideal of public debate. These reforms flowed from the currents of change that had overwhelmed Japan since its opening to the West.

A new government by new men of talent

Who would make a government by public discussion work once forces from the past had been overcome? To gain legitimacy, the new government needed to construct a sphere for open discussion and to promote channels for the employment of human resources.

The imperial court, which for so long had outsourced executive functions to warrior households, hardly contained within it adequate personnel for governance. To build a modern nation-state surrounded by Western imperial powers, the court had to transcend internal barriers separating domains and bring talent from across the archipelago to a national centre.

The task of recruiting men of talent indeed constituted the core problem in building a political structure based on public debate. The Proclamation of the Restoration of Imperial Rule (*ōsei fukko no daigōrei*) itself had described securing human resources as 'a matter of foremost urgency' and had called for a meritocratic system of employing personnel irrespective of status.

A model for this new system was laid out in 'An Outline of Eight Steps to a New Government' (*Shin seifu kōryō hassaku*), a text from 1867 commonly attributed to Sakamoto Ryōma. In this treatise, based on his earlier 'Eight Steps Aboard a Ship', Sakamoto delineated two types of personnel the new administration would need.

The first type was made up of 'men of talent renowned across the realm' (*tenka yūmei no jinzai*). Amid the upheavals of the end of the Tokugawa era, scholars and 'men of spirit' (*shishi*) had traversed the nation, and as human talent had thus scattered across the archipelago, knowledge of that talent, too, had grown. Sakamoto sought to exploit this network and summon men well-versed in Western knowledge as well as young, up-and-coming leaders to the national centre. Once assembled, these men could apply their expertise to the task of governing.

The second type of human resource was that of 'wealthy daimyo' (*yūzai no shokō*), a term Sakamoto used to refer to *yūhan*, heads of powerful tozama domains. It was these domain heads, with their formidable military and economic might as well as their superior personal capabilities, who could determine the success or failure of the nascent political transformation. What roles they would play constituted a major topic of concern to him and the state.

It was not just military might but also intellectual prowess that Sakamoto sought in these human resources. What was needed was for people of talent, regardless of their status-group affiliations, to express their views and to build an open sphere of discourse – and thus to chart a new course for the nation. The championing of a meritocratic system to employ human resources irrespective of status origins was epochal.

Japanese society from the Tokugawa era back had long been founded on an unyielding status system. In the later years of the Tokugawa, as the limitations of that system had begun to show, avenues for promoting men of talent independent of status had emerged. But those avenues were extremely narrow.[7] They did not suffice for a government of public opinion, which needed a vast concatenation of human resources with intellectual capabilities fit for the task of governing. The employment of talented men indeed constituted 'a matter of foremost urgency' for a new regime.

The Conference of Three Offices (*sanshoku kaigi*): A prototype for organs of public debate

The state embarked on building its structures of rule by first laying out three offices (*sanshoku*): the office of chief executives (*sōsai*); of senior councillors (*gijō*); and of junior councillors (*san'yo*).[8] It was a stopgap measure, to be sure: the powers and authorities of each office were fuzzy.

To the post of chief executive rose Arisugawa-no-Miya Taruhiko, the tutor (*hodō*) of the Meiji emperor. To senior councillor rose Ninnaji-no-Miya Yoshiaki and Yamashina-no-Miya Akira, both from the imperial family. These were symbolic appointments, meant to represent the ideal of the restoration of imperial rule. The appointees had few chances to exercise independent influence.

Decision-making devolved on senior councillors selected from noble and samurai households (*kuge, buke*). Towards the goal of a government by public opinion, these senior councillors formed a council known as the Upper Conference (*ue no kaigi*).[9] The council included Nakayama Tadayasu, Ōgimachisanjō Sanenaru and Nakamikado Tsuneyuki, appointees from the nobility. These men had all been involved in the so-called Secret Imperial Rescript to Assail the Bakufu (*tōbaku no micchoku*). But they were not chosen to reward meritorious action (*ronkō kōshō*). Rather, in the throes of a political watershed shrouded in uncertainty, someone needed to prop up the state. These appointees played that role.

Real power lay in the hands of Iwakura Tomomi. Perhaps because he was of relatively humble origins, he was at first chosen only as a junior councillor. But he rose swiftly to the post of senior councillor. When Sanjō Sanetomi, who had been ejected from the imperial capital in the Kinmon Incident of 1864, returned to Kyoto, Iwakura banded with him to form the central axis of the new administration. Iwakura then planted his allies in the state affairs commission (*goyō gakari*), which took charge of administrative affairs for the Conference of Three Offices, tightening his grip on power through administrative means.

Both Iwakura and Sanjō had been members of the anti-bakufu faction. They had been placed under house arrest (*kinshin*) during the reign of the Kōmei emperor, but they were pardoned with the succession of the Meiji emperor. As they gained influence, upper nobility in such high positions as the regency, the chancellorship and the court-bakufu liaisonship all fell from power, usurped by men of talent among the fervent nobles of the anti-bakufu faction. Such displacements showed that the *coup d'état* restoring power to the imperial court was not a phenomenon confined to warrior society. It was an all-encompassing upheaval that swept noble society, too, into its fold.

Five men from samurai households were also chosen as senior councillors: Tokugawa Yoshikatsu of Owari, Matsudaira Yoshinaga of Echizen, Asano Nagakoto of Geishū, Yamauchi Toyoshige of Tosa and Shimazu Tadayoshi of Satsuma. All were former or active heads of large domains who exercised real authority. At the end of the month, Date Munenari of Uwajima was added to their number.

Two factions thus made up the Upper Conference: anti-bakufu nobles (*tōbaku-ha kuge*), who were backed by the influence of the Emperor, and domain heads (*shokō*), who held economic and military might. They were sharply divided.

The Upper Conference was a decision-making body, but these nobles and daimyo who constituted it had no executive experience. They needed the practical dimensions of any matter discussed and sorted out for them before it reached them. This responsibility devolved on the Lower Conference, which was made up of the junior councillors.[10]

Appointed to the Lower Conference from the nobility were such up-and-comers in the anti-bakufu faction as Hashimoto Saneyana. Chosen, too, was Saionji Kinmochi, who later went on to become prime minister. He was just 20 years of age. From among the samurai, eleven were chosen. Daimyo selected as senior councillors were enjoined to appoint junior councillors from their respective domains: from Owari, two junior councillors were appointed, including Tanaka Fujimaro; from Echizen, three, including Nakane Yukie; from Geishū, three, including Tsuji Shōsō; from Tosa, three, including Gotō Shōjirō; and from Satsuma, three, including Saigō Takamori and Ōkubo Toshimichi. To be sure, all appointees were powerful samurai who had substantial experience leading their respective large domains. But in the context of the collapsed Tokugawa status system, these were selections without precedent.

The Conference of Three Offices was thus inaugurated, giving form to a new mode of rule. Moulded laboriously from pieces of a newly risen nobility and samurai from powerful domains, it was a composite structure erected on a subtle equilibrium between the authority of the imperial court and the power of domainal heavyweights.

A public-debate imbroglio

From the outset, the anti-bakufu nobles (*kuge*) and the powerful daimyo (*yūhan shokō*) who made up the Conference of Three Offices were sharply divided. They clashed first over how to treat the house of the Tokugawa.

The first meeting of the new regime was held on palace grounds the night of the ninth day of the twelfth month (= 3 January 1868), the day of the Proclamation of the Restoration of Imperial Rule (*ōsei fukko no daigōrei*). This was the so-called Kogosho Conference (*Kogosho kaigi*), or the Conference of the Smaller Palace. It opened with the declaration of an intent to carry out public debate (*kōgi*) to its fullest extent, according the spirit of the Charter Oath.[11] Yamauchi Toyoshige, on the samurai side, immediately asserted that for public debate to be properly carried out, the attendance of Tokugawa Yoshinobu, the largest domain-holder, was indispensable. Matsudaira Yoshinaga then furthered this line of argument.

The house of Tokugawa was the strongest military force and the largest domain-holder in the land. If it were to have entered the conference, it would have overwhelmed discussions and steered the course of the new state. Ōkubo Toshimichi and Iwakura Tomomi, among others, feared such formidable power. They sought to block Tokugawa entry. But Yoshinobu had built clout. He had demonstrated his willingness to cooperate with the new regime by surrendering power to the imperial court. To throw out the man behind that decision would have dealt a grievous blow to state legitimacy, especially when samurai were already on guard against the potentially preponderant influence of the imperial court. The two sides faced off, and neither side budged. As the final hour approached and night began to fall, they at last arrived at a resolution.

The Kogosho Conference yielded a compromise: the two sides would continue to call for Yoshinobu to step down voluntarily and to surrender his land to the imperial court (*jikan nōchi*), but they entrusted the handling of negotiations over this settlement to Matsudaira Yoshinaga and Tokugawa Yoshikatsu, *shinpan* daimyo sympathetic to the erstwhile bakufu. On the tenth day of the twelfth month (= 4 January), Yoshinaga and Yoshikatsu headed to Nijō Castle to communicate this decision to Yoshinobu. Yoshinobu called for time, insisting that a delay in implementing the decision would allow him room to mollify his subordinates.[12] Proceeding with negotiations at this point while keeping the military branch of the defunct bakufu at bay required great circumspection on both sides. That same day, troops from the Chōshū domain had entered the imperial capital. With fears of unforeseen contingencies mounting, Yoshinobu removed the military forces of the former bakufu from Kyoto and withdrew temporarily to Osaka.

The withdrawal to Osaka helped avert military confrontation while buying time for the political manoeuvring of powerful daimyo. Terrified that the two sides would needlessly take up arms and that the nation would plunge into civil war, the powerful tozama daimyo (*yūhan*) called for a gathering of the heads of large domains including the Tokugawa house, in conformity with the spirit of public debate. After clarifying the new mode of operations in their proceedings, they asserted the necessity of engaging in debate over the nature of the new government.

Yamauchi Toyoshige submitted a proposal (*ikensho*) articulating the principles laid out in this assembly on the twelfth day of the twelfth month (= 6 January), and ten other domains, led by Kumamoto, followed with petitions of a similar kind. Because a new government could not be formed without the participation of the daimyo, these petitions were of great significance: their influence helped expunge any reference to punitive measures against the house of the Tokugawa from the Proclamation of the Restoration of Imperial Rule.

On the heels of these proposals, four figures from the Kumamoto domain, including Yokoi Shōnan, were appointed as junior councillors, as was one figure each from Yanagawa, Tottori and Ōgaki. The samurai thus strengthened their formation in the stand-off: these were personnel who could restrain the manoeuvring of anti-bakufu nobles.

Indeed, circumstances did not favour the anti-bakufu faction. The Emperor, the source of the faction's power, had not made an appearance during the debates of the Kogosho Conference. Unable to endure the brouhaha of the arguments, Chief Executive Arisugawa-no-Miya decided to sabotage the conference, threatening to call it quits. With neither Emperor nor chief executive present, the anti-bakufu nobles jittered at the prospect of having their power usurped by the powerful tozama daimyo. They concocted a scheme to carry out decision-making on their own, without any interference by the powerful domain-heads.

On the eighteenth day of the twelfth month (= 12 January), without any notice to the powerful tozama daimyo, the anti-bakufu nobles gathered for a secret conference and won approval from the Emperor to apprise world powers of the establishment of a new government in Japan. Only after having obtained this imperial sanction did they refer the matter to the daimyo and the senior councillors. They thus sought to stifle opposition from their samurai opponents by gaining advance approval from the Emperor.

But the machinations of the nobles came crashing down. With the exception of Shimazu Tadayoshi, every daimyo senior councillor (*shokō gijō*) expressed unequivocal opposition to the plan. All insisted that they could not declare a new government to the world when the foundations of authority at home were still wobbly. The notice to foreign powers was thus interrupted before it went out, imperial sanction notwithstanding. As the treatise submitted by Yamauchi had revealed, the crux of contention lay not in the actual content of the plan. It lay in the decision-making processes leading to it and in the means by which public debate had been carried out. The go-it-alone decision-making of the anti-bakufu nobles made them their own enemy.

In its Proclamation of the Restoration of Imperial Rule, the imperial court had heralded public debate as the guiding spirit of a new government. But precisely because it so championed the ideal, the more the imperial court pushed ahead independently with a limited interpretation of the idea, the more the foundations of its legitimacy wobbled, and the more the cooperation of powerful daimyo became necessary for maintaining the centripetal forces of power. And thus, with every new manoeuvre the anti-bakufu faction made, the more influence the powerful daimyo and samurai junior councillors gained.

The Battle of Toba-Fushimi and the beginnings of an executive structure

In accordance with the will of these powerful daimyo (*yūhan shokō*) and samurai junior councillors (*buke san'yo*), the Upper Conference now proceeded towards welcoming the Tokugawa household into the new government.

The call that Ōkubo and other members of the anti-bakufu faction had made for the Tokugawa to return their lands to the Emperor (*ryōchi henjō ron*) was thrown out. There was willingness to retain necessary elements of the structure of the erstwhile regime rather than repudiate it entirely. On the first day of the first month of Keiō 4 (= 25 January 1868), Iwakura even went as far as to accept the appointment of Yoshinobu as a senior councillor. He hoped at last to realize a government based on public debate.

But military force crushed these political manoeuvres. On the twenty-fifth day of the twelfth month of the previous reign year (= 19 January 1868), the hardline faction of the erstwhile bakufu seized on the provocations of the Satsuma domain in Edo to set fire to its domainal residence. The volatile state of affairs spread to Osaka on the twenty-eighth day and then to Kyoto on the thirtieth, invigorating belligerent factions on both sides. On the second day of the first month (= 26 January), the Tokugawa side embarked from Osaka to present the Declaration of Hostilities against Satsuma to the Emperor, and on the third day (= 27 January), fighting broke out with the Satsuma army at Fushimi. So began the Battle of Toba-Fushimi.

In an instant everything changed. With the title of *Seitō dai shōgun*, Great Subjugating Generalissmo, placed on his shoulders by the anti-bakufu faction, Chief Executive Arisugawa-no-Miya hoisted the standard of the imperial throne and marched his troops against the bakufu. At first the imperial army lacked the military strength of the pro-bakufu side. Some even contemplated the need to remove the Emperor to a safer location. But as the Yodo domain, the Tsu domain and other erstwhile bakufu loyalists began defecting to the imperial side, the battle lines were redrawn in imperial favour. The evening of the sixth day of the first month (= 30 January), Yoshinobu fled from Osaka Castle and retreated to Edo by sea. Fate was sealed.

On the heels of victory at Toba-Fushimi, the new government moved toward gaining ascendancy over the entire country. On the seventh day of the first month (= 31 January), it announced a proclamation to track down Yoshinobu (*Yoshinobu tsuitō rei*), putting pressure on the domains to conform to the imperial course of action. In every direction and to every part of the country – to the San'indō, the Tōkaidō, the Tōsandō and the Hokurikudō; to Chūgoku, to Shikoku and to Kyushu – the government dispatched troops to quell unrest. In a single stroke, it swept into its fold the allegiance and subordination of domains across the archipelago.

With total sovereignty now firmly within sight, and with victory in war yielding new directly controlled lands for the state, the Conference of Three Offices (*sanshoku kaigi*), which before had been no more than an arena for public debate, took on new executive functions.

On the ninth day of the first month (= 2 February), Sanjō Sanetomi and Iwakura Tomomi were promoted from senior councillors to deputy chief executives (*fuku sōsai*). Sanjō and Iwakura came to hold final decision-making power in the government instead of Chief Executive Arisugawa-no-Miya, who had directed the military forces against Yoshinobu. Triumph in the Battle of Toba-Fushimi thus brought the anti-bakufu faction victory in the debates over the structure of rule. Seeing the need to codify its new mode of governance explicitly, the state clearly articulated the divided powers of the Three Offices: chief executives would 'preside over all matters of governance and decide on all administrative affairs' (*banki o sōsai shi issai no jimu o kessuru*); senior councillors would 'supervise the administrative affairs of each separate department and determine its proceedings' (*jimu kakka o buntoku shi giji o teiketsu su*); and junior councillors would 'participate in administration and fulfill administrative duties in each department' (*jimu o sangi shi kakka o bunmu su*).

Concepts of procedural and executive governance thus emerged in response to the exigencies of rule. The seventeenth day of the first month (= 10 February) saw the establishment of the departments of the Three Offices (*sanshoku bunka*), which divided government executive or administrative (*gyōsei, jimu*) and legislative or procedural functions (*rippō, giji*) into seven different fields:[13] the Office of Divinity (*jingi jimu*), which dealt with rites (*saishi*); the Office of Domestic Affairs (*naikoku jimu*), which handled lands under the direct control of the state; the Office of Foreign Affairs (*gaikoku jimu*), which handled diplomacy; the Office of the Army and Navy (*kairiku jimu*), which handled military matters; the Office of Accounts (*kaikei jimu*), which handled finance and tax collection; and the Office of Law (*keihō jimu*), which handled trials and judicial matters; as well as the Institutions Bureau (*seido ryō*), which investigated and recommended government officials for selection and promotion.

The head of each executive division was named the *sōtoku*, or general superintendent, and the next-in-line was titled the *kakari*, or commissioner; a senior councillor took the role of general superintendent and a junior councillor took the role of commissioner. It is here, in the emergence of this administrative chain of chief executive–general superintendent–commissioner (*sōsai–sōtoku–kakari*), that we find the birth of the present-day model of political organization in Japan, that of prime minister–minister–deputy minister. The Upper Conference, made up of senior councillors, came to fulfil the duties of what is today the Cabinet (*kakugi*); the Lower Conference, made up of junior councillors, played the role of today's Conference of Deputy Ministers (*jikan kaigi*). It is not an overstatement to say that the system that emerged at this moment gave birth to Japan's present-day executive structure.

This dicing-up of executive duties proceeded alongside designs to centralize decision-making power. Those designs became manifest on the twenty-fifth day of the first month (= 18 February), in the establishment of the Bureau of Chief Executives (*sōsaikyoku*), founded as a secretarial organization under the direct oversight of the chief executives. Under the authority of Chief Executive Arisugawa and deputy chief executives Sanjō and Iwakura, several other auxiliary structures were installed, including the post of the *hohitsu*, or aide, for providing advice and assistance in decision-making processes touching the Emperor; the *komon*, or counsellor, for offering counsel in response to queries from the chief executives; the *benji*, or clerical assistant, for carrying out general administrative affairs; and the *shikan*, or historian-scribe, for keeping records.

The identities of those chosen as *hohitsu* and *komon*, as aides and counsellors, reveal to us that the Bureau of Chief Executives was set up as an executive body to centralize governmental power. To the post of aide (*hohitsu*) were appointed senior councillors from the notable samurai households of Nakayama and Ōgimachisanjō; to that of counsellor (*komon*) were appointed Kido Kōin of Chōshū; Ōkubo of Satsuma (who was later replaced by Komatsu Tatewaki); Gotō Shōjirō of Tosa; and other leaders of powerful domains. That such important personnel as Kido, Ōkubo and Gotō were placed not in the Three Offices but on the Bureau of Chief Executives reveals an intent to wrest decision-making once and for all from the Three Offices, still dominated by the erstwhile status order, and to make the Bureau of Chief Executives the site in which general governance was carried out. The new government thus began evolving away from a conference body that deliberated on the direction of government towards a consolidated political body that executed political and administrative affairs.

We cannot overlook the important role of clerical assistants (*benji*) in this system. These were men responsible for the general affairs of the new government. To their post were appointed members of the nobility aligned with Iwakura and serving as commissioners of the Three Offices (*sanshoku goyō gakari*). Doubling as junior councillors in the various executive departments, the clerical assistants took charge of all requests (*gansho*) and queries (*ukagaisho*) that came to the government. They constituted the nucleus of all executive affairs: to tap into them would be to grab a hold of the entire new government. Through their eyes did Iwakura, and Iwakura alone, see.

But there was a problem. Precisely twenty-five junior councillors had been allotted among the newly established executive departments, leaving each department with multiple superintendents general (*sōtoku*), or head executive officers (*gyōsei chōkan*). Domestic Affairs, Foreign Affairs, and Accounts each had five superintendents; Divinity and the Army and Navy each had three; and Law and the Institution Bureau each had two. With too many head officials, the departments tumbled into disorder. There was no way of bringing about a unified executive state.

To clarify the chain of command in this confusing system, the organizational structure of the government was reshuffled again on the third day of the second month (25 February). The Bureau of Chief Executives and the seven departments were rechristened the Eight Bureaux (*hachi kyoku*), and a more intricate hierarchy was introduced across the departments: superintendent–aide–deputy aide–magistrate–deputy magistrate (*toku–yū–gon no yū–hanji–gon no hanji*).[14] To each bureau were assigned two senior councillors. The superior of the two took the higher-ranking role of superintendent (*toku*), and the inferior took the role of aide (*yū*). Of the junior councillors assigned to the bureaux, the senior in rank became deputy aides (*gon no yū*), and the junior became magistrates (*hanji*) and deputy magistrates (*gon no hanji*). This new chain of command elucidated hierarchical relations within departments. And it solidified the basis of a new administrative structure.

Even while meandering, the new Meiji government had managed, within just three months of its birth, to install a deliberative body of government, to consolidate a central executive body and to set up various administrative departments. With the inauguration of the Three Offices–Eight Bureaux system (*san shoku hachi kyoku sei*), an arrangement for the functions of execution and administrative procedure had been put in place – and with it a prototype of the first modern political structure in Japanese history.

From samurai to bureaucrat

The origins of the recruitment system (*chōshi seido*)

The new Meiji state had erected structures of executive government and outlined their procedures, but it had not assembled adequate manpower to put those structures reliably to work. The problem of recruiting human resources, 'a matter of foremost urgency', had seen no progress. Leaders of powerful domains had received positions commensurate to their influence – it was at this stage that the problem of human resources was stuck.

The state was in dire need of personnel with specialized knowledge who would enter the new executive departments and plan, propose and execute new policies. Indeed, the administrative burdens of the state had ballooned so quickly that accounts survive today of Ōkubo himself taking up the task of writing draft proclamations. The shortage of manpower cut deep.

The new regime announced the Recruitment System, the *chōshi seido*, its first strategy to recruit personnel, on the seventeenth day of the first month (= 10 February), the day on which it established the seven executive departments we just encountered. The policy called for the employment of talented personnel from across the country regardless of status background: the talent of not just domainal samurai but even men not serving in government posts would be excavated from the population. Once employed, these men would take on the operation of the various government departments in their capacities as junior councillors, deputy aides, magistrates and deputy magistrates. Anticipating vast increases in the demands of administrative work, the government did not set a target for the number of men it would need to recruit.

The Recruitment System applied the spirit of the Proclamation of the Restoration of Imperial Rule to the practice of personnel recruitment by encouraging all, regardless of their status affiliation, to express their opinions and participate in political affairs. By thus repudiating the status-based constraints of the bakuhan system, the new regime opened the door to meritocracy. It would rule by public debate: people chosen by meritocracy would take up the task of running the government. With this breakthrough in a new system of recruitment, the state sought to usher in an epochal transformation.

Samurai in anguish

But the act of declaring a new recruitment system did not in itself bring talented men hurrying to the government. The reasons lay in the particular contingencies of this pivotal point in history.

The personnel whom the state sought were men of talent, men with knowledge and experience fit for governance. Those who had such qualifications were, by and large, samurai in the domains. But because the samurai were affiliated by status with their domains, not with the central state, the government could not employ them directly: it could only draft them via the domains into the central state. From the perspective of the domains, to supply the state with personnel in this way would symbolize clear and enthusiastic support for the new regime. True, the more men the domains supplied to the state, the greater their influence could be. But in the foggy climate of the day, when none knew what lay ahead, few domains were willing to hoist their flag so gaudily in the government camp.[15]

Exacerbating the concerns of the domains was agitation over 'expelling the barbarians' and 'toppling the bakufu', which continued to convulse most domains internally. The personnel whom the state sought to siphon away were indispensable resources to the domains themselves. In such a time of upheaval, what domain could afford to surrender the very men who, because of their management experience, were needed to keep the domain in order?[16]

In such circumstances, even powerful tozama domains limited their supply of human resources to the state. After the declaration of the Recruitment System policy, the Chōshū domain, for instance, requested that the new regime privately communicate to it not just the names of those whom it wanted to recruit but also the anticipated roles of the recruits and the reasons for their placement in those roles. Chōshū could claim publicly that it was being circumspect, trying to ensure that no one entered a role for which he was not suited. But its real intent was to restrain the new regime. In practice, Hirosawa Saneomi and other such men who held the highest posts in domainal government were rebuffing the central state's attempts to recruit them.[17]

Domains without the power of such tozama strongholds as Chōshū were, of course, even more hesitant. Loath to degrade themselves by participating in and submitting to a government dominated by Satsuma, Chōshū and a parvenu nobility, these smaller domains decided to buy time.

The recruited samurai were themselves conflicted. They were less autonomous individuals than bearers of the long lineages of their warrior households. Each of these households had nurtured lord-vassal relations with the domainal head for over two centuries. For samurai who had been reared in traditional Confucian education as elite members of these warrior households, to renounce their domainal lords and enter into the new government would constitute betrayal.[18] The higher their rank in the domain, the harder it was, indeed, to contemplate leaving that rank.

No matter how much will of his own an individual samurai had, it was not easy to overcome the framework of the domain and relations with one's lord to enter service with the new government. The domain and the samurai alike needed propitious circumstances and an established system to help justify entry into government employment.

The personnel strategy of the new regime

Circumstances panned out in favour of the new regime. Because the fight against bakufu forces had turned to its advantage, the new government was able to take an even firmer stand in demanding personnel from the domains. The state went to work setting up a system towards this end.

First, chief executives took up the task of appointing men to government posts. Because recruited men would serve in practical administrative roles as magistrates and deputy magistrates, it would originally have been the role of the superintendents, the heads of the executive departments, to make these appointments. But their superiors, the chief executives, took on the role.

That chief executives played this role was significant in two ways. First, because the chief executives represented the Emperor, any appointment coming from them could take the form of a summons for direct employment from the Emperor himself. In an age of loyalism to the Emperor (*kinnōshugi*), none could easily dismiss an imperial summons. Second, because the superintendents of the departments came from noble families or served as a powerful tozama daimyo, appointments from them could have been seen as tendentious: some might have thought an appointment was being made with particular interests in mind or under certain forces. An appointment from a chief executive implied not the operation of these interested forces but an invitation into a new government at the helm of an entire nation.

Indeed, the new government was acutely conscious that it needed to go further in severing the bonds linking recruited samurai to their domainal lords and in bringing them fully into the fold of the administration. In the second month, the regime sent official notice to recruited men that they would be regarded as ministers of the court (*chōshin*) from the day they were employed, making it clear that they were in the service of the imperial court, not of their respective domains.[19] By the end of that month, the number of men employed by the regime had risen to sixty.[20]

Status as a minister of the imperial court was not merely a formal designation. Despite dire financial straits, the new regime awarded extraordinary salaries to its employees: a recruit received a prodigious 500 yen per month, while a chief executive received 1,000 yen and a senior councillor received 800 yen, though their salaries were halved during the Boshin War. Each recruited samurai was treated as a junior councillor; since most daimyo and nobles were themselves junior councillors, the recruited samurai occupied the same plane within the government that those daimyo and nobles did. It is not difficult to imagine the pride this distinction instilled in newly employed men, most of whom came from lower-level samurai households. These were changes that constituted a destruction of the Tokugawa status system.

Yet the new regime did carefully exploit certain vestiges of the traditional social order. Most representative of this strategy were the ranks (*joi*) the regime bestowed on its recruited men. In the intercalary fourth month, recruited samurai working as junior councillors were awarded official ranks. Nine were appointed to the lower Junior Fourth Rank (*ju shi i no ge*): Komatsu Tatewaki of Satsuma; Gotō Shōjirō of Tosa; Kido Kōin of Chōshū; Ōkubo Toshimichi of Satsuma; Hirosawa Saneomi of Chōshū; Yuri Kimimasa of Echizen; Fukuoka Takachika of Tosa; Soejima Taneomi of Saga; and Yokoi Shōnan of Higo. Another nine were appointed to the lower Junior Fifth Rank (*ju go i no ge*), including Yoshii Tomozane of Satsuma and Itō Shunsuke, later known as Itō Hirobumi, of Chōshū.

Under the bakuhan system, the Junior Fourth Rank had been awarded to Tokugawa senior councillors (*rōjū*) from *fudai* domains as well as daimyo from tozama domains with *kokudaka* values over 100,000. Just as the new regime sought to sever its personnel from their domains, it exploited the traditional status system to solidify them in their new positions. In an environment where the power of tradition still endured, rank constituted an extremely important means by which the new administration gave power and influence to the new recruits shouldering its burdens.

The problem that remained was the affiliation of these new men. Mutsu Yōnosuke, or Mutsu Munemitsu, of Kishū, or Wakayama, who served as a recruited samurai, wrote to Iwakura with the following words:

> The realm offers up praise and admiration for the imperial will, which has opened paths of expression and employment for men of talent. Nonetheless, it is deeply regrettable that this system has not yet achieved wide renown, that the employment of talent has not yet been thoroughly undertaken, and that the powers of those talents have not yet been able to attain their fullest extent.

> When we consider the reasons [for this failure], we see that it is not because remuneration from the imperial court has been thin or because people have failed to exert adequate effort. It is because people's positions [in the regime] have not yet been definitely fixed, such that they cannot apply their talents to the position to which they have been appointed.

What is desirable is that these customs of the past be entirely swept away, that the residences of recruits be offered to the imperial capital, that their domain stipends be discontinued, and that their abodes be moved. In this way will their duty [to the state] be firmly determined and their hearts and bodies both be given up in service to the imperial court. I believe that this is the foremost requisite for solidifying the basis of the imperial court.[21]

The end of the civil war and the consolidation of human resources

Circumstances changed dramatically starting in the fall of the first year of the Meiji era (= 1868). Scores of new recruits began entering the new government, reversing the personnel shortage the state faced earlier in the year. The pro-bakufu holdout of Aizu fell in the ninth month, making regime change all but an accomplished fact. Domains began deluging the central government with new human resources.

The policy of *hanseki hōkan*, the surrender of domain registers to the Emperor, allowed the government to recruit human resources from domains without being rebuffed.[22] The policy was enacted in the sixth month of the following year (= July 1869). Each domain 'reverted' institutional control over land and people to the imperial court, rendering the Recruitment System obsolete: the purpose of the system had been to wrest talented men away from domains, but now the registers of those men already belonged to the central state, not the domains. Around this time, 683 men occupied positions of magistrate or above in the state, according to the Suharaya version of the *Record of Officials* (*Kan'inroku*), which was published in the fifth month, just before the implementation of *hanseki hōkan*. If we remove nobles, members of the imperial family and other court officials from this tally, we are left with over 600 men: this was the number of recruited men now in the state. Although the *Record of Officials* makes no note of them, we know from the *Dajōruiten* and other extant official documents that recruited men also took lower positions such as deputy magistrate, clerical assistant and historian-scribe; if we add these posts to the tally, then we can conceivably place the number of recruited men in the government at over one thousand. The personnel employment programme of the new regime was comfortably on track.

The most powerful forces among the recruits were samurai from Satsuma, Tosa, Echizen, Owari and Geishū domains whose heads had been appointed as senior and junior councillors. Following these domains in power were Kumamoto, Tottori, Uwajima and Saga. Besides those domains, Chōshū in particular as well as Okayama in the west, Kaga on the Japan Sea-side and Ōgaki in the Tōkai region, contributed large numbers of personnel.

These changes in personnel of course greatly influenced the constituent ratios of junior councillors. The domains that supplied multiple junior councillors were the nine listed above, as well as Chōshū and Okayama. These eleven domains became the central axis around which the government revolved.

Other domains contributed men, too. Many samurai were recruited from Kaga, Ōgaki, Hikone and Tatebayashi, but by and large these recruits did not become junior councillors; they remained at the level of magistrate, deputy magistrate or clerical assistant. As the number of recruited samurai grew, a distinction thus began to arise between those who engaged in decision-making processes as junior councillors and those who handled administrative processes as magistrates. Even if they all participated in the government in the identical capacity of 'recruit' (*chōshi*), those who had supported the government before its course had been determined became politicians (*seijika*) who partook in decision-making, whereas those who had dithered, joining only once the future had been ascertained, became bureaucrats who tended to the practical functioning of the state.

Large numbers of talented men thus gathered under the fold of the new government once its foundation had been solidified and its form determined. The new regime razed the status system and opened its doors to the recruitment of human resources. In the process, a new sociopolitical order began to emerge wherein participation in this incipient stage of state-making became the standard for one's future place in it. From hereon, it was these pioneers of this early stage who would take control of the various executive divisions of the government and set them in motion. Human resources assembled from across the realm were incorporated into this order, giving rise to a clique that would come to be known as the Meiji oligarchy (*hanbatsu*).

The rise of Restoration bureaucrats: Breaking free of the old order

What kind of human resources did the new regime recruit? How did it find them? And how did those recruits find arenas in which to apply their skills and talents?

The category of 'recruit' can be divided roughly into two groups according to the role the recruit played. Figures such as Ōkubo, Saigō and Kido belonged to the first group. As representatives of powerful tozama domains, they formed a stratum that took on decision-making for the new regime. Today they are widely celebrated as the heroes (*genkun*) of the Restoration. But each of them had perished by around Meiji 10 (= 1877). Their role in carrying the burden of a new state lasted no longer than its earliest years.

It was the recruited samurai who followed them, those whom the original heroes had promoted and who took action under their helm, who set the Meiji government on its tracks. If we consider the real meaning of 'bureaucrat' (*kanryō*) as one who carries forward the actual practice of rule and administration, then it was precisely these men who were the 'bureaucrats of the Restoration' or the 'Restoration bureaucrats' (*Ishin kanryō*), born of the exigencies of a new age.

Entering a government that rewarded them for their administrative talents, members of this second group distinguished themselves by taking on the burden of governance. They thus gradually matured as professional politicians. It was they who gave being to the Meiji constitutional system, racking and exerting their minds after seizing the helm of a state shorn of its original heroes. It was these pioneers who blazed the trail from bureaucrat to politician.

Let us now witness the birth of the Restoration bureaucracy by depicting three of its representative figures in their younger years. These were men who strained every nerve to build modern Japan. Let us consider Yuri Kimimasa, Itō Hirobumi and Ōkuma Shigenobu.

Yuri Kimimasa: The first recruit and the open door

The first man to be recruited to the new regime was Yuri Kimimasa, known at the time as Mitsuoka Hachirō.[23] He hardly shares the renown of Itō or Ōkuma today, but he participated actively in state financial affairs, applying himself to the first printing of the Meiji currency (*dajō kansatsu*). He was also deeply involved in drafting the Charter Oath and in designing and planning systems for the new regime. He undoubtedly appears on any list of the leading figures of Meiji financial history.

Yuri was born to a samurai family in Echizen domain in 1829, the twelfth year of Bunsei. His otherwise nondescript life was greatly transformed by an encounter with a man of particular erudition: Yokoi Shōnan.

Yokoi was a samurai from Kumamoto domain, but he was invited outside the domain by Matsudaira Yoshinaga, who knew of his efforts to reform domainal administration through practical learning (*jitsugaku*). Visiting Fukui domain in Kaei 4 (= 1851), Yokoi observed that the dogmatic adherence to precedent (*zenrei tōshū*) that undergirded domainal governance only stultified thought. He concluded that real

Figure 1.1 Yuri Kimimasa in the early Meiji era, *c.* 1868. *Source:* Yuri Masamichi, *Shishaku Yuri Kimimasa den*, Iwanami shoten, 1940, p. 169.

reform required a grasp of actual circumstances and a form of rule that was based on those circumstances.

Yokoi advocated scientific and practical learning (*kagaku, jitsugaku*), ideas that appealed to Yuri Kimimasa, Hashimoto Sanai and other up-and-coming samurai reared in the domainal schools that proliferated during the late Edo era. But these were schools that championed the 'unity of education and governance' (*gakusei itchi*); they existed to train men for rulership, and they offered a deeply conservative education whose purpose was to preserve the status quo. This system could not help domains fix their floundering finances or resist the encroaching threat of Western powers.

In this context, young, frustrated samurai were attracted to the practical learning (*jitsugaku*) propounded by Yokoi, which sought to confront actual circumstances head-on, encourage thought and break open an effective new strategy for governance. This was a moment when Sakuma Shōzan, a scholar of Western learning (*yōgakusha*), was gaining renown in Edo for his mantra of 'Eastern virtue, Western arts' (*Tōyō no dōtoku, seiyō no geijutsu*). He argued that, to escape crisis, Japan had to introduce Western practical learning to supplement its traditional system based on Chinese learning. Such dreams of practical learning did not remain confined to Edo. They spread across the whole polity.

As intellectual tides turned towards practical learning, a question remained: would domains be able to change direction and apply this new mode of education? Yuri and his fellow young samurai, inspired by Yokoi, set to work in Echizen. They overhauled the domain's traditional agricultural encouragement policy, proposing and implementing a new government strategy based on research and analysis. Their reforms succeeded. The finances of the domain quickly improved.

Accompanied by Matsudaira Yoshinaga, Yuri set out for the imperial capital and for Nagasaki in Bunkyū 2 (= 1862). He mingled with samurai of spirit (*shishi*), becoming acquainted with new trends in the realm. And he gained fame as a man of spirit himself. This blessing of fame became a curse. After the retirement of Yoshinaga and the subsequent conservative turn of the domainal administration (*han shissei bu*), Yuri was regarded as a threat and placed under house arrest (*chikkyo*). On the cusp of upheavals both within Japan and abroad, he found himself trapped at home. He was crestfallen.

It was Sakamoto Ryōma who lifted his spirits. Sakamoto had come to know Yuri through Yokoi and admired his skills in governance and finance. Sakamoto and Yuri met in the tenth month of Keiō 3 (= October–November 1867), when Sakamoto was dispatched to Echizen as an envoy. Sakamoto asked Yuri about management policies to help establish a new government. He wrote down Yuri's ideas, and he submitted a recommendation to Iwakura Tomomi calling for the government to employ Yuri.

Iwakura accepted the recommendation, and in the twelfth month (= early 1868) the command for Yuri to ascend to the capital descended on Echizen domain. On his departure, Yuri made two remarks to the Echizen government: first, insofar as he was in the service of the new regime, he would not be swayed by the interests of the domain; and second, while he was employed in the new government, he would not take on administrative work for the domain. He claimed he could not help his home domain because he had not partaken in domainal administration for many years, and he hedged that he did not want to burden his domainal lord while away. But his real reasons lay in his intent to completely sever relations with his domain.

To the imperial court, Yuri pointed out that the affiliations of junior councillors still remained ambiguous. He called for a clear separation of the new regime's recruits from samurai in the domains. The imperial court accepted this suggestion, and they took in Yuri as a 'recruit' with a status and affiliation independent of his domain. From here on, all new men entering the new regime from the domains would be called *chōshi*, or recruits.[24]

On the eighteenth day, Yuri elected to enter the exclusive service of the new regime, and he was welcomed as a professional bureaucrat. In both his talents and his status, he was the ideal first recruit. He was 38 years old at the time. Only about two months had passed since an assassin had knifed and killed his old friend Sakamoto Ryōma.

Yuri was appointed not only as a recruit and a junior councillor but also as a member of the first generation of financial officers, the *goyō kinkoku toriatsukai*. In the Eight Bureaux system, he became a magistrate (*hanji*) in the Office of Accounts (*kaikei jimukyoku*), dedicating himself to the procurement of funds for the regime, the first printing of the new national currency and other measures essential to building the earliest financial structures of a new government.

Yuri accomplished one more important task. In order to uphold and perpetuate the legitimacy of a new regime, it was crucial to open the door to personnel recruitment and public debate even wider. The regime sought to make it widely known that this new government was altogether unlike anything before it. Yuri, the regime's very first recruit, believed that this task was none other than his.

Towards the Charter Oath

It was the eighth day of the first month of the first year of the Meiji era (= 1 February 1868). The conflagration at Toba-Fushimi had yet to die down. Yuri insisted that the battle raging was not a struggle of private interests between the erstwhile bakufu and an anti-bakufu clan but a fight to realize a new form of government. He argued that the new government needed to clarify the specific direction the state would take. He sought to go further than the Declaration of the Restoration of Imperial Rule: to the entire realm he wanted to reveal a concrete path forward.

Yuri enunciated his ideals in 'Giji no tai tai'i', or 'Outline on the Body of Proceedings', which delineated five points: that every person should have autonomous will (*kokorozashi*); that hearts and minds should be united in managing the nation-state; that knowledge should be sought throughout the world; that people of talent should be widely sought out and employed; and that governance should be carried out by popular debate. He adopted the emphasis on practical application he learned from Yokoi, he called for the employment of personnel regardless of their status background, and he demanded the inauguration of public debate to its fullest extent, a debate that would arise from abolishing the monopoly on power held by samurai and nobility. With this enunciation, Yuri invigorated dreams of a new age and adumbrated a vision of a new, open nation.

Yuri's 'Giji no tai tai'i' underwent revisions by Fukuoka Takachika, a commissioner of the Institutions Bureau (*seido kakari*); Kido Kōin, a counsellor for the Bureau of Chief Executives (*sōsai kyoku komon*); and Sanjō Santetomi and Iwakura Tomomi, deputy chief executives (*fuku sōsai*). On the fourteenth day of the third month (= 6 April 1868), the day before the full assault on Edo Castle, his ideals were publicly enunciated in the Charter Oath (*gokajō no goseimon*):

(1) Deliberative assemblies shall be widely established and all matters decided by public discussion.
(2) All classes, high and low, shall be united in vigorously carrying out the administration of affairs of state.
(3) The common people, no less than the civil and military officials, shall each be allowed to pursue his own calling so that there may be no discontent.
(4) Evil customs of the past shall be broken off and everything based upon the just laws of Nature.
(5) Knowledge shall be sought throughout the world so as to strengthen the foundations of imperial rule.[25]

With the exception of the fourth clause, the entire text of the Charter Oath came directly from the ideas in Yuri's draft. To cast off the customs of the past; to seek knowledge throughout the world; to pursue one's goals; to unite as one and build up a nation; to carry out decision-making by public opinion – it was a declaration that served as a manifesto for a new nation-state.

Announced as an 'oath' by the Meiji Emperor to the gods (*tenchi shinmei*), the Charter went on to be long venerated as the embodiment of the spirit of the Restoration, quoted in state political documents and in the Risshisha petition, the spark that ignited the Movement for Freedom and Popular Rights. The Oath acted not only as the ideational foundation of the Meiji constitutional system but also as evidence cited in the post-war era that a 'democracy with Japanese characteristics' (*Nihon-gata minshushugi*) already existed before the US Occupation demanded democratization. The document survived as a philosophy of Japanese modernity well past its immediate context.

Why has the Charter Oath been assigned such significance? In discussions to this day, two clauses have garnered particular attention: the first, because it guided future parliamentary and constitutional politics by upholding the principle of public debate; and the second, because it contributed to the construction of the nation-state by calling for the unification of all people behind the government.

To be sure, if we look at the unfoldment of Japanese modernity from the surface layer of constitutional politics, these two clauses stand out. But to establish a modern nation-state with an executive centre and to bring about rule by parliamentary government, the state needed knowledge and expertise to support it. That knowledge and expertise came from the exertions of young men who, through education, sought to rise for themselves in a new world (*risshin shusse*). We cannot overlook the exertions of these young men when we think about the making of the modern Japanese nation-state.

From this perspective, then, it is less the second clause and its call for spiritual unity that propelled Japanese modernization and galvanized the masses than the third clause, which opened a path for people to set goals and strive for their realization. This was the ideal that Sakamoto emblazoned in his 'Outline of Eight Steps to New Government': Sakamoto and indeed Yuri had envisioned a nation in which all people, freed from the shackles of the status system, could find their arena for action. The Charter Oath trumpeted this ideal for all to hear.

Itō Hirobumi: From lower-level samurai (*sotsuzoku*) to junior councillor (*san'yo*)

Perhaps no figure better represents the ideal of rising in the world through wilful exertion (*risshin shusse*) than Itō Hirobumi, or Itō Shunsuke, who ascended over the course of his life from a samurai (*shizoku*) to prime minister. He, too, was a man of talent brought in by the new regime and made a formal recruit, a *chōshi*. His ascent into government was enabled by the door of opportunity opened by the Proclamation

Figure 1.2 Itō Hirobumi in the early Meiji era, 1870. *Source:* Shunpo-kō tsuishōkai, ed., *Itō Hirobumi den*, vol 1., Tōseisha, 1940, p. 514.

of the Restoration of Imperial Rule and by the spirit of meritocracy that pervaded his age. In precise accordance with the spirit of the Charter Oath, Itō, pursuing his calling, vigorously carrying out the administration of state affairs and seeking knowledge throughout the world, emerged as a veritable hero of his time.

Itō was born in Tenpo 12 (= 1841), to a lower-level samurai household in Chōshū domain.[26] Having studied at Yoshida Shōin's academy, the Shōka Son Juku, he embarked on a clandestine voyage to Britain in Bunkyū 3 (= 1863), with Inoue Kaoru and other men from his domain. Struck by the might of the imperialist powers, Itō and his band came to regard the ideology of 'expelling the barbarian' as but a delusion. They turned to support for Opening the Country (*kaikokuron*). Six months later, encountering reports of war between Satsuma and Britain and of the foreign bombardment of Shimonoseki, they returned to Japan. Raising the flag of Opening the Country through Peace and Amity (*kaikoku washin*), they ran about to mend national affairs.

But the actions of Itō at this bakumatsu moment were hardly spectacular. He was recalled from the front lines during the Second Chōshū Expedition and tasked instead with procuring materiel from Britain. He partook in negotiations with Satsuma after the battle but only as a companion of Kido. He still did not stand in a position of domainal leadership as a politician, as Kido and Ōkubo did.

By the force of his own efforts and talents, Itō asserted his place in the world. In the first month of Meiji 1 (= 1868), he learned that armed conflict between the bakufu and Satsuma-Chōshū was impending, and he departed from Shimonoseki for Kyoto. Just over a week after the Battle of Toba-Fushimi, on the eleventh day, he arrived at the port of Kobe.

Kobe was on edge. Just a day before Itō arrived, a foreign solider cut in front of a regiment of Okayama-domain troops passing through the town. The troops opened fire. Incredibly, their gunfire even turned on Harry Parkes, the British envoy to Japan, who had scurried down to the site of the skirmish. The imperial powers reacted swiftly. They detained domainal warships anchored at Kobe and demanded a response from the Japanese state. This was the Incident at Kobe, as it is known.

Up to this point, it was the bakufu that had taken charge of all diplomatic affairs. But the tent government had been trounced at Toba-Fushimi, and under Yoshinobu its chief retainers had all retreated to Edo. All of a sudden, in its very first diplomatic test, the fledgling Meiji regime faced harsh demands from imperialist powers. It had to seize control of the situation and obtain recognition as Japan's only legitimate political authority. The stakes were enormous.

Itō arrived onto the scene. Witnessing the extraordinary circumstances in Kobe, Itō immediately visited Parkes, whom he knew, and gained a grasp on the situation at hand. He then carried an official message from Parkes to Higashikuze Michitomi, general superintendent of foreign affairs (*gaikoku jimu sōtoku*). Itō recommended that the state formally inform all major powers that regime change had occurred during the Restoration of Imperial Rule (*ōsei fukko*). Thus could it quickly and appropriately resolve the crisis at Kobe.

To the new regime, discombobulated by this state of emergency, Itō had arrived as nothing short of a *deus ex machina*, message from Parkes in hand. At once he was appointed as foreign affairs commissioner (*gaikoku jimu gakari*). Along with Iwashita

Michihira and Terashima Munenori of Satsuma as well as Mutsu Munemitsu of Kishū, he set out to gain official recognition for the Meiji state from the ambassadors of the six main powers: France, Britain, Italy, the United States, Prussia and the Netherlands. Iwashita bore experience from his time as a central domain minister (*karō*) who had arranged the end of hostilities with Britain after the Satsuma-Britain War; Terashima had been an instructor at the Institution for the Investigation of Barbarian Books (*bansho shirabe sho*), and he had also functioned as a diplomat, meeting with the foreign minister of Britain in the bakufu's delegation to Europe. The team's negotiations with the six powers succeeded. The new regime won recognition from each of them. Higashikuze reported back to the central state with high praise for the prowess of Itō and his band.

Likely as a result of these successes, Itō leapt up the administrative hierarchy and was appointed to the role of junior councillor on the twenty-fifth day of the first month (= 18 February). Up to this point, it had only been Hirosawa Saneomi and other upper-level samurai in roles of domainal leadership who had emerged from Chōshū to become junior councilors. Itō was an unusual selection.

The following month, Itō was chosen for the role of a recruited junior-councillor magistrate in the Foreign Affairs Bureau (*chōshi san'yo gaikoku jimukyoku hanji*). Then he took on a dual role as magistrate in Osaka prefecture and foreign-affairs magistrate (*gaikokukan hanji*) before finally being appointed governor of Hyōgo prefecture in the fifth month. With Kobe as his stage, Itō took the front line of diplomacy. In the fifth month again, he was decorated with the lower Junior Fifth Rank. Only two years had passed since he had been promoted from *sotsuzoku*, or lower-level samurai, to full samurai. He was but 26 years old. It is said that his parents held a small banquet in their hometown to celebrate his rise to a rank equal to that of a daimyo.

What propelled Itō so quickly through the hierarchy was no doubt the knowledge he had gained from visiting Britain and the negotiation skills he had cultivated in the bakumatsu era. But more than these advantages, two other factors helped his talents flourish: a particular historical juncture that made his knowledge direly in need and his network of contacts within and beyond his domain, which gave him opportunities to apply his knowledge. All this was enabled, foremost, by his unremitting efforts as a Chōshū samurai attendant to Kido.

Asserting a full-blown meritocracy

Despite his Chōshū affiliation, Itō did not cling to his domain. He took action as a bureaucrat of the new national regime. Indeed, it seems that Itō even disdained domains that greedily guarded power and condemned the traditional status system in which they operated.

Revealing his contemptuous attitude was the petition for surrendering domain registers to the Emperor (*hanseki hōkan no kenpaku*), which Itō arranged in the eleventh month of the year. It called for all domains to return political and military authority to the imperial court. Thus could they quickly establish a unified nation-state that would advance the process of civilization and enlightenment while confronting Western powers.

The question of surrendering domainal registers to the Emperor was discussed among recruited samurai as if it were an altogether natural matter. Such powerful men as Terashima and Kido as well as men such as Mutsu Munemitsu, who had ascended to the role of commissioner of foreign affairs at about the same time as Itō, had already proposed similar schemes. Many domains had already begun autonomously returning their registers to the central state.[27] But Itō's proposal drew exceptional attention and came under intense criticism, to the extent that it ultimately led to his resignation.

The target of denunciation was the part of Itō's proposal that addressed the station of the samurai. Itō repudiated the nepotism (*monbatsushugi*) of earlier times. He demanded the introduction of a meritocratic personnel employment system that would prioritize talent and ability in placing human resources. His was an unabashed, full-blown meritocracy: he called for stronger and more robust samurai to enter the standing army; for those with administrative talents to enter the government as officials (*kanri*); and for all those remaining without applicable skills simply to return home to their domains. As men who had sustained the genealogy of their households for some 250 years, samurai could hardly accept such iconoclasm, which threatened to raze a social system to which they ascribed great importance. Itō's revolutionary ideas came to be identified with the radical faction (*kyūshinha*) of the new regime and thus garnered both attention and vituperation.

As a result of the sustained efforts of Ōkubo and others, the four domains of Satsuma, Chōshū, Tosa and Saga led the way and formally submitted a proposal for the surrender of domain registers to the Emperor; Itō followed them and submitted a recommendation for how the state should proceed after the surrender. It was the first month of the second year of the Meiji era. The content of Itō's proposal summarized the debate that had unfolded in the departments of the new regime.

A faction of conservative domains (*shukyūha*) sharply denounced the proposal as excessively progressive. Itō took the criticism as a badge of pride. But as censure began pouring in from his home domain of Chōshū, the situation escalated to a point where his opponents even ascended to the imperial capital to rally for his ousting. Faced with such adverse circumstances, Itō acceded to a temporary resignation. His enemies had decried the suggestions that samurai be stripped of their special rights and that a policy of equal opportunity (*kikai kintō*) be implemented to liberalize and open up employment practices.

From early on, Itō had realized the untenability of 'expelling the barbarian' and had partaken in direct negotiations with the imperial powers. He had been employed by the new regime because of the knowledge and negotiation skills he had acquired. From low-ranking warrior (*sotsuzoku*) to a full-fledged samurai (*shizoku*), from a domainal vassal (*hanshi*) to a recruited man of talent (*chōshi*) – Itō had risen through the ranks and put faith in a new era of openness that would sweep away fiefdoms, status and other such traditional structures of power. It was this thinking that would evolve into a conception of parliamentary government – with him at its very centre.

The daring of Ōkuma Shigenobu: Plucking up opportunity

Among the powerful tozama domains of the bakumatsu era (*yūhan*), the Saga domain was of a particularly strange hue. It stood for a spirit of indomitable self-sufficiency, but it was not far from Nagasaki, and therefore not far from the influence of Nagasaki, the

Figure 1.3 Ōkuma Shigenobu in the early Meiji era, *c.* 1868. *Source:* Ōkuma-haku hachijūgonen shi hennsannkai, ed., *Ōkuma haku hachijūgonenshi,* vol. 1, 1926, front page.

sole part of Japan open to influence from the foreign world. Led by the broad-minded daimyo Nabeshima Naomasa, or Nabeshima Kansō, Saga succeeded in carrying out domainal reforms based on the promotion of productivity and industry (*shokusan kōgyō*), and it thus established itself as a *yūhan*. It was an unusual domain characterized by the simultaneous existence of a rigid, conservative status system and an enlightened orientation towards reform.

Hailing from these climes, Ōkuma Shigenobu, or Hachitarō, went on to distinguish himself as a leading Restoration bureaucrat. He was born in Tenpo 9 (= 1838) to a middling warrior family of some 400 *koku* that specialized in gunnery (*hōjutsu*).[28] He was nine years younger than Yuri Kimimasa and three years older than Itō. His origins were vastly more privileged than those of Itō – but precisely because of this privilege, he was constricted by an austere education in his domain.

In Ōkuma's days, the boys of Saga programmatically entered domainal schools at the age of 16 and remained there until they were around 25 years old. Their education centred on the Confucian classics. The schooling was harsh. If a warrior did not graduate, his stipend would be slashed and any dreams he had of entering government service (*shusshi*) would be thwarted. In a samurai world where appearances mattered, this sort of failure was unforgivable. Youths were required to demonstrate unalloyed fealty to the status quo. It was a rigid system that stunted bourgeoning talent and yielded unending mediocrity, Ōkuma later recalled.

In bakumatsu-era Saga, as elsewhere in the realm, Revere-the-Emperor (*kinnōha*) ideology reigned. Ōkuma rode these pro-imperial currents and studied national learning (*kokugaku*), or nativism, under Edayoshi Shin'yō, older brother of future councillor (*sangi*) Soejima Taneomi. Swayed, he denounced the Confucian education of the domain. It cost him his spot in school. He was expelled.

Ōkuma did not repent and return to Confucian learning after his expulsion. But he did not return to national learning, either. He ran after Dutch learning (*rangaku*). His relatives opposed this new direction, arguing that his future would vanish before him if he did not return to school. But with his mother's understanding and support, Ōkuma was able to sustain his Dutch studies.

The switch to Dutch learning was a turning point in Ōkuma's life. Having seen the necessity of Western learning in the light of shifting trends, Ōkuma's native Saga domain had decided to send young men with a background in Dutch learning to Nagasaki, where they would then pursue British learning. Now an instructor in Dutch studies at the domainal institute for Dutch learning, Ōkuma was an obvious selection to this Nagasaki group.

Ōkuma was dispatched in the wake of the botched Second Chōshū Expedition, a time when Japan had plunged into a state of extreme volatility. At this uncertain moment, he received basic instruction in Christianity, the United States Constitution and international law from Guido Verbeck, an American missionary. Verbeck told Ōkuma that in order to engage in conversations with Europeans and Americans, Ōkuma had to understand the religious and constitutional thought that would undergird their interactions and that he had to gain mastery over international law as a language for negotiation. Besides these academic pursuits, Ōkuma also engaged in trade as the point-person for Saga domain. He thus polished his negotiation skills both in the classroom and in practice. Other men, too, had gathered to study under Verbeck around this time, including Soejima Taneomi, Etō Shinpei and Ōki Takatō, all of Saga; Ōkubo Toshimichi of Satsuma; Itō Hirobumi of Chōshū; and Katō Hiroyuki, a retainer of the bakufu. These were men who went on, as Restoration bureaucrats and human resources, to carry forward the new Meiji regime.[29] Nagasaki served as their school, the school of a new enlightenment faction.

In the first month of Meiji 1 (= around February 1868), when the Battle of Toba-Fushimi ended with victory for the new regime, Ōkuma was once again dispatched to Nagasaki, this time for work. News of the defeat of bakufu forces had reached the commissioner (*bugyō*) of Nagasaki, who responded by stepping down from his post, creating a void in administration and diplomacy. To fill the void, the domains of the western provinces (*saigoku*) had joined together to set up an administrative bureau at the port. Representing Saga, Ōkuma worked together with Matsukata Masayoshi of Satsuma, Sasaki Takayuki of Tosa and others to take the helm of this new office. Each of them had overseen trade and commerce in his domain and had thereby gained skills in language and accounting.

Ōkuma stood out even among such talent. He put his exceptional negotiation skills to work, skills that stemmed from his knowledge of international law and from his practical experience conducting trade. His abilities came to the attention of Sawa Nobuyoshi, superintendent general of the regime's Kyushu pacification armies (*Kyūshū chinbu sōtoku*), and he entered the service of the government as a foreign-affairs magistrate (*gaikoku jimu hanji*) and deputy officer (*fuku sanbō*). The Saga domain hailed the employment of Ōkuma as an opportunity to build ties with the new regime.

Under Sawa at Nagasaki, Ōkuma was charged with handling customs. He swept up and sorted through the piles of unfinished business that had accumulated under the bakufu-era commissioner's office (*bugyōsho*), gaining a favourable reputation among people both within and beyond the bureau. As a result of these successes, no doubt, Ōkuma was appointed as a recruit and a junior councillor while in Nagasaki. It was but two months after Itō had received the same appointments. Ōkuma was exactly 30 years old.

What pulled Ōkuma away from his field of action in Nagasaki and to the central government was a diplomatic crisis, just as it was with Itō. On the thirteenth day of the third month (= 5 April), not long after Sawa took up his post as superintendent, the new regime announced the establishment of the Department of Divinities (*jingikan*) and the policy of the unity of rites and rule (*saisei itchi*). Then, on the fifteenth day, it indicated its intention to ban Christianity. Having received this dictate to proscribe Christianity, Sawa ordered the conversion of all Hidden Christians (*kakure kirishitan*) still concealed in the Nagasaki area since the Shimabara Rebellion of 1637 to 1638. Twenty-six believers in Urakami refused to convert.[30] Thus began the incident known as the Fourth Destruction at Urakami (*Urakami yonban kuzure*).[31] As the regime cracked down on the Christians, Western imperialist powers demanded that it respect freedom of belief and preserve the right to proselytize. The regime needed circumspection and careful judgement. To offer advice to the state, Ōkuma ascended to the capital along with Inoue Kaoru of Chōshū, himself also a recruit, a junior councillor and an assistant for the Foreign Affairs Bureau.

The regime awaited Ōkuma and his band before opening consultations on how to respond. Ōkuma vigorously maintained that the laws of the land had been firmly fixed and that the demands of foreign imperialists constituted nothing but unjustified interventionism in domestic affairs. He insisted that to yield would not only make the regime lose face, it would arouse a state of dire uncertainty in a realm still rocked by the forces of 'expelling the barbarian'. Ōkuma presented a compelling argument, and it garnered wide support. But the problem now lay in how to conduct negotiations with the foreign powers. The new regime entrusted Ōkuma with this task.

The negotiations unfolded on the third day of the fourth month (= 25 April), at Higashi Hongan Temple in Osaka. On the side of the imperialist powers stood Parkes. In response to Parkes, who insisted that all civilized states had to respect freedom of belief, Ōkuma conceded the import of Christianity but riposted with a history of how Christianity had thrown the unity of the Japanese state into disarray. He indicated further concerns that Christianity would now spark a conflict between itself and the native religion of Japan. The negotiations dragged on for six hours. No resolution came of them, but the imperialist powers stopped pressing forward with their demands thereafter. Out of consideration for the imperialist powers, the Japanese side spared the believers at Urakami the death penalty, exiling them instead.

To the new regime, the appearance of Ōkuma on the political stage was like the discovery of an unexpected trove of treasure. Kido, who had accompanied Ōkuma in the negotiations, even described him as bearing a 'cheerful' (*yukai*) attitude while he expatiated on the benefits and harms of Christianity and resisted the highhanded coercion of Parkes. From here forward, the central leadership of the regime held Ōkuma close at hand.

With the experience and knowledge he cultivated in Nagasaki, Ōkuma manoeuvred through difficult negotiations with agility, inspiring a sense of fearful admiration in all those around him and thereby gaining a foothold in the new regime. He was promoted to deputy governor of the foreign service (*gaikokukan fukuchiji*), and then he transferred to the Ministry of the Treasury (*ōkurashō*) by the end of the year to help resolve mounting trade problems. As a senior aide in the treasury (*ōkura daiyū*), he applied his abilities to monetary reform, becoming a man of practical talents on whose shoulders rested the new regime. He gathered Itō and other young hands in the Restoration bureaucracy into the tile-roofed walls of his abode, which came to be known as the Ryōzanpaku, named after the legendary Liangshanbo of the Song Dynasty, a place where great heroes and men of ambition would gather.[32]

An age of conservatism, an age of reform

No sooner had the new regime been established than it began to recruit men of talent into its fold, transcending the status system of its forebears. For 'men of ambition' (*yūshisha*) born in an age wherein the status of their households at birth had determined their occupations, there was, in the words of Ōkuma, 'no happier thing' than the Meiji Restoration.[33] It was precisely for this reason that these men gave their whole lives for the new government. And thus was the Meiji bureaucracy born. The service these men undertook for the new regime, carrying its burden on their shoulders, was so central that some said the government constituted 'rule by magistrates' (*hanji seiji*). The influence of bureaucratic service was sweeping.[34]

Of course, for every Itō in the government who lifted himself up from lower-level samurai status, there was no shortage of holdovers from Tokugawa domainal elites (*karō kyū*). These elites had done little to contribute to the rise of the new government, even though they had played important roles in the bakumatsu regime as representatives of their domains.

Their negligible place in the making of the Meiji state resulted from the long-enduring stability of the bakuhan system, in which they originally operated. In that system, which was propped up by Confucian ideology, preservation of the status quo through dogged adherence to precedent was deemed a virtue; work was carried out according to assigned status affiliations; and 'not changing' in itself was highly prized. Domainal schools offered students up to the age of 20 a sound education centred on Zhu Xi Neo-Confucianism; they sought not to provide practical learning in government policy but to instil in their students the mental preparedness to be a ruler. They valued not the skill of governance (*keisei no sai*) but its virtue (*tokumoku*). In this context, 'good' came only from progressing through a set curriculum and excelling in it. Young men walked down this fixed path single-mindedly. No reward awaited those who thought and acted for themselves. Quite the contrary: free-thinking youth would be ejected from the system.

Although it succeeded in producing reliable government officers, this formalized system in domanial schools stultified any spirit of breaking free from established structures. Schools produced men bent on preservation. In a time of transformation, these men found themselves bereft of the educational preparedness to act on their own and to break open a new age for themselves. They could hardly match the freely thinking, freely moving, freely choosing men of spirit around them.

Of course, it was not the case that they were lacking in ability. They fell behind primarily because they could not rival the unbounded freedom of the *shishi*, who had no obligations to protect their domains or their households. Indeed, lower-level samurai formed the preponderance of those who pursued Western learning in its earliest days. If an upper-level samurai had undertaken Western studies, he would have been disparaged as a 'Dutch-addict' (*ranpeki*): Western learning was practical learning, not a proper field of study for those of high status.[35] That lower-level warriors came to form the core of the Restoration bureaucracy reflected, then, a distortion of the Tokugawa status system amid the transformations of a new era.

Little wonder that the new regime faced backlash from men who lived by the traditional order. As vigorous criticism from traditional elements mounted, men of talent willing to enter the new government dwindled. And although the state needed specialized knowledge to help build the structures of a new administration, it lacked objective standards by which to determine whom to employ. In these circumstances, the state relied increasingly on personal connections as it made its personnel hires. We witness here the emergence of a clique of men pejoratively called 'oligarchic bureaucrats' (*hanbatsu kanryō*).

From the perspective of those living in the traditional world, to abjure one's domain and lord and to throw oneself into the service of a new regime constituted acts of betrayal. Many believed that bureaucrats had gained their posts not through talent but through this sort of shameful perfidy. Such a hostile view of bureaucrats blended in with feelings of intense jealousy and resentment. And these feelings lingered long.

The new regime had gained legitimacy from its victory in the Boshin War and from its successes in recruiting men of talent. But danger was now lurking. In its relations with individual domains, it seemed headed towards a stand-off that would amount to a fight between the old order and the new. To safeguard its fledgling legitimacy, it became even more pressing to emblazon the principle of public debate and to urge on political participation across the realm.

Public debate and new personnel

The 1868 constitution system and the centralization of structures of rule

On the eleventh day of the fourth month (= 3 May 1868), Edo Castle fell. Not a drop of blood was shed. Tokugawa Yoshinobu retreated to Mito as Aizu and other domains in the north-east persisted in their allegiance to the bakufu. But the war with the defunct bakufu was over. On the first day of the next month, the intercalary fourth month, Parkes presented the Meiji Emperor with an official communication from the Queen designating him as her envoy (*shinninjō*) to the sovereign. In the international field no less than the domestic one, the new regime was gaining legitimacy as the sole ruler over the realm.

Iwakura, Ōkubo and other members of the anti-bakufu faction continued to hold the reins of power in the new regime. As circumstances settled, planning began under their leadership for new structures that would support a new administration. Towards this end, the Constitution of 1868 (*seitaisho kansei*) was promulgated on the twenty-first day of the same month. It was based on a draft from the Institutions Bureau (*seido ryō*).[36]

The word *seitai* in the phrase *seitaisho* was a direct translation of the word 'constitution'.[37] The constitution declared, 'All power in the realm will be reverted to the Council of State (*Dajōkan*). Thus will the scourge of governance being divided along two paths be not. The power of the Council of State will be divided among three branches: the executive, the legislative, and the judicial. Thus will the scourge of lopsided [government] be not.'[38] In other words, even while concentrating power in the newly formed Council of State, the constitution divided power equally among three branches to avoid the problem of excessive power falling on one branch. This was the general structure of state outlined in the document.

The Legislative Council, or *Giseikan*, was established to take charge, of course, of legislation. It was made up of two parts: the upper chamber, which conducted decision-making, and the lower chamber, which responded to referrals and inquiries. Composed of senior and junior councillors, the upper chamber was a sweeping decision-making body in which consultations on every facet of national governance unfolded, from constitutionalism and law to personnel affairs, diplomatic treaties, and war and peace. The lower chamber was composed of representatives from each domain. It deliberated on requests for counsel and other queries from the upper chamber. Although all fundamental decision-making processes were carried out in the upper chamber, a wide range of opinions were solicited from and consolidated in the lower chamber, allowing for a mode of public debate with both a centralized concentration of decision-making power and a broad sweep of political participation. Such were the designs behind the Legislative Council.

Dividing power could have yielded a dysfunctional government. To prevent such a situation, the state had to give careful consideration to the relationship between the Legislative Council and the Executive Council (*gyōseikan*). Crucial in this regard were Sanjō and Iwakura. The chief executive position was disbanded, and they were moved from their positions as deputy chief executives to the newly formed post of *hoshō*, or chief aide. The *hoshō* served as head of the executive officers, but he was chosen from among the senior councillors, who served as legislative officers. Thus, even while dividing power among the three branches of government, the state designed top leadership posts that amalgamated the divided powers. It supplied itself from the outset with a mechanism to regulate power and ensure its sustained grip on political authority.

The Executive Council carried authority over many of the departments it inherited from the previous administrative structure: the Departments of Divinities, of Accounts, of Military Affairs, of Foreign Affairs and of Law. But it absorbed the Bureau of Chief Executives (*sōsaikyoku*) into the Executive Council itself; the Office of Domestic Affairs (*naikoku jimukyoku*) into the Department of the Provinces (*chihōkan*); and the Institutions Bureau (*seido jimukyoku*) into the upper chamber of the Legislative Council. Amid this reshuffling, the state decided that all executive officers with ranks of assistant officer or magistrate (*hankanji*) and up would go by the English-language title 'minister' in foreign dealings. We can discern in this decision the sensitivity to foreign diplomacy with which the state set about building its executive structures.

The building of administrative structures proceeded in the provinces just as it did in the central state. Pacifying armies dispatched to each region brought lands once controlled by the bakufu under the helm of the new regime. The state thus gained direct control over new territory, where it established military and legal authority, expanded popular education and moral suasion mechanisms, supported industrial productivity and developed structures for the collection of taxes.[39] To advance these new projects, the pacifying armies were transformed from military forces designed to enforce security into executive organizations. The deputy superintendent (*fukusōtoku*) of the Hokurikudō pacifying army, for instance, became the governor of Echigo province, and his counterpart in the Tōkaidō became the chamberlain (*jōdai*) of Kōfu. As in the central government, these provincial governments took men from noble lineage as their head officers and then recruited samurai from neighbouring domains to carry forward the actual processes of governance.

The regime renamed its directly controlled lands 'prefectures' (*fu, ken*) to highlight their importance. Under the new administrative structures of the 1868 Constitution (*seitaisho kansei*), pre-existing domains were added to these prefectures, making the Department of the Provinces cover both domains and prefectures (*fu, han, ken*). Increasingly crowded out by the directly controlled prefectures, the domains, too, gradually came under the immediate purview of the new state.

Human resources and the centralization of power

Why did the state need to carry out these reforms? From its inception, the new regime had made proclamations and recruited men of talent according to the exigencies of the moment. Its governing structure had become warped and ungainly as a result, bloating to an unnecessary size. The process of building new structures of rule required a commensurate process of tidying up and reorganizing both those structures and the men in them.

Indeed, the state had gained a prodigious amount of weight. A month before the proclamation of the Constitution of 1868, Matsudaira Yoshinaga, senior councillor, had submitted a proposal to the deputy chief executives calling for reform of the government and for better selection of state personnel.[40] He was sounding an alarm: as government structures were settling more firmly into place, the administrative tasks of the Council of State were ballooning, the state was being inundated by imperial mandates (*chokuyu*) and reports (*gosatasho*), and chaos was taking hold. The blame for the mess lay in reckless, undisciplined employment practices, Yoshinaga said.

By this point, the number of senior councillors in the state had increased to twenty-nine and that of junior councillors to eighty-four. Over one hundred men in the Three Offices now had a hand in decision-making. No doubt, administrative demands had increased. But that was precisely the problem: the state needed more bureaucrats to take up practical administrative functions, not more senior and junior councillors, who had decision-making capacities in the Legislative Council.

Why had the number of senior and junior councillors risen to this point? There were two reasons. First, more than half of those who had been newly appointed as senior or junior councillors were daimyo or nobles (*shokō, kuge*). To expand its support base, the new regime had actively sought to fold powerful daimyo into the state. As it furnished those daimyo with high ranks, it endowed them with commensurate responsibilities in their domains. It was an important strategy for a fledgling regime: it at once expanded the state's influence and averted a free-rider problem by giving leaders concrete responsibilities.

The second reason lay in the policy of awarding merits (*ronkō kōshō*) to members of the nobility. Nobles lobbied hard to gain remuneration from the state, demanding rewards based not only on an assessment of their actual activities in the bakumatsu and Restoration eras but even on the degree of the fealty of their forebears and lineages. Nobles had long held a distinguished place in society, but in their years under warrior rule they had fallen into economic despair. Rescuing them from destitution was seen as a necessary step for preserving the dignity of the imperial court. Thus the state appointed many of them as junior councillors. We have already seen how well junior councillors were compensated.

These employment practices, based on the personal interests of nobles and the state, stood in contradiction to the principle of meritocracy that the new regime heralded. From a practical standpoint, too, it was a fatally inefficient system for a government that had to manage a range of executive functions even amid financial limitations. There was no way that active decision-making could proceed in an assembly made up of one hundred motley men. And what is more, as great numbers of men with only minimal political consciousness assembled together, so too did the risk of venality and factionalism grow. The integrity of the regime could easily have fallen apart. The state had ballooned to a point where both its functionality and legitimacy were tottering precariously. It threatened to collapse under its own weight.

The reforms of the 1868 Constitution sought therefore to revamp both the structure of the state and the selection of personnel. The regime pushed forward with audacious reforms. It reduced the number of senior councillors to eleven and that of junior councillors to just ten. Among the eleven senior councillors were Sanjō and Iwakura, nobles who had recently taken the post of *hoshō*, as well as four other nobles who had been senior councillors since the inception of the state: Nakayama Tadayasu, Ōgimachisanjō Sanenaru, Nakamikado Tsuneyuki and Tokudaiji Sanetsune. Filling the remaining seats were five of the original daimyo senior councillors: Yoshinaga, Hachisuka Mochiaki of Tokushima, Kamei Koremi of Tsuwano, Nabeshima Naomasa and Mōri Motonori. Many of the sixteen men ejected from posts as senior councillors were transferred to provincial officer posts.

Remaining as junior councillors were Komatsu and Ōkubo of Satsuma; Gotō and Fukuoka of Tosa; Kido and Hirosawa of Chōshū; Soejima Taneomi of Saga; Yuri of Echizen; and Yokoi of Kumamoto. Excluding Yokoi, who entered the government after being especially sought out, the junior councillors were, without exception, the most powerful men from the most powerful tozama domains; all had been deeply engaged from the earliest stage in the establishment of the new regime. Each was honoured with the junior Lower Fourth Rank on the same day of his reappointment.

Sixty-nine men were ejected from their roles as junior councillors: thirty-one domainal samurai and thirty-eight nobles. Itō, Ōkuma, Inoue, Terajima and other Restoration bureaucrats who had been originally employed for their talents were transferred to the Executive Council. But many other men who had entered the government as representatives of their domains, men such as Nakane Yukie of Echizen, lost their posts in the government.

The new regime thus preserved its legitimacy while consolidating decision-making processes and deepening its pool of talent for practical governance. It had recklessly proliferated government posts to gain support in the wake of the *coup d'état*. Now, with the winds of political authority blowing in its favour, it turned to building new structures for substantive political action.

Widening participation: Realizing the ideal of public debate

Although the state had begun putting up the façade of a centralized political authority, its foundation remained wobbly. People and land still remained affiliated with the domains. It needed both to aid in domainal rule and to secure political participation from the domains themselves.

A solution lay in the Constitution of 1868, which sketched out a policy for opening up public debate across the entire nation. The lower chamber of the Legislative Council was designated as the arena in which debate would occur. Whereas the upper chamber functioned as the joint deliberative body of the senior and junior councillors, the lower chamber was made of assemblymen known as *kōshi*, or tributary men. Gathered together under a chairman of the lower chamber, these tributary men each represented their respective domains and together constituted a government congress (*gikai*).

The 'tributary men' (*kōshi*) were a category instituted together with the recruits (*chōshi*), but the roles of the two groups differed vastly. Unlike the recruits, who took charge of the practical affairs of the new regime, the tributary men were assemblymen who sought to put the ideal of public debate (*kōgi yoron*) into practice.[41] Whereas no fixed quota was set on recruits, who were appointed based on their talents and abilities, tributary men were chosen by the domains, and their numbers were fixed based on the *kokudaka* of each domain: three for large domains of over 400,000 koku; two for mid-sized domains of over 100,000 koku; and one for smaller domains. Thus influence in the assembly was allotted to domains based on their size.

The state called for tributary men to solicit public opinion in their own domains (*hanron*) and then to partake in the deliberations of the lower chamber based on that opinion. It was a system that placed heavy responsibility on the shoulders of the tributary men. Liaisons (*rusui yaku*) from each domain did reside in Kyoto in the earliest days of the regime, but many of those liaisons could not have represented domainal popular opinion. They would have been more an encumbrance to than a vehicle for reciprocal communication between the central state and the domains. The state therefore called for domains to appoint new public servants to represent domainal opinion, giving official notice that the tributary men should fulfil this function.

The notice from the new regime on this matter enumerated points of considerable interest. The central state did not simply call for conformity to its demands. It sought to invigorate the expression of public opinion within domains. It called for debate among domains based on actual circumstances in each holding. And it asked domains in that debate not to conform with one another blindly. We clearly see here the delineation of an ideal in which each domain would offer the assembly a lucid, independent opinion and thereby participate fully and judiciously in public discussion. Thus would the concept of open public debate be realized.

But what exactly was discussed in the lower chamber? According to the 1868 Constitution, the chamber would deliberate not only on tax law, communications, coinage and currency, weights and measures, military service, the construction of castles and other such matters that pertained directly to the domains. Treaties, war and peace, and other affairs of national governance, too, were deliberated. The envisioned domain of discussion was vast.

Still, the lower chamber was a consultative body whose being was premised on inquiries from the upper chamber on which it would consult. Without the upper house, the lower house had no reason to be. This arrangement derived from a sense of fear that the lower chamber could become a breeding ground for anti-regime sentiment. It was true that the state had opened up new arenas for public debate, but those arenas had limits.

In the fifth month, the lower chamber received requests for advice on strategies to set up a navy, on means to conduct government finances and on ways to keep the hearts and minds of the people pacified. From the sixth month, the assembly met three times a month to deliberate on these matters. But it quickly descended into turmoil. Inquiries were withdrawn in the eighth month. Within just three months, public debate in the lower chamber was dissolved.

This failure did not suggest a renunciation of the principle of public debate or a new conception that it was unnecessary. Attempts and struggles to realize the ideal of public debate persisted as legislative structures were renamed the House of Public Debate (*kōgisho*) and the House of Representatives (*shūgiin*) and the National Diet was ultimately established. The lower chamber was but the first attempt in this process.

--

Who conducted the actual task of ruling the realm and establishing legitimacy for the new Meiji regime? It was men of talent assembled from across the nation as recruits and tributary men, as *chōshi* and *kōshi*. With the knowledge they gained from practical experience and with the capacity for action they cultivated in the bakumatsu era, it was recruited samurai who broke free of the structures of their domains to become the motive force sustaining a new regime. Dispatched to the national centre with generations of household and domainal heritage on their backs, tributary men partook in the new process of public debate, sharply deliberating on the best means of governance.

Ōkubo, Saigō, Kido, Sakamoto – these are the heroes of whom we speak when we tell of the champions of the Meiji Restoration. But the Restoration was not achieved by their efforts alone. There were others: Restoration bureaucrats who shouldered the burden of practical governance, men of talent who carried on their backs the future of the new regime, domainal vassals across the land who drew up plans to find new ways in the world as the social order shifted beneath their feet. It was these men who broke open a new age of *risshin shusse*, of rising in the world by autonomous will.

Developing Human Resources for a New Regime

The personnel employment system of the new state: Overcoming status

On the twentieth day of the first month of the second year of the Meiji reign (= 2 March 1869), the domainal lords of Satsuma, Chōshū, Tosa and Hizen submitted their call for the surrender of domainal registers to the imperial court (*hanseki hōkan*). In the third month, the Emperor completed his second procession to Tokyo (*Tōkyō gyōkai*), making it the de facto capital of the nation. All that remained of a civil war raging since the previous year lay in Hakodate, the last holdout of Enomoto Takeaki. Meiji Japan was well on its way to becoming a consolidated nation-state with a centralized administration.

But things did not go so smoothly. Forces demanding the expulsion of barbarians (*jōi*) ran rampant across the realm. Men carried an expectation verging on conviction that the state would carry out the policy of expelling barbarians. Meanwhile, few domains had understood that the surrender of domainal registers and the transfer of power to a centralized administration meant their demise. Most assumed that daimyo authority over their lands would be reaffirmed before long, just as it was when one shogun succeeded another. To guide the forces favoring expulsion to the reality of conciliation and to establish a centralized administration in peace, the Meiji government sought to create an administration with knowledge, power and legitimacy.

To bolster legitimacy, the state sought first to widen the path of political participation. It found it necessary, as explained in Chapter 1, not only to advance public debate but also to cast a wide net across the nation and hire talented men into the bureaucracy, where those men would engage in planning and implementation. Opening the double door of legislation and execution to the public became a means of advancing state legitimacy. A regime that had used the samurai recruitment system (*chōshi seido*) to secure human resources for the short term now had to develop talent for the mid- and long term. And as it did so, it searched for knowledge for modern Japan itself.

Towards a Restoration bureaucracy: The public selection of state officials

For a new regime that had heralded a meritocratic system independent of status affiliation, a particularly thorny problem lay in the daimyo of powerful tozama domains (*yūhan*). It was these daimyo who supplied the financial resources, human talent and military might that undergirded the new regime. The state could hardly afford to disregard their will.

Personnel changes after the reforms of the 1868 constitutional system revealed this problem. Four men, including Yamauchi Toyoshige of Tosa domain, were reappointed in this period as senior councillors (*gijō*). Ikeda Yoshinori of Tottori domain, who had made considerable contributions in the Boshin War, was also added to the senior councillors. With more reappointments and additions from the nobility as well, the number of personnel in the state once again began to balloon: the number of senior councillors climbed from eleven to nineteen, and that of the junior councillors (*san'yo*) from ten to seventeen. Before long, the centralization of decision-making envisioned in the 1868 Constitution had become tangled up in enduring forces from the past.[1]

Sweeping reforms were not possible so long as these long-standing wielders of power formed the nucleus of the state. To break through the impasse, Ōkuma Shigenobu, Iwakura Tomomi and other members of the reform faction planned to carry out an election of state officers, as ordained in the 1868 Constitution. Their aims were threefold: to reduce the number of men in the state and thereby build a system wherein reform could proceed quickly; to buttress the legitimacy of government authorities by holding open elections; and to raise a sense of unity in the regime through mutual elections.

The first open election of state officials (*kanri kōsen*) occurred on the thirteenth day of the fifth month (= 22 June 1869). Suffrage was granted to officers ranging from chief aides (*hoshō*) down to magistrates (*hanji*). Electors were to choose from among nobles and daimyo (*kugyō shokō*) for the positions of chief aide, senior councillor, department head (*kanchiji*) and head of the inner court (*naiteishoku chiji*). For the posts of junior councillor and deputy head of department (*fuku chiji*), they could choose from among all those with voting rights.[2] Elections were held on the premises of the Council of State (*dajōkan*). Voters were to record their selections on a ballot and submit the ballot in a box.

The Meiji Emperor himself appeared at the elections. They began with voting for the chief aide. With seemingly unanimous approval, forty-nine votes, Sanjō Sanetomi was elected to the position; his appointment then descended from the Emperor. Voting for the senior and junior councillors occurred the following day. The number of senior councillors was fixed at three: elected were Iwakura and Tokudaiji Sanetsune, each with forty-eight votes, and Nabeshima Naomasa, with thirty-nine. Domainal lords who had been appointed through the post-1868-Constitution merits-and-rewards system (*ronkō kōshō*) failed, without exception, to be elected.

The six junior councillors elected were Ōkubo, with forty-nine votes; Kido, with forty-two; Soejima Taneomi, with thirty-one; Higashikuze Michitomi, with twenty-six; Gotō Shōjirō, with twenty-three; and Itagaki Taisuke, with twenty-one. The election of Ōkubo, Kido, Soejima and other such men of talent, all of whom had promoted the policy of surrendering domainal registers to the Emperor (*hanseki hōkan*), signified an affirmation of the trajectory towards centralizing power. With these elections, the reform faction of the regime achieved its real purpose: arresting the powers of the domainal lords, preserving their own freedom to rule and endowing legitimacy to new policies they would enact.

On the fifteenth day of the fifth month (= 24 June), the day after the elections concluded, assignments were made to the six posts of deputy head of department. It was in these positions that authority over the six executive divisions resided. Ōkuma Shigenobu was appointed to the Department of Accounts (*kaikeikan*); Ōmura Masujirō of Chōshū to Military Affairs (*gunmukan*); Terajima Munenori to Foreign Affairs (*gaikokukan*); Sasaki Takayuki to Legal Affairs (*keihōkan*); and Hirosawa Saneomi to People's Affairs (*minbukan*). Each hailed from one of the four leading domains of the Restoration: Satsuma, Chōshū, Tosa or Hizen. Thus the positions were filled with bureaucrats who excelled in both talent and experience. The human foundation for an administration geared towards reform was firmly established.

The surrender of domainal registers to the Emperor and the rise of the Employment-Edict system (*shokuinrei taisei*): Transformations in decision-making

With its structures in place, the new regime opened an expanded upper chamber (*jōkyoku*) assembly of the Legislative Council on the twenty-first day of the fifth month, or 30 June, even inviting the lords of all domains to join.[3] Enomoto Takeaki had surrendered three days earlier. The civil war had ended. The assembly marked the departure point of a new Meiji government with political authority over the entire nation. The state now sought to win concerted support for its centralization of power.

The assembly meeting proceeded with participants expressing their opinions on three topics of inquiry from the Emperor: the prosperity of the Imperial Way (*kōdō kōryū*), the full-time appointment of domain governors (*chihanji sennin*) and the development of Ezochi (*Ezochi kaitaku*). But actual debate in the conference was avoided. There was wisdom in this 'general consultation, executive decision' system (*tōsai gōgi sei*), a system inherited from the ancient past wherein all opinions were heard and noted but decisions were ultimately made by designated potentates. The system succeeded in averting the stand-offs and conflicts that had marred earlier decision-making processes.[4] It expedited decision-making by setting up new structures of public debate while perpetuating top-down modes of arbitration. Such was the pragmatism of the regime.

Having here confirmed the absence of significant opposition to its designs, the government implemented the policy of surrendering domainal registers to the Emperor on the seventeenth day of the sixth month, 25 July. The policy granted erstwhile daimyo and noblemen special privileges as members of the peerage (*kazoku*), but it folded them into the modern nation-state as constitutive members. Restoration bureaucrats who had once felt torn by their dual allegiance to the central government and their domains now became affiliated only with the central state, both in name and in practice. On the same day, the now-unnecessary personnel recruitment system was disbanded.[5]

With the surrender of domainal registers to the Emperor, the government became the sole political authority over the entire nation in both theory and reality. Now faced with the problem of governing the whole realm, a regime that had heralded in its 1868 Constitution the ideal of the tripartite division of power pivoted towards gearing its structure of rule more pragmatically to reality. It was in this vein that the Employment Edict (*shokuinrei*) was proclaimed on the eighth day of the seventh month (= 15 August).[6] The edict inaugurated the Two Departments and Six Ministries System (*nikan rokushō sei*), composed of the Council of State and the Department of Divinities (*jingikan*) as well as the ministries of People's Affairs (*minbushō*), of the Treasury (*ōkurashō*), of Military Affairs (*hyōbushō*), of Judicial Affairs (*gyōbushō*), of the Imperial Household (*kunaishō*) and of Foreign Affairs (*gaimushō*).

The state severed spaces of public debate from the Council of State. The change constituted a dramatic shift. The upper chamber of the Legislative Council was dissolved, and the lower chamber was reorganized, transforming from the House of Public Debate (*kōgisho*) into the House of Representatives (*shūgiin*), which became no more than a consultative organ of the Council of State. Its role was extremely limited.

The Council of State turned into an executive body with vast authority and decision-making power. In its upper ranks stood one minister of the left (*sadaijin*) and one minister of the right (*udaijin*), who assisted the Emperor and who arbitrated on matters of imperial governance (*taisei o handan suru*). Below them were three major-counsellors (*dainagon*) and three councillors (*sangi*) who contributed opinions to the state and carried out decision-making. The six ministries operated beneath these leaders. At the helm of each ministry stood a lord (*kyō*). Beneath him were two ranks of deputy ministers (*jikan*), the senior and junior aides (*daiyū, shōyū*); two ranks of administrative officers (*jimukan*), the senior and junior deputies (*daijō, shōjō*); and two ranks of secretarial officers (*shokikan*), the senior and junior scribes (*dairoku, shōroku*). Thus a clear line from drafting and planning all the way up to decision-making was mapped out. The One-Hundred Noble Titles (*chōtei hyakkan*), ranks that had been handed down since the court of the seventh-century Tenji emperor, were all abolished, and new ranks that would form the foundational structure of a modern bureaucracy were installed: the *chokuninkan*, officials who were appointed by imperial decree through recommendation from the Cabinet and were in principle granted their assignments through personal meetings with the Emperor; below them, the *sōninkan*, those similarly appointed by recommendation to the Emperor by the Cabinet but without a meeting with the Emperor; and below them, the *hanninkan*, those appointed by heads of executive departments. These reforms dissolved the remaining links between governmental position and status or pedigree. They gave birth to a structure in which personnel, no longer constrained by provenance, were appointed by ability.

Loci of power and decision-making changed, too. As executive state functions became increasingly specialized, the posts that nobles and domainal lords had held as heads of the ministries (*shōkei*) became largely symbolic. Actual power over the Council of State lay in the councilor posts (*sangi*) held by Restoration bureaucrats; power in each executive department lay, meanwhile, with the senior and junior aides (*daiyū, shōyū*).

The desires of the regime to overcome the long-standing status-based social order infiltrated all dimensions of state and society. It was at this point, for instance, that Maejima Hisoka left Shizuoka domain and entered into service at the Ministry of People's Affairs. He is well known today as the founder of Japan's postal system; he also went on to serve as head of the postal bureau of the home ministry (*naimushō ekiteikyoku chō*) and as deputy minister of communications (*teishin jikan*). Maejima had been a leading official in the Shizuoka domain, which had been under the direct control of the Tokugawa household, but he was appointed to a status as low as ninth-tier rank (*kyūtō shusshi*). He was deeply resentful. But this umbrage vanished after he attended his first ministry meeting and experienced the atmosphere of the gathering. He recalled the experience with the following words:[7]

> It was the fifth day of the first month of Meiji 3 [5 February 1870] when I first entered the bureau. I had not anticipated it, but I attended as a senior officer of the bureau, and only Shibusawa Eiichi, who was a *sōninkan* posted dually in the tax ministry [and in my bureau], was posted to my ministry as well. But in attendance at the meeting were Ōkuma and Itō as well as Date [Munenari], the lord at the helm of both the finance and people's affairs ministries. Without the least grandiloquence or braggadocio, and without any discrimination between high or low, they opened their hearts and deliberated on the pressing matters of the hour. Joy was restored to my heart. I felt immensely glad.

The Ministry of People's Affairs was home to Ōkuma and Itō, the foremost paragons of the new regime, and in working with them to attend to state governance, Maejima perceived extraordinary possibility. To deliberate with them in an unrestrained atmosphere, to be judged not by status but by ability—to Maejima, who had had to find a way for himself in the rigid status system of the erstwhile bakufu, these were propitious signs by which he could feel the changes of a new era. There was nothing more attractive to the spirited youth of the day, to these young men with will and ambition who dreamed of radical transformation, than the liberal airs that blew through the new regime.

Change, not confined to the national centre, rippled out to the provinces. In the tenth month of Meiji 1 (November-December 1868), the government gave the domains official notice of a new System for Employment in Domainal Governance (*hanchishoku sei*), a plan for the reform of domainal administration.[8] In this ordinance, too, the state ordained that domains must employ men of talent without regard to their lineage, and it mandated that domains report all shifts and changes in governance to the Council of State. The government thus revealed its intent to directly oversee an overhaul in personnel employment practices across the realm.

With the central state now holding sovereignty over the entire nation, the domains, acceding to this state directive, embarked on an alternation of generations in their leadership. This renewal of human resources expedited reforms of domain administration, and across every part of the nation, a new generation of talented men suited for a new age began to accumulate fecund executive experience.

What kind of personnel should we assemble? Deliberations in the House of Public Debate (*Kōgisho*)

With the Employment-Edict System thus laid out, the Restoration bureaucrats, made up predominantly of samurai (*shizoku*), took centre stage in the regime. But these bureaucrats could not make the government run on their own. To satisfy growing administrative demands, they needed to develop a large number of human resources with practical executive capabilities.

Who would take up such executive functions? Along with the problem of participation in decision-making, that of executive government had become a point of interest across the nation. Would the state find effective means to select men of talent from across the realm? Or would it gather men through private interests and personal connections? The legitimacy of the regime hinged on these questions.

The House of Public Debate took interest in these matters, and it conducted insightful deliberations on the prospect of introducing an examination system for state employment.[9] Using its discussions as our entry-point, let us examine the problem of personnel employment in the early Meiji era.

As explained earlier, the House of Public Debate was inaugurated as an arena for the practice of public debate. In it, tributary men (*kōshi*), representing their respective domains, gathered and deliberated on state affairs.[10] Two-hundred and twenty-seven men from the domains gathered for the first assembly, which convened in the third month.

On the twelfth day of the fourth month (= 23 May 1869), Kanda Takahira, deputy chair (*fuku gichō*) of the House of Public Debate, submitted the 'Petition for a Chinese-style Examination System' to the House. The document called for an examination system for the employment of bureaucrats.

Kanda was among the leading new intellectuals of the bakumatsu-Restoration era. He had pursued Dutch learning early on and worked as an instructor in the Institution for the Investigation of Barbarian Books (*bansho shirabe sho*), and then in 1868, the first year of the Meiji reign, he entered employment with the regime as a recruit (*chōshi*), joining the Department of Foreign Affairs before transferring to the Department of Accounts.[11] He was a progressive Restoration bureaucrat whom the state deployed in its most critical fields. Indeed, it was Kanda who drafted the operational guidelines for the House of Public Debate when it was being installed. He himself then took up the post of deputy chair of the House, and the first bill he submitted was this proposal for an examination system.

Kanda opened the bill with this argument: various methods for employing human resources have been taken up from long ago, but the civil examination system carried out in China has received exceptional acclaim, even in the West. In our nation, Kanda wrote, we must use the opportunity afforded by the establishment of a new government to inaugurate a system for the employment of talented people. We should then put that system into effect alongside laws for government assembly (*kaigihō*). We must thus follow the precedent of the Chinese imperial examination system (*kakyo*, Ch. *keju*) to gather men of extraordinary talent, and we must use the parliamentary system of the West to bring the hearts and minds of people together. On these two pillars must we build the nation-state.

To provide a basis from which deliberations in the House of Public Debate could proceed, Kanda laid out specific details for his proposal. He recommended that exams be conducted once a year; that the exam not only encompass national learning (*kokugaku*) and Chinese learning (*kangaku*), but also emphasize a set of subjects needed for practical governance: economics (*keizaigaku*), composition (*bunshōgaku*), astronomy and geography (*tenmon chiri gaku*), military studies, legal studies, medical studies and natural history (*hakubutsugaku*); that examinees sit three rounds of exams; that those deemed excellent be employed on a probationary basis as state bureaucrats below the fourth rank; and that the names, origins and posts of those who reached this endpoint be widely broadcast. By dressing the system in Chinese garb, Kanda drew in members of the conservative faction, but by incorporating exams, he simultaneously laid the basis for employment by meritocracy.

The proposal constituted a chasm separating an old order, one in which members of the House of Public Debate had been reared, and a new order, one emerging before their eyes. Over this chasm, the public debaters wavered. They could not altogether abandon the traditional structures of their domains: they unanimously called for domains to retain the right to nominate exam-takers in this new system.

But even as they hesitated, many of the representatives indicated enthusiastic support for the examination system itself, praising it as 'a just plan' and 'a good system'. After all, they shared a common desire to secure influence in the government by sending their own personnel into its fold. They welcomed an exam system that would allow for the fair and equitable employment of their men.

The men of the House of Public Debate expressed incisive opinions on the exam system, even considering how the new system would be applied to post-Restoration Japan. Some insisted that testing various martial arts (*bujutsu*) on the exam would be necessary to prevent statesmen from going the way of Qing bureaucrats, whose literary pursuits had enervated and emasculated them. Others, basing themselves on the way of the warrior (*shidō*) and emphasizing the importance of human qualities, argued that virtuous deeds (*tokkō*) should be considered on the exam. Still others advocated for greater emphasis on debate and discussion skills (*benron*), and others further called for the inclusion of practical subjects such as accounting (*kaikeigaku*), legal codes (*hōritsugaku*), commerce (*shōgyōgaku*) and mining (*kōzangaku*).

No doubt, there was opposition to the exam system, too. Foremost was the fear that it would abet a spirit of shameless desire to rise in the world (*shusse*). But not many rallied behind this conservative line of dissent. The exam-system proposal was ultimately approved with 146 votes in favour. Only nine opposed, and thirty-three abstained.

The resolution never evolved into a concrete plan. No other resolutions from the House of Public Debate did, either. But the domainal identity and political consciousness expressed in these deliberations had tremendous influence on the subsequent formation of the Meiji bureaucracy. The state realized that, if such a pronounced sense of domainal consciousness existed, it would make sense to exploit it by selecting men of talent from the domains, having them compete against one another and making them develop into men useful to the government. This method called for the establishment of schools across the provinces that would provide students with a foundational education. From those schools, the state would then assemble and nurture those who earned the most outstanding grades. The result would be the emergence of a modern education system.

The tributary students (*kōshinsei*) of the University-South College (*Daigaku Nankō*): An assembly of national elites

Developing human resources through Western learning (*yōgaku*)

This indeed constituted the human-resource development strategy that persisted throughout the history of modern Japan: the state would excavate talent from the provinces through an institutionalized education system, and it would then develop that talent into human resources who would become the men to build a new era.

The origin of this system lay in a proclamation dated the twenty-seventh day of the seventh month of Meiji 3 (= 23 August 1870), and titled, 'Tributary Students (*kōshinsei*) to be Placed in the University-South College (*Daigaku Nankō*).'[12] The Daigaku Nankō, or the University-South College, was an organ for education in Western learning. It was a descendant of the Institution for the Investigation of Barbarian Books and the Institute for Development (*Kaiseijo*) and a forerunner of the University of Tokyo.[13] There were already over 3,000 students pursuing Western learning at the University-South College when the 1870 proclamation was made, but the government nonetheless commanded each domain to send its most distinguished students of Western learning to the institution. It made clear its intention to use the University-South College as a centre for developing human resources through Western learning.

The term *kōshinsei*, or 'tributary students', referred to students who represented their respective domains at the university, just as *kōshi*, or tributary men, represented their domains in the government. The idea was this: to gain a good name for itself among its rivals, each domain had to dispatch its brightest young men to the university, men who could match up to their counterparts coming from other parts of the nation. The concentration of so much talent in a single place would make these men redouble their academic efforts in a spirit of one-upmanship, and this competition would in turn lead to the development of exceptional talent. It was a sweeping strategy based on both the fixation of domains on interdomainal relations and on the voraciously competitive spirit of young men.

The origins of this scheme to systematize human-resource development through widespread education had already appeared in the state's 'Regulations on Universities' (*daigaku kisoku*) and 'Regulations on Middle and Primary Schools' (*chūshōgaku kisoku*), both ordained in the second month. The regulations mandated the establishment of middle and primary schools in every prefecture (*fu, ken*). They called for students in primary school to learn the basics of five subjects: ethics (*kyōka* [*kyōgaku, shūshin*]), law (*hōka*), natural sciences (*rika*), medical sciences (*ika*) and liberal arts (*monka*). Students in middle school would then pursue more specialized learning. Those with the best grades would take exams, which were held across the country, and then proceed to university, where they would spend three years studying a subject of their choice. And those who were deemed exceptional even at university would be employed by the government. A plan was thus conceived for students to move through an educational process from elementary school to middle school to university – and for the state thereby to assemble talent from the provinces.

But the universities, which were to act as the state's collecting basins for human resources, were not yet ready. The three universities of the day each had a separate educational programme: the University-Main College (*daigaku honkō*) handled national and Chinese learning; the University-South College, the Daigaku Nankō, offered instruction in Western learning; and the University-East College (*daigaku tōkō*) trained students in medicine. There was no standardization or unity across the three academies. Deep fissures ran through the Main College in particular, where nativist education or national learning (*kokugaku*), which prided itself as the intellectual undergirding of the Restoration, had begun to assail Chinese learning (*kangaku*), the official form of education for the bakufu.[14]

The announcement of the 'Regulations on Universities' exacerbated the stand-off in the Main College. Because the regulations called for a single, comprehensive university focused on Western learning, the conflict between national and Chinese learning snowballed into a broader fight that involved the problem of Western learning. The fight also constituted, from a general perspective, a confrontation between two camps: that of university instructors, who were caretakers of the national nerve-centre of learning, and that of the government, which sought to advance a new education policy. Amid the birth pangs of a new system of higher education, the movement towards a systematized educational structure experienced a momentary setback. Matsudaira Yoshinaga, the man in charge of education policy and the official who oversaw the universities, resigned in the seventh month. Around the same time, the Main College, at the centre of the imbroglio, closed its doors indefinitely.

The proclamation with which we began this section, 'Tributary Students to be Placed in the South College', was announced in the same month that the Main College shut down. The comprehensive university system envisioned in the 'Regulations for Universities' thus proceeded with the University-South College, the Daigaku Nankō, at its vanguard.

Toward equal opportunity in learning: Ogura Shohei and Hirata Tōsuke

So began a process wherein brilliant minds from across the nation would gather together, embark on new kinds of learning, grow in competition with one another and live out their ambitions. Functioning as the means by which such men could 'pursue their own calling' (*risshi*), as promised them in the Charter Oath, was the *kōshinsei seido*, or the 'tributary-student system'.

The system itself arose from the calling of a young man: Ogura Shohei, a samurai from Obi domain in Hyūga province. Ogura was a talented youth who went to Edo in pursuit of Yasui Sokken, a Confucian scholar also from Obi at the Shōheizaka Academy (*Shōheizaka gakumonjo*) whom he greatly admired.[15] Ogura was then appointed by his domain as a liaison (*rusui yaku*) to Nagasaki, where he studied English and mingled with men of spirit (*shishi*) from various domains. From this experience, he came to believe that Obi should invest in cultivating human resources not in spite of being a small domain but precisely because of its size. He successfully called for the daimyo to dispatch young samurai to Nagasaki, where they would study widely and learn English. These young men were sent to the Chienkan, an institution at which Guido Verbeck taught. Ogura, too, embarked on study there.

After Verbeck took up a teaching post at the University-South College upon an invitation from Ōkuma and others, Ogura followed him there and enrolled. He was astonished to find that most of his peers originated from powerful tozama domains. Without connections to or oversight from established scholars, youths like him from small domains faced a forbiddingly steep climb into the university. He was chagrined. Was this not a violation of the intent of the Charter Oath that 'all be allowed to pursue their own calling'? Distinguishing himself at the University-South College, Ogura

Figure 2.1 Ogura Shohei in the early Meiji era, *c.* 1871. *Source:* Komura Jutarō kō denkihon henshū iinkai, ed., *Komura Jutarō*, Kōmyakusha, 2013, p. 32.

went on to become vice-deputy for universities (*daigaku gon-no-daijō*), where he maintained that young men of promising talent should come to the university from every domain across the land. He quietly crafted a proposal to this end.

Also involved in this proposal was Hirata Tōsuke.[16] Hirata was a samurai from Yonezawa domain in Dewa province who was close to Ogura. He eventually rose to such heights as to be dubbed one of the 'four heavenly kings' (*shitenō*) of Yamagata Aritomo. But troubles lay at every stage of his path. First among them was his early affiliation with the anti-imperial rebels of the Mutsu-Dewa-Echigo Domain Alliance (*Ō-U-Etsu reppan dōmei*).

After losing the Boshin War, the Yonezawa domain had found a new way by reforming domainal governance and encouraging Western learning. Hirata became a pioneer of this new learning. He gained renown as one of the paragons of the Kōjōkan,

Figure 2.2 Hirata Tōsuke from the ministry of Finance, 1879. *Source:* Kunaichō, ed., *Meiji 12nen Meiji tennō gokamei jinbutsu shashin-chō* 2013, p. 72.

the Yonezawa domainal school, where he studied English under Watanabe Kōki, later the head of the Imperial University (*Teikoku daigaku sōchō*). Hirata's achievements led to his dispatch as a tributary student to the University-South College, where he found himself surrounded by students from domains that had sided with the imperial state in the Boshin War. His origins in an anti-imperial domain notwithstanding, his talents were discerned by Ogura, who picked him out of the crowd and treated him without prejudice or disdain.

Together, Ogura and Hirata submitted a plan to the government for a policy of equal-opportunity learning (*kikai kintō saku*). The government, mired in the turmoil surrounding the university system, adopted the proposal and announced it as the tributary-student system.

Based on the suggestions of Ogura and his band, the tributary-student system emerged as a mechanism to assemble talented, promising men from all across the nation. Domains of over 150,000 *koku* would each send three men to the University-South College; domains of over 50,000 *koku,* two men; and those of fewer than 50,000 *koku,* one man. The stipulations were that students had to be between 16 and 20 years old, of exceptional talent and upright conduct, and of robust health. Students already pursuing Western learning were to be given preference. If domains already had men at the University-South College, they were permitted to transfer them to tributary-student status.

The 'tribute' (*kō*) in the term 'tributary student' (*kōshinsei*) suggested more than just tributaries flowing from the peripheries to the center. It would seem reasonable to expect that a government siphoning talented men away from the domains would draw from its own coffers to provide for them, but the state commanded domains themselves to finance the 170 *ryō* it took to educate a student per year, a figure that covered everything from tuition to lodging and material fees.[17] The tributary-student system quite literally involved offering students up as tribute. With it, the personnel- and cash-strapped state killed two birds with one policy.

Domains vied to send out their young men despite the heavy burdens on them. They did so, of course, partly to propitiate a new regime that had gained ascendancy over the entire realm. But they were also driven by a spirit of interdomainal competition. Facing a new political reality, they could not afford to fall behind in the contest to produce men of talent. It was in this way that, seemingly overnight, the University-South College transformed into a battleground for prodigies from across the realm, each of whom carried the honour of his domain on his back.

Portraits of the tributary student

It was the winter of 1870, the third year of the Meiji reign. Over three hundred young men from across the nation gathered at the University-South College, located at Gojiingahara, near today's Gakushi kaikan, outside Hitotsubashi, by the imperial residence. 'Before us lies a place of gathering for the most talented men of the realm, a spectacular sight of the wellspring of civilization (*bunka*)', recalled Hirata of the vast assembly of youth.[18] With such a great number of men gathered, some would gain great renown through their successes, but others would slip away and vanish in the course of their studies, and others still would even die before reaching the fullness of age. Let us sketch a portrait of some of these men.

Widely known as the most exemplary tributary student is Komura Jutarō.[19] Hailing from the Obi domain, he was a relative of Ogura Shohei, the man who drafted and proposed the tributary-student system. Ogura found promise early on in Komura, sending him out to pursue Dutch studies under Verbeck.

It was with Ogura's recommendation that Komura was selected as a tributary student. He enrolled in the university at 16 years of age, right at the lower threshold of the age range. But he achieved grades that thoroughly lived up to Ogura's high commendation, and he proceeded to study at Harvard Law School as a member of the education ministry's first study-abroad contingent (*dai'ikki monbushō ryūgakusei*). After returning to Japan, he became an officer in the foreign ministry, serving as foreign minister in the Cabinet of Katsura Tarō, in which capacity he signed the Portsmouth

Figure 2.3 A portrait of the tributary students, 'kōshinsei,' 1870. *Source:* Tokyo Imperial University, ed., *Tokyo teikoku daigaku 50 nen-si*, vol. 1, 1932, p. 116.

Peace Treaty, as is well known. Among other foreign ministry bureaucrats who strove for Russo-Japanese amity, Takahira Kogorō, too, got his start as a tributary student.

Following Komura as the most iconic tributary student is probably Hatoyama Kazuo.[20] Originally known as Miura Kazuo, he was chosen as a tributary student by the Mashima domain in Mimasaka province. Mashima was a domain of just 10,000 *koku*, even smaller than Obi. It had no men with training in Western learning. And so it sent off fifteen-year-old Hatoyama, below the minimum age cut-off and with no background in Western learning, as its choice. At first, Hatoyama was placed in the lowest level class in the university. But he was spurred to action by this mediocre start, and he unleashed an effort so formidable that it was said that 'not only does he have a memory far surpassing that of anyone else, but he studies harder than everyone, too, leaving [others] with no way to compete'. Indeed, Hatoyama excelled past his older classmates. Before long he surpassed even Komura, attaining the most distinguished rank in the Education Ministry's first dispatch of students and becoming its cynosure. He became the first Japanese to attain a juris doctor degree, a feat he achieved at Yale Law School, after which he returned to Japan to become a professor in the law faculty of Imperial University, an officer in the Foreign Affairs Ministry, and then a member and ultimately the head of the House of Representatives. He thus gained a government foothold for a family dynasty that persists to the present day.

If we consider the tributary students by the field in which they were educated, we see particular attention was given to nurturing talent in law. Faced with the paramount problem of treaty revision, the new regime sought personnel who could quickly prepare a legal code that would support the treaty revision process. Numerous students went on to found a private law academy to this end: Hozumi (originally Irie) Nobushige, who at some 26 years of age became division head (*buchō*) at Tokyo Imperial University, and Kabuto Kuninori, who dedicated himself to the drafting of civil law (*minpō*), as well as Okamura Teruhiko and Kishimoto Tatsuo. Theirs were careers that resulted, no doubt, from their personal experiences as tributary students – students who, as pioneers of new pursuits of learning, understood first-hand the importance of education.

Particularly salient among the tributary students who became executive bureaucrats (*gyōsei kanryō*) were those who entered the Education Ministry. They often took Euro-American models as their guide. These students included Kinoshita Hiroji, who studied high school education and went on to become the first head of Kyoto Imperial University; Isawa Shūji, who popularized the songbook of the Ministry of Education (*Monbushō shōka*); and Nakagawa Hajime, who led opposition against the Romanization of Japanese. Sugiura Jūgō, founder of the journal *Nihonjin* (*The Japanese*), also studied at the University-South College as a tributary student.

We find among the tributary students, too, the first Japanese doctorate-holders in engineering, physics and natural sciences. Among these men, Furuichi Kōi, who laid the foundation for public works and civil engineering (*doboku*) in Japan, achieved particular success as a bureaucrat. The most distinguished figure among the nation's army combat engineers, Ishimoto Shinroku, was a classmate of Furuichi who hailed from the same town.

By producing such prodigious talent, the tributary-student system provided modern Japan with a foundation in knowledge. If it had not sought to gather youth from all across the realm as it did and spur their study through interdomainal competition, the system would surely not have achieved such formidable results in only the first attempt at implementation. It was a resounding success just as Japan began its plunge into modernity.

The encounter with Western learning, the stone wall of Chinese learning

How were tributary students selected? The central state provided no detailed standards besides the mandate that students be between 16 and 20 years old and preferably have a background in Western learning. It left the selection process to individual domains. But domains varied widely in the extent to which they had encouraged Western studies, and that variation starkly influenced their selection processes. In the Zeze domain of Ōmi province, for instance, the daimyo and even regular warriors had displayed a deep interest in Western learning, despite their proximity to the imperial centre of Kyoto. In the Jungidō, the domainal school, there were ten men pursuing Western learning for the twenty in Chinese studies and the meagre three in national learning. Western learning had established a foothold in the domain.

The main force in Zeze's Western studies was Kuroda Kikuro, an instructor in the domainal school. After having mastered the family tradition of Confucian learning, he studied Dutch learning from Ogata Kōan and Itō Genboku, and he set out for Edo in the bakumatsu era to gain knowledge at the Institution for the Investigation of Barbarian Books.

Kuroda gave particular attention to Sugiura Jūgō. Sugiura was studying Confucian learning under him at the Jungidō when one day he turned to him and implored, 'Chinese studies are great, but at least teach me a bit about Dutch studies.'[21] Kuroda acquiesced. He taught him not only Dutch but English and French and even mathematics and astronomy.

Kuroda had not gained his vast knowledge on his own. He had benefited from the learning that had accumulated at the Institution for the Investigation of Barbarian Books, which had gathered together scholars of Western learning from across the realm. Just as the Shōheizaka Academy had acted as the propelling force behind the Confucian stream of scholarship, scholarship on Western learning had developed in its own nerve-centre, the Barbarian Books Institute, and spread across the realm from there. One of the men whom Kuroda brought to the Institute in its late years was Sugiura, who went on, with Kuroda's recommendation, to be chosen as a tributary student. He was only 16 years old at the time of his selection.

Such domains as Zeze where Western learning had gained an early foothold were exceptional. Instituting Western learning in domainal schools was a long process: the power struggles between Chinese and national learning within domains first had to be overcome, and then instructors in Western learning had to be brought into the school. It was a process similar to that which unfolded in the universities of the early Meiji era. But even when the early Meiji era did arrive, education in many domains continued to revolve around a Confucian-studies core. Young men in this new age, sensitive to the shifting winds of their times, were repulsed by the stagnant Confucian atmosphere of their domains. They set about persuing Western learning on their own.

The young men of Western learning: Self-directed study

One such man who pursued Western learning independently was Isawa Shūji, a tributary student from Takatō domain.[22] Like most domains, Takatō had placed Chinese learning at the centre of domainal education. Isawa was an academic prodigy serving as superintendent of resident students at his school (*ryōchō*), but his interests lay not in Chinese studies but in Western learning. These interests could not be served: Takatō lacked experts who could instruct him. Isawa was left to devour whatever translated works he managed to obtain, such as Henry Wheaton's *Elements of International Law*. When he was dispatched to Edo in Keiō 3 (= 1867), as part of the domainal military, he wandered the streets alone in search of an English-Japanese dictionary and Francis Wayland's work on economics, or so it is said. A man of the provinces, he hungered for knowledge of things unknown, and he actively sought that knowledge out.

But there were limits to self-study. When news arrived that the daimyo of Takatō would send his troops up to the imperial capital, Isawa volunteered to join the division, believing that he would be able to pursue Western learning once there, even as a soldier. His wish was granted: he was enrolled in the troops, and he entered a Dutch studies academy in Kyoto. His tenure was short-lived. Before long, the Takatō contingent received command to return to their domain. Isawa desperately sought a way to stay in Kyoto to continue his Western learning, but he could not win permission to do so.

Isawa returned to his domainal hometown, where he soon learned of the Proclamation of the Restoration of Imperial Rule. Adamant not to fall behind at a time of swift change, he worked hard to convince his father to send him to Tokyo to study. He won his father's blessing in Meiji 2 (= 1869).

In Tokyo, Isawa's passionate energy won him the chance to study under a singular master in his field: Nakahama Manjirō, or John Manjirō, of the erstwhile bakufu. Among the very few in his day to have had first-hand experience living in America, Manjirō served as an instructor in the Institute for Development (*Kaiseijo*). But he did not take any personal students of his own. Isawa could not enrol in the Institute for Development because he was an independent student, not one supported directly by the domain. His solution was to visit Manjirō repeatedly and to entreat private mentorship. Manjirō eventually agreed, and Isawa became a personal and therefore unusual student of Manjirō, under whom he gained a vast knowledge.

Just half a year later, Manjirō was sent off to Europe to observe and report back on the Franco-Prussian War, leaving Isawa at a loss for where to go and what to do. It was at this moment, fortuitously, that notice had gone out to the domains to send tributary students to the capital. There were almost no suitable students in Takatō, which had not had resources to dedicate to Western learning. The domain did have one student at Keiō Gijuku, but he exceeded the age limit. Another possible candidate declined because he was the son of an instructor at the domainal school responsible for the selection process itself. This left Isawa to fill the lone spot for a tributary student from tiny Takatō domain. Isawa had been studying in hardship, living only on his samurai rice stipend (*fuchimai*); now he had won a new opportunity with expenses fully covered. Rejoicing, he entered the University-South College, where he encountered *Elements of International Law* and gained knowledge in pursuit of his goal of entering the Foreign Ministry. It was the autumn of his twentieth year.

There were other cases in which domains dispatched tributary students who had no prior training in Western learning. Surprisingly enough, Hozumi Nobushige, later the head of the law school of the Imperial University (*Teikoku daigaku hōka daigaku chō*), was one such student.[23]

Hozumi was the first son in an upper-level samurai (*jōshi*) household in Uwajima domain, a domain often hailed as the foremost centre of Dutch learning. Many scholars of Dutch learning came and went in Uwajima: Ninomiya Keisaku, a disciple of Philipp Franz von Siebold; Takano Chōei, a fugitive after the 1839 Crackdown on the Barbarian Society (*Bansha no goku*); and Murata Zōroku, known also as Ōmura Masujirō, who founded the Japanese army – all had links to Uwajima. But strangely enough, Uwajima's centre for English and Dutch studies did not attract men from within the domain itself. Except among those closest to the daimyo, the dominant intellectual orientation was towards Chinese studies. Young men of ambition (*yūshi no seinen*) ran not after Western learning but after Wang Yangming-ism and its revolutionary potential. Underlying this intellectual orientation was the notion that Chinese learning, a form of preparation for governance, was the pursuit of upper-level samurai, whereas Western learning, deemed a practical pursuit, was suitable more for lower-level samurai.

This division of learning based on status affiliation, which manifested itself in the aversion of upper-level samurai to Western studies, takes us back to Sakuma Shōzan's *Mea Culpa* (Seikenroku), a text he wrote a year after the arrival of Matthew C. Perry.[24] The core concern of that tract, which is familiar to many for its advocacy of 'Eastern virtue, Western science', was the question of how to break through the intellectual stagnation wrought by the rigid formalism of Confucian studies.

Sakuma did not deny the importance of learning from China and Japan. What he denounced was how Confucian scholars wallowed in recondite magniloquence with little concern for reality. In the wake of the crisis of Perry's arrival, Sakuma called for deep study in mathematics to help strengthen maritime defences – a call that acted as an incisive cut into samurai who, partaking complacently in the authority of traditional learning, failed to respond to the reality of the crisis before them.

Still, to dabble in Western learning at this time departed from the common sense and social consciousness of upper-level samurai, who understood their social roles in the context of the long-enduring bakuhan status system. High-status samurai regarded Western learning as practical learning, as did Sakuma. Western learning was like arithmetic: something lower-level samurai acquired to help them with practical governance. Those who stood at the top of government needed not these skills but high morals. Such was the ideology of governing by virtue (*tokuchishugi*) that upper-level samurai espoused.

The recollections of Isawa provide further insight into these intellectual currents. At a moment when the fire of anti-barbarian sentiment had yet to die down, to go and read the strange horizontal script of the imperialists was, Isawa reflected, something only weirdos did. Even among those chosen as tributary students, there were some who simply could not accept the task of reading the books of savages (*iteki*). They quit. Others even began knifing foreign instructors at the University-South College. Such incidents occurred frequently.

It was out of these rocky intellectual tides that tributary students had to be picked. Those whom we have encountered here came largely from lower-level samurai households or were otherwise children of domainal school instructors. Their Western pursuits may seem visionary to us today, in an age when all partake in Western studies, but in an era when anti-barbarian sentiment remained strong and when a Chinese-studies order remained firmly intact, their learning was a learning for social misfits and eccentrics.

And just as they learned outside the social mainstream, so too was the will of Western-oriented tributary students extraordinary. To know worlds unknown, to break open an unseen future for their nation – it was this pioneering spirit they carried. They together built up an index of the academic fields of the Meiji era, from the humanities to the sciences, from law to astronomy, from politics to business to education. Their curiosity about the unknown became a motor propelling them, some of the first scholars in their fields, to leading roles on their historical stage.

310 students from 259 domains

The range of fields in which these tributary students made their careers is bewildering. And their entryway into those fields was the learning on which they embarked at university. What was this learning? What sort of education was conducted at the University-South College? Let us examine the studies of these tributary students.

From north to south, from the Tate or Matsumae domain in Hokkaido to the Satsuma domain in Kyushu, from 259 of Japan's 261 domains, students numbering 310 gathered at the University-South College.[25] In the diversity of the customs and climates of their origins, in the heterogeneity of the extent of their prior learning and of their status affiliations, these youths made the university a motley microcosm of Meiji Japan. They differed in their speech and in their hairstyles and clothes. Some wore high-collared shirts (*haikara*) and swept-back *nadetsuke* hair, while most wore the typical attire of the so-called 'Meiji student' (*Meiji no shosei*): topknot (*mage*), sword (*haitō*), haori top (*sesaki baori*) over horse-rider hakama bottoms (*umanori bakama*).[26]

In this environment, men from domains at war with each other no more than two years earlier, domains such as those in Tōhoku and Kyushu, found themselves studying together in the same classrooms and living together in the same dormitories. Inevitably, on their backs they carried the weight of the honour of their domains.

The academic performance of these young men bore directly on how others, or at least others on their college campus, judged the domains they represented. Pedagogy at the University-South College was conducted in the original languages of assigned texts, so students were sorted into tiered classes according to their linguistic ability. This system fuelled their competitive fire. To be slung into a class of low achievers was to have the honour of one's domain besmirched. Komura, who had accumulated knowledge and experience in Nagasaki, was placed in the highest class: group 1. But Suigiura was assigned to lowly group 14, and Hatoyama to group 15, rock bottom of the hierarchy. Each climbed his way up the educational ladder from there.

The sense that each student represented his domain extended beyond academics and into daily life. 'The bro from X domain ate a snake, but the bro from Y domain couldn't stomach it' – at times, the young men even resorted to such inane contests of endurance to one-up one another. So pervasive was their consciousness of domainal identity that it became their guiding principle of action.[27]

Competing with such heavy loads on their backs, some began to fall behind. Those of relatively senior age or of particularly distinguished lineage especially struggled to keep up.[28] Often deeply cultured in Chinese learning, these older students found the content of introductory English and French texts childish. Frustrated, they veered away from the standard system of studying everything in the original language and undertook a fallback system of simply learning the content in Japanese.

Younger students or students of lower status had little reason to resist the system and approached their studies in earnest. Being selected as a tributary student had afforded them a once-in-a-lifetime opportunity. To squander it would be to lose a chance they could never again recover.

Learning at the University-South College

The exertions of young men in bakumatsu times had partially consolidated a basis for students in the early Meiji era to pursue Western learning.[29] Along with Verbeck, the first foreign instructor in the nation, a number of capable indigenous teachers had arisen in the bakumatsu era, including Tsuji Shinji and Katō Hiroyuki.[30] As the earliest leaders in Western studies, homegrown instructors had gained experience through trial and error. Now they were ready to help tributary students build capacity under their tutelage.

Foundational books, notably Webster's dictionary, had begun to proliferate in the bakumatsu era, and tributary students were able to secure copies with domainal funds. But even as a sound basis for learning had begun to solidify, students who would engage in this new field of learning remained relatively few. Tributary students therefore won considerable solicitude from the state and from their domains as they devoted their energies to this new field. Theirs was an extraordinarily fortunate generation.

The education this generation received was a systematized one in which, at least in principle, students read original texts in English, French and German, as we have seen. The regulations of the University-South College (*Daigaku Nankō kisoku*), ordained at the same time that the tributary-student system was inaugurated, mandated that subjects at the College be divided between a general education curriculum (*ippan kyōiku katei*) made up of 'regular courses' and a collection of specialized courses (*senmonka*) in law, science and humanities.[31] Liberal-arts topics among the regular courses ranged from basic reading and writing to conversation and composition; science topics ranged from addition, subtraction, multiplication and division to algebraic geometry and physics.

Once a student completed regular courses, he moved on to specialized subjects. In legal studies, he could pursue constitutional law, criminal law, civil law, procedural law, commercial law, international law, economics, statistics and legal theory; in science: physics, botany, zoology, chemistry, geology, mechanics, astronomy, trigonometry, conics, cartometry and calculus; and in the humanities: rhetoric, logic, Latin, national histories and philosophy.

Courses ran between 9.00 am and 11.00 am and between 1.00 pm and 3.00 pm, a two-hour midday break dividing the two blocks. Four hours a day might seem scanty, but students needed ample time for preparation and review, as courses were conducted in foreign languages and class sizes were small, with twenty-five in a language class and twelve in math and reading. Sugiura, for instance, studied so hard without sleeping at night or returning to his room at break-time that his roommates began to worry about him – such stories survive to the present day. Indeed, all day and through the night, students studied and studied, truly exerting themselves for knowledge.

Why did these students dedicate so much energy to their academic pursuits? A certain sense of pride and self-satisfaction pervaded the University-South College during this era: young men came to feel privileged that they were the ones learning and preparing to become the new rulers of Japan. For these youths, who lacked a high rank in warrior society, these new studies could lead directly to new lives both for themselves and for their nation.

In the dreams they dreamed of the future, these young men idolized Ōkuma Shigenobu. Having gained rank among the Meiji bureaucrats by dint of his own talents, Ōkuma enjoyed great popularity. Komura and his friends displayed a photograph of Ōkuma on the table in their dorm. On the photo was written, 'Presented to my friend, Mr. Komura Jutarō, by Ōkuma Shigenobu.' They basked in the envy of students around them – though it was, of course, Komura himself who had written the note.[32] Such was the spirit of vivacity that flowed among these men in these earliest moments of a new nation.

The lives of tributary students: Prototypes of the college student

The lives of the tributary students revolved around their university and its dorms. It was hardly a glamorous life.[33] They lived in communal rooms of six or eight *tatami*, roughly 10 or 13 square metres. Lining the walls on either side of their rooms were closets; they used the upper shelves as study surfaces. Their roommates were their primary rivals. You do not go to sleep before your roommate, you do not wake up after your roommate – their rooms became battlegrounds of academic willpower.

The dormitory, the common home of students from all across the realm, became an arena for discussion on domainal affairs, an arena not unlike the government's House of Public Debate. When the Meiji state dissolved domains and installed prefectures in 1871 (*haihan chiken*), fiery discussion engulfed the dorms: 'What's going on with your domain?' 'How'd his domain end up?' And when a newspaper reading room was installed, it morphed into a salon. Every Friday, Sugiura and his friends used it to convene a discussion group they called the 'Tea-Talk Association' (*sawakai*).

To sustain the spirit of its students, the university appointed class heads (*kyūchō*) and gave them leadership over the student body. In the law programme, it was often Komura and Hatoyama who filled this role; in the science programme, it was often Furuichi. The boys under their leadership, living in an era of upheaval, were rugged and rough around the edges, their everyday lives so wild that facetious superlatives they awarded to one another included the lofty category, 'Best at Throwing Stones'. To rein in this brash virility required some more brash virility.[34]

Even though their expenses were covered by their domains, students were hardly well off. Many were so poor, in fact, that their superlatives even included the category: 'Has Only Two Sets of Clothes'. But more urgent than clothes were empty stomachs. The class heads splurged their university-bestowed allowances on extravagant parties at restaurants, where they satisfied the voracious appetites and demands of the young men. Many became so caught up in the excitement that they got drunk beyond capacitation. One man was hauled back home one evening and, finally regaining sobriety, cried out: 'I'm just now remembering what happened – I inconvenienced you all, and although I was drunk, that's still not okay. I will commit seppuku to atone for my wrongdoing.' His friends laughed raucously. Scenes such as these unfolded day in and day out.

Meals were provided in the dorms, but they could not fill bottomless stomachs. Roasted sweet potatoes, both cheap and filling, became a go-to choice to slake collegiate hunger. Boys would dawdle out after dinner to buy sweet potatoes, bring them back and unwrap them at the table in the centre of their rooms. Others would then gather around to eat their fill. They would eat to satisfaction and then sit around and talk and debate, and then they would get hungry again, and then they would eat some more. And then, before they called it a night, as they cleaned up their books, they would scoff down whatever bits and pieces were left. And then they would go to sleep.

The superlatives the boys wrote for one another indeed tell of their attributes. The students of course had academic interests. There were some who were indignant about the state of the nation and the world, and there were those who studied and studied and studied. There were maths nerds and bookworms and Chinese-studies experts. They had other, more sweeping interests, too: *shibai* theatre, *gidayū* dramatic narrative and *yose* vaudeville; rickshaws and *tanka* poetry and drawing; the game of *go* and sumo and fishing. They ate soba and azuki bean soup (*shiruko*) and mochi, but they also ate Western-style meals and bread and other things that students across the sea ate.

There was no shortage of charm in their habits of daily life. They drank and drank and drank and never bathed. They were sleepyheads and slobs and farters. They lost their tempers at the slightest things. They doodled. They sauntered out of the cafeteria munching on food. 'They needlessly use foreign words' – we can hardly help but chuckle at this one. Study hard, play hard, stuff your face – even in their daily lives, they were stereotypical college kids.

Collegians studying abroad

The dissatisfaction of tributary students and university reform

But in their relentless pursuit of knowledge, tributary students were about to hit a wall. The University-South College only gave students the most cursory of introductions to different fields of learning. The more the students studied, the more they wanted to delve deeper into their topics. Their boundless curiosity evolved into an unquenchable thirst for ever higher levels of education.

In 1871, the fourth year of the Meiji reign, students launched a movement to reform their university. At the forefront of the movement were Furuichi, Saitō Shūichirō and others of the most distinguished students in the academy.[35]

They demanded improvements to the quality and quantity of their education. First was the question of quality. They called for the university to bring instructors who could offer courses rivalling those at institutions in America and Europe. Thus, they said, would the Daigaku Nankō live up to its name as a university. 'To call this a university when its courses hardly surpass those of elementary schools in foreign lands! We will be the laughing-stock of generations to come', they wrote.[36] We can feel the angst of these young men as they ran up against an academic barrier they could not overcome.

Then there was the problem of quantity. The petitioners believed that a good education came from masterful instructors teaching small classes, but the state lacked the financial means to recruit enough instructors from abroad, and there were only so many indigenous instructors. The petitioners argued that because the number of teachers was limited, so too should the student body be whittled down by an elimination of inferior students. They set their sights on students who had drifted away from the proper standard of learning in foreign languages and had resorted to a fallback standard of studying in Japanese.

It was a straight-shooting, brazen call for reform – and a form of inexplicable humiliation to the students it targeted for elimination. At a time when the national climate was still volatile, implementing such a radical proposal would have exposed its proponents to danger. But Furuichi and his band signed the proposal with blood and pushed forward with steely determination. For days on end they worked to persuade important figures in the government to implement their plan.

Their plan came to fruition. They benefited from fortuitous timing: in the seventh month of the year (= August–September 1871), the decree to abolish domains pulled the legs out from under the tributary-student system. Domains no longer existed to send out tributary students. An altogether new system needed to arise to facilitate student dispatch and indeed to support the entire national education system. The Ministry of Education (*monbushō*) was founded in the same month, tasked with building this new system.

Leading the new reforms was Etō Shinpei of Saga, a bureaucrat who held fifth-tier rank in the Council of State (*chūben*) and was head of the Institution Bureau (*seidokyoku chō*). Etō was the first-ever senior aide (*daiyū*), or second in command, of the education ministry. He brought Katō Hiroyuki, Machida Hisanari, Matsuoka Tokitoshi, Nagayo Sensai, Tsuji Shinji and other up-and-coming stars of Western learning into the ministry, solidifying its central support.

The ministry cracked down on student selection. It dissolved the Daigaku Nankō, the University-South College, and instead installed simply the 'Nankō', or South College. It allowed only the best students to re-enrol, eliminating those with lesser abilities. It proposed a series of reform measures to the Council of State: to abolish the alternative system that had emerged of studying in Japanese rather than the source language; to expand educational offerings in English as well as in German and French; to renovate the school and dormitory systems across the country based on Western blueprints; and to enforce stricter selection processes for resident students, alongside other reforms. The Council of State approved these suggestions. The proposals of Furuichi and his group thus came to be realized in a dramatic overhaul of education.

On the twenty-fifth day of the ninth month, or 7 November, the University-South College closed its doors, opening up the problem of student selection. Hatoyama explained in his diary: 'The school has been closed due to reforms in the education system, and as a result, I am leaving the dorms. But at this time, we have received orders that students must not return to their home prefectures. The performance of all students will be investigated, and those who are judged favorably will be selected for reenrollment.'[37] Exceptional students would be allowed to re-enrol without any examinations; the rest would have to sit exams. Komura, Hatoyama and Furuichi, of course, took no exams to re-enrol.

As we can see in the dissolution of the alternative system of studying in Japanese, the ministry sought to overhaul the University-South College with an eye on student language ability. Sugiura had excelled at the university but had struggled with languages. He was not allowed to re-enrol automatically and was placed in the exam-taking group. He scraped by and made it into the South College. Other students such as Miyazaki Michimasa, who later as an instructor at Sapporo Agricultural College (*Sapporo nōgakkō*) helped rear such important figures as Shiga Shigetaka, failed the exams but were granted special readmission after fellow collegians appealed on their behalf. Of the 1,000 University-South College students, only 450 were accepted into the South College. It was a brutal elimination.

These reforms dramatically changed the spirit among students. A jovial mood survived, but life in the dorms became more disciplined and competitive. Upperclassmen were appointed as dorm heads who supervised other students. Over the generations, dorm heads came to include Inoue Kowashi, an icon of the Meiji legal bureaucracy; Ogura Shohei, father of the tributary-student system; Kukiri Ryūichi, who ascended to the heights of the education ministry; Hamao Arata, who became head of the University of Tokyo; and others. Distinguished in both personal qualities and perspicacity, they constituted a who's who of experts not only in Western but in national and Chinese learning. Underclassmen grew and developed under the helm of these men – men who had all taken their earliest steps on the same path.

The study-abroad movement: To pursue knowledge throughout the world

University reform thus took off. From its opening in 1870 to its dissolution in spring 1871, the University-South College had increased the number of foreign instructors on its staff, starting with W. E. Griffis, who transferred in from Fukui domain. These foreign instructors contributed greatly to the development of education in Japan. As time passed, the college changed its name a number of times, reshuffled its subjects of instruction and finally merged with the Tokyo Medical Academy (*Tokō igakkō*) to form the University of Tokyo in 1877.[38]

The more the college emphasized the importance of texts in their original languages, the more the imaginations of students ran after the distant places about which they read. Before long these students set their sights on studying in those places in person. Let us look at Komura's recollection on the matter:

> Soon it was the eighth year of the Meiji reign [1875], and I had already read most of the books [available], and I could listen to the remarks of foreigners and more or less understand them. I realized at this point that I had learned all that I could while ensconced in this tiny realm called Great Japan. Thus I developed a deep determination to lead the way and go to the West, to breathe in its civilized air, to learn of its strengths, and, to make up for our weakness, to build up a one-hundred-year plan for our nation.[39]

Six years of education behind them, these men boasted academic prowess that surpassed what the domestic field of learning could offer them. The time 'to seek knowledge throughout the world so as to strengthen the foundation of imperial rule', trumpeted in the Charter Oath, had arrived.

But the students lacked the financial means to study abroad on their own. Governmental study-abroad dispatches were at the discretion of individual ministries, which sent out bureaucrats already on the job according to their needs. This was the extent of the national study-abroad system; no framework existed for university students to be sent overseas.[40] To create such a framework, Furuichi and other study-abroad hopefuls pursued a series of strategies. They launched appeals to government authorities. They planned out a programme for loans from wealthy commercial patrons. They even appealed to cabin boys on foreign ships. Nothing worked.

With every road blocked, Furuichi went to consult with Tsuji Shinji, his erstwhile teacher and head of the Tokyo House of Books (*Tōkyō shosekikan*), today's National Diet Library (*Kokkai toshokan*). Tsuji intimated to Furuichi that there were signs of impending change in government policy on state-sponsored study abroad, and he suggested that now was the time for university students to engage in a concerted movement. Furuichi returned to his dorm, mobilized Komura, Saitō, Kikuchi Takeo and Hasegawa Yoshinosuke, all of whom shared his will to go abroad, and launched a movement for government-funded dispatches abroad.

Just as Tsuji had suggested, the government was nearing a fundamental overhaul of its study-abroad system. At this point, the state investment in sending individuals to study abroad had failed to yield good results.

One reason lay in the quality of those chosen to study abroad. The government first announced its study-abroad regulations in the twelfth month of 1870 (= January–February 1871). They included stipulations on the academic ability and age of study-abroad students but also on other matters: students were not to defame the honour of the nation while travelling in the West; those deemed delinquent or profligate were to be sent home immediately and punished; and students were absolutely not to engage in procuring monetary loans or other resources.

That the government had to lay out such sweeping regulations touching on the everyday lives of students reveals the sorry state of the men studying abroad. This depravity was a result of the student selection process: in the absence of clear guidelines, men of power recklessly sent abroad whoever had the closest connections with them. It is true that there were evaluations in place for students who returned home but, indeed, the results of those evaluations were hardly prodigious.

Another problem lay in financial resources. The nascent Meiji government needed to take in as much knowledge as it could from Western powers. The various ministries all sent out state-sponsored study-abroad students for this purpose. These students strained government finances. The desire to study abroad and the financial pressures that came with it only increased after Fukuzawa Yukichi published his *Seiyō jijō* (Conditions in the West), raising admiration and envy of the West, and after the Iwakura Embassy made its tour of Europe and America. In 1873, there were as many as 373 people on state-sponsored study abroad.[41]

The ten finest picks for study abroad

The state-sponsored study-abroad programme was bloated and unwieldy. To set things in order, in the twelfth month of 1873, the Ministry of Education called for all students abroad to return home, at least temporarily. Saionji Kinmochi had been studying in France. The communication from the education ministry jolted him to self-criticism. He reflected on his laziness and delinquency, reprimanding himself for flaunting superficial knowledge to disguise his immaturity, calling on himself to engage in deep investigation of a concentrated field of learning. It was not only Saionji. The study-abroad students of the early Meiji era all shared a profound desire to learn, but as vast worlds of knowledge swept before their eyes, they stood bewildered, unable to choose their own paths.

Just as it tried to rein in students abroad, the government redoubled its resolve to send domestic university students overseas. The reason here, too, lay mostly in money. To bring outstanding foreign instructors to a small country in the Far East required stupendous offers of remuneration. And even if the state managed to inveigle instructors with troves of cash, it often turned out that their talents did not match the needs of the state.

In such a situation, it made little sense to waste fortunes on foreigners who would desultorily bring in bits and pieces of specialized knowledge. It made more sense to send out Japan's own university students, who would acquire knowledge systematically and then return home to become professors and train more indigenous students. From a long-term perspective, it was a policy shift that would have an extraordinary pay-off.

In December 1874, the Ministry of Education resolved to find exceptionally promising students and send them off to study abroad. It conducted exams on campus, and it made its picks of the ten top students: in law, Hatoyama, Komura, Saitō and Kikuchi; from science, Hasegawa, Matsui Naokichi and Nanbu Kyūgo; in engineering, Haraguchi Kaname and Hirai Seijirō; in polytechnic studies, Furuichi; and in mining, Andō Kiyoto. The law students all went to the United States: Hatoyama to Columbia University, Komura to Harvard University, and Kikuchi and Saitō to Boston University. Furuichi went to France to study civil engineering at the École Monge. Andō went to Germany's Universität Freiburg to learn about mining.

The education ministry had designated ten spots, but in fact eleven men studied abroad. Saitō Shūichirō had been a central figure in the study-abroad movement, but he had missed the final cut. He was added to the roster of ten after a ferocious follow-up movement.[42]

Three seats had been set aside for law students. Hatoyama, ranked first in academic performance, had a sure spot; so too did Komura, ranked second. The remaining spot was seen as a toss-up between Kikuchi and Saitō. Saitō sought to win a seat by ousting Hatoyama, nonpareil academically but younger than he was. He set about in every direction to usurp Hatoyama. Indeed, Saitō himself relates this episode in his recollections; there can be little doubt about it. Hatoyama was a child of a small domain of Mimasaka, but he was born to a warrior household from the domain's residence in Edo (*Edozume hanshi*) and was reared in refined Edo ways. With a dignified sash (*kakuobi*) and top (*haori*), his attire was always proper and dignified; beyond appearances, he studied hard, and his memory was one-of-a-kind. Other students rightfully envied him. Saitō campaigned to topple him from his seat by claiming that he was a rote memorizer with no leadership ability, top of the class in grades but anaemic and effete, lacking the qualities to be an authority figure. Later Saitō would confess deep shame over his actions, but such was the fiery desire to study abroad among men at the time.

Things ultimately worked out for Saitō, who made it into the study-abroad contingent by the skin of his teeth. We can only imagine the chagrin of the classmates he left behind. They could only wait for the second dispatch, which occurred in 1876. That round was opened to applications from across the country, but ultimately no one from outside the university applied. The winners came from familiar internal faces:

in law, Hozumi, Okamura Teruhiko and Sakisaka Naoshi; in chemistry, Sugiura and Sakurai Jōji; in engineering, Sekiya Seikei, Masuda Reisaku and Taniguchi Naosada; and in physics, Okino Tadao and Yamaguchi Hanroku.

Unlike the first-round students, who mostly went to the United States, this second-round contingent headed to Britain. Hozumi went to King's College London; Okamura and Sakisaka went to Middle Temple, an Inn of Court in London; and many of the students in engineering and physics went to the University of Glasgow.

Britain was the world's greatest empire at the time; America was still a developing country. It is said that the first-round students, who had superior grades and had led the movement for study abroad, were outraged to hear that the second-round students got to go to Britain. In the students' new homes, new struggles began.

Learning abroad: Komura, Hatoyama, Furuichi

The zeal with which Komura Jutarō had pursued his studies at the University-South College did not abate when he went to Harvard. So great was his fervour that a doctor needed to advise him to refrain from reading so much at night. And there are stories surviving today of Komura telling second-round student Sugiura that he so regretted

Figure 2.4 Komura Jutarō (centre) at Harvard University, *c.* 1875. *Source:* Komura Jutarō-kō denkihon henshū Iinkai, ed., *Komura Jutarō*, Kōmyakusha, 2013, front page.

Figure 2.5 Hatoyama Kazuo at Columbia University, *c.* 1875. *Source:* Hatoyama Haruko, ed., *Hatoyama no isshō*, 1929, p. 23.

not placing first in his class that he tried to return home. But as the ardour of these study-abroad students stayed strong overseas, the stakes of their studies ratcheted up. They only had to uphold the reputations of their domains at the University-South College. Now they needed to champion the honour of their entire nation.

A year after Komura went to Harvard, he was joined by Kaneko Kentarō, of Fukuoka domain, who went on to become minister of justice and a member of the Privy Council. Komura and Kaneko shared the same dorm, but while Kaneko expanded his social network across the school, Komura ensconced himself in the dorm or in the library and single-mindedly read specialized texts.

Once he finished his legal studies, Komura felt that he needed to supplement his theoretical education with practical training. He chose to find employment, not to pursue graduate school. From among the many law offices around him, he found work in the office of Edwards Pierrepont, attorney general and ambassador to Britain under President Ulysses S. Grant. For two years, he learned about legal procedure and opinion through hands-on experience, acquiring the language and skills to conduct negotiations. Sources on his relationship with Pierrepont are scanty, but given the later trajectory of Komura's career, we would do well to imagine the influence that working for a top-tier attorney and diplomat had on him.

Whereas Komura gained practical knowledge in legal affairs and negotiation, Hatoyama explored international law. He took interest in developing a legal system that would go beyond Euro-American influence and would suit Japan's own contingencies. Hatoyama described his feelings at the time of his selection for study abroad with the following words:

> At this time, law is still a hazy field. It has not yet been clearly defined. I therefore wish to study international law, for at a time when our international relations are growing more active, it has become more crucial than ever. And yet, because there are still very few in our nation who have undertaken this most urgent field of study, we have no choice at present but to hire westerners and use them for counsel. Is this not a source of shame for the Japanese? Thus I embark on this trip with firm determination. I have steeled myself: I will not return home without having explored the very depths of international law.[43]

Hatoyama headed to Columbia University. There were already several Japanese studying there, including Sōma Nagatane of Hikone domain, who went on to become a member of the House of Representatives and the first head of Senshū University, and Shimizu Atsumori, a member of one of the three branches of the Tokugawa household (*gosankyō*) and later a count (*hakushaku*) in the peerage. With them, and with a handful of others – such as Kōmuchi Tomotsune, who had been dispatched by the Home Ministry to investigate commercial affairs and who later became a member of the House of Representatives and head of the Legislation Bureau (*hōseikyoku*), and Megata Tanetarō, who was sent by the treasury minister and who later became head of the Central Tax Bureau (*shuzeikyoku*) – Hatoyama formed the Friday Society (*Kin'yōkai*), a study group whose members gathered to discuss and battle out legal theory. Their discussions centred on how to reform domestic law and included such issues as the debates on proscribing concubines and the inauguration of the bar for lawyers (*daigennin*).

Hatoyama passed his graduation exams at Columbia in Meiji 10 (= May 1877), and after pursuing further study in French and Latin, he enrolled at Yale Law School. He received word of his father's passing that same year, but he charged on at Yale without returning home. He obtained his master's degree in law the following year, 1878, and his juris doctor degree in 1880.

At Yale Law, Hatoyama always carefully researched relevant legal precedent before attending class, and he established a presence for himself even in seminar-style courses. At his final degree ceremony, he delivered a speech titled 'A Comparison of the Family Systems of Rome and Japan' in front of some five thousand people. He returned home bristling with pride.

Meanwhile, Furuichi, who had been at the centre of the study-abroad movement, had gone to France to pursue studies in engineering. He was aiming for admission to the École Centrale des Arts et Manufactures, the top school in the field. He went first to study at the École Monge, where he ranked sixth among some two hundred students after a year of study. His prowess gained him a spot at the École Centrale. His outstanding academic performance was even reported in newspapers in Japan.[44]

Furuichi invested his energies in studying principles of engineering education. Spurring him were the ideas of H. X. Maillot, his erstwhile teacher at the School for Development (*Kaisei gakkō*). Someone with the talents of Furuichi could set up an engineering school like École Centrale in Japan and help promote engineering education across the realm; then a foundation would be established for Japan to develop through science and technology – these were the dreams Furuichi dreamed, with Maillot's backing. In France, he delved into a wide range of academic pursuits: construction, architecture, public works, railways and other fields. He then returned to Japan and was appointed head of the School of Engineering (*Kōka daigaku*) in Meiji 19 (= 1886). His dreams came true.

Furuichi was not just an educator. After graduating from the École Centrale, he spent his final year in France at the University of Paris. There, surprisingly enough, he studied political economy. He sought not simply to devote himself to technology and education but to link those pursuits to policy. Through his studies in Paris, Furuichi gained comprehensive training as a bureaucrat with both administrative and technical expertise. He applied that training as head of the engineering school; as a leading technocrat in civil engineering, in which capacity he helped to develop and deepen the use of technology; and as head of the Public Works Bureau and the Railway Bureau as well as deputy officer in the Postal Bureau, where he flourished both as a technocrat with sophisticated executive skills and as an executive with mastery of technical skills. With the study-abroad experience he had so fervently sought, Furuichi broke open the world of civil engineering and public works for a nation at its most incipient stage.

The afterlives of tributary students: Hatoyama and Komura, intertwined

Between 1880 and 1881, the study-abroad students began returning home one by one, their five years abroad now over. The new knowledge the state had so eagerly anticipated was at last arriving.

Doctorate from Yale Law in hand, Hatoyama was welcomed back to Japan with an immediate teaching post in the Department of Law at the University of Tokyo (*Tōkyō daigaku hōgakubu*). Indeed, these men had brought home with them the very cutting edge of research and education. They had arrived as ordered, fulfilling the state's original intentions when it sent them out.

Hatoyama applied the methods he learned at Yale Law to his pedagogy. Using cases of judicial precedent as subject matter, he took up the Socratic method to engage his students in discussion, approaching them half as teacher, half as fellow learner. These discussion-based seminars, opened up by new knowledge from the West, won great popularity. Many of the men who later took charge of the modern legal system were reared in these seminars: Katō Kōmei, prime minister, foreign minister, member of the House of Representatives and member of the House of Peers; Suzuki Mitsuyoshi, lawyer, member of the House of Representatives and head of the Police Bureau of the

Home Ministry; and Okayama Kenkichi, head of the new Association of Tokyo Lawyers (*Tōkyō daigennin shin kumiaikai*) and a member of the House of Representatives, to name a few.

Hatoyama had to step down from his university post the following year, when a speech he gave at a graduation ceremony ignited a firestorm. But his knowledge, yielded from a government investment, would not go squandered. In 1885, he was appointed, upon invitation from Foreign Minister Inoue Kaoru, as head of the Investigation Bureau (*torishirabe kyoku*) of the Foreign Ministry. The bureau was tasked with researching and investigating international law in pursuit of treaty revision. Katō Kōmei, Hatoyama's student at Tokyo University, served as deputy head. Throughout his time at the bureau, from the imbroglio over hiring foreign judges on Japanese courts to the attack on Foreign Minister Ōkuma by Kurushima Tsuneki of the Gen'yōsha, Hatoyama applied his talents to active work for treaty revision. His early desire to study international law and change the face of Japan in the world was at last realized.

Hatoyama resigned from his work on the bureau after the attack on Ōkuma and the collective resignation of the Cabinet. His official excuse was to take responsibility for the failure of treaty revision. But there was undeniably another factor: his admiration for Ōkuma, pioneer of wilfully rising in the world (*risshin shusse*) through Western learning.

From here, Hatoyama sought a new field of action in the House of Representatives as a member of the Ōkuma faction. With the inauguration of the First Ōkuma Cabinet in June 1898, the first party cabinet in Japanese history, Ōkuma then took a dual role as prime minister and foreign minister; Hatoyama served as his deputy foreign minister, and with much of the actual work of the ministry delegated to him, he was recognized as foreign minister in all but name. At the same time, he won plaudits as a successful politician in the Diet.

Then we have Komura. We know him today for his shining successes as foreign minister at the Portsmouth Peace Conference, but the first half of his life as a bureaucrat involved, surprisingly, a string of disappointments and frustrations, frustrations at least relative to the early successes of Hatoyama.

Awaiting Komura on his return from America was the tragedy of Ogura Shohei, whom he had admired as his teacher. Etō Shinpei had posted Ogura to important positions in the government, and Ogura burned with desire to help inaugurate a modern education system. But he became tied up in the Saga Rebellion of 1874 and was incarcerated. Although he returned briefly to the government thereafter, he went on to fight for Saigō Takamori in the Southwest War and perished on the battlefield.

Ironically enough, it was the Justice Ministry (*shihōshō*) that took in the forlorn Komura after Ogura's death – a ministry now itself without its erstwhile leader, Etō Shinpei. It had set about putting together a legal code, and it needed personnel well versed in foreign law. It plucked up Komura and put him to work in the criminal (*keijikyoku*) and civil bureaux (*minjikyoku*). In 1884, following an invitation from his tributary-student comrade Saitō Shūichirō, Komura then entered the Foreign Ministry, which had embarked in earnest on treaty revision. Komura undertook translations of laws and orders (*hōritsu meirei*) and public documents (*kumon*) in the Translation Bureau, which Saitō headed.

Further tribulations were on the horizon for Komura. Saitō vacated his post in the Translation Bureau after he was promoted to head of the State Affairs Bureau (*seimukyoku*). Sauntering into the void came Hatoyama, Komura's younger rival, the man whom Komura could never quite match academically. Hatoyama already had a simultaneous primary job as head of the Investigation Bureau (*torishirabe kyoku*), but he filled this post too. Komura's pride was deeply insulted, so much so that he dubbed himself 'perennial underling Komura' (*sangi Komura*). He eventually did become head of the bureau, but only in 1888, when Hatoyama became a legal scholar and his dual appointment was dissolved.

It has been said that Komura's plodding rise through the ranks resulted from his lack of support from the central oligarchy. He may have been bogged down by his relationship with Ogura, who had sided with Saigō against the state. But even so, he rose even more slowly than other tributary students from outside the oligarchy, such as Hatoyama and Saitō. The most significant reason for his frustrations lay in his own ideals. Around this time, Komura joined forces with Sugiura and other collegians from the University-South College to form the Japan Club (*Nihon kurabu*), an organization devoted to advocating Japanese nationalism (*kokkaron*). Through Sugiura, the Japan Club became linked to Miyake Setsurei, Shiga Shigetaka and other men of the Seikyōsha as well as to Kuga Katsunan and Takahashi Kenzō. Together, they founded the journal *Nihonjin* and the newspaper *Nihon*, through which they upbraided the foreign policy of Inoue. It is little wonder that one who mingled in these quarters faced obstacles in the government.

But in every curse lurks a blessing. Political upheavals eventually ousted Saitō and Hatoyama from the Foreign Ministry, but Komura weathered the storm. Because he had taken an anti-Westernization, anti-Inoue stand, and because he had applied his specialized talents to administrative rather than political work, he was able to remain in the ministry. He was taunted as the 'Minister of Japanese-English Translation' and the 'Officer of Scribbling' (*tōhitsu no ri*); he was derided as the man at the helm of the 'Bureau of Konjac', a reference to the gelatin or konnyaku that was used in the printing of translations; but even still, he unflinchingly fulfilled his official duties as a translator.

And in every blessing lurks a curse. Eighteen-ninety-two saw the appointment of Mutsu Munemitsu as foreign minister in the second Cabinet of Itō Hirobumi. His rise opened the era of Mutsu diplomacy and with it a new chapter of tribulations for Komura. Mutsu sought to shake up his ministry. In it he placed Hara Kei, who rolled out reforms and dissolved the Translation Bureau. Komura faced unemployment.

But a job suited to his talents precipitated. He took up a post as a counsellor (*sanjikan*) at the Japanese Embassy in the Qing Empire. It was October 1893. At first Komura interpreted the move as a demotion, but finding himself in China on the cusp of the Sino-Japanese War, he set about applying his innate investigative talents to an analysis of the circumstances of the Qing state. As tensions between Japan and the Qing mounted, Komura showed off his intelligence-gathering abilities and his rich specialized knowledge. Honda Kumatarō, a diplomat who later became Komura's secretary (*hishokan*), wrote of Komura, 'Mutsu jettisoned Komura, but Komura wound up in a fortuitous place. The very day after he was thrown out, his real worth was suddenly realized again, and he was placed in extraordinary capacities by Mutsu.'

From here, Komura ascended to the chair of the Political Affairs Bureau (*seimukyoku*), from which he managed the crises of the Sino-Japanese War, its peace treaty and the tripartite intervention by France, Germany and Russia. He climbed steadily to ambassador extraordinary and plenipotentiary (*tokumei zenken kōshi*), and then to deputy foreign minister (*gaimu jikan*), building up the era of the 'Komura Foreign Ministry' (*Komura no gaimushō*), as it is known.

The rise of the First Ōkuma Cabinet of 1898 ushered in the era of party cabinets, and deputies across the ministries were shuffled and dropped in favour of party members. Ōkuma himself took the post of foreign minister, and he chose Komura as his deputy. The appointment was a result of the trust Komura had won from Ōkuma when Ōkuma served as foreign minister in the second Cabinet of Matsukata Masayoshi. It was, no doubt, a moment of supreme bliss for Komura, who had admired Ōkuma from his days as a tributary student, when he adorned his table with a picture of him.

But the new ruling party wielded formidable power, having ascended by toppling the oligarchic government. It rebuffed the attempt to allow Komura, a bureaucrat and not a party member, to be appointed as deputy foreign minister. Ōkuma encouraged Komura to join the party, but Komura declined. He decided to take a post as ambassador to the United States.

Fretting about how circumstances would unfold after his departure, Komura asked Ōkuma who would succeed him in the ministry. Ōkuma invoked the name of Hatoyama, and Komura set off for America relieved. One can imagine his thinking: foreign policy should sail forward independent of the fickle winds of partisan power politics; with Hatoyama at the helm of the ministry, there was little need to worry. And so it was that the paths of these two men, men who had been rivals since their earliest days as tributary students, met again.

The two men had chosen different roads in life. Where Hatoyama had found an arena for his talents in partisan politics, Komura had kept his distance. But with the establishment of the so-called Komura Foreign Ministry, Komura's own presence became indispensable if political power ever slipped from the hands of the parties. With the 1901 inauguration of the First Katsura Tarō Cabinet, Komura was summoned back to Japan and installed as foreign minister. The mark he made on Japanese history thereafter, by signing the Portsmouth Treaty, is well known.

Meanwhile, change blew Hatoyama off course after so many years of apparently smooth sailing. After the collapse of the First Ōkuma Cabinet, the Meiji Emperor and the genrō came to mistrust Ōkuma-faction politicians. Those politicians fell away from the centre of political action. Then Itō Hirobumi founded the Rikken Seiyūkai in 1900. Perhaps sensing that the main current of party politics was now flowing in favour of the Seiyūkai, the new mainstream party, Hatoyama abandoned Ōkuma. He joined the Seiyūkai with the help of an old acquaintance, Hara Kei.

This transfer of allegiance came precisely as the Seiyūkai, the ruling party of the First Cabinet of Saionji Kinmochi, began to trounce the Rikkenhontō. Hatoyama made a clear declaration in favour of the Seiyūkai, pledging his allegiance to it and to constitutional government. But his defection came under vehement attack: he was a leader in the opposition party who had flipped to a new party just as the latter was gaining ascendancy in the Diet. Imprecations flew. Some claimed that Hatoyama had defected with a new spot as justice minister readied for him. His reputation as a tributary-student elite was badly damaged.

But opportunity came again later. When the imperial command to form a cabinet once again descended on Saionji in 1911, he began to gather ministers from the Seiyūkai. Hatoyama, rich in both knowledge and renown, was a powerful candidate. But he was deeply unwell. He had stomach cancer. He still campaigned to become a cabinet minister, but Hara Kei convinced him that it would be an act of impiety towards the Emperor for a bed-ridden man to take a seat in the cabinet. He dropped his cause.

Hatoyama died in October. He never became a cabinet minister. Soon afterward, the Saionji Cabinet collapsed under demands to add two more divisions to the military, and the Taishō Political Crisis exploded. The time for full-blown party politics had at last arrived. But Hatoyama, dead, was nowhere in sight.

As if in pursuit, Komura died the following month. He served in his second stint as foreign minister until the August preceding his death, and he perished with the Foreign Ministry still bustling with his disciples. It had been a life ever in ascent: he had risen through the ranks of the peerage from baron (*danshaku*) to count (*hakushaku*) to marquis (*kōshaku*).

A fleeting moment of opportunity to mine the depths of academic pursuit had come and gone in the earliest days of the Meiji era. Tributary students, pioneers of their era, had seized that moment and collected troves of knowledge. As the curtain began to fall on the Meiji era, they left those troves for the generations that would follow them. And they exited the stage.

Building a Constitutional System:
The 1870s and 1880s

The rise of Restoration bureaucrats:
Coordinating power, dividing roles

Dividing and centralizing legislative and executive government

The implementation of the policy of surrendering domainal registers to the imperial court (*hanseki hōkan*) ushered in a new phase for the Meiji regime. The government now had to embark on a thoroughgoing process of building new structures of rule. It grappled with how to develop a political system that would function as the centralized administration of an entire nation. It had to transform the hodgepodge Council of State (*Dajōkan*) into a unified organ, and it had to systematize relations between the national centre and the provinces.

We can discern the beginnings of a movement towards a new structure of centralized rule in a proposal from Ōkubo Toshimichi in the tenth month of Meiji 3 (= 1870). In his treatise, Ōkubo assigned particular importance to processes of decision-making. The supreme arbiter of the nation, the Emperor, was but a child. Ōkubo believed that if the regime wanted to proceed resolutely with reforms while maintaining unity, decision-making responsibilities had to fall on a small number of men. These officials would bear responsibility for making decisions while maintaining close communication with other members of the state administration.

Ōkubo imagined a system wherein a chief aide (*hoshō*) would take a post equivalent to the present-day prime minister (*sōri daijin*) and a councillor (*sangi*) would take a dual appointment as both councillor and head of one of the departments in the executive state (*shō no chōkan*), a post equivalent to a minister in the present-day Japanese Cabinet (*kokumu daijin*).[1] Up to this point, in accordance with the principle of the tripartite division of power, the post of councillor, which bore directly on government decision-making, had been conceived as integral to the legislative branch (*rippōfu*) and independent of the executive branch (*gyōseifu*). Ōkubo sought to change this conception.

To make reform work, state officials needed to have intimate knowledge of and solid control over the practices of executive government. But the men acting as councillors and as heads of executive departments (*shōkyō*) were former domainal lords and members of the nobility, men who had at best a tenuous understanding of executive governance. Their relative ignorance had already sparked tension between the Conference of Three Offices (*sanshoku kaigi*) and the departments of the executive branch (*gyōsei kakushō*). Government functioning was floundering. By calling for the head of each department in the executive arm to hold a dual appointment as a councillor, Ōkubo sought to build a bridge between the executive and legislative branches and to break through the stagnant state of political affairs. It was an epoch-making proposal.

Ōkubo did not plan to appoint men already serving as councillors to the heads of the departments. Nor did he intend to appoint those already serving as department heads as councillors. His scheme was more brazen. He plotted to promote Restoration bureaucrats who had been gaining power within the departments to the helm of their respective divisions and then to grant them simultaneous posts as councillors. By using young talent to combine the executive post of department head with the legislative post of councillor, Ōkubo could build a new government wherein responsibility and authority, decision-making and implementation, legislative and executive power were all united. He had long yearned for a government with the ability to get things done. Now he had arrived at a model for such a government: a government dominated by the executive branch (*gyōsei shudō*).

In the second month of the next year, Meiji 4 (= 1871), Etō Shinpei of Hizen, Gotō Shōjirō of Tosa, and others tasked with research in governmental institutions (*seido torishirabe*) gathered under the watch of Ōkubo and hammered out a broader plan for the reform of the state. They developed a streamlined system wherein ministers (*daijin*) would oversee the general government (*taisei*); the dually posted councillors/department heads (*shōkyō ken sangi*) would carry out decision-making; and each executive department would put those decisions into effect.[2]

Kido Kōin dissented. He feared that Ōkubo's scheme would give too much power to individual departments and thereby fracture the government further rather than weld it together. Kido maintained that if heads of departments, who were relatively steeped in executive experience, were to participate in legislative government, they would overwhelm state ministers, who lacked such specialized knowledge. The legislative branch would then lose its ability to supervise and check the power of the executive arm.

Ōkubo and Kido both recognized the need for a government with decisive leadership capacity, one that would winnow its human talent to draw out the best few men to partake in decision-making processes. In the sixth month, they dismissed the majority of state councillors, leaving only Saigō Takamori and Kido in that role. With Kido at the centre, debates on structural reform of the government commenced in the seventh month. But because Kido clung unyieldingly to his ideas on the tripartite division of power and the strengthening of the legislature, consultations floundered, never moving past rarefied discussions of systems theory.

The dissolution of domains, the installation of prefectures and the birth of provincial officials

As reforms in the central government sputtered, the state began to receive a spate of proactive proposals from the domains that outlined reforms they planned for their own local administrations. It was a radical movement towards change: reform plans from Inaba and Higo domains, for instance, respectively present-day Tottori and Kumamoto, even went as far as to call for the resignation of domainal lords.

Behind the movement lay differences in the success with which administrative reform had occurred in the domains.[3] Every domain had embarked on some sort of reform after the central state announced the new system for employment in domainal government (*hanchishoku sei*). But none could so easily cast off the influence of traditional lineage systems. Financial reform in particular, which relied on an overhaul of samurai household privileges (*karoku seido*), had run aground. The situation was no better in such leading domains as Satsuma and Chōshū, which had produced Ōkubo, Kido and other leading government officials. In these circumstances, pushing ahead with domainal reforms became a means by which powerful domains such as Inaba and Higo could flaunt their accomplishments and gain further power and influence.[4]

The domains were given a sense of urgency by the actions of vigorous young bureaucrats in the central government. Nomura Yasushi, Torio Koyata and others from the national centre went to Satsuma and Chōshū to persuade power-holders there to lead an initiative to dissolve the national system of feudal domains and consolidate power. Their efforts provided a lifeline to Kido Kōin, who was struggling to advance reforms on his own. He cast his lot with theirs, and together they surreptitiously prepared for *haihan chiken*, the dissolution of domains and the installation of prefectures. Even Sanjō Sanetomi and Iwakura Tomomi, leaders close to Kido, were notified of the plot only two days before its implementation.

On the morning of the fourteenth day of the seventh month (= 29 August 1871), the heads (*chiji*) of Satsuma, Chōshū, Hizen and Tosa domains (a proxy, in the case of Tosa), followed then by the heads of Owari, Higo, Inaba and Awa domains, and finally by all domainal lords resident in the capital, were summoned and notified by Sanjō Sanetomi, minister of the right (*udaijin*), of the Imperial Rescript for the Dissolution of Domains and the Installation of Prefectures (*haihan chiken no chokugo*). Domains that had persisted for some 250 years were, one and all, swept away. In their stead new prefectures would be established. On this same day, Ōkuma Shigenobu of Hizen and Itagaki Taisuke of Tosa were appointed as councillors alongside Saigō and Kido. The announcement left little doubt that the four domains that had born responsibility for the regime change of 1868 – Satsuma and Chōshū along with Hizen and Tosa— intended to retain power into the indefinite future.

The dissolution of domains threw the world of the samurai into disarray. What would become of their status affiliations, their occupations, their lineages? In an instant they had been ejected from places of stability into a world of flux. Their greatest anxiety lay in their uncertainty over how they would be treated once their erstwhile lords were relocated to the national capital.

The state forged ahead with streamlining and reconfiguring a new map. The dissolution of domains had yielded a whopping 302 prefectures, a geography of unfathomable inefficiency for a new centralized administration. To rationalize rule, the regime had to dismantle the structures of domainal organization and engage in large-scale reconstruction. It set about amalgamating domains based on boundaries and place names inherited from the ancient past, carving out such reinvented spaces as Kai and Harima. By the eleventh month, the state had succeeded in reducing the number of national prefectures to seventy-two *ken* and three *fu*. To the extent possible, it rechristened each domain when it transformed it into a prefecture, seeking not to allow domain names to carry over into the modern era.

A new bureaucratic structure common across the entire nation was installed in each of the new prefectures.[5] At its summit stood a prefectural head (*kenrei*) and a deputy prefectural head (*gon-no-kenrei*, or simply *gonrei*). The prefectural head enjoyed formidable power, including the right to appoint and dismiss the deputy head as he pleased.[6]

Who would be appointed to this important post? Once the domainal lords had departed their posts, the provinces they left behind waited with eager anticipation to see what kind of men would become their new rulers. The men who would come to the helm had to be endowed with both aptitude and pluck.

Ōkubo, Kido and other such men at the heart of the central regime had themselves come from the provinces. They firmly grasped the situation at hand, and they proceeded with circumspection. Before making any appointments, they first dispatched capable men from among the state counsellors (*sanji*, not to be confused with councillors, or *sangi*) to shore up the personnel basis for new prefectural administrations and to scope out the opinions of erstwhile domain executives. Their plan was to maintain a degree of continuity from the disbanded domains to ensure a peaceful transition to a new system. The time of upheaval favoured them: precisely because it was a moment of turmoil, it was not hard to identify men in every domain who had made particularly outstanding achievements. They thus managed to proceed relatively smoothly with a change of guard. These transformations not only spread the ideology of meritocracy and a system of rewarding exceptional achievement across the provinces but also fanned the flames of autonomous will and individual success (*risshi*) among youth in the prefectures.

With the foundation of the administration laid out, appointments descended consecutively for prefectural heads (*kenrei*), deputy heads and counsellors. Most appointees came from outside the prefectures they served. Without direct ties to the land, these bureaucrats developed a system wherein they governed in close association with men more intimately affiliated with the prefecture. The principle of not appointing prefectural heads to prefectures from which they originated (*hishusseichi shugi*) emerged at this point and persisted as a tenet of provincial administration until the post-war era, when the prefectural governorship became a popularly elected post.

To flaunt their talents, prefectural heads pursued new policies soon after they were appointed. The proliferation of school education was one such policy. Appointed heads of prefectures were often bureaucrats from the enlightenment faction (*kaimeiha*). They bore exceptional interest in enlightening the masses in their provinces: they believed that this was their mission.[7] Education was a way for them to transform erstwhile domainal vassals (*ryōmin*) in a feudal system (*hansei*) into citizens of a prefecture (*kenmin*). An imperial rescript promulgated in 1873 declaring that the duty of provincial officials lay in enlightenment (*kaimei*) provided a tailwind to their endeavours.[8] The prefectural heads undertook their executive tasks with a perception of themselves as shepherds of hoi polloi.

As the state proceeded with streamlining the prefectural system and slashing executive posts, some prefectural heads were knocked off their posts by young upstarts intent on flaunting their executive skills. In others cases, prefectural heads (*kenrei*) and their underling counsellors, later known as governors (*chiji*) and division heads (*buchō*), were transferred across the nation in single units, creating continuity in human resources. Such was the case of Yasuba Yasukazu, born in Kumamoto in 1835 and later head (*kenrei*) of Fukushima, Aichi and Fukuoka and of Hokkaido (*Hokkaidōchō chōkan*); and of his underling Fukano Ichizō, born in Kumamoto in 1852 and later a secretarial officer (*shokikan*) in Fukushima, head of the internal affairs division of the Hokkaido government (*Hokkaidō naimu buchō*), and governor (*kenchiji*) of Fukuoka and Aichi.[9] Such men functioned as cadres of specialists in provincial governance and revolutionized their field.

The Three-Ministries System (*san'in sei*) and the origins of the division of management (*buntan kanri*)

The central government finally moved ahead with reforms of itself once it had put the dissolution of domains and establishment of prefectures into effect. On the twenty-ninth day of seventh month of Meiji 4 (= 13 September 1871), the state inaugurated the Three-Ministries System of the Council of State (*Dajōkan san'in sei*). It splintered the Council into three parts: the Central Ministry (*Sei'in*), the supreme decision-making organ of the state; the Ministry of the Left (*Sa'in*), the legislative organ; and the Ministry of the Right (*U'in*), the executive organ, in which the heads of the government departments (*kakushō chōkan*) assembled.[10]

At the summit of the Three Ministries stood the Central Ministry, 'which the Emperor oversaw and which superintended the myriad affairs of the realm (*Tennō ringyo shite banki o sōhan*)', according to the Regulations for the Organization and Administrative Affairs of the Council of State (*Dajōkan shokusei narabi ni jimu shōtei*). The Ministry was composed of the minister of the state (*Dajō daijin*), who stood at its helm; two ranks of councillors that together composed the ministerial officers (*gikan*) – the *nagon*, a category that was quickly dissolved, and the *sangi;* and secretaries (*shokikan*) ranked from the Privy Grand Chronicler (*sūmitsu daishi*) down. Sanjō Sanetomi assumed the office of minister of the state (*Dajō daijin*).

The Central Ministry not only functioned as a supreme decision-making organ but also coordinated the general affairs of the state. All matters, whether legislative, executive or judicial, were referred from the Ministry of the Left and the Ministry of the Right to the Central Ministry, which then proceeded with decision-making. If the legislative Ministry of the Left raised an issue related to executive administration, that issue passed through the Central Ministry to the Ministry of the Right. And if the executive Ministry of the Right submitted a matter that bore on legislation, that matter would likewise pass through the Central Ministry to the Left for resolution. The Central Ministry was thus designed to regulate legislative and executive functions across the state.

Because it bore such an important function, Kido believed that the Central Ministry needed an auxiliary organ with specialized knowledge that could support its functioning. He looked into the installation of a secretarial bureau (*hishokyoku*) with secretarial officers (*shokikan*) who would specialize in investigating government affairs. But fears that Kido's plan would inordinately expand the powers of the Central Ministry prevented it from materializing. To win support for reform required careful attention to the equilibrium of power in the state.

The head (*kyō* or *chōkan*) and senior aide (*daiyū* or *jikan*) of each executive department together made up the Ministry of the Right, which was tasked with 'planning laws for present affairs (*tōmu no hō o anshi*) and investigating the actual benefits and drawbacks of executive administration'. These men did not take part in the Central Ministry. The proposal set forth by Ōkubo, which would have unified legislative and executive government by combining the posts of councillor and department head, was thus repudiated. But the department heads did gain wide-ranging authority not only over their own respective policy domains but also over personnel matters. 'Heads of departments (*kyō*) hold total and exclusive authority to preside over all affairs in their divisions. No intrusion into the authority of another division will be permitted' – thus was the division of power among the executive divisions clearly delineated in a document titled 'Laying out Regulations for Appointments to Heads of Departments and Head of the Development Bureau'.[11]

The regime blocked the dual appointment of councillors and department heads, but its expansion of the powers of department heads as chief officials in the executive state allowed departmental turf wars and territorialism, long a latent source of concern, to rage. Once the dissolution of domains and installation of prefectures laid the basis for policies to cover the entire nation in scope, departments strengthened their strategic resolve and jostled to win funds to put their particular visions into reality. Budgeting became a quagmire.[12] The blueprint of the regime dictated that budgeting matters be handled by the Ministry of the Right and referred to the Central Ministry only in cases where there was an outstanding problem. But right from the outset, matters of budgeting failed to proceed down this predetermined route. Indeed, the limits of the budgeting system were exposed in the Chastise Korea debates of 1873.

Another objective of institutional reform was to enforce the careful selection of personnel, a problem that had vexed the regime from its earliest days. Significant personnel changes accompanied the construction of the Three-Ministries System. Sanjō Sanetomi rose to the helm of the Central Ministry as minister of the state (*Dajō daijin*); Iwakura Tomomi became minister of the right (*udaijin*); and the leading men from each of the four domains that had put the dissolution of domains into effect found their places solidified: Saigō of Satsuma, Kido of Chōshū, Ōkuma of Hizen and Itagaki of Tosa. In the Ministry of the Left were placed such strong-willed, opinionated men as Gotō and Etō who had long been involved in research on systems administration (*seido torishirabe*). These appointments revealed an intent to turn the Ministry of the Left into a legislative organ of real substance that abjured empty doctrinarism.

Men from the four domains of Satsuma, Chōshū, Hizen and Tosa by and large monopolized posts in the staffs of each of the departments besides those of Divinities (*jingishō*) and of the Imperial Household (*kunaishō*), which were rather idiosyncratic. Not only men from other domains but also erstwhile daimyo and members of the nobility were ejected from the nucleus of political power. The new departmental officers were all bureaucrats who had engaged in practical work to support the Restoration administration since its inception. It was for this reason that they came to be censured as an oligarchic autocracy (*monbatsu sensei*). Regardless, that men of such exceptional talent came to constitute the Restoration regime signalled the beginnings of the coalescence of a modern nation-state.

Old personnel went and new personnel came as the state took form. Once the division between legislative and executive government had been made clear, men in the department offices came to acquire specialized skills as bureaucrats, and they began to develop into politicians who would take on the processes of decision-making. These new veterans then moved on to new posts, and in their vacated seats arrived young upstarts who, fresh from journeys to the West or years of university education, had gained the latest knowledge and skills in various fields of modern learning. There thus emerged a dynamic process of nurturing, employing and promoting human resources.

Reform even extended to the configuration of departments. On the ninth day of the seventh month (= 24 August), the Department of Judicial Affairs (*gyōbushō*) merged with the Censorate (*danjōtai*) to form the Department of Justice (*shihōshō*).[13] Interdepartmental friction had often flared into fights between Judicial Affairs, which of course held all judicial matters under its jurisdiction, and the Censorate, which superintended government administration. Because turf wars occurred frequently, and because the central state absorbed the judicial authorities that had been held by individual domains until their dissolution, it became necessary to standardize the legal (*hōtaikei*) and judicial (*saiban*) dimensions of governance. These measures were no less crucial for treaty revision.

We have already seen in the previous chapter the origins of the Department of Education (*monbushō*), which emerged as a state organ for developing and implementing a nationwide educational policy in the wake of the dissolution of domains. In the eighth month of 1872, the year following the founding of the education department, the nation was divided into eight separate university sectors, and middle and elementary school districts were also put into place. A new national education system was promulgated, and the department embarked on building and consolidating new organs of education.

The Department of People's Affairs (*minbushō*), responsible for taxes and for the nationwide family registration (*koseki*) system, was dissolved on the twenty-seventh day of the seventh month (= 11 September 1871), and absorbed by the Department of the Treasury (*ōkurashō*), which unified tax collection and state financial affairs under a single departmental roof. The Treasury, organized in five divisions (*shi*) – taxation (*sozei*), the exhortation of industry (*kangyō*), the printing of money (*shihei*), the family registration system (*koseki*) and the postal system (*ekitei*) – turned into a juggernaut of a government office, sweeping into its jurisdiction even local government officials (*chihōkan*) from across the nation. At the helm (*kyō*) of the department stood Ōkubo Toshimichi.

The Three-Ministries System more or less solidified the structure of the central Meiji state. Since the dissolution of domains and the installation of prefectures had opened up the possibility of applying a single policy indiscriminately across the entire Japanese nation, the government departments lunged ahead with expanding their fields of influence. They issued proclamation after proclamation, demand after demand. The prefectures, still rocking after the collapse of the domainal system, were left discombobulated. The central state issued so many demands so recklessly that prefectural officials had to decide on their own which to heed and which to ignore, left with no choice but to find a way on their own to relax the restrictions placed on them. So lamented Torio Koyata, whom we encountered earlier.[14] Disgruntlement in the provinces began to mount. The power of the state to effect reform and to make system-wide adjustments, whether in the provinces or in the national centre, was now to be put to the test.

The Iwakura Embassy and institutional research

With Iwakura Tomomi, minister of the right, as the lead ambassador, the foreign embassy of the Meiji regime embarked from Yokohama on the twelfth day of the eleventh month of the fourth year of the Meiji reign (= 23 December 1871). Its first destination was America, which enjoyed relatively good relations with Japan. From there the embassy proceeded through various European states in anticipation of the revision of the Ansei-era Five Powers Treaty, due for re-examination in the fifth month of the following year. The result of the voyage is well known. Negotiations to disband consular courts with extraterritoriality ended in failure for the Japanese side, but the first-hand experience of Western civilization and Western institutions by so many government officials contributed to a new course for the Meiji regime, a course exemplified by the slogan 'Rich Country, Strong Army' (*fukoku kyōhei*).

If the result of the embassy is well known, its motivations are not. From the outset, gaining knowledge of and experience in the West was a stated objective of the embassy. Let us set the clock back two years and witness the lead-in to the Iwakura Mission.

In the third month of 1869, the Meiji government summoned Guido Verbeck, an American of Dutch extraction in Nagasaki, to serve as an instructor at the University-South College (*Daigaku nankō*). Many Meiji government officials, including Ōkuma, Ōkubo and Itō, had studied under Verbeck. Verbeck ascended to the capital in response to their call. His vast knowledge influenced scores of students at the University-South College, not least the tributary students assembled there from across the realm.

It was not only students who learned under Verbeck. Politicians and statesmen often went to him to ask for instruction on the constitutional state, international law, education and various other dimensions of Western civilization. It was an era of bewildering change: the Boshin War was headed towards a conclusion, and events moved in quick succession from the opening of the House of Public Debate (*kōgisho*) to the surrender of domainal registers (*hanseki hōkan*) to the inauguration of the Two Departments, Six Ministries system (*nikan rokushō sei*). Meiji leaders thirsted for knowledge about how to set up the systems of their state.

Verbeck well understood the circumstances of the regime. To bring Western civilization to Japan, it was not enough simply to acquire superficial knowledge by reading books, he argued. Japanese needed to go the West themselves and understand it by seeing it with their own eyes. In the fifth month, just two months after his arrival in Tokyo, Verbeck laid out these thoughts in a formal recommendation to Ōkuma Shigenobu.[15] He called for the state to dispatch an embassy abroad. But the government, still in its earliest years, could not afford to send away so many of its statesmen for an extended period of time. It did not take up Verbeck's recommendation immediately.

Only after the dissolution of domains and the installation of prefectures did circumstances allow an extended embassy abroad. In the eighth month of 1871, Ōkuma persuaded Sanjō Sanetomi, minister of the state, to allow him to become the ambassador on a foreign expedition that would negotiate treaty revision. The purpose was not only the revision of treaties but also the first-hand acquisition of Western knowledge. Ōkuma, who had distinguished himself in the field of diplomacy but had no overseas experience, no doubt felt an exceptional urge to go out and see the West for himself.

But Ōkubo Toshimichi, fretting about Ōkuma's mounting power, moved to thwart his manoeuvring. Ōkuma enjoyed the rank of councillor, but his status was altogether different from that of Saigō or Kido. Saigō and Kido had benefited from their origins in Satsuma and Chōshū, which had led the way from domains to prefectures. Ōkuma, meanwhile, had won widespread admiration by dint of his own practical capabilities. Around him had rallied the younger generation of the enlightenment faction. There was no denying his power and influence: if Ōkuma were to succeed in negotiations for treaty revision amid these circumstances, he would dramatically alter the balance of power in the regime.

Ōkubo and his allies succeeded in winning Sanjō to their side. They turned the Ōkuma Embassy into the Iwakura Embassy.[16] Iwakura was promoted to the lofty post of minister of the right upon his appointment to the embassy. He had occupied the significant post of head of foreign affairs (*gaimukyō*) up to that point; his displacement of Ōkuma was not unreasonable. Ōkuma, dreams shattered, went on to find a new field of action in domestic affairs.

Bureaucrats conducting institutional research

A new face replaced that of Ōkuma at the head of the foreign embassy, but its underlying purpose did not change. A Sovereign's Letter (*kokusho*) dated the eleventh day of the fourth month clearly articulated three objectives for the Iwakura dispatch: first, to present a letter from the sovereign of Japan to those states with which he had entered into treaties; second, to learn about Western state institutions and civilization and to bring back to Japan what would contribute to modernization; and third, to engage in negotiations for treaty revision.

To allow it to fulfil the second objective in particular, the embassy was populated not only with Ambassador Iwakura and his retinue of deputy diplomats but also with many bureaucrats chosen from various government departments. The embassy was charged with investigating five specific fields in the West: structures of government administration; government finance and accounting; industry and technology; education; and the army and navy. Relevant departments vied with one another to send out their most promising men.

The embassy needed men to take up practical tasks, especially that of translation. To this role it primarily summoned erstwhile retainers of the bakufu (*kyū bakushin*) who had study-abroad experience. These men had gained deep specialized knowledge through their work as translators, but in the embassy they came to play significant roles not only as linguistic mediators but also as investigators in their own right. Ga Noriyuki, for instance, who taught Hoshi Tōru English as a professor in the Institute for Development (*Kaiseijo*), accompanied Kido Kōin in his investigations of foreign constitutions. After returning to Japan, Ga himself embarked on a translation of Montesquieu's *The Spirit of the Laws* and went on to dedicate his energies to producing translations that formed the basis of the Japanese legal code (*hōten hensan*).

Commissioners (*rijikan*) appointed from the various departments came to form the centre of the institutions research team (*seido chōsa*).[17] The actual task of conducting research devolved on five men – Tanaka Mitsuaki, Yamada Akiyoshi, Tanaka Fujimaro, Hida Tameyoshi (or Hamagorō) and Sasaki Takayuki – and their attendants. Most of these men were new bureaucrats in their late twenties to late thirties who had gained practical administrative skills in the new regime. Rich in experience, informed of practical affairs, and skilled at absorbing information, it was they who were most fit for this task.

Particularly remarkable among the attendant staff was Inoue Kowashi. Born in Kumamoto in 1844, Inoue studied national learning (*kokugaku*) at his domainal school but went on to master Western learning at the School for Development (*Kaisei gakkō*), where he became head of institute and gained wide renown for his prowess. He distinguished himself from his earliest days in the Department of Justice and was added to the Iwakura Embassy to conduct research on codes of criminal procedure (*keiji soshō hō*).

Upon his return to Japan, Inoue not only dedicated his energies to establishing this field of law but also applied his interest in structures of rule to the production of the text *Ōkoku kenkoku hō*, by which he became recognized as the preeminent authority in Japan on the Prussian Constitution and gained the trust of Ōkubo Toshimichi. The death of Ōkubo brought with it an era of misfortune for Inoue, but his efforts allowed him room to flourish under Iwakura and Itō when they later sought to inaugurate the Meiji Constitution.

The Department of Education, which was founded around the same time the Iwakura Mission prepared to depart, was tasked with the formidable work of building a nationwide education system. The Ministry of Education dispatched assistant (*taijō*) Tanaka Fujimaro to lead a group of five specialists, including Nagayo Sensai, to join the embassy as attendants and conduct research. Tanaka was a power holder in his domain who had acted as its representative at the Kogosho Conference, which we witnessed in Chapter 1. As a greater scribe in the Privy Council (*sūmitsu daishi*) and through other roles, he became influential in the new regime as well.[18]

Tanaka embarked on active research while on the embassy. Together with his assistants – Niijima Jō, born in 1843, later the founder of Dōshisha, and Tomita Tetsunosuke, born in 1835, later president (*sōsai*) of the Bank of Japan, both studying in America at the time – Tanaka carried out a painstaking institutional study, which resulted in a fifteen-volume report titled *Riji kōtei*, or *Commissioner Proceedings*.

Among the concrete results of their research were the proclamation of the Rescript on Education (*kyōikurei no happu*), approval for the operation of private academies and the introduction of music education in Japan.

Young bureaucrats and the infatuation with the West

Accompanying Tanaka on the journey to the West was Nagayo Sensai, born in 1838, a bureaucrat and specialist in healthcare and public health whose contributions to the modernization of those fields left an exceptional legacy. Nagayo hailed from a family of Chinese medicine (*kanpō*) practitioners in the Ōmura domain of Hizen. He went on to study at the Tekijuku, the school of Ogata Kōan, where he became head of the school (*jukutō*) at a young age. From there he proceeded to Nagasaki to train in medical studies. With the founding of the Department of Education, he was recruited by Etō Shinpei, senior aide (*daiyū*) in the department, and entrusted with the reform of medical education.

Nagayo left a record of the process that led to his selection as an attendant on the Iwakura Embassy.[19] From it we can glean the intensity of the desire he and his comrades had to go to the West. Nagayo had heard from a friend about the impending Iwakura dispatch and its prospective research on state institutions. He sprang to his feet, hired a rickshaw and made his way to Inoue Kaoru.

> When I arrived at the residence of Inoue [Kaoru] at Kaiunbashi, Yoshikawa [Akimasa] was already there in the guest room. I asked him if he had come in the hope of becoming an attendant on the ambassadorial dispatch. Yes, he responded, asking if I was there for the same reason. I nodded, smiling faintly. When I put my request [to join the mission] before Inoue, he said that Itō [Hirobumi] would be in charge and that I should go to consult with him. [...] I waited for Itō to return home and won an interview with him. Upon his instructions, I then went and visited Kido at Kudansaka the following morning. Fortunately, he said that he hadn't heard yet of any volunteers who were doctors. He told me that I should meet with Tanaka [Fujimaro], who would probably be appointed by the Department of Education as an embassy commissioner, and with Ōki [Takatō, head of the education ministry], and put in a request with them. He said that he would speak with them himself but that since it was probably better for me to be in touch with them myself soon, I should head in their direction immediately. From there I visited both of them. Scurrying about all day through the evening, I managed to arrange the substantial part [of participation in the embassy].[20]

Up to this point, Nagayo had been bewildered by the speed of change in medical education under the new Department of Education. Tokyo was already bustling with zealous young medical specialists. Nagayo had felt that there was no remaining space for him to find success. He had found himself stranded in a place 'with no way to move forward and with fear of falling back'.

But the Nagayo who returned from study in Germany and the Netherlands was a different man. He rose to head of the Tokyo Medical School (*Tōkyō igakkō*) and of the Bureau of Public Health (*eiseikyoku*) and took up leading roles in building infrastructure to suppress contagious disease and developing the administration of medical science and public health (*eisei*). To Nagayo, the embassy was an exceptional opportunity to push his knowledge to the frontier of learning and to become a human resource of great promise for the nation.

For such rising bureaucrats just entering the government, the chance to transcend the limitations of text and learn *in situ* marked the consummation of many years of longing. It offered, too, a critical means for them to raise their own worth in a world where the value of executive and administrative capabilities was quickly rising.

At the same time the Iwakura mission went abroad, the Army Academy (*rikugun heigaku ryō*), too, sent members of its ranks to France, where they studied military command and organization (*gunrei, heisei*). Matsuda Masahisa of Ogi domain, later lauded alongside Hara Takashi as a leader of the Seiyūkai, was one such man, as was Sone Arasuke, who was involved in negotiations with the Seiyūkai as treasury minister in the first Cabinet of Katsura Tarō.

We have already seen in Chapter 2 how both before and after the Iwakura Mission the departments of the government actively sent their young bureaucrats to Europe and America to gain new knowledge and develop as human resources. The Iwakura Embassy became a catalyst for realizing the desires not only of these individual departments, which had transformed into full-fledged policy and planning institutions after the dissolution of domains, but also of the bureaucrats in those divisions, who committed themselves to becoming superior human resources and putting their abilities into full force.

The motley origins of the study-abroad students

It was not just up-and-coming bureaucrats who wanted to journey to the West. Travelling on the Iwakura Mission were study-abroad students who sought to break open new paths in their lives by studying overseas. Particularly well known among them were Tsuda Ume and her contingent of women students. Indeed, if we look at the whole contingent of study-abroad students on the mission, we find startling diversity in their origins, and we gain a clearer sense of the nature of a foreign embassy during a period of transformation.[21]

Erstwhile domainal lords formed the core of the study-abroad contingent.[22] These were men who had vacated their daimyo seats, yielded to new prefectural governors and gathered in Tokyo after the domains were dissolved and replaced with prefectures. What to do with these surplus officials had become a grave problem. Former ministers of the bakufu had set about searching for solutions.[23] Western learning, and by extension a voyage to the West, gained particular salience as a possible new future for old feudal lords.

One could not simply tell a former daimyo to get up and go to the West on his own, of course. He needed his former vassals with him. It was ensured that he would be properly attended by such men. Maeda Toshitsugu of Kanazawa domain, for instance, was accompanied by such men as Sekizawa Akikiyo, born in 1843, who had studied in Britain during the bakumatsu era.[24] Attending Torii Tadafumi of Mibu domain was Morita Tadaki, who had been to America on the *Kanrinmaru*.

These were no mere attendants. Sekizawa, for instance, was appointed as a commissioner for expositions (*hakurankai goyō gakari*) and worked to introduce Japan to the world at the Vienna World Exposition of 1873. On the side, he dedicated himself to research on how to develop export industries for Japan. Seafood processing caught his eye.

When he visited the Swedish and Norwegian pavilions at the Vienna Expo, Sekizawa was struck by how processed marine goods had gained success as exports; at the Austrian pavilion, he learned about artificial salmon incubation. In 1876, he headed to the Philadelphia World Expo, where he encountered canned salmon, on exhibition by the Canadians. He picked up methods for artificial incubation and technology for can manufacturing and took them back to Japan. With the Training Institute for Fishing Industries (*Suisan denshūjo*) as his centre of activity, he worked towards the industrialization of fishing, gaining renown as the father of the Japanese fishing industry. His example reveals how far-reaching the Iwakura Embassy was in scope.

Particularly noteworthy, too, were children of the nobility who studied abroad on the embassy. Born in 1858, Matsugasaki Tsumunaga went to Prussia and was at first ordered to pursue military studies (*heigaku*) as part of a policy to rear children of high-ranking nobility as military men.[25] But he was stricken by disease there. The diagnosis bade ill: a future as a military man would have been difficult. He changed course and turned to architecture, enrolling at the Technical University of Berlin. For eleven years he immersed himself so deeply in his study-abroad experience that it is said that he even lost mastery of Japanese. Upon his return to Japan, he rose to the head of the construction division of the Cabinet's ad hoc Bureau of Architecture (*naikaku rinji kenchiku kyoku kōji buchō*), in which capacity he took on planning for the concentrated construction of government buildings at Kasumigaseki and founded the Association for Building Houses (*zōka gakkai*), the forerunner of the Architectural Institute of Japan (*Nihon kenchiku gakkai*).

Not all who went abroad enjoyed such success, of course. Among those who foundered was the 1845-born Shimizudani Kinnaru, who had gained prominence in the bakumatsu era as a youth from noble lineage and who had gained particular renown as general superintendent of the Hakodate judicial office (*Hakodate saibansho sōtoku*). Shimizudani proposed the dispatch of pacification armies to Ezochi and was subsequently appointed as general superintendent of those forces. But he was trounced by the army of the former bakufu, led by Enomoto Takeaki, soon after his arrival in Ezochi. He was forced to retreat to Aomori, the bitter ignominy of defeat lingering with him. Shimizudani was appointed deputy at the Hokkaido Development Agency (*Kaitakushi jikan*) after the fall of Enomoto, but within two months he lost the post to Kuroda Kiyotaka. He moved south, taking up Western studies at the Osaka Academy for Development (*Ōsaka kaisei gakkō*). While he was in Osaka, it was discovered that he had known that Enomoto had been lending out almost 10 million square metres (3 million *tsubo*) of land to Prussian merchants and that he had done nothing about it. He was placed under house arrest (*kinshin shobun*).[26]

Shimizudani descended from a distinguished pedigree: his father was a councillor (*sangi*) and his grandfather a major-counsellor (*dainagon*). In light of his heritage, those around him offered him support. They encouraged him to study abroad in Russia. Perhaps they foresaw a renewed life for him in the Development Agency. But posterity has no record of any achievements from him during his time abroad. After returning from his four years of study, he inherited the mantle of his family, but he attained no official positions of note. He died in 1883 at 38 years of age.[27]

The politicians of the Restoration regime sent their own children, too, to study abroad: Tomotsuna, the firstborn boy from the primary wife of Iwakura Tomomi and later a counsellor to the imperial court (*kyūchū komonkan*); Hikonoshin, or Toshinaga, the firstborn son of Ōkubo Toshimichi and later a member of the House of Peers (*kizokuin*); Nobukuma, the second-born son of Ōkubo, who was later known as Makino Nobuaki and took up posts as minister of the imperial household and home minister; and Isaburō, the second-rank adopted child (*yōshishi*) of Yamagata Aritomo, who became deputy home minister and head of the communications ministry. It is said that Nobukuma had heard that both his father and older brother were on the embassy. He submitted a request to join them, thinking that staying all alone at home would be rather sad.

Those who journeyed West – and those who did not

The children of Meiji leaders profited from their provenance. If they wanted to go abroad, they could. Everyone else had to fight a fierce competition to go abroad. It was a race that determined the course of their lives. Those who fought the hardest were students brimming with a desire to learn and study. It was they who won, at the end of a spirited campaign to gain spots on the embassy, the trophy of study abroad.

Hirata Tōsuke, the man who first proposed the tributary-student system, ran single-mindedly after an opportunity to study abroad.[28] By his academic prowess he had broken away from the main pack of students. He had risen to head of dormitory at the University-South College with hopes of a bright future pinned on him. But as he witnessed his peers – Ogura Shohei of Obi, Niwa Ryōnosuke of Saga – one by one get the summons abroad without any word himself, his impatience began to boil over. Countless times he petitioned Yamaguchi Naoyoshi of Saga, the man charged with supervising the university (*daigaku kantoku*), and reiterated his yearning to go abroad. But he could not even win an interview with Yamaguchi.

Hirata figured it was because of his roots: he hailed from Yonezawa domain, an enemy of the imperial court during the Restoration. In the fifth month of 1871, he quit the South College, set his sights on Russian studies and waited for his time abroad to come. Then came word of the impending Iwakura Embassy. He could not *not* be on it.

Hirata wrote a letter to Iwakura outlining a proposed Russia policy. He entrusted it with Watanabe Kōki, who had trained Hirata in English back during his Yonezawa days. His request for study in Russia was now written and submitted, and it was out of his hands. By this point, Watanabe had secured a spot on the embassy as a secretary (*shokikan*), and he was willing to act as an agent for Hirata. Hirata, whose academic record outshone that of his peers, finally found his wishes come true. He was added to the embassy as a leader of study-abroad students.

Hirata did not end up studying in Russia. After arriving in Berlin, he met with Shinagawa Yajirō and Aoki Shūzō, both of whom were already studying in Germany. They convinced him that Russia could hardly be counted as a developed country, that it was not worth studying there and that it was in fact in Germany, a nation in the midst of a meteoric rise, that he should examine. Persuaded, Hirata changed his study locale. He studied politics, national law and international law under Rudolf von Gneist at the University of Berlin, and from there he scaled the heights of academic achievement, ultimately earning his doctorate from Heidelberg University. Hirata's was the first academic degree in politics awarded to a Japanese. Upon his return to Japan, he became, even among other bureaucrats with legal expertise, the cynosure of a Meiji government seeking to establish a constitutional system based on the Prussian model. He later ascended to the top of the Yamagata faction of bureaucrats.

What happened with Hirata happened strangely often among study-abroad students. So many of those who journeyed West found resonance in fields other than those they had originally chosen, and they ended up bringing knowledge of those new fields back with them. Perhaps that was the whole point of going abroad. Indeed, such was the case with 1847-born Nakae Tokusuke, known better as Nakae Chōmin, Rousseau of the Orient. Nakae had felt that he had exhausted the limits of French-language study in Japan. He went to France, and he came back with popular rights theory. Just as the political expertise of Hirata did, Nakae's knowledge became a tool that broke open a path to autonomy for the nation.

How were these men able to leave behind such astounding legacies? We can glean an answer in the fiery desire to study abroad of Ōkuma Shigenobu, leader of the cadre of young bureaucrats. No doubt Ōkuma valued the new knowledge awaiting him in Europe and America. But there was something else. Misgivings about reform pervaded not just the nation at large but even the government itself: would Japan, so different from the West, really find a fit in Euro-American institutions? It was not just sceptics who voiced incredulity. Even progressive bureaucrats, those who themselves championed the adoption of Western institutions, could not quite overcome their qualms. They needed the assurance that came from going and seeing for themselves. It was not as if the confidence they gained translated to persuasiveness back home, of course. Their brimming sense of conviction triggered an equal and opposite reaction. Journeying to the West helped rear scores of valuable human resources, endowing them with liberal shares of a knowledge that would advance reform. But at the very same time, it deepened the chasms separating men on the home front.

Towards the upheaval of 1881

An aggressive executive government and the dysfunction of the Central Ministry (*Sei'in*)

The dissolution of domains and installation of prefectures strengthened the determination of the various executive departments to pursue their own policies. They actively studied foreign institutions, as on the Iwakura Mission; they carried out their own policy research; and they employed the talents of scores of men with experience in the West. As the earliest Restoration bureaucrats became increasingly politicized members of the Central Ministry and the Ministry of the Right, up-and-coming executive bureaucrats wielding new knowledge began to gain a foothold in the departments themselves.

The departments could not satisfy their need for professional bureaucrats only by hiring those with experience in the West. They set about cultivating their own talent. With treaty revision as its foremost objective, the Department of Justice sought to raise up scores of judges and attorneys with a grasp of Western law. It opened up its own school in 1871, the Meihōryō, a forerunner to the Department of Justice School of Law (*shihōshō hōgakkō*), and embarked on training legal professionals within Japan. Gustave Émile Boissonade, Georges Bousquet and other newly appointed instructors from France began teaching classes with an emphasis on nurturing practical capacity.[29] Students at the school received stipends from the state and enjoyed guaranteed posts as government officials upon graduation. Little wonder that exceptional youth from across the nation began flocking to the school.

Intent on assembling a Western-style army and spurred on by the recommendation of military junior aide (*heibu shōyū*) Yamagata Aritomo, the Department of the Military (*heibushō*) began implementing Western-style education at the Osaka Military Academy (*Ōsaka heigaku ryō*). The department hoped to train army officers in preparation for nationwide conscription in 1873. A band of men including Katsura Tarō, who was born in Chōshū in 1847 and went on to become army minister and prime minister, began their education at the academy and proceeded to Germany and France to deepen their studies. Their academic training was different from that of the tributary students, whose schooling spanned a wide range of topics from the humanities to the social sciences to the natural sciences. The training of military men responded to the demands of governmental policy, which needed professional bureaucrats who had been nurtured for particular purposes.

As individual departments proactively hammered out their own policies, their budgetary demands for the 1872 fiscal year bloated beyond restraint. The Department of the Treasury (*ōkurashō*) was tasked with coordinating the state budget, but its head, Ōkubo Toshimichi, had gone to America and Europe as part of the Iwakura Embassy. Senior aide Inoue Kaoru was left to bear the brunt of endless demands for money.[30]

Faced with such circumstances, Inoue demanded that each department provide evidence for how it calculated its proposed budget, and he delegated the task of coordination to the Central Ministry. It was a decision made in perfect accordance with the logic of the Three-Ministries System. But Sanjō Sanetomi, who led the Central Ministry, feared a backlash from the individual departments and settled for ad hoc manoeuvres to propitiate them, granting them one-time funds rather than devising a systematic budgetary plan. Irate, Inoue and his band threatened to resign, at which point the Central Ministry reverted budgetary matters back to the Department of the Treasury. The plans of the Central Ministry lacked coherency and failed abjectly.[31]

How did these circumstances arise? To chalk the situation up to the personality of Sanjō would be overly hasty. This was an era in which the employment of promising human resources was proceeding quickly. As talent flowed into the post-domainal

Restoration government, bureaucrats with specialized knowledge began to gather beneath politicians at the rank of department head. Policy-making bodies thus began to take form in each of the departments. These policy groups could back their demands with specialized and indeed legitimate justifications. To manage their requests required playing politics.

When it was politics that drove executive coordination other problems emerged. Each of the politicians making up the class of department heads represented not simply a particular domain but a particular strain of domain-based oligarchic factionalism (*hanbatsu*). If the regime planned to decline the demands of a department, it had to do so after having considered not only the personal interests of the individual at the head of the department but also the fealty or recalcitrance of the domain from which he hailed. The politicians themselves well understood the game they were playing and brandished threats of resignation as trump cards. Administration became increasingly difficult as executive government became caught up in the still-lingering influence of erstwhile domains. The politicians who had begun their careers as Restoration bureaucrats bore both political savvy and specialized expertise, which had taken them to the apex of both political power and the professional bureaucracy. They had become indispensable organs in the machinery of the Meiji government.

And it was precisely for this reason that coordination and decision-making needed to happen in the Central Ministry, an institution that brought all of these men together. All shared in this understanding. In May of the following year, 1873, the regime therefore revised the employment system of the Council of State (*Dajō kanshoku sei*), designating councillors as 'officers of the Cabinet' (*naikaku no gikan*). The revision served to concentrate decision-making power over legislative and executive affairs in the Central Ministry.[32]

And yet the Central Ministry still could not manage the government. The situation only worsened. Inoue and others, who had submitted a proposal for financial reform, left their government posts. Chaos spread. The demands of executive government, which constituted one side of a problem of justice, became caught up in factionalist power struggles, complicating the situation further. The Department of Justice under Hizen man Etō Shinpei was more than willing to expose in its full nakedness a graft scandal involving Chōshū-faction politicians and the Department of the Treasury – we need look no further than this for an example of the oligarchic factionalism that marred the state.

The political rupture of 1873: A failure of general coordination

The individual departments, proclaiming the indispensability of their policy-making wherewithal and demanding budgets of their own, had entered into negotiations with the Department of the Treasury to gain state funds. The Treasury, meanwhile, had sought to inculcate financial discipline and tighten the state belt. After state councillors were designated 'officers of the Cabinet', the situation had escalated to a stand-off between the individual departments and the Central Ministry. What began as an attempt to coordinate state administration tumbled into domainal-factionalist sparring.

Just as the situation was spiralling into total confusion, the Chastise Korea debates were thrown into the mix. In August, an internal decision was made to dispatch Saigō, his eye on war, to Korea. Expectations mounted. Perhaps a war abroad would help break the deadlock in both internal and foreign affairs.

Ōkubo had returned to Japan in May, ahead of Iwakura, to resolve the unfolding budgetary crisis. He opposed the plan to chastise Korea. His experience abroad inclined him towards building a rich country with a strong army (*fukoku kyōhei*), and the Chastise Korea plan would have encumbered that vision by burdening state finances and by generating friction with foreign nations. But Ōkubo saw that circumstances did not favour his vision yet. He bought time until Kido and Iwakura returned.

With the return of Iwakura in October, Ōkubo submitted a proposal to revamp the general coordination of the Central Ministry and the executive departments. It centred on the very plan he had advocated all along: to have councillors serve simultaneously as departments heads. Rather than attack the Chastise Korea proposal head-on, he wanted to overcome the dysfunction of the Central Ministry first and thereby to resolve a host of other problems, including instability in the domestic social scene; disequilibrium in government revenue and expenditure; and an excess of imports flooding the nation.

The Ōkubo proposal aimed to appease members of the Meiji caretaker regime just as it sought to reform the state. The plan would strengthen authority in the Central Ministry by sustaining the appointment of councillors as 'officers of the Cabinet', and it would grant simultaneous posts as councillors to wielders of power in the executive branch including Etō Shinpei, head of the justice department; Ōki Takatō, head of the education department; and Gotō Shōjirō, chair of the Ministry of the Left (*sa'in gichō*).

The problem Ōkubo faced was outside the government, not within it. The restive discontent of samurai in the provinces (*chihō shizoku*) could not be suppressed. The dissolution of domains and the installation of prefectures had destabilized their status, and the inauguration in 1873 of the proposed conscript army further undermined them, robbing them of their occupational privileges. And yet the state had no choice but to mobilize samurai themselves to suppress rebellions (*ikki*) against the conscription edict.

Saigō saw a solution to this mounting problem in his plan to chastise Korea, and he insisted obdurately on having himself dispatched as an emissary to Korea. The Central Ministry became embroiled in debate. Saigō finally managed to win consent for his plan from Sanjō Sanetomi, minister of the state, and the Cabinet reached a decision backing him. Then Ōkubo submitted his resignation. As the situation deteriorated, Sanjō tumbled into a state of confusion, and he was unable to submit the Cabinet decision to the Emperor. The regulations of the Council of State (*Dajōkan shokusai*) included a provision allowing the minister of the right or of the left to stand in for the minister of the state in administering affairs when the minister of the state was absent. The task of reporting the Korea decision to the Emperor therefore devolved to Iwakura, minister of the right. Banding with Ōkubo, he plotted to submit to the Emperor a personal opinion statement opposing the Saigō dispatch and the affirmative Cabinet decision. Within the imperial palace, men scuttled about behind the scenes to ensure that the Iwakura counter-proposal would be adopted. And indeed it was:

on 24 October, approval was granted, in opposition to the Cabinet decision, for a postponement of the emissary dispatch to Korea.

Their decision rebuffed by the Emperor, Saigō Takamori, Itagaki Taisuke, Etō Shinpei and Soejima Taneomi, the last of whom that very month had been appointed as a councillor, resigned from their councillor posts and left the regime. Thus unfolded what is known as the political upheaval of 1873 (*Meiji rokunen no seihen*). Stand-offs within the regime reached a breaking point. Resolution came only through a manoeuvre with no precedent: the Emperor unilaterally rejected a Cabinet decision.

Change swept through the membership of the upper tier of the regime as a result of the political schism. All department heads, with the exception of army head Yamagata Aritomo, were granted simultaneous posts as councillors. Yamagata rose to a councillor post in July of the following year, 1874, along with Ijichi Masaharu, chair of the Ministry of the Left, and Kuroda Kiyotaka, head of the Hokkaido Development Commission (*Kaitakushi chōkan*). The vision that Ōkubo had long advocated was at last realized. A system of government that united legislative and executive functions by appointing men in dual posts as department heads and councillors was inaugurated.

The founding of the Home Ministry (*naimushō*): The birth of 'the authority among the authorities'

From this upheaval was born the sweeping government organ that stands for modern Japan itself: the Department of the Interior, or the Home Ministry (*naimushō*).[33] Social policy, local government, the administration of the police, of hygiene, of public works – the scope of the Home Ministry stretched across vast swaths of national executive governance. Dubbed 'the authority among the authorities' (*shōchō no naka no shōchō*), the department came to function as the nucleus of domestic administration.

The idea that a department (*shōchō*) should be installed to oversee the general coordination of domestic executive governance had been taken up by the Ministry of the Left in 1872. Even under the caretaker government, investigation into such a prospective department had gained steam, with Etō Shinpei leading the charge. The impetus lay in the desire of Etō and his band to chip away at the power of the burgeoning Department of the Treasury. They were backed up by provincial officials (*chihōkan*) who sought to unify and standardize provincial administration. The caretaker regime managed to assemble a plan for a department of the interior that would centralize the administration of the police and of the provinces. But political instability prevented the plan from evolving into a proposal.

Ōkubo, who rose to the helm of a new political system after the schism of October 1873, had long acknowledged the need for a department that would centralize domestic administration.[34] He had learned that the caretaker regime had discussed plans to install a department for domestic administration (*naiseishō*), and he had ordered attendants on the Iwakura Mission to investigate and collect information about the domestic administrative systems of America, England, France and Russia. He had thereby amassed research on whose basis the conception of the new department coalesced. In November 1873, the Department of the Interior, or the Home Ministry, was founded as the main pillar on which the post-upheaval political system would rest. It became a vast assembly-ground of executive functions. It was composed of seven divisions: six *ryō* and one *shi*. Five *ryō* subdivisions were transplanted from the Department of the Treasury: industry promotion (*kangyō*), household registration (*koseki*), communications (*ekitei*), public works (*doboku*) and land (*chiri*); one *ryō* came from the Department of Justice, public security (*keiho*); and one *shi* came from the Ministry of Industry (*kōbushō*), that of surveying (*sokuryō*). The scale of the department went well beyond the original plans, which merely sought to split up the Department of the Treasury and to centralize provincial administration.

The expansive scope of the Home Ministry was the result of two historical contingencies. First, maintaining the peace and security of the realm had become a matter of extreme urgency after scores of men in the Konoe Army resigned from their posts amid the Chastise Korea schism and after samurai began resisting the conscription edict. Second, once the Iwakura Embassy brought home the notion of 'rich country, strong army' as a national policy, the state needed to develop local governments and work with those governments to advance industry encouragement policies for farmers, artisans and merchants. In response to this need, six divisions were installed in local governments: general affairs (*shomu*), encouragement of industry (*kangyō*), tax collection (*sozei*), public security (*keiho*), education (*gakumu*), and expenditure and revenue (*shutsunō*). The Ōkubo Home Ministry, which oversaw these various divisions, was thus born as a wide-ranging, comprehensive department that shored up state administration, cultivated the power of the people and exercised its own power across the entire nation.

At the inception of the Home Ministry, the posts of senior and junior aides (*daiyū*, *shōyū*) remained vacant. Five *daijō*, men one rank below the junior aides, respectively led each of the department subdivisions known as *ryō*, equivalent to *kyoku*, or bureaux. These men acted as supports for Ōkubo. None of them – apart from Hayashi Tomoyuki, from Chōshū domain, who headed the Public Works Bureau, and Kitashiro Masaomi, from Tosa domain, who headed the general affairs division (*shomuka*) – came from the domains of the Meiji oligarchs. They were instead either erstwhile retainers of the bakufu or men originating from shinpan domains. All had deep experience in practical administrative affairs, and they gained renown as men of talent who obtained their posts by meritocracy. That so many bureaucrats from oligarchic domains (*hanbatsu kanryō*) had defected from the regime after the 1873 upheaval allowed the rise of these kinds of personnel.

What distinguished the staffing of the Home Ministry was a system wherein human resources flowed between the national centre and the provinces. Even in its earliest days, the department was staffed with men who had gained success as officials in the provinces. They were employed by the Home Ministry to apply their experience to the reorganization and unification of provincial governance. Such men included Kawase Hideharu, who went from Kumamoto prefectural head (*kenrei*) to head of industry promotion; Murata Ujihiki, who went from prefectural counsellor in Tsuruga prefecture to head of public security; Kitashiro, whom we have already encountered and who began as deputy head of Aomori; and Matsudaira Masanao, who went from counsellor in Niigata to head of the main accounting division (*shukeika*).

Others moved in the opposite direction, returning to the provinces as provincial officials after working at the Home Ministry: Matsudaira; Nitta Yoshio, who went from head of the records division (*kirokuka*) to deputy head (*gonrei*) of Kagawa; and Takei Morimasa, who went from head of the supplies procurement division (*yōdoka*) to governor (*kenchiji*) of Fukui. Matsudaira in particular achieved continual and conspicuous success during his thirteen years in Miyagi prefecture and five in Kumamoto prefecture. He then returned to the Home Ministry as a deputy minister (*jikan*). By sustaining this system of scuttling personnel back and forth between the centre and the peripheries, the Home Ministry supplied its policy-proposing core with experiential knowledge from provincial officials. This structure, which yielded an intimate collaborative relationship with the provinces and let practical on-the-ground experience inform state policy, helped support the regime in its 'rule by Home Ministry'.

The reforms advanced by the Home Ministry extended all the way to personnel selection in the prefectures. The suppression of the Saga Rebellion of 1874 was followed by a large-scale reshuffling of staff in the Saga prefectural government. The majority of posts below the level of prefectural head came to be held by people originating from outside Saga prefecture. And in Sakata prefecture of the Tōhoku region, widely known as a 'recalcitrant prefecture', a peasant movement led to the installation of Satsuma man Mishima Michitsune as prefectural head and to the overhaul of personnel.

Having long awaited an opportunity to strike, the regime moved ahead in August 1876 with a plan for a mass amalgamation of prefectures. It reduced the existing fifty-nine prefectures to just thirty-five. Its ostensible objective was to rationalize the scale of provincial financial administration. But its more essential purpose was to eliminate 'recalcitrant prefectures' where the influence of the defunct domains lingered and the forces of anti-regime agitation remained rampant. The Home Ministry had to make prefectures abide by its edicts and injunctions if it wanted to implement a national standardized system of provincial and local governance. The resistance of recalcitrant prefectures encumbered this effort. It was for this reason that, under the revamping, Saga was folded into Nagasaki, Tsurugaoka into Yamagata, Tottori into Shimane, and Myōdō (which later became Tokushima) into Kōchi.

The dissolution of twenty-four prefectures meant the elimination or replacement of vast numbers of upper-level provincial officials. The Home Ministry filled posts with young rising stars, such as Koike (Watanabe) Kunitake, originally of Takashima domain and head of Kōchi prefecture. And it indicated that it would begin governance performance reviews with a three-year term as their basis. Five years after the dissolution of domains and establishment of prefectures, an era of avoiding radical change had ended. Now the Home Ministry took the lead in selecting personnel foremost by ability.

Underlying the various reforms by Ōkubo and his government was a desire to consolidate decision-making power and to secure talented bureaucrats who could get things done. To employ capable human resources regardless of their origins was indispensable in advancing the policy of 'rich country, strong army'.[35] When Ōkubo had visited Britain, he had seen that what undergirded a nation well known for its parliamentary politics was a sturdy bureaucratic structure made up of talented people.

Indeed, he was deeply inspired by this observation. The main purpose of his reforms was to employ not only outstanding politicians but also bureaucrats with robust knowledge and skills. And he sought to establish a cooperative working relationship between the two.

The equilibrium and management of power after the death of the Restoration heroes

In regions where vestiges of the old order persisted, people found the reforms of the new regime impetuous and brazen. Resentment smouldered. After the defection of councillors in the upheaval of 1873, the political discontent of the defectors became linked to the discontent of people in the provinces. Samurai rebellions, beginning with the Rebellion at Saga, and a movement for the establishment of a parliament, represented most notably by the Petition for the Establishment of Parliamentary Government in 1874, both had ripple effects across the country. But once the Southwest War of 1877 ended in government triumph, words trumped weapons as the preferred means of resisting the state, and the Movement for Freedom and Popular Rights amplified its calls for parliamentary governance.

The government itself acknowledged the need to open a parliament. It accepted the will of Kido Kōin, who had called for the full development of consultative government since the earliest years of the Meiji era. In 1875, the Emperor issued a promulgation for the gradual establishment of constitutional government (*zenji rikken seitai juritsu no mikotonori*). The government installed the Chamber of Elders (*Genrōin*) to 'widen the sources of legislation', the Court of Cassation (*Daishin'in*) to 'strengthen the powers of arbitration', and the Assembly of Provincial Officials (*chihōkan gikai*) to 'seek the public good through the sentiments of the people (*minjō*)'. A tripartite division of power was thus accomplished, though of course it had limits, and an assembly that would take up opinions from the provinces was built up again.

These changes spelled the demise of the ministries of the right and of the left. Two years later, the Central Ministry, too, was dissolved, and the assembly of the councillors and of the ministers of the right and of the left was redubbed the 'Cabinet' (*naikaku*). Deliberations and decision-making would proceed there.[36]

But the entire structure faced another upheaval just six years later, in 1881. Kido died of illness in 1877. That same year, Saigō perished on the battlefield. A year later Ōkubo was stabbed and died. The composition of the Meiji regime changed dramatically and suddenly. In February 1880, the dual appointment scheme of councillors and department heads was dissolved, and by the fall of 1881 the regime had become a hodgepodge of men functioning exclusively as councillors, those holding dual appointments and those working exclusively as department heads.

A new system had to be set in place once the dual appointment of department heads and councillors was abolished. Six divisions were installed in the Council of State: foreign affairs, domestic affairs, accounting, military affairs, judicial affairs (*shihō*) and legislative affairs (*hōsei*). A councillor took charge of each field over which he had standing influence. Sano Tsunetami, who came to lead the Department of the Treasury, was appointed with the recommendation of Councillor Ōkuma Shigenobu, his hometown buddy; Tanaka Fujimaro, who took the helm of the Department of Justice, was recommended by Councillor Ōki Takatō, who had held the post before him. Substantive power remained in the hands of the councillors.

To establish a balance of power even while dividing roles was regarded as an especially important problem of personnel management during this era. As part of a plan to appease the Tosa faction of the state, the regime proactively employed Fukuoka Takachika as head of education; Kōno Togama as head of agricultural and commercial affairs (*nōshōmu*); Hijikata Hisamoto as senior aide in the Home Ministry; and Hosokawa Junjirō as senior aide in the Department of Justice.

Unlike the councillors already occupying their posts, these new hires were deployed in fields far from their original areas of expertise. Fukuoka was well versed in judicial and legislative affairs, but he was appointed to the Department of Education; Hosokawa had expertise in education policy, but he was sent to the Department of Justice; and Kōno had a proven track record in police and judicial matters, but he was placed in agriculture and commerce. To the posts of senior and junior aides in these departments were assigned administrative bureaucrats (*jitsumu kanryō*) originating from within the given department. It was they who held real power within the ministry. By liberally handing out titles but safely guarding the substance of power, the state managed to secure the stability of its executive functioning.

Such emphasis on establishing a balance of power was needed because no prominent politicians remained in the Meiji government after the death of Ōkubo Toshimichi and because the state needed to form a united front against growing attacks from outside the government. Sanjō and Iwakura were coordinators and managers, not the kind of men who would themselves lead in advancing policies. Itō and Ōkuma stood at the apex of the Restoration bureaucrats, and although their talents had distinguished them from the rest, they were still young, and their political powers had limits. As it faced impending treaty negotiations with Korea and the Qing Empire abroad as well as a surging Popular Rights Movement at home, the supreme task before the regime was to establish an equilibrium of power through a system of unified collective leadership (*shūdan shidō taisei*) and to ensure the stability of government operations.

The political upheaval of 1881: Stand-offs over structures of rule

But a financial brouhaha and a debate over the ideal form of government proved again to be the undoing of unified leadership. Ōkuma Shigenobu had taken charge of state finances after the death of Ōkubo Toshimichi. He had proceeded with a positive fiscal policy and, to the extent possible, granted departments the budgets they requested. In the harsh light of the experiences of 1873, he could not help but take such an approach. He had to ensure the stability of executive operations.

Prolonged years of positive fiscal policy, coupled with an increase in the printing of paper money to furnish the military costs of the Southwest War, led to sharp inflation. Obloquy poured in not only from popular-rights activists but also from members of the state itself. The abolition of the councillor/department head dual appointments was a desperate measure by Itō and Inoue to remove Ōkuma from the Department of the Treasury and to impose financial retrenchment. But the Satsuma faction, which favoured a positive fiscal bent, obstructed the manoeuvre. They arrived at a compromise measure: to install Ōkuma and Itō as members of the accounting division of the Council of State (*Dajōkan kaikeibu*) and to place Ōkuma's fellow countryman Sano at the helm of the Department of the Treasury.

The state was left playing perpetual catch-up in financial affairs, responding to problems after they arose. Ōkuma sought to secure adequate funds for the regime by collecting foreign bonds, and he tried to cut back on expenditure by reforming the structure of financial administration. His plans ended in failure, impeded in the former case by opposition to loans from foreign countries and in the latter by resistance from state departments accustomed to positive fiscal policy.[37] Ōkuma finance ran aground. His failure stemmed from the structural problems of a Meiji regime that had abandoned state coordination measures out of fear of a backlash.

Around this time, amid a surging movement for the establishment of a parliament, the regime used the name of Minister of the Left Arisugawa-no-Miya Taruhitoshinnō to order each of its councillors to submit a proposal for the opening of a parliament. These proposals transformed simmering financial stand-offs into a political imbroglio.

Kuroda Kiyotaka ignited the fire. In Meiji 13 (= February 1880), Kuroda called for a return to a positive fiscal policy and argued that it was too soon to begin setting up a national parliament. He claimed that if the regime used a positive fiscal policy to create new jobs, it would suppress the Popular Rights Movement and would not need to scramble to inaugurate a parliament. Inoue, who favored a fiscal austerity plan in July, opposed Kuroda, arguing that their present reality exposed the failure of positive fiscal policy and demonstrated the urgent need for a parliament. The political fault lines up to this point were the same as those enduring since the upheaval of 1873.

But the situation quickly exploded into an all-out crisis. The state administration collapsed. At the centre of the upheaval was none other than Ōkuma, the man in charge of state finances. After he rose to the shared helm of the accounting division of the Council of State with Itō, Ōkuma moved ahead with a series of measures: a turn to financial retrenchment, the establishment of the Department of Agricultural and Commercial Affairs, a government sell-off of factories and structural reforms aimed at the opening of a parliament. In December, Itō put out a proposal calling for the gradual, measured establishment of a constitutional political system. It seemed that Ōkuma, Itō and Inoue had together put into place a structure for fiscal retrenchment and for the gradual opening of the Diet. Ōkuma was soon designated as the man responsible for consultations on this gradual process.

But Ōkuma dithered and dithered without submitting his own proposal on parliamentary government. After repeated prodding and encouragement, he at last submitted the proposal in March 1881, but even then only as a secret communication to the Emperor. His was a radical proposal calling for the hurried opening of the parliament. He demanded the inauguration of a constitution by the end of that year, an election of Diet members by the end of the following year and the opening of the parliament two years later. And he called for a party cabinet system wherein parties, made up of individuals with shared policy views, would form the main basis of governance.[38]

The state convulsed as the most powerful man in the administration put forth a proposal more radical than anything anyone had imagined. Ōkuma intended to build up a state administration that had actual leadership capability. He planned to maintain collaborative ties with Itō, Inoue and other members of the Chōshū clan by working on the opening of a parliament. At the same time, he would gain support from the Satsuma clan by working towards a return to a positive fiscal policy and by securing revenue sources through public debt.[39] He hoped to break through the political gridlock by finding equilibrium between the competing political forces of Chōshū and Satsuma and between the two political problems of state finance and parliamentary government. Thus would he build up an administration with real leadership power.

But the grandeur of his plan triggered equally great opposition. To open a parliament in just two years and to introduce a cabinet system based on political parties constituted a repudiation of the political forces propping up the regime at the time. For Iwakura and his band, who had painstakingly tried to balance old and new forces in the regime, it was a proposal that could not be accepted. Oligarchic politicians (*hanbatsu seijika*) still in the regime were similarly alarmed. They had suspicions. Parvenu bureaucrats and intellectuals linked to Fukuzawa Yukichi had begun to gather around Ōkuma; they were plotting a parliamentary system in which powers of political administration would alternate. Had Ōkuma banded with Fukuzawa in an attempt to seize control of the administration?

Inoue Kowashi took this sense of alarm and, craftily, shrewdly, transformed a policy stand-off into a full-blown political upheaval. Inoue had encountered Prussian constitutionalism as a member of the Iwakura Embassy. To oppose the Ōkuma party-cabinet proposal, which resembled the British model, Inoue Kowashi put forth a proposal advocating a Prussian-style constitutional monarchy (*rikken kunshu sei*). He worked behind the scenes to have his model adopted. He won Iwakura and Itō to his side, and, with a net cast around Ōkuma, he managed to win support for his relatively gradualist Prussian scheme even from Inoue Kaoru, a believer in the British model, and from members of the Satsuma clan, vocal advocates of the speedy inauguration of the Diet. Forces were now decisively in Inoue Kowashi's favour.

On 11 October, Ōkuma and the band of bureaucrats around him were chased out of the regime. This was the political upheaval of 1881. The following day, an imperial proclamation announcing the inauguration of a Diet in 1890 was released, and the countdown to the inauguration of a constitutional government began.

The demise of the parliamentary cabinet system (*giin naikaku sei*)

The actions of Ōkuma and his band were too secretive, too hasty. It was in part for this reason that they met with such severe resistance, even though it was they who had originally been slated to lead the move to a constitutional government.

The source text to which supporters of the parliamentary cabinet system referred was *On Parliamentary Government in England* (*Eikoku giin seiji ron*), a work by Alpheus Todd. The original English-language version had been given to Ōkuma by Minister of the Left Arisugawa-no-Miya as a reference for research into constitutional systems. Ōkuma had the work translated by up-and-coming bureaucrats such as Yazo Fumio and

Ozaki Yukio.[40] It became a foundation for the political thinking of these men.[41] Inoue Kaoru, too, had favoured an English-style parliament right until the political upheaval. With such influential men supporting it, the English parliamentary model had been seen as the prescribed course for the state. But it was slapped down as excessively radicalist after the schism of 1881, and the Prussian model of constitutional monarchism, which attracted leaders because of its seeming gradualism, came to displace it.

This swapping-out of political systems left a knotty legacy for the history of modern Japanese politics. If a Diet were to be inaugurated, then it would function as a tax-collecting assembly (*chōzei gikai*), and its debates would centre on problems of state finance. In such a case, the only way the government could put its ideas into practice and advance its policies would be through its relationship with the parliament. And if the parliament were to be inaugurated while oppositional popular political parties (*mintō*) were still inveighing against what they called oligarchic despotism (*yūshi sensei*), then the state would soon find itself stuck in a quagmire.

The point of a parliamentary cabinet system was to prevent a situation wherein the state and the political parties would face off against one another. Ōkuma envisioned a system in which the head of the majority party would become prime minister and in which the government would control both legislative and executive functions, a system wherein 'all governance emerged from one source' (*shosei ichigen*). To Ōkuma, who had been at the helm of state finances, it made perfect sense that the majority party in a parliamentary Cabinet should control state administration and push ahead with raising taxes, pursuing foreign bonds and securing funds for a positive fiscal policy. Of course, in such a case, the majority party would be made up of government politicians – and be headed by none other than Ōkuma himself.

Putting such a plan into practice would require careful explanation, painstaking behind-the-scenes negotiations and deliberate implementation. It was for this reason, we can reasonably suspect, that Ōkuma kept delaying the submission of his proposal and ultimately chose a secret imperial communication as his method for submission. But his circumspection came across as surreptitiousness, and it became his own undoing.

And despite his pro-parliament posture, Ōkuma could not even win support for his proposal from the popular parties leading the parliamentary movement. Itagaki and his Freedom Party (*Jiyūtō*) insisted that a parliament had to be inaugurated first and that it should then enact a constitution.[42] Ōkuma, in opposition, expected that the presiding administration would inaugurate a constitution and then proceed with opening a national Diet. To the popular parties, the Ōkuma proposal came across as a duplicitous reform measure designed to ensure that regnant political forces continued to prop up Ōkuma's own authority. What appeared to the regime as an excessively rash plan came across to the popular parties as tepid, insipid. Caught in the middle, Ōkuma won support from neither. He withdrew from the regime. And with him, so too did the battle over a parliamentary cabinet system become drowned out by political wrangling.

Still, even though Iwakura and his coterie struck down the Ōkuma proposal and deemed the Prussian model of constitutional monarchism better suited to the Japanese reality, they left a door open to the British model of parliamentary politics, claiming that the Prussian system 'was inadequate for the future'. How to deal with this fundamental structural problem of the relationship between the regime and the parliament was a question they left for a later date, a time when the constitutional system would be inaugurated and the government would need to work out its own functioning.

Partisan officers (*seitōkan*) and permanent officers (*eikyūkan*): Folding changes of administration into the system

The Ōkuma proposal has garnered considerable historiographical attention mainly because of its call for the quick inauguration of a parliament and for its presentation of a parliamentary cabinet system. But the proposal was filled with other suggestions and ideas, ones typical of a man like Ōkuma who stood at the centre of the national administration and who, as a Restoration bureaucrat, understood executive government well. Particularly striking among his other ideas was 'Proposal Three: the separation of partisan officers (*seitōkan*) and permanent officers (*eikyūkan*)', which dealt with the relationship between political power and the structures of bureaucracy. It was a richly suggestive proposal with revelatory ideas about the proper relationship between regime and bureaucracy.[43]

If a Cabinet based on political parties wanted to hold real leadership power and manage the affairs of the state, it had to take control of the executive government. Ōkuma proposed that a wide range of posts, from councillors as well as heads and aides of departments (*shō kyō yū*) to heads of bureaux (*kyokuchō*), be filled with party men coming from the parliament. He saw these posts as political ones and the men in them as 'partisan officers' (*seitōkan*). Ōkuma believed that because posts concerned with practical executive matters – from ministers and councillors, to heads of departments (*chōkan* or *kyō*), to deputy heads of departments or vice ministers (*jikan* or *yū*) – all had a hand in decision-making on policy, they should be vacated and refilled every time political power changed. The British system operated on the principle that posts from administrative vice minister or permanent secretary (*jimu jikan*) down should not be affected by changes in political power. But Ōkuma imagined a system that went beyond mere duplication of the British system.

This set-up reflected the new reality of the Meiji government. Fourteen years had elapsed since the Restoration. The departments were being filled by specialized professional bureaucrats. It was around this time that Komura, Hatoyama and Furuichi had begun trickling back from their study-abroad destinations.

The Restoration bureaucrats had begun taking up posts as councillors and department heads (*shōkyō*). They bore profound specialized knowledge in their fields, and they grew deep roots in their respective departments. They selected to the posts of senior and junior aides, the auxiliaries of the department heads, men with whom they had deep relationships. They would do and die together.

Meanwhile, as executive government became increasingly professionalized, talented men with deep specializations were being installed as heads of bureaux (*kyokuchō*) as well. These men operated with a high level of discipline, and, as a result, substantive decision-making power began migrating down from the heads of departments to them. Facing this reality, Ōkuma and his band believed that, in order to make a party cabinet system work, the political structure from the top of the department descending down to the level of the departmental bureau head had to function as a single executive unit that would change whenever administrative power did.

Even as he sought to raise uniformity in the government by turning departmental officials into 'partisan officers', Ōkuma and other bureaucrats did not forget the path to professional bureaucracy that they themselves had travelled. Bureaucrats had an important reason for being in the state: they could apply their specialized knowledge to executive government, and they could if necessary express their opinions on various affairs. Ōkuma therefore allowed bureaucrats below the level of bureau head to secure lifelong posts as 'permanent officers'. But in exchange, he prohibited them from holding simultaneous posts in the parliament. He sought to isolate lifelong bureaucrats from the influence of party politics and changes in political power. To enable wide-ranging debate was to fulfil the intent of the Charter Oath; to allow men to secure lifelong posts in the state was to ensure continuity in executive government. The two aims were separate.

The Ōkuma proposal thus regarded the minister or department head (*daijin*), the deputy minister (*jikan*) and the bureau head as a single unit within the administrative structure of the state. Once their expertise carried them up the ranks of their department to the post of bureau head, bureaucrats faced a choice: they could opt to become politicians, or they could live as professional bureaucrats. Whether in the political parties or in the governmental departments, the human resources produced by this system came to support rule by party politics. The structure Ōkuma sketched out was a profoundly practical vision of partisan political rule.

But the boundary between the realm of politics and the realm of executive government is blurry. Time, people and government policy all draw and redraw it. The demarcation between political affairs and administrative affairs (*seimu, jimu*) became the main battle-line over which proponents of oligarchic rule and proponents of party politics fought in their contest for control over the state. Bureaucrats were often buffeted by the forces of these power struggles. And on occasion it was modern Japan itself that was rocked in the competition.

Ōkubo Toshimichi had spent many years favouring stability over change. Coming after his death, the 1881 political upheaval presented the Meiji regime with an opportunity to press ahead with reforms. Once Ōkuma and the British model he had trumpeted were defeated, the remaining politicians in the regime took up the task of planning out a new structure of rule, one that, modelled after the more circumscribed Prussian model, put a certain distance between the politicians and a prospective Diet.

At the core of this new task was the problem of how to construct the relationship between executive and legislative government. As the regime built a robust executive branch composed of talented professional bureaucrats, its members began to imagine the stand-offs bound to arise with the legislative branch. They started building a new constitutional system in earnest.

Building a cabinet system: Attempts at a responsible government

The House of Counsellors (*Sanji'in*): Constructing an organ for legislative research

In the wake of the upheaval of 1881, the regime dissolved the six-part division of councillor (*sangi*) responsibility and resurrected the dual appointment of department heads and councillors. It put special emphasis on maintaining stability as it moved ahead with reforms. Matsukata Masayoshi, the newly appointed head of the Ministry of the Treasury, enacted deflationary policies, and on the basis of the stability engendered by fiscal belt-tightening and political cooperation, preparations for the introduction of a constitutional system took off.

In October 1881, the regime installed the House of Counsellors (*Sanji'in*, not to be confused with the later House of Councillors, or *Sangi'in*). Having received the imperial proclamation for the inauguration of a Diet, the House of Counsellors was to take on the actual task of installing the new state system. With a view towards standardizing laws and ordinances, it was granted the authority to conduct advance research into bills submitted by the central regime (*seifu*), the departments (*kakushō*) and the House of Elders (*Genrō'in*). The research it conducted acted as a general coordination mechanism, much as that of the Cabinet Legislation Bureau (*naikaku hōsei kyoku*) in the Japanese government today does. It thus provided backing to reform proposals. As preparations proceeded for impending negotiations over treaty revision, the House of Counsellors took shape as an organ of the state charged with reform of state institutions.

Human resources were deliberately poured into the House of Counsellors. Itō Hirobumi stood at the head (*gichō*). Below him assembled promising new bureaucrats well versed in legal systems: Inoue Kowashi, Ozaki Saburō, Yasuba Yasukazu, Itō Miyoji, Ōmori Shōichi, Kiyoura Keigo and Sufu Kōhei.[44] It was not only men who had travelled to the West who joined the House. Men with deep training in Chinese and national learning (*kangaku, kokugaku*) such as Kiyoura, who had served as head of academy (*jukutō*) at Hita no Kangien, joined its ranks. We can discern an intent by the regime not to allow members of the state to be carried away by currents of Western learning. It wanted them to understand and sort among the best and worst of different systems.

The House of Counsellors first set about standardizing structures of executive government and systems of laws and ordinances, which had grown messy. Regulations governing the authorities of department heads and senior and junior aides varied by department. In November, the House moved to standardize these regulations, promulgating and enacting the Regulations on Administration in the Departments (*shoshō jimu shōtei*) as a form of unified standard. Here it was clearly codified for the first time that department heads bore both advisory (*hohitsu*) and executive (*shikkō*) responsibilities. It was also ordained, with regard to modes of legislation, that legal regulations (*hōritsu kisoku*) would have to be announced openly as declarations (*fukoku*) and that each department would have to make proclamations (*futatsu*) of its guidelines for functioning (*jōrei*). Hereafter, the House of Counsellors functioned as a general coordinator of the regime through its mastery of the legislative system and served as the leader of reform.

The departure of a constitutional research team

As the regime shored up the foundations of the nation, in 1882 it dispatched to Europe a team of constitutional researchers with Itō Hirobumi as its head. A select group of men accompanied him: Itō Miyoji, Kawashima Atsushi, Miyoshi Taizō, Yamazaki

Naotane and Yoshida Masaharu.[45] Hirata Tōsuke, a junior official in the treasury secretariat (*ōkura shō-shokikan*) who had earlier participated in the Iwakura Mission, joined them too.

The 1882 voyage to Europe is generally remembered as a constitutional field trip by Itō Hirobumi, but his research team carried a sweeping list of no fewer than thirty-one different research themes. 'To look into the foundations of all constitutional and monarchical states in Europe and their constitutions, to consider their development, to observe their current functioning and present conditions, to research the benefits and harms of their systems' – with such a mandate, the team aimed not only to study constitutional systems but also to conduct vast-ranging research into systems of governance as a whole, seeking to gain knowledge and understanding that would allow them to develop these systems in Japan. And they did not only examine Prussia. They extended their research to all states operating on constitutionalism. Even as they placed the Prussian system at the centre of their investigation, they conducted flexible research that sought to absorb experiences of a diverse range of constitutionalist states.

Faced with such a formidable task, Itō anguished. The previous winter, Itagaki had led the founding of the Jiyūtō, the Freedom Party. And just two days after Itō's departure for Europe, Ōkuma inaugurated the Constitution and Reform Party, the Rikken Kaishintō. Ōkuma and his party then established the Tokyo Professional School (*Tōkyō senmon gakkō*) and set about training their own human resources. It was not hard to imagine the talented men trained there arising en masse if a Diet were inaugurated, running for positions and applying their skills in the parliamentary arena. Itō and his team had to act quickly and build up a government that could absorb and respond to the criticisms these men were bound to make in a prospective Diet. Itō felt these pressures piling onto his shoulders, and onto his shoulders alone. It is said that he was drowning in alcohol in the days leading up to his journey to Europe.

This exasperation revealed that Itō had made a full transformation from a professional bureaucrat to a politician. He now faced a situation in which three political factions with three different views of constitutionalism were facing off against one another: the Constitution and Reform Party (*Rikken kaishintō*) faction of Ōkuma, Fukuzawa and Ono Azusa; the Freedom Party (*Jiyūtō*) faction of Itagaki, Ueki Emori and Nakae Chōmin; and the internal state faction of Iwakura and Inoue Kowashi. Itō had to go abroad and come back with a vision and knowledge superior to those of the battling factions. The pressure was staggering. But facing Itō was a golden opportunity: if he succeeded in acquiring the insights he needed, awaiting him at home was a status as a politician whom no one could hope to rival. That he took along with him not Inoue Kowashi but Itō Miyoji, a confidant he had searched out himself, signalled the fiery ambition he carried.

Building a nation-state, training its bureaucrats: From hermeneutics to practical learning

Itō hustled about the length and breadth of Europe, visiting Germany for three months, Austria for another three, Germany again for yet another three, Britain for two and

Russia for one. As he traversed the continent, he dispatched Yamazaki Naotane to Belgium and Saionji Kinmochi to France on separate research trips.

Rudolf von Gneist at the University of Berlin and his student Albert Mosse became Itō's teachers, as did Lorenz von Stein at the University of Vienna. In London, it is said, Itō attended a lecture by Herbert Spencer.

The research topics before Itō included general themes such as the structure of the Cabinet, the problem of the scope of authority, the question of responsibility and the relationship between the Cabinet and the parliament. Other themes went as far as to address concrete problems such as parliament election laws, the distinction between laws and regulations (*hōritsu, kisoku*), and the structure and scope of the authority of individual executive departments. Influenced especially by Lorenz von Stein, Itō studied the organic theory of the state (*kokka yūkitai ron*), which regarded the establishment of equilibrium among the monarch, the parliament and the executive government as the primary purpose of a constitutional system.[46]

Von Stein argued for the inauguration of a constitutional system in which the political participation of citizens would give rise to a sense of national will, and he emphasized the necessity of setting up executive structures to put that will into actual practice. Towards these ends, he stressed the need for the systematic training of professional bureaucrats and for the establishment of the field of *Staatslehre* or 'state studies' (*kokkagaku*) (not to be confused with the 'national studies' or 'nativism' [*kokugaku*] of an earlier era) that would investigate the question of governance. Von Stein's thinking revealed his concern with circumstances in Germany at the time. Hermeneutics dominated German universities. The system continually produced passive bureaucrats who, without any practical learning, obsessed over purely theoretical problems.

The lectures of Von Stein spurred Itō and his team; policy-making meant grasping the relationship between state and society and realizing the public good in that society. To realize this public good, it was necessary to establish a field of 'state studies' and, on its basis, produce bureaucrats who would take action in the government. The benefit of being a relative latecomer in introducing a constitutional system was that Japan could learn from the mistakes of nations gone before it. Japan had to overcome the errors that bogged Prussia down.

These problems were intimately linked to the question of employing bureaucrats. The Meiji regime had succeeded in collecting human resources through the recruitment system (*chōshi seido*), and it had invested considerable energy in nurturing those resources at the University-South College. Then influences from the domains gained strength in the system. Personnel employment based on personal interests, wherein selection depended on a network of connections and acquaintances, pervaded the regime. Scores of incompetent bureaucrats started leeching off the government. Such inefficiency and injustice in the personnel system became a target of opprobrium among popular-rights activists, who called for the inauguration of an examination-based employment system.[47]

What conversations did Von Stein and Itō have about these problems of bureaucracy? In his arguments about the powers of executive government, Von Stein suggested that, even while the monarch retained the right himself to appoint ministers closest to him, administrative bureaucrats should all attain a baseline of education and be selected only if they pass an examination. From this thinking emerged the bureaucratic system of modern Japan, with both officers appointed freely (*chokuninkan*) and those appointed after taking exams (*sōninkan*).

Itō Hirobumi returned home in August 1883 having fortified his conception of a new structure of rule. At the core of the government he would place a cabinet system (*naikaku seido*), executive ministries (*shōchō kikō*) and a system of state officials (*kanri seido*). The figure of an exasperated, tormented Itō all but vanished. In its place emerged a confident statesman assured of his ability to trounce both popular-rights activists and conservative elements within the state. It was a confidence born from the knowledge he had gained in his discussions with Von Stein and from the observations he had made of constitutional government across Europe.

German studies began to flourish across Japan. The humanities and science divisions (*bungakubu, rigakubu*) at the University of Tokyo made German language a compulsory subject. Summoned from Germany, Karl Rathgen began offering courses in public administration (*gyōseigaku*) and political science (*seijigaku*). Joining Hermann Roesler, already employed by the government, Karl Rudolph and other bureaucrats from Prussia arrived in Japan as counsellors to the Meiji regime and, responding to requests from the government, contributed to a range of endeavours including drafting legislative bills.

It was primarily professional bureaucrats with experience in the West who sustained the now full-blown process of amending the structures of state. Among these reformers were Inoue Kowashi, Itō Miyoji, Iwakura Tomosada, Arakawa Kunizō, Watanabe Renkichi, Makino Nobuaki, Yamawaki Gen and Kaneko Kentarō.[48] In March 1884, these men gathered in the newly established Bureau for the Investigation of State Systems (*seido torishirabe kyoku*), and under Itō Hirobumi, head of the bureau, they devoted their energies to building a constitutional system. Arakawa, Watanabe and Yamawaki had begun their higher education in the University-East and University-South colleges (*Daigaku tōkō, Daigaku nankō*), and from there had gone to study abroad in Germany and Austria. Makino and Kaneko had accompanied the Iwakura Embassy and studied in America. They all returned from their study-abroad destinations to become potent human resources, taking up posts as administrative bureaucrats (*jitsumu kanryō*) in legislation (*hōsei*). The wide-ranging cultivation of human resources in the early Meiji era had borne fruit. The knowledge and insights of these men found practical application as they designed the structures of a regime they wanted to rebuild.

Towards a cabinet system: The realization of responsible government

The Cabinet (*naikaku*) was the first administrative organ installed in the new constitutional government. The Cabinet of the Council of State (*dajōkan naikaku*), which had councillors serving under a minister of state, a minister of the right and a minister of the left, could not serve the purposes of a constitutional monarchy. It was a system mired in contradictions. The ministers, who acted as auxiliaries to the monarch, knew little about matters of governance. The councillors, those who actually took on the practical work of state administration, had no direct way of communicating with the monarch. No system of responsible governance could be borne by this configuration. As minster of the right, Iwakura Tomomi had striven for reform of the internal administration of the state. Once he died in 1884, the necessity of reform became ever starker.

On 22 December 1885, the regime abolished the Council of State system (*dajō kansei*) and inaugurated a cabinet system (*naikaku seido*) headed by a prime minister. The system marked the origin of a structure of responsible government (*sekinin seiji taisei*) wherein the ministers of the state (*kokumu daijin*), made up of the prime minister and the heads of each of the executive departments (*kakushō no chōkan*), ran all executive state affairs under the watch of the Emperor.[49]

To allow him the ability to coordinate the government as a whole, the system bestowed vast powers on the figure at its summit, the prime minister. As head of the Cabinet, the prime minister reported to the Emperor, determined the direction of the state and supervised the entirety of governmental administration. It was a system of 'grand-chancellorism' (*dai saishō shugi*). That government regulations for the Cabinet were called 'The *Powers* of the Cabinet' (*naikaku shokken*) illustrates the extent of the role of the prime minister.

The regulatory and supervisory powers of the prime minister were not limited by those that were officially articulated. Because all laws and ordinances (*hōrei*) required the countersignature of the prime minister, in practice no laws could be established without his approval. It was a stark departure from the Council of State system, wherein the minister of state and ministers of the right and left had virtually no effective powers of coordination and execution.

The post of minister of the state (*dajō daijin*) had been largely an honorary one throughout the Japanese past, and Sanjō Sanetomi, who rose to the post after the Restoration, did not deviate from this tradition. In this sense, 'to guide the direction of the state and to superintend the departments of executive government', as the powers and functions of the prime minister were described in 'Powers of the Cabinet', marked a departure from a long political tradition extending from ancient times, a departure fitting for the inauguration of a constitutional polity. And indeed it was none other than Itō Hirobumi, the man who had planned the entire system, who became the first prime minister in the structure he designed.

Few changes were made in other departments. Most heads of departments in the Council of State system held on to their posts as department ministers in the constitutional system. Replacements occurred only in the navy (*kaigun*), in agricultural and commercial affairs (*nōshōmu*), in education (*monbu*) and in communications (*ekitei*). Saigō Tsugumichi, who became the new appointee for the navy, was in fact transplanted from his previous post as head of agricultural and commercial affairs. It was, then, only to three departments that new appointments were made: Mori Arinori, to education; Tani Tatewaki, to agricultural and commercial affairs; and Enomoto Takeaki, to communications. Changes among the deputy ministers (*jikan*), equivalent to the senior aides (*daiyū*) before the reforms, were similarly few. Apart from Iwamura Michitoshi, a senior aide in the justice department (*shihō daiyū*) who was transferred to the post of head officer of the Hokkaidō prefectural government (*Hokkaidō chōchōkan*), the leading bureaucrat of every ministry stayed on to become its deputy.

The reasons for such continuity are clear. If it wanted to push ahead with institutional reform, and if it wanted to be ready to respond to the deliberations that would occur in the national Diet, the state needed to refrain from making reckless personnel transfers and instead carefully nurture state ministers and government officials with deep expertise in state affairs. Yamagata Aritomo, home minister for seven-and-a-half years; Matsukata, minister of the treasury for ten years and ten months, his term then extended to fifteen-and-a-half years; Ōyama, army minister for eleven years and three months, extended to fifteen years and four months; Saigō, navy minister for ten years and two months between his posts in the Home Ministry; Yamada, justice minister for seven-and-a-half years – from roughly the time when Itō returned from his constitutional exploration trip in 1883 to the end of the first Yamagata Aritomo cabinet in 1891, a range of government ministries were headed by a single man who served a lengthy term of service. By contrast, if we exclude ministers in military posts, from 1891 onward no pre-war minister held the same post in the same department for over five years. We can see that offering men extended terms of service was an exceptional measure by which the state prepared for the inauguration of a parliament.

With Yamagata, Matsukata, Ōyama, Saigō and Yamada at its centre, executive governance found stability, and reform moved ahead smoothly. With such long terms of service, it is little wonder that these men left profound, wide-ranging influence on their departments. Their terms marked the origins of bureaucratic cliques (*kanryōbatsu*), a phenomenon most strikingly represented by the notorious Yamagata faction.

Subjected to great change was the Imperial Court. Sanjō Sanetomi, who had long held the post of minister of the state, became an interior minister charged exclusively with handling affairs of the imperial court (*kyūchū jimu sennin no naidaijin*). Ahead of the inauguration of the cabinet system, Itō Hirobumi replaced Tokudaiji Sanetsune as head of the imperial ministry (*kunai kyō*). As a result of the visitations of the Emperor to the Cabinet (*tennō no naikaku shinrin*) and the separation of the imperial and the political arms of the state (*kyūchū, fuchū no betsu*), the influence of the imperial court on state politics was curtailed. These were changes aimed at laying the groundwork for a politics of responsibility.

The members of the Cabinet could not bring about a responsible government on their own. The Cabinet had to install auxiliary organs that would enable it to conduct research, to make proposals and to manage the state. The Council of State had a secretarial organ attached to it, but that organ was no more than an administrative body charged with handling documents, keeping records and managing the operation of the state assemblies.

It was for this reason that the regime installed a Cabinet Legislation Bureau (*hōseikyoku*) as it inaugurated the cabinet system. The new bureau amalgamated the Assembly of Counsellors (*sanji'in*), which had operated under the Council of State, with the Bureau for Investigation of State Systems (*seido torishirabe kyoku*), which operated under the Cabinet. This new organ was placed under the authority of the Cabinet. With a view to standardizing laws and ordinances across the government, it was tasked with investigating bills submitted by the ministries. For important policies that would be driven by the Cabinet, the Bureau itself conducted research and made proposals.

Particularly outstanding counsellors (*sanjikan*) who had taken part in planning institutions for the constitutional polity became responsible for the process of judicial review (*hōrei shinsa*). These counsellors included Hirata Tōsuke, Yamawaki Gen, Makino Nobuaki and Sone Arasuke, the last of whom had studied in France and later went on to be treasury minister and resident general (*tōtoku*) of Korea; the counsellors also included young up-and-coming bureaucrats with study-abroad experience. To the ministries, the judicial review these men conducted constituted a hurdle no less formidable than that of the parliament.

Hereafter, starting with the dual appointment of Shiba Junrokurō as a counsellor in 1889, a flurry of professors in the law faculty of the Imperial University, including Hozumi Yatsuka, Minobe Tatsukichi and Ikki Kitokurō, were granted dual posts as state counsellors. By supporting the practical dimensions of its work, these appointees contributed to raising the authority of the Cabinet Legislation Bureau. The bureau solidified its powers by continuing from here to draw out the very best talent from among the available bureaucrats for itself.

The head of the Cabinet Legislation Bureau wielded considerable powers to express his thoughts both within and beyond the Cabinet, and at times he even used legislative reform as a political weapon to make changes in the state system. With capabilities not only in research, investigation and drafting of proposals but also in judicial review, the new Cabinet was poised to function effectively as an arena for the general coordination of the entire government.

The birth of 'grand deputies'

Following the establishment of the cabinet system came the building of bureaucratic structures. At the same time that he inaugurated the Cabinet, Itō issued each of the departments a set of standards known as 'Five Points on the Discipline of State Officials' (*Kanki goshō*). The standards were meant to regulate the work of bureaucratic institutions. An ad hoc committee for the investigation of official institutions (*rinji kansei shinsa iinkai*) was set up in January 1886, and with Inoue Kowashi, Itō Hirobumi and Kaneko Kentarō at the centre of the committee, by that same summer it had succeeded in putting into place the framework for a modern Japanese bureaucracy. The five points Itō delineated were as follows: to keep clear the scope of bureaucratic work, a clause aimed at standardizing national administrative groups as well as staffing in the departments; to make prudent selections of personnel; to peel away red tape (*hanbun*); to cut down on wasteful spending; and to adhere fastidiously to official discipline. In February 1886, an official system was promulgated that fixed the fundamental structure of each executive department. A system of officers consisting of deputy ministers (*jikan*), bureau heads (*kyokuchō*), division heads (*kachō*), counselors (*sanjikan*), and secretaries (*shokikan*) was installed, a system that persists to the present day. The basic bureaucratic structure of the state ministries, too, was determined; each ministry was to be composed of the ministerial secretariat (*daijin kanbō*), the general affairs bureau (*sōmukyoku*) and other individual bureaux.[50]

Deputy ministers came to play particularly important roles. The departmental system devolved two separate functions on the deputies as part of a design to use them to connect the Cabinet and the individual ministries. The first role called for them to serve as representatives of the cabinet minister in their given ministry. All tasks within the scope of the work of a cabinet minister, with the exception of actual attendance at cabinet meetings and the promulgation of ministry ordinances, could be delegated to a deputy minister. It was especially significant that deputies could even sign official documents in place of their seniors. Both in name and in practice, the minister and his deputy came to be seen as a single unit in the scope of their powers and responsibilities.

The second role enjoined on deputies was to act as coordinators of administrative affairs. They were, without exception, appointed dually as head of the general affairs bureau (*sōmukyoku*) in their ministry. The general affairs bureau was composed of a documents division (*monjoka*), a travel division (*ōfukuka*), a records division (*kirokuka*) and a reporting division (*hōkokuka*). Tasked with 'unifying all departmental administrative affairs', the bureau functioned at the heart of the system of state ministries, and its head served 'to coordinate all departmental administrative affairs' under the helm of the ministers.

That deputies came to play these two disparate roles at the same time meant that they had powers to coordinate administrative tasks (*jimu*) even as they functioned as representatives of political affairs (*seimu*). The state thus turned away from Ōkuma's proposed separation of political and administrative tasks. With 'grand deputies' serving as heads of the general affairs bureaux, the relationship between deputy ministers and ministers served as a powerful bond linking the Cabinet to individual departments. As a result of this configuration, the Assembly of Deputies (*jikan kaigi*) came to play a critical role in laying the groundwork for deliberations in the Cabinet.

The Public Documents System: The establishment of systematized laws and ordinances

Unifying the various executive organs of the state was only half the task of preparing structures of rule for a constitutional polity. In the years after the Restoration, the Meiji regime had issued a range of laws, ordinances and official notices in response to the exigencies of rule. As over twenty years of paperwork accumulated, and as laws became entangled with one another, the situation became so complicated that not even professional bureaucrats could gain a handle on it. To add to the muddle, the provinces too had their own customs and practices suited to their own contingencies. Every time a law or ordinance went forth from the central regime, hundreds of questions and rejoinders came in from the provinces. From the provinces to the ministries, from the ministries to the Council of State – as questions and comments shuttled across levels of government, it generally took an entire year for the interpretation and application of a given law to gain traction. Reform could not proceed under these circumstances.

According to the *Index of Japanese Laws and Ordinances: Early Meiji Edition* (*Nihon hōrei sakuin [Meiji zenki hen]*) compiled by the National Diet Library, the Council of State was issuing some two thousand laws and ordinances every year during the latter half of its rule. The deluge of responses to these ordinances that swept over the ministries defies imagination. The workload that fell on the ministries was formidable.

They tried to compensate for the inadequacies of their structure by throwing manpower at the problem. But it was an acutely inefficient system. The need for fundamental, thoroughgoing reform was dire.

In February 1886, the state promulgated as its first imperial edict (*chokurei dai'ichigō*) the Public Documents System (*Kōbunshiki*), which standardized the form of all government documents. A clear system of laws and ordinances was established wherein senior councillors (*Genrōin*), later members of the Imperial Diet, issued laws (*hōritsu*) after engaging in debate; the government determined edicts (*chokurei*); the prime minister issued cabinet ordinances (*kakurei*); and ministers of the individual departments issued ministerial edicts and regulations (*shōrei, kisoku*). The system also helped to standardize the means of communicating official proclamations by calling for their inclusion in an official state publication (*kanpō*), and it served to rein in the profusion of questions from the provinces by attaching supplementary explanations to a given law or ordinance. It was a scheme to stabilize and rationalize rule by law.

--

Having weathered two political upheavals, one in 1873, the next in 1881, the Meiji regime set about building a constitutional polity established firmly on consolidated executive organs and a carefully incubated Diet. The structures of a new form of government were thus put into place.

Now the state had to think about how to raise up, employ and set to work those human resources who would fill and support the structures it had erected. The new challenge it faced was how, amid the surging Popular Rights Movement, it could develop the field of *Staatslehre* and assemble the best talent from across the country. The goal of a national constitution and an imperial Diet was firmly within sight. Now the state needed to develop a strategy to cultivate the men who would take charge of those new institutions.

Higher Education and the Constitutional Era

The birth of scholar-bureaucrats

The spirit of clause nineteen

Within just over two decades of its birth, the Meiji regime had inaugurated a national cabinet, developed a standardized system for all public documents (*kōbunshiki*) and installed structures of bureaucracy in each of its government ministries. Institutions of executive government firmly in place, it turned in July 1890 to holding the first ever general elections for the House of Representatives (*Shūgiin*), and with the Meiji Constitution taking effect in November, it opened the Imperial Diet opened that month. A new chapter in the history of modern Japan began. The era of the constitutional state had arrived.

Itō Hirobumi and Lorenz von Stein had envisioned a government that would first develop its executive branch and then build structures for legislation on that basis. To realize this vision, it was necessary to nurture professional bureaucrats who would take charge of the executive state. That task implied not only gathering human resources with deep specialization and broad-ranging knowledge but also, from a broader perspective, opening up the bureaucracy and allowing political participation through the executive state. Towards this end, the Meiji Constitution decreed in its nineteenth clause, 'Japanese subjects may, according to qualifications determined in laws or ordinances, be appointed to civil or military offices equally, and may fill any other public offices.'[1]

The clause may seem rather strange to us today, but it carried profound significance for people in an era constrained by lineage and social status. Itō Hirobumi, who led the drafting of the constitution, hailed it as 'the choice fruit of the reforms of the Restoration' (*Ishin kaikaku no bika*) because it allowed men to become military and bureaucratic officials irrespective of their geographic or familial origins.[2] Itō Miyoji, too, extolled the clause as a means of expunging the pernicious effects of bureaucratic lineages on executive government and on the cultivation of human talent. He wrote that the regime 'had opened the doors to the employment of human resources, and it was here [in this clause] in particular that the constitution guaranteed these open doors'.[3]

With barriers to entry into the world of officialdom lowered, men could become bureaucrats or military officials regardless of their origins or social status, if only they gained knowledge and expertise. This open door was the hallmark of the spirit of the

Meiji Restoration, the manifestation of Fukuzawa Yukichi's vision of autonomous will (*risshi*) and of a new nation based on learning and knowledge, the fruit of the proclamation of the Five-Point Charter Oath that 'all shall be allowed to pursue their own calling so that there may be no discontent'.

Skirting the road to officialdom

We can identify the starting-point of reforms towards a more open bureaucracy in the second clause of the 'Five Points for the Discipline of State Officials' (*Kanki goshō*), which we encountered in Chapter 3. That clause called for the state 'to make prudent selections of personnel', or, in other words, to be cautious in whom it appointed to the bureaucracy. Earlier in the Meiji era, the practice of appointing personnel based on private interests had flooded the regime with human resources it did not need, leading to dire inefficiencies. There was widespread concern that, with the government clogged, 'scholarly masters' (*seigaku no shi*) across the nation would find nowhere to apply their experiences. Their talents would go unexploited. The regime needed to find a way to shore up a system for employing human talent, to jettison unnecessary resources and to gather together personnel who would benefit the government.

Employing human talent gained another valence of significance once the inauguration of the Imperial Diet came within purview. In its stand-off against popular political parties (*mintō*), the government wanted to win human resources over to its side and steal them away from its opposition. Talented youth had begun marching into the opposition parties after the defection of Ōkuma Shigenobu in 1881. The first renegades acted as catalysts, allowing the parties to absorb ever greater numbers into their ranks.

Politicians in the government began to panic when university students, who were supposed to have been under their control, started slipping away and entering the popular political parties. Collegians had shown a predilection for debate and argument even from the days of the tributary students (*kōshinsei*). But under the influence of the Movement for Freedom and Popular Rights, their knack for debate erupted into a fever for politics and oratory. Their political speeches began expanding in scope and gaining in intensity. Then came the political upheaval of 1881, in which Ōkuma, ever popular among students, was ejected from the Meiji government. The political utterance of students turned to philippic.

Ōkuma and his anti-regime associates were hardly heedless of these developments. With Ono Azusa as their window, they seized opportunity and extended their arms into the national university. Of eleven students studying law and politics in 1882, or Meiji 15, six played a direct role in the founding of Ōkuma's Constitution and Reform Party (*Rikken Kaishintō*) and the Tokyo Professional Academy (*Tōkyō senmon gakkō*).[4] The six were joined by another of their comrades who had dropped out of studying literature.[5] It is said that Ernest Fenollosa, who was in charge of political science at the University of Tokyo at the time, berated these men in his speech at the university graduation ceremony, depicting their actions as treachery.

That so many men forsook the path to officialdom, gave up on its reliable promise to a stable future and dived headlong into the uncertain future of oppositional political parties demonstrated the allure of the movement Ōkuma had launched. But it also revealed something about the regime itself. Young men deeply mistrusted the Meiji government. Witnessing how youths steered clear of it, the regime recognized that it had to provide young men with benefits and occupations commensurate with the specialized professional education they had received.

As the life courses of the tributary students demonstrated, university in the early Meiji era functioned as a learning ground where men acquired new knowledge and applied it to a wide range of fields. Students pursued their intellectual passions wherever they led. Some became scholars who dedicated their lives to learning and academics; others applied their knowledge of the law and became lawyers, or *daigennin*; still others gained expertise in sericulture and made new lives for themselves in the flourishing world of enterprise. Even specialists in law and politics saw the bureaucracy as no more than one among a number of possible career paths. Katō Kōmei, for instance, an Aichi man born in 1860 who went on to become prime minister in the twentieth century, graduated top of his class in law in 1881 but did not enter the bureaucracy, choosing instead to work for Mitsubishi. He only flipped to the Foreign Ministry six years later, after an encounter with Mutsu Munemitsu.

It was entirely reasonable for students who spent their formative years in a liberal atmosphere of learning to opt not to enter into a regime dominated by oligarchic domainal factionalism. Indeed, whereas students originating from such oligarchic strongholds as Satsuma and Chōshū invariably became state bureaucrats, those from other origins rarely followed such a course. Even those who did choose the road to the bureaucracy mostly entered the Ministry of Justice, where oligarchic influence was thin. What reason did students have to surrender the freedoms they had painstakingly won at school simply to enter a hotbed of oligarchism?

In a regime dominated by oligarchs, those hailing from regions other than the oligarchic strongholds found themselves without reputation, clout or freedom. To expunge the sense of disadvantage common among such men, it was necessary not simply to open the doors of the state more widely but to search for ways to make the route to the bureaucracy seem more attractive, to make it appear as an enviable path that only a talented few could travel.

The establishment of the Imperial University: An institution for rearing bureaucrats

To summon people to the road to bureaucracy, the regime needed to develop national institutions of higher education and construct a system wherein only those who had honed professional skills could attain official posts and thereby gain exceptional benefits. The 'Five Points for the Discipline of State Officers' called for an exam system to employ men with a professional education. It ordained that the exams should take the age of the applicant, his character and conduct, his physical health and his talents and abilities as standards for selection.

At this stage, each government ministry had its own official academy to educate bureaucrats professionally. Members of the army were trained at the military academy (*shikan gakkō*); those of the navy, at the academy for soldiers (*heigakkō*); those of the Ministry of Justice at law schools; and technical bureaucrats (*gikan*) at the School of Engineering (*kōbu daigakkō*). This system allowed men to attain high degrees of specialization, but it made it difficult to train generalists with knowledge that could encompass the whole nation. Itō and others who had trumpeted the need for *Staatslehre*, or 'state studies' (*kokka gaku*), acutely felt the need for reform.[6]

The Itō band decided to inaugurate a new general university aimed principally at cultivating bureaucrats. From the very day after the promulgation of the Five Points for the Discipline of State Officials, members of the regime led by Inoue Kowashi began standardizing and unifying the university system. In March 1886, they promulgated as the third Imperial Edict a decree on the Imperial University; the first two edicts proclaimed the Official Documents System and the inauguration of the bureaucratic system of the ministries. The erstwhile University of Tokyo was merged with the Ministry of Justice School of Law (*shihōshō hōgakkō*) and the School of Engineering (*kōbu daigakkō*) to inaugurate the Imperial University (*Teikoku daigaku*). The Tokyo School of Agriculture and Forestry (*Tōkyō nōrin gakkō*) was added to it in 1890 to form a sweeping generalist university with six divisions of undergraduate or graduate education: law, medicine, engineering, humanities, science and agriculture.

The new Imperial University became an arena for hammering out and disseminating the 'state studies' envisioned by Itō and Von Stein. To advance his vision, Itō seized the opportunity afforded by the formation of a new cabinet to appoint Mori Arinori as minister of education. Itō was sojourning in London to conclude his constitutional investigation in Europe when he met Mori, then the Japanese ambassador to Britain. Backed up by his own personal experiences as a foreign emissary, Mori propounded a theory of national education that Itō found agreeable.[7] Conservative elements attacked Mori, denouncing his theories as excessively gung-ho about Westernization, but Itō summoned Mori into the education ministry as a commissioner (*goyō gakari*). Mori began laying the groundwork for educational reform.

The Imperial University was swept under the jurisdiction of the education ministry, now with Mori at its helm. To the chancellorship of the university (*sōchō*) the ministry appointed Watanabe Hiromoto, who transferred from his post as governor of Tokyo (*Tōkyō fuchiji*).[8] He had no prior experience in education administration. His appointment stunned the general public. By appointing the university chancellor simultaneously as head of the subsidiary College of Law (*hōka daigaku*), authorities signalled that the Imperial University, and especially its College of Law, which was composed of the faculties of law and politics, was to serve as an institution for training executive officials through 'state studies'.[9]

It is significant that the Imperial University Edict proclaimed not only scholarship, research and instruction but also actual practice as the missions of the university. The university implemented a tiered curriculum that advanced in stages and allowed prospective officials to gain systematic mastery of the social sciences, especially law, politics and economics. The curriculum in the law faculty began with constitutional law and advanced to legal theory. That in the Faculty of Politics moved from national law (*kokuhōgaku*) to national finance (*zaiseigaku*).

Japanese men who had experience studying abroad began to fill the ranks of university professors. The talented men who had gathered as young tributary students in the University-South College now stood at the forefront of scholarship and education. They led the design and implementation of new structures of the university and set about nurturing a new generation. In the College of Law, Hozumi Shigenobu became the first ever head of professors (*kyōtō*), later ascending to head of the college (*gakuchō*); Hatoyama Kazuo ascended to a professorship before becoming head of professors; and Furuichi Kōi became the first head of the School of Engineering (*kōka daigaku*). Within fifteen years, an ambitious plan to send Japanese students abroad and bring them back to replace foreign professors was bearing fruit.

Opening the doors of the university: A rapid increase in school capacity

The most dramatic change in university education was the sudden expansion of the doors of higher education to the outside world. Up to this point, the University of Tokyo had graduated only a measly number of students per year: some ten or so from the schools of humanities and of law and about fifty altogether across all divisions of the university. The Imperial University rapidly expanded the number of students per graduating class to some four hundred men, an eight-fold increase. The Faculty of Law swung its doors open particularly wide, taking in 150 men a year.[10] Higher education in Japan changed suddenly and decisively.

The overhaul of tertiary education relied on the assumption that there would be secondary schools (*kōtō chū gakkō*), later known simply as high schools (*kōtō gakkō*), that would supply men ready for university. High schools themselves needed reform. Financing the surging number of students became an added problem. Up to this point, boys who had made it to university had relied on the national state or on their home prefectures to provide for their expenses, or they had used stipends that samurai received from their erstwhile domainal lords to finance themselves. But those funds ran dry. Financial support narrowed as economic distress beset the nation and as the state dissolved feudal domains and set up prefectures, curtailing samurai stipends. By 1885, only some 10 per cent of the total university student body was receiving financial aid from customary sources. The finances of the university itself fell into dire straits.

Watanabe, chancellor of the Imperial University, grasped the situation and took action to resolve it. He went after private enterprises and official state institutions, places where university students were likely to apply their talents after graduation.[11] He solicited donations and scholarships: if companies wanted to recruit talented men, they had to make investments in those men early on. Scholarships thus became available both because of the ambitions of state agencies and private business and because of the passionate will of Watanabe. Many of those scholarships survive to this day. Watanabe himself had once been a young man from Fukui who journeyed to Edo to pursue Western studies. He carried a belief greater than that of most in the power of learning to nurture men of talent.

To youths in the provinces, university became a life goal. Village leaders began improving their schools, establishing scholarship associations (*ikueikai*) on the basis of existing structures and granting funds to talented boys so that they could proceed to higher levels of education.[12] These wealthy village leaders extended their funds not only to samurai but also to commoners. Sometimes, it was individuals who came to the financial aid of talented students, and occasionally, some even sought to marry talented young men into their families to preserve their lineages. Meritocracy began to pervade the furthest reaches of the realm.

Why were rural leaders so eager to send their young men to university? Talented youths who left their hometowns and found new places to apply their talents became sources of pride for those at home. The newly opened doors to university and the newly paved path to bureaucracy meant that even men from the provinces now had the chance to receive higher education and to participate in state affairs as bureaucrats. These were opportunities once reserved for a select few. Just as the Movement for Freedom and Popular Rights provided new paths to political participation through the legislative arm of the state, so did the opening up of the bureaucracy expand opportunities through the executive arm. It was with their eyes on the state that rural leaders, who themselves had deep connections with provincial politics, readily shipped their young men off to university, often without regard for the reality that a reservoir of young talent was draining away from the peripheries.

The introduction of the Probationary Employment System (*shiho seido*)

Just as change overcame the supply of state officials, so too did systems to take in these men require adjustment. Employment of state bureaucrats was systematized and standardized for the first time in July 1887, when the Regulations on the Examination, Probationary Employment and Apprenticeship of State Officials (*bunkan shiken shiho oyobi minarai kisoku*, hereafter Regulations on Probationary Employment) was promulgated.[13]

Following the Itō-Von Stein model, the regulations decreed that prospective bureaucrats must first complete specialized education at university, succeed in government-mandated examinations and pass through a probationary period of employment before being formally hired by the state. Higher-level applicants, or 'career hires', had to sit exams commensurate with their higher levels of education before being tentatively hired; regular applicants, or 'non-career hires', were selected to apprenticeships after sitting lower-level regular exams. In either case, applicants had to pass through a three-year probationary period before being selected as *sōninkan*, officials appointed by recommendation to the Emperor, or *hanninkan*, those appointed by the executive departments. There were exceptions. Graduates from the law or humanities faculties of the Imperial University were exempt from taking all examinations, and graduates from private law schools, too, had the regular exams waived. The very fact that they had received a professional education was deemed sufficient evidence of their talents.

An intricate system for cultivating and employing men through professional education, examinations and probationary training became firmly established. Even public newspapers, which bore the deep imprint of anti-state popular-rights activism, extolled the system for its thoroughgoing meritocracy.

The Probationary Employment System did not merely regulate entry through the doors of the bureaucracy. It had two important effects on the functioning of a new bureaucracy in a constitutional state.

The first effect lay in facilitating the rise of a new generation in the bureaucracy. The ballooning administrative demands of the early Meiji period had led to desperate, reckless employment of state bureaucrats, many of whom were ineffective in the increasingly complex executive arm of the modern nation-state. The 'rationalization of state executive administration' heralded with the introduction of the Cabinet aimed to purge the regime of decaying, useless state officials.[14] By laying out clear standards for the abilities required of state officials, the regime managed to throw off dead weight and replace old officials with young bureaucrats bearing new knowledge and skills. By the first decade of the twentieth century, close to all senior bureaucratic positions were filled with university graduates.

The second benefit of the Probationary Employment System was that it guaranteed a degree of continuity in the executive state. Formulating a structure wherein all entrants into state administration had either to hold a university degree or to pass state examinations limited prospective bureaucrats to a narrow band of people with a professional education. This barrier to entry prevented large-scale changes in the bureaucracy from accompanying every change in cabinet power.

This system, like so many others, was the brainchild of Itō Hirobumi, who had seen how a spoils system plagued governance in the United States. He feared that the regular changes of administrative power in a parliamentary system might lead to a similar spoils system in Japan. And if, as a result, men with no prior executive experience were to begin trying to snatch up bureaucratic posts, the very model conceived by Itō and Von Stein of the supremacy of the executive arm would collapse. Itō and his fellow statesmen had themselves endured such a situation in the pre-1881 Meiji regime.

Examinations in the Probationary Employment System

How, then, were the examinations in the Probationary Employment System actually conducted? Let us take up the first ever round of higher-level examinations (*dai'ikkai kōtō shiken*), which were conducted in 1888, as an example.

The newly founded Civil Officer Examination Bureau (*bunkan shiken kyoku*) took charge of setting up the examinations.[15,16] Watanabe, chancellor of the Imperial University, held a simultaneous post as head of the bureau. After working with the Cabinet in May to confirm the number of employees each ministry anticipated hiring, the bureau announced its examination prospectus on 1 July. Exams would be held from 1 October. Ninety-three men would be hired as probationary officers in the judiciary (*shihōkan*) and twenty-six as executive officers (*gyōseikan*), of whom five would be affiliated with the Cabinet, three with the Foreign Ministry, eight with the Home Ministry, three with the treasury, five with the Justice Ministry and two with agricultural and commercial affairs. The prospectus was released in the official state publication, and it was communicated to high schools identified as possible suppliers of personnel for the regular exams as well as to private law schools targeted for recruitment to higher-level exams. Among those private law schools were Meiji Law School (*Meiji hōritsu gakkō*), which became today's Meiji University; the English Law School (*Igirisu hōritsu gakkō*), which changed its name to the Tokyo Institute of

Law (*Tōkyō hōgakuin*) the following year and evolved into today's Chūō University; and Senshū Academy (*Senshū gakkō*), today's Senshū University.

Once they received the official exam prospectus, would-be test-takers began collecting curricula vitae, proofs of graduation and other necessary documents and started sending in their official applications. Forty-one men applied in the first year of exams, with nineteen in the executive officer pool and twenty-two in the judicial. Of those men, one came from the nobility, twenty-five from samurai backgrounds and fifteen from commoner backgrounds. Although most applicants were of samurai descent, it was significant that commoners, too, applied.

The first hurdle applicants had to overcome was the written exam, which lasted seven days from Monday, 1 October, to Monday, 8 October. Sunday was a day off. Exams were prepared on ten different topics: civil law (*minpō*), procedural law (*soshōhō*), criminal law (*keihō*), criminal procedures (*chizaihō*), commercial law (*shōhō*), constitutional law (*kenpō*), public administration (*gyōseigaku*), finance (*zaiseigaku*), economics (*rizaigaku*) and international law (*kokusaihō*). Applicants took only those exams that their desired employee required of them.

The morning of the first test day, applicants assembled at 8.30 am at the higher-level exam site set up at Akasaka Aoi-chō. The exam lasted for three hours, from 9.00 am to 12.00 pm. Test-takers could not carry anything into the exam site, but they were permitted to use the full published text of all state laws and ordinances as well as the official state newspaper, which were made available in the test room.

Test questions were in Japanese. Examinees were assessed on their mastery of theory, their understanding of existing laws, their ability to take on practical work and the speed and accuracy of their responses. 'Provide an outline of the organization of the British cabinet and ministries'; 'Provide an outline of local governance in Britain'; 'In Britain, which kinds of appointed officials can become members of parliament, and which kinds cannot?' – questions covered the formation of cabinets, provincial governance systems, parliamentary issues and problems facing the state at the time.

Every subject was graded out of 100 points, and members of the exam committee themselves did the grading. If a student scored over an average of 60 points across all his subjects, he passed; if he scored below 50 on any single test, he failed the entire exam. The highest score in the first ever round of exams, 75.1 points, went to Ōuchi Ushinosuke, a samurai from Fukushima who went on to became a magistrate (*hanji*), a counsellor (*sanji*) in the Legislation Bureau (*hōseikyoku*), and head of external affairs for the governorship of Tokyo prefecture (*Kantō-to tokufu gaiji sōchō*). Ōuchi also went on to study in Germany and to become highly valued by Gotō Shinpei in Taiwan, where he conducted research on indigenous customs and practices, and in Manchuria, where he was a researcher (*chōsa jigyō*) for the South Manchuria Railway Company.

Of the thirty-six men who took the first written exams, nineteen were applicants for judicial officer positions and seventeen for executive positions. Five from the original applicant pool dropped out. Fifteen from the judicial pool passed, but everyone in the executive pool failed. None of those who failed was able to move on to the oral exam round. The door to the executive bureaucracy was surprisingly narrow.

Oral exams occurred between Monday, 22 October, and Friday, 26 October, split up over a five-day period. As in the written exams, examinees in the oral round gathered on the test day in a waiting room before being transferred, in order, to their interview room. Once he entered, an examinee found the members of the exam committee lined up before him, headed by the committee chair. The examinee took a seat in front of the examiners and fielded a barrage of questions. The interview lasted between thirty minutes and an hour. Marks from each of the exam committee members were averaged, and a decision would thus be made about whether the applicant should pass.

On 20 November, about a month after the entire process concluded, the names of all those who passed were announced in the official state newspaper. Nine men had succeeded: six samurai and three commoners. All were in the judicial pool. They did not necessarily stay permanently in their initial posts, as transfers among ministries occurred frequently. Kanokogi Kogorō, for instance, was hired as a judicial officer but entered the Ministry of Agricultural and Commercial Affairs and then moved to the governorship of Gifu prefecture; Arimatsu Hideyoshi, also a judicial officer, transferred from head of the public safety bureau (*keihokyoku*) to head officer in the legislation bureau. Such men started out their careers in the judicial offices before entering the executive arm. The regular civil-officer exams (*futsū bunkan shiken*), which led to employment as an apprentice, had more test takers: 358 examinees, of whom 150 were samurai and 208 were commoners. Thirty-five men passed the exams: thirteen samurai and twenty-two commoners.

It had been projected that ninety-three men would be hired as judicial officers and twenty-six as executives, but only nine men actually passed the judicial exams. The number was far too low. Yet the rate of exam success was not particularly low compared to rates in other countries at the time. The concern, it seems, was less about securing an adequate quantity of regular employees than with ensuring their quality.

What enabled this emphasis on quality over quantity was an alternative path in the system. Applicants to the Probationary Employment System who had graduated from the law or humanities faculties of the Imperial University, and those to the regular officer system who had graduated from approved private academies and high schools, had the exam stage waived. These applicants could enter state ministries with just an interview.

The state filled its quotas by taking men through this route. Of the fifty-eight men who applied to the Probationary Employment System by this means, of whom twenty were to the executive arm and thirty-eight to the judicial arm, all were employed by the state. Of the eighty-four applying for lower-level apprenticeships, twenty-nine were hired. Perhaps it was because they were the very first applicants, many of these exam-waiver scholars became mainstays in the world of bureaucracy: Hayashida Kametarō, in the Cabinet; Ikki Kitokurō, in the home ministry; and Hiranuma Kiichirō, Komatsu Kenjirō and Yokota Hideo, all in the justice ministry.

Voices of the test-takers

The regime thus carved out a path for men of talent to enter its fold. Why did the youth themselves choose to enter it? And how did they proceed down the path prepared for them?

Let us first consider candidates such as graduates from private law academies who sat the written exams. Around the time of the first exams, the number of total annual graduates from private law academies was surpassing some 1,500. Most graduates went on to become judges or lawyers. But once the regulations for the probationary exam system were put in place, some students began aspiring to become judicial or executive officials.

In 1887, Shioiri Tasuke, a graduate of Meiji Law School and later a probationary hire as a magistrate (*hanji*), wrote an exam guidebook titled *Secrets of the Exams for Higher-Level and Regular Civil Officers and Lawyers*.[17] Such books began proliferating in the first decade of the twentieth century, and Shioiri led the pack with his manual. From his stories of his experiences in the exam system, we gain a snapshot of the lives of young men stepping up for the probationary-system exams.

Succeeding on the tests, Shioiri claimed, involved 60 per cent academic expertise, 20 per cent good writing and 20 per cent sheer luck. He provided troves of practical advice to his readers. He emphasized that there were no cut-and-dry correct answers to exam questions. He exhorted applicants to follow the sequence of questions strictly, to strive for simplicity and clarity, to refrain from quibbling with the question asked and to do their utmost to avoid merely listing off examples and instead to provide lucid theory in their answers. Shirori published his book just a year after the Public Documents Edict standardizing state laws and ordinances was promulgated. It was a moment at which examinees were tormented by anxiety over how they would be graded on questions about law, politics and economics, when interpretations and understandings of those fields remained in flux.

No formal textbooks existed to help examinees. Shioiri dumped a long list of required reading on would-be test-takers. For constitutional law, he recommended Itō Hirobumi's *Commentaries on Constitutions* (*Kenpō gikai*) as well as Walter Bagehot's *The English Constitution*, translated by Okamoto Eitarō as *Eikoku kenpō no shinshō*; Johann Kaspar Bluntschli's *Lehre vom modernen Stat*, or *Theory of the State*, translated by Hirata Tōsuke as *Kokkaron*; and John Stuart Mill's *Considerations on Representative Government*, translated as *Daigi seitai ron*. For administrative law, he suggested Rudolf von Gneist's work on British constitutionalism translated by Egi Makoto as *Eikoku gyōseihō kōgi*; and Von Stein's *Gyōseigaku*, published by the Genrōin. But these were hardly texts that men of the day could read and understand on their own. Private law academies began offering a series of courses by professors from the Imperial University and by bureaucrats themselves, reflecting the demands of students for information on how to succeed on the new exam system.

On oral exams, Shioiri wrote that examiners sought to judge not only the ability of applicants to apply their knowledge to practical situations but also their personal qualities and their aptitude for work as higher-level state officials. He recommended that examinees approach the interview with courage and audacity, to pay respect to the examination committee and to answer questions with clarity.

Applicants were faced not only with test questions having no clear answers but also with vexing ambiguity about the number of seats open to them and about the extent of their competition. The state exams were shrouded in mystique. 'As the road to certification by the state becomes wider, so too does it become more difficult to navigate' – records of lament survive to this day.[18] Still, regardless of the difficulties along the way, probationary employment represented an enticing opening for the slightly liberated dreams of young men who, if they lacked connections to the oligarchy, would otherwise never have been able to enter officialdom. Shioiri encouraged prospective test-takers with hortatory promises, telling them that even if they were poor college students today, if only they gained knowledge and learning, then they too could become state bureaucrats. These were words that came from the heart of a man who himself had his dreams come true.

Even graduates of private law academies could be employed as regular bureaucrats, though not higher-level bureaucrats, with only an interview. But many chose not to settle for this easier path. To young men who had worked so hard to persuade their families of the legitimacy of their dreams, who had borrowed prodigious sums to fund their studies, who only then had finally made it to the capital – to such men, going home without having succeeded on the probationary employment exams, the tests at the very pinnacle of the system, was simply not an option.

Many graduates of private law academies sought to secure their futures by applying simultaneously for multiple exams: the Probationary Employment exams, the exams to become judges or prosecutors (*hankenji*) and the exams to become lawyers (*daigennin*). Which of those panned out was a secondary concern. All test-takers had to do was to pass, to win a place in Tokyo for their talents and to find success. That was their supreme ambition.

Rocks on the road, and a new path to the bureaucracy

Students at the Imperial University hailed the Regulations on Probationary Employment and the road to bureaucracy that it opened up. The new state of affairs benefited those studying politics even more than it benefited those studying law. Law students had long enjoyed prospects as lawyers, judges or holders of other legal professions, but students of politics had never had a predetermined path after their studies were complete. For students of politics who had kept their heads in their books and flowed along the path of higher education, it had been profoundly disorienting suddenly to find freedom in their life courses.

The year before the inauguration of the Regulations on Probationary Employment, Kanai Noboru, an assistant (*joshu*) of Karl Rathgen, an instructor in administrative law (*gyōseihō*), composed 'The Future Direction of Students of Politics' (*Seiji gakusei shōrai no hōkō ika*), a document in which he put forth impressions from his interactions with his students.[19] He painted a bleak picture of young students of politics with a narrow window into the world of scholarship and without connections to the world of bureaucracy. The students anguished as they contemplated their paths forward.

Students had flocked en masse into the popular political parties amid the effervescence of the Popular Rights Movement not only because of their political passions but also because they had few other places to go. Waiving exams for students who had graduated from university and laying out a carpet to the bureaucracy served as an effective strategy to bring equilibrium to the supply of young men anxious about the future and the demand of a regime desperate to recruit human resources.

The regime began extending its reach into the Imperial University to pull students into the administration. It dispatched Kaneko Kentarō, a drafter of the constitution serving as a ministerial secretary (*hishokan*), for the task. He spent three years from 1887 teaching Japanese administrative law (*gyōseihō*).

Kaneko's classes were fresh, unusual. Unlike academic professors, who steeped their courses in theory, Kaneko based his classes firmly in practical topics such as the scope of authority of central and local governments and the rights and responsibilities of executive officials. He himself gloated that his classes gave students 'enough to understand the general affairs and actual conditions of our national administration'.[20] Such a novel course sparked the interest of students. Almost all students in political science began to aim for posts in the executive bureaucracy. Kaneko's tenure was so successful that applicants began exceeding the number of available positions.

Salaries and benefits in the government improved, too. Up to this point, because university graduates had been employed as *hanninkan*, their salaries never rose above about 20 yen per month. But once they began entering the regime through the probationary employment system, they were treated as *sōninkan*. Their starting salaries roughly doubled to some 450 to 600 yen per year. In an era in which entry-level employees at large banks were making some 35 yen per month, theirs was extraordinary remuneration. Increasing numbers of students began to choose the path to bureaucracy as the regime cultivated their interest in state administration and threw money at them. And thus was born the scholar-bureaucrat (*gakushi kanryō*), steeped in professional education.

The road to professional bureaucracy: Beyond oligarchic control

Hiring: Instructors and professors

Let us now consider students who actually became bureaucrats after passing through the probationary employment system. All of those who graduated from the Imperial University College of Law in 1888 proceeded on to the road to officialdom. The class included such distinguished men as Uchida Kōsai, Hayashi Gonsuke and Hayashida Kametarō.[21] But even among these heavyweights, Ikki Kitokurō stood out. Ikki, from Shizuoka, entered the Home Ministry, became its deputy minister and then proceeded to become minister of education, home minister and a Privy Council member.

Ikki was born in Keiō 3 (= 1867), in Kakegawa. He studied at the Kihoku Academy (*Kihoku gakusha*), which was run by his father, Okada Ryōichirō. Okada Ryōhei, the minister of education, was his older brother. Ikki left Shizuoka and headed to Tokyo, where he graduated from a preparatory school for the Imperial University (*daigaku yobimon*) and enrolled in the humanities division of the university. After the Edict on Universities was promulgated, he re-enrolled in the law school.

At the Imperial University College of Law, Ikki attended the lectures of Kaneko Kentarō.[22] Enamoured by the worldview Kaneko espoused and the practical academics he advocated, Ikki took up the advice Kaneko offered him and applied to the Home Ministry. Kaneko introduced Ikki to Suematsu Kenchō, head of the of Prefectural

Governance Bureau (*kenchikyoku chō*) and son-in-law of Itō Hirobumi. Ikki visited Suematsu, who asked him, it is said, about strategies for financing the establishment of more secondary schools. A proposal was floating in the government for building more secondary schools, a step seen as necessary towards increasing the number of students proceeding to university. But funds were tight. What should the state do? It was an exam question – but posed in real life. Ikki proposed that local governments themselves should finance the construction of their schools, an answer that coincidentally accorded with what the government itself was planning. He was hired.

Ikki suggested rather self-deprecatingly in his memoirs that his hiring was part of a general desire to promote the brand-new probationary employment system. But he had graduated top of his class from the Imperial University, and he was afforded exceptional treatment commensurate with his exceptional standing as he was welcomed into the Home Ministry. His upward climb thereafter demonstrated that the ministry had not erred in its initial judgment. Ikki went on to hold a dual post as a professor at the Imperial University along with his role in the government, just after Kaneko did. He served as a bridge between the university and the government.

Another heavyweight of Japanese politics who entered the bureaucracy through the probationary employment exam system was Wakatsuki Reijirō. From Shimane and born in 1866, Wakatsuki was an 1892 graduate in French law who ascended to the post of prime minister. He wanted to be hired into the Ministry of Agricultural and Commercial Affairs, which had a reputation for employing personnel proactively and then advancing them through the ranks more quickly than other ministries.[23] But Wakatsuki was too late. By the time he began applying, Kaneko, then the minister of agriculture and commerce, had already made internal negotiations with the Imperial University and decided on his new hires. Wakatsuki's dreams were destroyed. He was then rebuffed by the Home Ministry and the Ministry of Communications until at last, through the good services of an older alumnus, he scraped into the Ministry of the Treasury. From there, Wakatsuki rose through the ranks to deputy and then head of the ministry before arriving at the post of prime minister. Few could have predicted his meteoric rise.

A particularly unusual case was that of Mizuno Rentarō, an Akita man born in 1868, an 1892 graduate in English law and similarly a probationary employment hire. From his days as a student, Mizuno had demonstrated exceptional talent, graduating at the top of his class. With a recommendation from Professor Hozumi Shigenobu, he entered the First Bank (*Dai'ichi ginkō*).[24] It was an unprecedented path for a new college graduate, the result of the demands from Shibusawa Eiichi, father-in-law of Hozumi, for talented human resources to populate the world of enterprise.

But it seems that Mizuno was not cut out for work in a bank. After just four years, he gained a reference from Professor Ume Kenjirō and transferred to the Ministry of Agricultural and Commercial Affairs, and then he switched again to the Home Ministry the following year. Here at last he settled down. He rose through the ministry ranks and became its most iconic bureaucrat.

The movements of these men reveal how instructors dispatched by the regime to the Imperial University served as a pipeline between the two institutions. The adjuncts could confirm the characters and talents of young men before they recommended them for state employment. As such a direct pipeline took shape, so too did recommendations and employment advice from professors become more common. A personnel employment system once based on the private interests of oligarchs transformed into one in which the regime hired university graduates who had received a professional education. The government certainly placed emphasis on the professional skills of its would-be employees, but it did not only seek knowledge. Through this new system, it secured a means to ascertain the characters of the men it planned to bring into its fold.

Conceit: Retirement advice for the oligarch-bureaucrats

Thus the regime systematized a means of collecting personnel from the Imperial University with expertise in legislative and executive government. Kanai Noboru, who had once despaired over the dim prospects of students studying politics, returned to the Imperial University after four years of study in Germany and became a professor in the College of Law. With the new state employment system before him, he rhapsodized: 'Students [today] face futures that overflow – overflow with hope (*tabō*), overflow with too much to do (*tabō*)'; 'Those who want to move ahead in life and enter university should, without hesitation, enter the study of politics.'[25] The era of legal studies had arrived.

The inauguration of a standardized employment system based on meritocracy and professional education had instilled in employees a self-conscious identity that they were scholar-bureaucrats, different from the oligarch-bureaucrats already in the regime. Theirs was a rank won not through connections or private interests but through hard work and study. Breaking free from the pejorative image of state officials fawning at the feet of oligarchic potentates, new hires began to regard their entry onto the road to bureaucracy as a means to participate in establishing a constitutional state.

Scholar-bureaucrats were intensely proud of their learning and their academic prowess. An exemplary case was that of one student who passed through the probationary employment system and rose to the rank of bureau head in the Ministry of Agricultural and Commercial Affairs. While still at college, he presented a dissertation titled 'The Past and Future of Meiji-era Officials', in which he argued that only those who had received the latest education in politics and law could fulfil the newest needs of the executive government.[26] It was a fiery polemic. He went so far as to call for the retirement of all previous bureaucrats who had not received a professional education.

Scholar-bureaucrats with a professional education were exuberant as the executive government became increasingly specialized and the legal system became increasingly Westernized. Snobbish, proud, these scholar-bureaucrats drew a line between themselves and those factional oligarchic-bureaucrats who had been employed because of their domain-based connections. They developed a new image of a new kind of autonomous bureaucrat, and they established a new precedent in the world of officialdom.

Professional bureaucrats before the era of scholars: Hara Kei and Gotō Shinpei

As the bureaucracy was filled with scholar-bureaucrats from professional universities, a new kind of executive government based primarily on law, the common language of these new bureaucrats, began to emerge. But there were other bureaucrats in the

Figure 4.1 Hara Takashi with his wife in Paris, 1883. *Source:* Kikuchi Gorō et al., eds, *Hara Takashi Zenden*, vol. 1, Nihon Hyōronsha, 1922, front page.

regime who had already risen through the ranks and who had gained a comparable degree of professionalization by a different route. Representative of this strain were bakufu ministers who had travelled abroad during the late Tokugawa era and other young men who had studied abroad as attendants to the Iwakura Mission or other embassies. Having travelling down diverse paths, by around 1880 these men began assembling in the bureaucracy. Their talents and abilities flourished once they were set to work on actual governmental tasks.

Hara Takashi, or Hara Kei, was one such administrative bureaucrat (*jitsumu kanryō*). Because the memory of Hara as a partisan politician, as the inaugurator of the first genuine party cabinet in Japanese history, remains so strong, the fifteen years he spent honing his skills as a bureaucrat remain shrouded in relative obscurity.

Born in 1856, or Ansei 3, Hara was the second son of a samurai family in Morioka domain.[27] He came from a distinguished household that had produced even a chief retainer of the domainal lord (*karō*). Morioka fell on hard times when, about ten years after Hara's birth, it suffered defeat in the Boshin War and became a hotbed of rebel armies. Hara pursued Chinese and English studies at his domainal school, but perhaps because of these unfavourable circumstances, he left home to pursue further studies elsewhere.

Figure 4.2 Gotō Shinpei with his wife, 1883. *Source:* Tsurumi Yūsuke, ed., *Gotō Shinpei*, vol. 1, Gotō Shinpei haku denkihensankai, 1937, p. 366.

Hara drifted. He embarked for Niigata, accompanying a French pastor, and then proceeded back to Tokyo, where he dabbled in English at the academy (*juku*) of Mitsukuri Shūhei, before he finally took up French law as his first systematic field of study. In Meiji 9 (= 1876), he enrolled in the law academy that the Ministry of Justice had set up to train legal professionals. Of the 104 men in his incoming class, the second class in the history of the school, he entered with the second best academic record. It was at this point, for the first time in his life, that Hara threw all of his energy into academic pursuit.

But his time at law school, too, was fleeting. After just two-and-a-half years, Hara was dismissed from the academy, having incurred the displeasure of the head of school. He entered a newspaper, the *Yūbin hōchi shinbun*, and gained fame by publishing political treatises. But the paper was overrun by Ōkuma associates when they were driven out of the regime in the 1881 political upheaval. Hara bridled at the change in staff. After just over a year, he left the paper, transferring over to the pro-regime *Daitō nippō*. And then that paper went under.

Change remained the unrelenting reality of Hara's life until he at last merged onto the road to bureaucracy. After the *Daitō nippō* folded in 1882, Inoue Kaoru, who was involved in the management of the paper, pulled Hara into the Foreign Ministry. Hara took up a role as commissioner (*goyō gakari*) in the Public Communications Bureau (*kōshinkyoku*), where his main task involved translating documents from French.

In November 1883, an unexpected opportunity knocked. Hara was appointed as Japanese consul in Tianjin following the outbreak of the Sino-French War. Then the Kōshin (or Kapsin in Korean) Incident broke out in Seoul, not long after Hara arrived in the Qing Empire. His flexible response to the crisis won recognition, and he gained further praise for his outstanding work in the negotiations led by Itō Hirobumi for the Treaty of Tianjin. With this distinguished track record, Hara moved up in the diplomatic world. He was dispatched to Paris, where, during a two-year tenure, he had the opportunity to experience European politics and diplomacy in person. He returned to Japan in 1887, and he came to occupy positions of trust under Inoue Kaoru and Mutsu Munemitsu. Setting his talents to reform of the Foreign Ministry, starting with the exam system for diplomats, he climbed through the ranks to deputy minister. It was five years after this point that Hara began participating in the Rikken Seiyūkai and making his inroads into party politics. The politicians who inaugurated the era of party politics began their careers as practical bureaucrats and climbed their way up from there.

The life course of Hara resembled that of Gotō Shinpei, who established himself in medical studies and then found success as a colonial bureaucrat.[28] From there he became home minister and then foreign minister. Gotō was born in 1857, the year after Hara was born, in Mizusawa, located south of Morioka. His talents were discovered by the young Yasuba Yasukazu, who had been dispatched to Mizusawa as a greater counsellor (*daisanji*), and he went to the Sukagawa Medical School (*igakkō*) to pursue medical studies. When Yasuba was transferred to Aichi prefecture as its governor, Gotō followed him there and enrolled in Aichi Medical School. He accumulated considerable practical experience across the country.

Gotō gained renown for the quarantine measures he implemented for soldiers returning from the Sino-Japanese War. He then dedicated his energies to public health administration (*eisei gyōsei*) under Nagayo Sensai and deepened his understanding of government administration, and with these experiences as leverage he became head of the popular affairs administration division of the governorship general in Taiwan (*Taiwan sōtokufu minsei chōkan*). The successes he accumulated as a colonial bureaucrat gave him future opportunities to take action as a politician steeped in specialized knowledge.

Both Hara and Gotō began their lives in lands that had fallen from national grace and been overrun by recalcitrant forces. Despite their unfortunate provenance, they won the opportunity to receive professional education when that education was just being developed, and, using that learning as their motor, they propelled themselves into the national government, gaining a foothold there. Their initial rank was hardly so lofty as the positions of intellectuals from among the erstwhile bakufu ministers or of scholars with university degrees. But in a world where few had specialized knowledge, they wielded their talents as they accumulated practical experience. Theirs were talents that emerged from specialized knowledge and a canny ability to put that knowledge into practice.

Another professional bureaucrat before the era of scholars: Kiyoura Keigo

The Meiji Restoration had created a world in which those who had pursued Western learning found themselves with advantages in life. But many youths simply had not had the opportunity to study Western knowledge. Even after the Restoration, many continued to pursue Chinese and national learning, as in bygone times. Those fields had formed the core of education at domainal schools, and many even believed that men below a certain age should not be exposed to invidious Western ideas. Even the University-South College, the leading bastion of Western learning, banned boys below

Figure 4.3 Kiyoura Keigo as the secretary in the Legislation Bureau of the Council of State, *c.* 1881. *Source:* Inoue Masaaki, ed., *Hakushaku Kiyoura Keigo den*, Hakushaku Kiyoura Keigo den kankō kai, 1935, p. 96.

the age of 16 from enrolling at the university, claiming that boys needed to focus on Chinese and national learning during their youngest years.

As oligarchs asserted themselves and as returnees from voyages to the West won renown and admiration, it became increasingly difficult to make a life for oneself through Chinese studies. Such is the lesson we glean from the life course of Kiyoura Keigo, who gained a sterling reputation as a student at the Hita Kangien, among the foremost academies of Chinese learning in the nation.[29]

Kiyoura Keigo was born in Kamoto, Yamaga, Kumamoto, in Kaei 3 (= 1850). He had academic ambition even from a young age. Bearing prodigious talent, he enrolled in the Hita Kangien and climbed the ranks all the way to head of campus (*shachō*).

Soon after the Restoration of Imperial Rule, Kiyoura established a private academy under Kumamoto Castle. But by the fifth year of the Meiji reign (= 1872), he had had a change of heart. He resolved to move to the national capital. His will was roused by word coming in from Tokyo of the activities of Hita Kangien alumni. Kiyoura headed to Saitama, where he paid a visit to Nomura Morihide, with whom he shared connections to Hita Kangien. Nomura was the first ever prefectural head (*kenrei*) of Saitama.

Nomura welcomed the arrival of Kiyoura, appointing him as a prefectural professor (*Saitama-ken daikyōju*) and entrusting him with reform of the prefectural education system. The official title Kiyoura obtained sounds lofty, but in fact he was no more than a lower-level prefectural officer occupying the fourteenth tier of official ranks. Rather than grumble about his lowly lot, Kiyoura pressed forward, building the foundations of the education system and gaining esteem as an administrative bureaucrat even in neighbouring prefectures.

In August 1876, Kiyoura headed for Tokyo, having been appointed to the Research Bureau of the Ministry of Justice and charged with investigating laws for the punishment of crimes (*shihōshō chizaihō torishirabe kyoku*). It was Yokota Kuniomi, a fellow Hita student who later became head of the Court of Cassation, who had summoned Kiyoura to the national centre. Under the counsel of French advisor Gustave Émile Boissonade, the Ministry of Justice was in the throes of amending national laws and ordinances, and it was bringing in men of talent from across the country for support. To establish a national legal system, the ministry needed not only men with experience studying in the West but also those well versed in Chinese and national studies. Kiyoura was an ideal resource. He thus won the opportunity to study law not in the abstract but in an applied field, with no less than the renowned Boissonade as his guide. Kiyoura became a specialist in criminal law (*keihō*) and went on to work for the Legislation Bureau of the Council of State before transferring to the House of Counsellors, where he mined the depths of his talent while working to improve national legal systems.

Finding a field of personal specialization allowed Kiyoura to expand the realm of opportunities before him. The Home Ministry snatched him up in 1883 as it hustled to build the national police system. The following year, it appointed him as head of the Public Security Bureau (*keiho kyoku*). Twelve years had elapsed since Kiyoura had left his home in Kumamoto. The national police, populated primarily by former samurai who had transformed into policemen, sorely lacked resources capable of developing an organizational scheme for the force. High expectations were pinned on Kiyoura and his expertise in criminal law and procedure.

This swift rise through the ranks was recompense for the extraordinary efforts Kiyoura had exerted, to which testifies the still-extant personal collection of books he donated to his hometown. The collection abounds with texts both in Japanese and in Western languages on various national police systems. The pages of those books in turn abound with notes and marginalia attributed to Kiyoura.[30] Known today as a Yamagata-faction bureaucrat, Kiyoura managed to ascend all the way to head of the Privy Council. He recollected,

> I had no factional or personal ties through my domain, through my family lineage, through my academic pedigree, through my relatives, or through marriage. I had not even a single strand of a network on which I could rely. And so I had no choice but put to one arm forward and then one foot forward and to crawl my way up by my own powers. Such were my circumstances.

Such words of self-flattery were not unusual for Kiyoura, who indeed blazed his own trail by dint of his own efforts, not through any interested powers.

Neither Hara and Gotō, who hailed from rebel strongholds, nor indeed Kiyoura benefited from the early solicitude of oligarchs. They were not among wielders of power when the Boshin War ended. But it was precisely for that reason that they exerted themselves in learning until they compelled those around them to recognize their talents.

For all the might oligarchs wielded, there were limits to the human resources they could claim on their side. A dearth of talent attenuated their powers. They shrewdly sought to fold capable men from across the nation into their camp. It was hardly by accident that Inoue and Mutsu discovered Hara; Yasuba and Nagayo, Gotō; or Nomura and Yamagata, Kiyoura. The Meiji regime could not have done without casting a wide net to catch personnel.

Unlike Kiyoura, who had no connections to the oligarchic factions even by marriage, Hara and Gotō both married into political clans. Sadako, wife of Hara Takashi, was the daughter of Satsuma strongman Nakai Hiromu; Kazuko, wife of Gotō Shinpei, was the daughter of Yasuba Yasukazu. Even from ancient times, families with distinguished pedigrees had used marriage as a device to bring talented men into their fold and preserve their lineage. But the life records of men such as Gotō and Hara suggest that they did not win power by marrying up. Their own powers and abilities brought prestige to the families they married into. Whom they married in itself acts as evidence of the extent to which their powers were recognized and respected. Even well past the Meiji era, it remained commonplace for upper-level bureaucrats to marry their daughters to talented officials working below them. Bureaucrats used such familial connections to accumulate political capital and to form a network of people who could collectively build clout.

The higher-level civil officer exams: The introduction of an exam employment system

From probationary employment to examinations

The probationary employment system inaugurated in 1888 allowed a steady flow of scholar-bureaucrats from the Imperial University to enter the ministries of the Meiji government. In the six years from 1888 to 1893, 126 scholars embarked on the path to bureaucracy through probationary employment. Of those, thirty-four entered the Home Ministry; twenty-seven, the treasury; sixteen, the Audit Board (*kaikei kensain*); thirteen, agricultural and commercial affairs; and thirteen, the Legislation Bureau. The remaining men went to other divisions.

Things went less smoothly for graduates of private academies. The Probationary Employment exams targeted at graduates of private law schools were disbanded in 1891, just three years after they were inaugurated. There were multiple overlapping reasons. Most employees from private schools came through judiciary exams, but those exams were separated from the probationary exams and transformed into stand-alone tests. Meanwhile, the number of men employed as executive officials plummeted quickly from fourteen in 1889 to six in 1890 to none whatsoever in 1891.[31] It was not as if the ministries had no need for probationary employees. Rather, because the ministries had gained approval to hire university students at any time they wished, their probationary-employee quotas had already been filled by the time exams began in October of each year.

The popular oppositional parties, which had hailed the introduction of an official government testing system, decried the year-round employment of university students as a violation of the purpose of probationary employment exams. They claimed that the measure trampled on the very spirit of the Meiji Restoration, as enshrined in clause 19 of the Constitution, which guaranteed an open door to officialdom. The ministries, on the other hand, grumbled that three years of mandatory employee probation were too long, especially since the trial period was applied even to graduates of the Imperial University, who were exempted from taking examinations. Just three years after its implementation, compromises with reality started watering down the ideal bureaucratic system sketched out by Itō Hirobumi.

The scholar-bureaucrats themselves had grievances. They did not get along with older bureaucrats from the domainal factions. Scholar-bureaucrats looked down on oligarch-bureaucrats for their lack of specialized knowledge and their blind adherence to precedent. And oligarch-bureaucrats belittled the ideas of scholar-bureaucrats as highfalutin academic theorizing unsuited to the reality of practical administration. The two sides clashed. To subvert the scholar-bureaucrats, oligarch-bureaucrats moved to persuade the Cabinet to rehire former oligarchic officials who had stepped down. They managed to have their proposal adopted. These resurgent reactionary forces undermined the probationary employment system, which had originally aimed at elevating the efficiency and quality of executive government by setting specialized knowledge to use.

The popular opposition parties plotted to strike back. Using the Imperial Diet as their launching pad, they went after the central regime, demanding even further liberalization of bureaucratic employment. They found an ideational anchor and practical advocate in Ōtsu Jun'ichirō, author of *On the Employment of State Officials in Japan* (*Nihon kanri nin'yō ron*). Ōtsu had won a seat in the Diet as a representative (*daigishi*) from the Constitution and Reform Party (*Rikken Kaishintō*). In the first plenary session of the Diet, he argued vociferously for further improvements to the bureaucratic system.

The response of the relevant state committee flummoxed Ōtsu and his coterie. The committee insisted that because the bureaucracy fell under the governing authority of the Emperor (*tennō taiken*) in its capacity as part of the system of official appointees (*kansei taiken*), it was inappropriate to use the Diet to discuss matters pertaining to it. The very notion of the supreme power of the Emperor blocked any further deliberations in the Diet.

The introduction of examinations for higher-level civil officers: Specialization and homogenization

The popular parties advocated opening up the bureaucracy, calling for bearers of new knowledge to fill its structures and continually reinvigorate its functioning. It was not just the opposition that rallied behind this liberalization. None other than Itō Hirobumi himself, who had conceived the probationary employment system, agreed with them.

Change began as circumstances deteriorated in the regime. The fourth session of the Imperial Diet opened in 1893 under the second Cabinet of Itō Hirobumi. Against the backdrop of rising tensions with the Qing Empire, the regime became locked in a fierce struggle against the popular parties over its demands for an expansion of the navy. The stand-off escalated to a point where members of the regime began to wonder whether they should dissolve the Diet or resign en masse. The onslaught from the popular parties continued and extended to a denunciation of the bureaucracy. Kōno Hironaka of the Freedom Party pilloried the regime, lamenting that 'education has become no more than a thrall to the whims and fancies of oligarchs, who have turned it into an instrument to promote their longevity', and that 'the world of government officialdom has become nothing more than a breeding-ground for the interests of private parties.' A bureaucratic system built up on high ideals had, he protested, degenerated into an organ to protect the private interests of the oligarchy.

The Rescript on the Construction of Warships (*kenkan shōchoku*) issued by the Emperor, which called for the regime and the Diet to cooperate and committed to adjusting the budget by slashing costs associated with the imperial house, helped bring the stand-off between the parties and the regime to a resolution. With the Rescript, the regime also promised the popular parties reforms in executive government. It installed a special committee in the House of Representatives that would debate the content of those reforms.

Itō did not let this chance slip away. The Diet had turned its attention to reform. The Emperor, who wielded supreme power over the bureaucratic system (*kansei taiken*), had indicated his support for change. It was a prime opportunity to knock out the oppositional forces of the factionalist oligarchs and to bring reform of the bureaucracy to completion. Itō banded with members of his staff and set out resolutely on full-blown reform.

The reforms intended to make a stark division between political officers (*seimukan*), who took up political roles such as regulation or negotiation, and administrative officers (*jimukan*), who took up practical executive tasks. They further sought to abolish vested string-pulling in personnel selection and to widen the search after human resources. The first objective would create a more specialized, professionalized environment by cordoning off administrative officers from the world of politics. The latter would fill the ranks of the ministries with specialized human resources who could satisfy ministerial demands.

In October 1893, the Edict on the Employment of Civil Officers (*bunkan nin'yō rei*) placed an employment examination system at the centre of a new mode for hiring officials.[32] The system combined the demands of the popular parties for an open door to officialdom with the desires of Itō and his co-planners for a bureaucracy with a high degree of professional specialization. The new strategy mandated that all prospective higher-level bureaucrats, be they graduates of private law academies or of the Imperial University, sit the exam for higher-level state officers. The probationary employment system was abolished. The simultaneous appointment of the head of the official Exam Bureau to the chancellorship of the Imperial University was dissolved and replaced with a simultaneous appointment between the head of the Exam Bureau and head of the Legislation Bureau (*hōseikyoku*), a move that signalled a desire to seek out human resources more widely, not simply at the Imperial University.

The new system took into account the desires of the state ministries and included mechanisms to respond more flexibly to the demands of the executive government. The probationary period for new bureaucrats, criticized as too long, was eliminated altogether, and new hires were permitted to enter the main bureaucracy immediately. Success on the exam itself became the main qualification for becoming a bureaucrat, and the state ordained that if for whatever reason a bureaucrat had to step down from his post, it retained the right to re-employ him if need be. It was for this reason that the system was dubbed one of 'employment by qualifications' (*shikaku nin'yō*). As a result of this system, the state was able to increase and decrease the membership of the bureaucracy according to the exigencies of its policies.

The vision of Itō and his band to raise the efficiency of the state by eliminating vested hiring strategies found form in the Edict on the Employment of Civil Officers. The rise of a more liberal, meritocratic employment system led newspapers across the country to laud what they called an unexpected and dramatic reform of the state.

Employing men through exams made the entryway into the state extremely selective, and as a result the bureaucracy became increasingly specialized and homogeneous. These changes were acclaimed as measures by which favouritist employment by factions was curtailed and efficiency boosted.

But these changes also resulted in the greater isolation of the world of officialdom. Because mid-career hires or employment from the private sector did not occur except during the Second World War, officialdom, at least at the level of the men who made it up, became cut off from the rest of society. The regime had managed to curtail employment through private interests, but greater professionalization came at the cost of diversity. The introduction of the examination employment system marked the precise origin moment of the homogeneity of the Japanese bureaucracy, a peculiar characteristic that persists to this very day.

Chaos in the first round of exams

The first round of exams, in 1894, did not proceed without confusion. Or perhaps it was not the system itself that was chaotic but the examinees who found themselves nonplussed by a system in the throes of change.

The examination system was welcomed by the regime and hoi polloi alike, but students at the Imperial University were less thrilled. They had lived their student lives on the assumption, proffered by the Probationary Employment System, that they could enter the regime without taking exams. All of a sudden they found their special privileges vanish. Their lives rocked by the abrupt change, they protested vigorously. The shift represented to them an unjust vitiation of an established system, the capitulation of the state to the popular parties, parties whose ranks were filled with men from private law academics. With the futures promised to them at enrolment now suddenly revoked, it is little wonder they responded with rage.

It is not as if the regime failed to take conciliatory steps. It exempted graduates of the Imperial University from the preliminary round of exams, which involved an essay test and which was required for graduates from private schools. But the waiver did not change the fact that Imperial University students had to sit for the main round of exams. It did not assuage their test-taking anxieties. And it did not heal their wounded pride now that they had to compete with graduates from private academies on the same exam field. The Imperial University graduates rallied for a return to exam exemption. They banded together and boycotted the exams. The largest contingent of test-takers suddenly declared collective war on the system. Right from the outset, the exams faced crisis.

The regime did not budge. Insisting that 'it is best to side with the just arguments of public opinion even if minor injustices arise along the way', it disregarded the grumbling of the Imperial University graduates and ploughed ahead with administering the exams. Men intent on participating in state governance had been streaming into the College of Law at the Imperial University. They had little way of achieving their ambitions except by means of the state bureaucracy. The regime was confident that, if it carried ahead determinedly, after a few years applicants would be left with no choice but to take the mandated exams, even if they raised a ruckus in the first year. Indeed, the timing for a new exam system could not have been better. The change occurred just after the continual flow of talent into the Imperial University had become all but certain.

The response of the boycotters bore out the predictions of the state. Six men that same year, and another three the following year, took the exams as the state had mandated and entered the bureaucratic ministries as affiliated officers (*zokkan*), entering the path to becoming a *sōninkan*. Among the first group of men was Sugiyama Shigorō, later deputy home minister; among the second was Kurachi Tetsukichi, later deputy foreign minister. The ministries recognized that they could not let such potent prospective manpower slip away, and they took practical interim measures to help bring these men in at a moment of transition.

What, then, of graduates from private law schools? Perhaps because they were required to take a preliminary round of exams, many dithered for the first year, reluctant to take the plunge. It was, after all, the first time they had to take exams since the dissolution of the previous system in 1891.[33] They figured they would take it easy for the time being.

Twenty-eight people sat the first round of exams. Only six passed: four from the Tokyo Institute of Law (*Tōkyō hōgakuin*), today's Chūō University, and one each from the Franco-Japanese School of Law (*Wafutsu hōritsu gakkō*), today's Hōsei University, and the Meiji Law School (*Meiji hōgakkō*), today's Meiji University. Five of these men were appointed as state officials. The top scorer on the exam was Kanbayashi Keijirō, the Franco-Japanese School graduate. Born in Kyoto in 1867, Kanbayashi had already gained fame as the author of *Notes on the Japanese District System* (*Nihon gunsei chūkai*). After passing through the Legislation Bureau and the treasury ministry, Kanbayashi transferred to Korea, where he rose from governor of Kankyōhoku province (K. *Hamgyŏngbuk do*) to deputy (*jikan*) in the House of Yi (*Ri ōshoku*). New graduates had also boycotted the consular and foreign-affairs officer exams conducted in that same year. But three graduates from the Imperial University as well as Funakoshi Mitsunojō, a baron (*danshaku*) born in Hiroshima in 1867, took and passed the exams.

The second ever annual exams, held the following year in 1895, proceeded without trouble. Thirty-seven men passed, of whom twenty-five were law graduates from the Imperial University and twelve were from private law academies. It is conventionally thought that graduates of private schools made up a negligible portion of the men who filled the bureaucracy, but they in fact constituted about 10 per cent of men employed from this point to the immediate pre-war period.

Together, the nineteenth article of the Meiji Constitution and the Edict on the Employment of Civil Officers realized the vision of the Charter Oath that 'all be allowed to pursue their own calling so that there may be no discontent'. As power in the world of officialdom transferred from factionalist oligarchic bureaucrats to scholar-bureaucrats, vast change swept through the bureaucracy, upending the relationship between bureaucrats and political parties in particular. The new composition of the bureaucracy became a major factor in the inauguration of party politics.

The challenge from private law academies

The diary of one bureaucrat gives us a closer behind-the-scenes look as young university graduates stepped up to official exams. The diary-writer was Okada Unosuke. Born in Hyōgo prefecture in 1872, Okada worked as an uncertified teacher at an elementary school (*jinjō shōgakkō no daiyō kyōin*) while pursuing studies on his own. He then enrolled at the Tokyo Institute of Law. He passed the higher-level officer exams upon graduation and served in various capacities as a Home Ministry officer, as an administrative officer in Nagano prefecture and as a Home Ministry division officer (*bukan*) in Ehime prefecture, before rising to governor of Ibaraki and then of Saga. In his diary he divulges candid, unrestrained thoughts from the time he took the higher-level exams to the time he was employed.[34] Let us use his diary to pry into the minds of young men training their sights on government employment.

Okada Unosuke spent the fall of 1869 in indulgence. He dissipated daytime watching vaudeville theatre and night-time getting drunk. Day passed day in a daze. That summer he had graduated top of his class from the Tokyo Institute of Law. Before him lay, it seemed, a scintillating future in the legal profession. But then September came, and with it the exams for the employment of lawyers and judges (*hankenji tōyō shiken*). He did not think he had done well. He turned to the bottle as he awaited word of failure.

Figure 4.4 Okada Unosuke, as the governor of Saga Prefecture, *c.* 1917. *Source:* Rekidai chiji hensankai, ed., *Nihon no rekidai chiji*, p. 993.

Exam results reached Okada in October. Just as he had predicted, he had failed. Okada cursed the hubris that his spectacular academic performance at law school had instilled in him: 'These results [of the exams], which invite the humiliation of defeat, put [my] disgrace today on display. Proud generals and indolent soldiers are always defeated. It was, I believe, none other than the mighty victory I won on my graduation exams that brought about the failure I experience today.'

Okada had no other path forward except through state employment. As he wasted his days in dissipation, one day he went to a vaudeville show (*gidayū*) performed by an all-female troupe. Such performances in which women performed bold songs enjoyed wide popularity among university students. Watching the show, Okada had an epiphany: 'If one [is willing to] endure degradation, overcome ignominy, and persevere and fight and persist through trials, then to transform the indignity of today into the success of tomorrow is not necessarily impossible. Battle always involves both victory and defeat. Should one suddenly begin to shed tears simply because of a single defeat?' Perhaps the show he watched was one about surmounting difficulty.

Whatever it was, Okada suddenly roused himself back to action and with a vigour and intensity as never before decided to take the exams again the following year.

In his quest to become a lawyer, Okada immersed himself in study, making daily visits to the Tokyo Library (*Tōkyō toshokan*) at Ueno, renamed the Imperial Library (*Teikoku toshokan*) the following year. But he still sought entertainment. Dragged down, perhaps, by the doldrums of unending study, he began to frequent political speeches as a form of diversion. His interest in politics was piqued. He was particularly moved after he attended a party on 10 December for law students. Ōkuma Shigenobu delivered a fiery talk on administrative reform as part of a speech panel at the party. Ōkuma was then serving as foreign minister in the second Cabinet of Matsukata Masayoshi and as head of the committee on streamlining executive government (*gyōsei seiri iinaki*). The bristling energy of state administration after the Sino-Japanese War allured Okada into the world of politics.

His interest in politics deepening, Okada began to feel restless sitting alone behind a desk with his head in a book. He opened study circles with his acquaintances and tried his hand at debate. His interlocutors were made up of old classmates from law school such as Kōno Hideo, later head of the audit board, or acquaintances at the Imperial University such as Okamoto Eitarō, later deputy minister of agricultural and commercial affairs. Okamoto was a distinguished man who had translated Walter Bagehot's *The English Constitution*, a text Shioiri had recommended as a reference work for students. Sparks flew among the debaters. After a debate with Imperial University students hosted by Okamoto at his lodging, Okada griped, 'One should not listen to such theoretical palaver. I have come more and more to know that [the talk of] university students is without profit.' With a growing sense of resentment towards Imperial University students, he began to gain a hold on his own self-confidence.

In July 1897, the names of the eighteen members of the committee on examinations for higher-level officers were publicly announced. The list included a host of professors from the Imperial University, including Hozumi Yatsuka, Hijikata Yasushi, Kanai Noboru, Terao Tōru, Tomizu Hirondo and Ikki Kitokurō. Okada collected their publications without delay and began plotting his path to officialdom.

Because he graduated from the private Tokyo Institute of Law (*Tōkyō hōgakuin*), Okada had to pass the preliminary round of exams, an essay test, before sitting for the main round. After agonizing and agonizing, he finally took up his brush on 5 August, the night before the test deadline, and completed the preliminary exam in a single sitting. He submitted the test and his application for the main round the following day. It is unclear what subjects he sat for; in his year, the exam on constitutionalism asked about the nature of legislative power (*rippōken*) and legislative procedures, and the exam on administrative law asked about the relationship between police authority and ownership rights. On 10 September, Okada received notification that he had passed the preliminary exam.

The main exam

The main round of exams began on Friday, 1 October. The first day involved a written exam known as the 'speed-essay test'. One-hundred-and-forty-four examinees were summoned to the House of Representatives at 7.30 am. The exam itself started at 9.45 am. It ended forty-five minutes later, at 10.30 am, after which the examinees left the exam room.

The exam on constitutionalism that year covered constitutional review (*iken rippō shinsaiken*), and the exam on administrative law covered the purpose of the police. The first day of exams was followed by two weekend days off, 2 and 3 October, during which Okada stayed at home and reviewed constitutional, administrative and criminal law. Because he had sent in a joint application for the employment exams for judges and lawyers, he spent Monday through Friday of the following week, 4 to 8 October, taking those tests at the Ministry of Justice.

The night of 6 October, the middle of his week of law exams, Okada received the results of the speed-exams. He had passed. He submitted the mandated application, made his selections for the subjects he wanted to take and began preparing for further exams the following week.

The main written tests in the main round of exams finally began on Friday, 15 October. Okada wrote the following recollections:

> The written tests for the higher-level examinations for officers will occur this afternoon at the House of Representatives. We will arrive there after 1 pm. There are 146 examinees altogether, including both those with university degrees [from the Imperial University] and those who had to sit the preliminary round of exams. I've heard that there are 58 scholars [from the Imperial University], so there must be 88 men from private law academies. The men with Western clothes and pretty coiffures – and there are not a few of them – must be Imperial University scholars now seeking to become public officials. [...] To fight for a spot in the Emperor's government against scores of these imposing scholars who spent over a decade of their lives immersed in study at the empire's supreme bastion of education! How dreadful.

Imperial University alumni had lost the privilege of entering the bureaucracy without exams, but often they were immediately hired in June by government ministries as affiliated officers (*zokkan*). The ministries did not assign them any work of significance after hiring them. They gave them time and space to study so that they could pass the exams later in the year. Now that he had won a seat next to such 'men with Western clothes and pretty coiffures', no doubt Okada was left reflecting on the year of back-breaking exertion that had brought him to this point, in contrast to their year of privilege.

Exams proceeded. On Friday, 15 October, the test was on administrative law. The next morning was criminal law; then civil law in the afternoon; and then after a day off for the New Harvest Festival (*shinjōsai*), international law and economics came on Monday, 18 October; and then constitutional law as well as criminal procedural law (*keiji soshō hō*), an elective subject, appeared on Tuesday, 19 October. Then at last the written exams were all over.

The exam on constitutional law reflected the times. No doubt influenced by the stand-off between the regime and the parliament, the exam prompted examinees,

'Discuss the differences between the efficacy of the budget and that of the law. In forming law, do support from the parliament and approval from ministers have different effects?' Having completed the constitutional law exam, Okada made a pit-stop at the women's vaudeville show that transformed his life, downed a drink and then went home. At his lodge he found a crate of *matsutake* mushrooms his older brother in Kobe had sent him. It helped ease his fatigue.

Results for the exams for lawyers and judges were supposed to have been released by this point. Okada waited and waited. Every day he went to a newspaper reading room to check the official state newspaper for results. Nothing. At last, on 9 November, he learned of the results for both the judiciary and executive exams at the same time. He had passed both. He rushed to send a telegram back home to Kobe.

But next came the oral exams. They began a week later, on Monday, 15 November. Like the written exams, they began at 7.30 am on the premises of the House of Representatives and ended at noon. Eighty-six men, thirty-one from the Imperial University and fifty-five from private academies, had passed the written tests, the examinees were told. The previous year, a total of fifty people had passed the entire set of exams. If they placed in the top 60 per cent of test-takers, they could make it into officialdom, it seemed.

Oral exams proceeded by subject. The first day was economics, examined by Kanai Noboru, Koike Seiichi and another committee member; day two was administrative law, examined by Hozumi Yatsuka, Nakane Shigekazu and Kiuchi Jūshirō; day three was civil law, examined by Hijikata Yasushi, Tomizu Hirondo and another member; and day four was criminal law, examined by Matsumuro Itasu, Maeda Kōkai and Ishiwata Bin'ichi. It seems that Okada sailed through the first four days without difficulty.

Then came day five. He was supposed to have been good at constitutional law. But examination committee member Ikki Kitokurō tripped him up. 'I suffered painfully at the hands of Professor Ikki today, and so now my prospects of passing the exam have been thrown into uncertainty,' he wrote. 'It's so disappointing I can't bear it.' He prepared for failure. Day six went better. The exam, on international law, was administered by Misaki Kamenosuke, Fujita Ryūzaburō and Terao Tōru. Okada handled questions from Misaki confidently and adeptly. But his performance did little to raise his spirits: 'There's nothing to be done about my failure yesterday,' he wrote. The final oral exam, on criminal procedures, was held on Monday, 22 November, and was administered by Matsumuro Itasu, Ishiwata Bin'ichi and another committee member. On that very day, Okada received word that he had not only passed but placed second among all test-takers on the exams for judges and lawyers. He resolved to enter the judiciary.

Judicial officer or executive officer

Unexpectedly enough, Okada passed the exams for higher-level officers, too. And so too did Kawano, his old acquaintance from the Tokyo Institute of Law. Together they rejoiced. On 27 November, with notice of exam success in hand, Okada headed to the Ministry of Justice for a meeting to determine his post in the Ministry.

The award ceremony to bestow certificates of exam success occurred at the Legislation Bureau on 30 November. Here Okada learned that of the fifty-four men who had passed the exam, he had placed tenth. Just as he was filled with a sense of accomplishment, doubts about his path forward began to arise.

The post assignment meeting at the Ministry of Justice had already come and gone. He was all set to continue on as a lawyer or a judge. Amid his seeming certainty, on 9 December, he received his appointment as an intern public prosecutor representative at the court of Ōtsu (*shiho kenji dairi Ōtsu saibansho zume*).

Okada thought he would simply take up the new post assigned to him. But his path suddenly veered in a new direction. He received a summons from the Home Ministry addressed by Misaki Kamenosuke, head of the bureau for prefectural governance, who had sat on the exam committee for international law. On 11 December, Okada paid a visit to Misaki, who encouraged him to leave the justice ministry and join the Home Ministry. Misaki assured him that if he spent just one or two years trying his hand at administrative matters in the Home Ministry, he would be promoted to counsellor in the prefectures, a rank equal to that of head of a ministry division (*bukachō*). Enticed by such prospects, Okada intimated that he would think about it a bit and then probably say yes. The Home Ministry had a reputation for providing chances for promotion to graduates of private law academies. His hopes mounted.

Faced with a similar choice was Nagai Kinjirō, a graduate from the year below Okada at the Tokyo Institute of Law who later became head officer in the governorship of Karafuto (*Karafutochō chōkan*). He had placed first on the exam for lawyers and judges and ninth on that for higher-level officers. The justice and home ministries both sought to employ him. On 13 December, Nagai and Okada together went to meet Okuda Yoshihito, an old acquaintance who was then a deputy minister of commercial and agricultural affairs. Okuda had taught at the Tokyo Institute of Law and befriended the two students then. He now gave them an inside scoop on the regime and promised to speak with Misaki to see where things stood for them.

When Nagai and Okada visited Okuda again on 15 December, he assured them that all was well. The Home Ministry was in good order. There was little danger of instability, and their prospects looked favourable there. Their anxieties assuaged, they paid a visit to Misaki and formally expressed their interested in being hired by the Ministry. They then submitted their resignation to the Ministry of Justice.

Okada entered the Home Ministry on 25 December with a dual appointment in the Home Ministry-affiliated Hokkaido bureau (*Hokkaidōkyoku*) and the bureau for prefectural governance (*kenchikyoku*). He was introduced to his new colleagues on his first day by other men affiliated with the ministry: Sayanagi Tōta, also a graduate of the Tokyo Institute of Law and later governor of Chiba, and Nishimura Mutsuo, graduate of the Tokyo Professional School and later governor of Saga. He worked in the ministry for just one day before it closed for the year the following week, on 27 December. That evening Okada attended a goodbye party for Sayanagi and Nishimura, who were taking up counsellor posts in the new year in Hyōgo and Ibaraki, respectively. No doubt Okada saw in them his own future. He himself went back to his hometown the following day for the first time in two years, now basking in glory.

Desperate to redeem himself after the ignominy of failure the first time, Okada had studied ferociously. It paid off. He passed both sets of exams he took. With outstanding grades, he and Nagai found themselves in a tug-of-war between the Home Ministry and the Ministry of Justice. With their own powers they had opened up a path from private law academies to the Home Ministry bureaucracy, that 'authority among the authorities'. Their trajectories showed that the door to officialdom was opening ever wider.

When viewed in the broader context of constitutional politics, Okada's switch from the judicial to the executive world reveals how far executive government and constitutional politics had come. The life course of Misaki, the head of the bureau of prefectural governance who first invited Okada to the Home Ministry, similarly signalled a world of change. Misaki had graduated from the law school of the University of Tokyo and become a state diplomat before transferring into the Freedom Party. Once Itagaki Taisuke entered the second Cabinet of Itō Hirobumi, Misaki followed him into the regime as a political hire to head the Prefectural Governance Bureau. He was a thoroughgoing partisan politician. His was indeed an era in which more men were traversing back and forth between the worlds of partisan politics and bureaucracy, of legislative and executive government. These new human resources pressed ahead with reform in the state ministries. State officialdom was transforming under the influence of party politics.

The things the oligarchic progeny carried

Men such as Okada, graduates of private law academies with no privileged domainal provenance, had to fight their way up the path to bureaucracy. But it is not as if those who hailed from privileged domainal factions had it much easier. Burdened with heavy expectations from men gone before them, and continually bathing in the harsh light of attention, they found that their privileged provenance became less an asset than an encumbrance.

Such was the case of Chōshū man Kamiyama Mitsunoshin, who passed the second-ever examinations. He was born in the second year of the Meiji reign (= 1869), and went on to graduate in English law before entering the Home Ministry. He eventually became governor of Kumamoto prefecture, a deputy minister of agricultural and commercial affairs and superintendent of Taiwan.[35] Deeply invested in training a new generation, his home region of Yamaguchi had, with its own powers, established in 1886 the third secondary school in the country, after the First High School in Tokyo and the so-called Third High School in Osaka, which was later moved to Kyoto. Kamiyama graduated from the school in Yamaguchi at the top of his class. To the Chōshū faction, which pinned hopes of their future on him, he was a rising star.

The Home Ministry hired Kamiyama immediately after he graduated from university in July 1895 and placed him as an affiliated officer (*zokkan*) in the bureau for prefectural governance. As with other affiliated officers fresh out of university, the Home Ministry did not give him any substantial work, enjoining him first to study for his impending exams. The kinds of benefits lavished on Kamiyama became a source of resentment for men such as Okada, but it was precisely these same benefits that became a heavy burden on men like Kamiyama. How could one fail the exams after having been given such advantages? It was not just Kamiyama's reputation at stake. It was that of Chōshū. Kamiyama eventually passed the exams, and he heard the result in advance of the formal award ceremony. His superiors in the bureaucracy leaked the news to him. He was at last able to let go of the anxieties distressing him. He wrote in his diary, 'I of course did not let myself be overcome by anxieties for the exam, but it isn't as if my mind hasn't now found some ease.'[36]

Another case was that of Tanaka Jirō, who passed his exams in 1898, the year after Okada. Tanaka hailed from Saga, where he was born in 1873. He graduated from the Fifth High School and entered the Imperial University as a student of British law. He graduated from university ranking seventh in his field. With an introduction from alumni, he entered the Ministry of Communications, whose helm he eventually took. He entered the ministry because of its reputation for encouraging young upstarts to study abroad.[37]

Just like Kamiyama, Tanaka began studying for the exams when he first entered the ministry. He lodged in the Ōiso Chōseikan with fellow students such as Shimomura Hiroshi, later head officer of general affairs in the Taiwan governorship and superintendent of the informatics institution (*jōhōin sōsai*). Together, they immersed themselves in study. They were scholars with university degrees, but they could take nothing for granted on the exams. There was precedent of failure for even outstanding men. Two years earlier, Kamino Katsunosuke, later deputy treasury minister, had failed, as did Egi Tasuku, later minister of justice, the year after Kamino. Desperate to avoid such ignominy and fearing that they would have to leave the government if they failed the exams, students plunged into their books. It was precisely because of their propinquity to power that scholars of oligarchic domainal origins felt the full weight of anxiety. Perhaps that was evidence that the exams were being administered fairly.

The depth of their anxieties yielded proportionately great conceit when they passed the exams by their own efforts, won a position in the regime and became professional bureaucrats. After the Russo-Japanese War of 1904 to 1905, almost all administrative posts in the bureaucracy at the level of bureau head and below were filled by men who had passed the state exams. It was these men who carried the future of executive governance. By 1914, the era of the Second Ōkuma Cabinet and the age of party politics, all deputy ministers were men who had passed university exams.

Portraits of the scholar-bureaucrats

One can hardly speak of the bureaucracy of modern Japan without mention of one its most fascinating factions: the Twenty-Eight Group (*ni hachi kai*). The association was not based on shared geographic provenance, as domainal factions were. Nor was it bound together by blood or marital ties, as the Yamagata faction was. It was a clan of men who all graduated in 1895, the twenty-eighth year of the Meiji era. They did not necessarily have the sort of snooty exclusivity characteristic of academic cliques. But more or less all of the Twenty-Eight Group found lofty careers in or near politics. They formed a relatively loose coalition of men with similar thoughts, ideals and points of view.

Figure 4.5 The Twenty-Eight Group's inaugural dinner for Prime Minister Hamaguchi Osachi (centre of the sofa), 1929. *Source:* Nanbara Shigeru et al., eds, *Onozuka Kiheiji*, p. 200.

The Twenty-Eight Group was the first cohort of scholar-bureaucrats to pass through the examination system; what was meant to be the first group, the 1894 graduates, had boycotted the exams. The government ministries welcomed this first batch of talent especially gleefully. And the talented men themselves built up a strong internal web of connections as they competed against and supported one another.

The group was a line-up of distinguished figures in government. From English law there were Kamiyama, whom we have encountered before; Hijikata Hisaakira, later president of the Bank of Japan; Seino Chōtarō, head of the Disaster Recovery Bureau in the Home Ministry; Kawamura Kingorō, deputy of the Imperial Household Ministry; Tadokoro Yoshiharu, deputy education minister; Hagiwara Moriichi, head of the Bureau of Commerce in the Foreign Affairs Ministry before passing on early; Shidehara Kijūrō, ambassador to the United States and prime minister; and Tawara Magoichi, head of the Cabinet Bureau of Colonial Affairs (*naikaku takushokukyoku*).

From French law there was Nishikubo Hiromichi, superintendent of police. From German law there were, most notably, Kubota Kiyochika, deputy home minister; Toyoshima Naomichi, head of the criminal-affairs division of the Court of Cassation (*Daishin'in keijibu*); and Odagiri Iwatarō, governor of Okinawa.

From political science there were Onozuka Kiheiji, chancellor of Tokyo Imperial University; Hamaguchi Osachi, deputy treasury minister and prime minister;

Shimoóka Chūji, deputy home minister and superintendent of executive affairs in the governorship general of Korea; Takano Iwasaburō, professor in the economics department of Tokyo Imperial University; Shōda Kazue, deputy and later head of the treasury ministry; Isawa Takio, superintendent of police; and Sugawara Michiyoshi, deputy treasury minister.

Each remains a symbolic figure in the bureaucracy of modern Japan.

After climbing their way through the bureaucracy, many of these men gained a foothold in politics as members of the Kenseikai or its successor party, the Rikken Minseitō. Hamaguchi Osachi became chair of the party and prime minister. Shidehara Kijūrō became foreign minister in a Kenseikai-Minseitō-led Cabinet and served as a leading proponent of cooperative diplomacy. Shimoóka Chūji and Tawara Magoichi darted from the executive bureaucracy and became Kensekai party officials and members of the House of Representatives affiliated with the Kenseikai. Isawa Takio, Nishikubo Hiromichi and other members of the nobility formed the Dōseikai, a Minseitō faction in the House of Peers that supported the party. There were only a few exceptions amid the overwhelming tilt to the Minseitō: Odagiri Iwatarō joined the House of Representatives as a Seiyūkai partisan, and Shōda Kazue too approached the Seiyūkai towards the end of the Taishō era.

The main reason for this Minseitō orientation lay in Hamaguchi Osachi, who acted as the prime mover of the group and who entered and became active in the Dōshikai, later known as the Kenseikai, the new party founded by Katsura Tarō. But it does not suffice simply to say that members of the group marched behind Hamaguchi and then circled around him in a ring of mutual support. They were bonded by their shared understanding of an ideal constitutional system, an understanding they gained during their university days. They all admired the British model of parliamentary politics.

Hamaguchi Osachi and Onozuka Kiheiji

Two men, Hamaguchi Osachi and Onozuka Kiheiji, battled for the claim as the most distinguished man of the Twenty-Eight Group. Both had graduated at the top of their high school classes, Onozuka at the First Secondary School in Tokyo, Hamaguchi at the Third Secondary School in Kyoto. They met at law school and hit it off immediately, coming and going to one another's dorms to engage in conversation and debate.

Even at the Imperial University College of Law, known as 'the exclusive domain of German legal studies', Onozuka devoted himself to the thought of Mill, Spencer and other English theorists, finding resonance in the constitutionalism and progressivism of Sueoka Seiichi, head of comparative national legal studies.[38] He graduated top of his law school class and received offers from Itō Hirobumi to be his secretary and from Yamagata Aritomo to be a counsellor. He declined both. He was uninterested in the bureaucracy; he liked politics. He even thought about putting himself up for election during his university days as a means of promoting party government. The idea of parliamentary politics had deep roots in his thought.

Hamaguchi had no less political fervour. His senior thesis examined the foundations of British parliamentary government, and it is said that on his official exams he even got into a row with Ikki, an examiner tasked with constitutional studies, over the question of political systems.[39] Onozuka and Hamaguchi parted ways and walked different paths through politics and academia after they graduated, but they maintained ties. When the Kenseikai, Hamaguchi's political party, took a stand in favour of popular elections (*futsū senkyo*), Onozuka supplied the party with theoretical and intellectual undergirding. And when Hamaguchi rose to prime minister, Onozuka lent support from the world of academia as chancellor of Tokyo Imperial University.

The Onozuka-Hamaguchi battle for distinction in the Twenty-Eight Group was dubbed 'First versus Third', after their respective secondary schools. Alumni of the First High School in Tokyo and those of the Third in Kyoto long regarded one another as rivals, fighting to one-up one another. When Onozuka and Hamaguchi entered law school in 1892, men from the first-ever graduating classes of secondary schools in Yamaguchi, Kanazawa and Kumamoto entered with them and hurled themselves into the intellectual competition. Just as the tributary students competed with the honour of their domains on their backs, students at the law school vied to preserve the reputations of their alma maters.

The year before they proceeded to the Imperial University, Hamaguchi and his fellow senior-year high schoolers published the *Seinen shisō*, or a journal for 'the will of youth', later renamed the *Jinshinkai zasshi*.[40] The magazine remains preserved at Kyoto University today, and in it we can find essays and articles by Hamaguchi, Shimo'oka, Isawa and others. The foreword of the publication declared, 'We youth are truly the successors of the founders of the Restoration. We are men who will carry forward the civilization of Japan. We have inherited it from our forebears, and we seek to pass it down to our progeny.' They gushed with the bright ambition of a new generation. With magazines and speech panels as their stage, Hamaguchi and his coterie gained confidence and expertise in their worlds of study.

A new era welcomed these young men. Chronic illness had prevented Sugawara Michiyoshi, for instance, from proceeding straight to university. But the delay serendipitously placed him among the Twenty-Eight Group. Born in 1869 in Miyagi prefecture, Sugawara later reflected on his student days:

> Among all those at university, I was forced to walk the longest path to higher education. I was stuck in school three years beyond what was ordinary. Regardless of whether it was good or bad, because of the delay, I was able to take the first ever higher-level officer exams for graduates of law school. If I had graduated from university just a year or two earlier, I might not have been able to take them. And not just that, the year we graduated was the year the Sino-Japanese War ended. By good fortune, we found ourselves at a time when the prospects of the nation were rising grandly. Because I graduated late, I had the chance to ride the gusting winds of the postwar nation, and looking back, I see how every curse in life really is a blessing.[41]

Members of the Twenty-Eight Group filled the ranks of the regime once the Rikken Dōshikai became the ruling party in Taishō 3 (= 1914) and Ōkuma Shigenobu formed his second Cabinet. Kawamura took the helm of the Imperial Household Ministry; Shimo'oka, the Home Ministry; Hamaguchi, the treasury; and Kamiyama, agricultural and commercial affairs. Together with three deputy ministers, as well as Isawa, who became superintendent of the national police force, the men gathered for a banquet at the residence of Kubota Kiyochika, the governor of Tokyo prefecture. They revelled in their glory, declaring, 'It isn't long before we take the helm of every ministry, school, and bank.'[42] They had trained in professional school together, taken exams together, and climbed the ranks of officialdom together all the way to its summit, vying and competing at every step. And along the way, they had pulled the constitutional state to a point of rule by party politics.

High schoolers in a booming age: Shōda Kazue

How did these rising bureaucrats spend their lives as students? Shōda Kazue, a member of the Twenty-Eight Group, left for posterity a diary of his student life.[43] Through it we witness how the horizon changed as young men entered the boom and bustle following the First Sino-Japanese War.

Figure 4.6 Shōda Kazue, as the department chief in the Ministry of Finance, *c*. 1903. *Source*: Shōda Tatsuo, '*Shōwa' no rirekisho*, Bungei shunjū, 1991, p. 24.

Shōda was born in the ninth month of Meiji 2 (= 1869), in Matsuyama domain. He was the fifth boy in a samurai family. He attended the first middle school of Ehime prefecture before proceeding to the First High School in Tokyo and then the Imperial University School of Law. From there he kept climbing. He entered the Ministry of the Treasury, where he rose to the rank of deputy and then became treasury minister in the cabinets of Terauchi Masatake and Kiyoura Keigo. He was transferred to the helm of the Ministry of Education under the administration of Tanaka Giichi. A childhood friend of navy officer Akiyama Saneyuki and the great haikuist Masaoka Shiki, Shōda, it is said, was responsible for introducing Shiki to Ōhara Kijū, who became Shiki's haiku master. He himself held distinctions as a haikuist.

It was 1886 when Shōda packed up and headed to high school in Tokyo. His life there revolved around the dorm he shared with his buddies from Ehime. Located in Hongō Masago-chō, not far from the secondary school or from the Imperial University, the dorm was the erstwhile residence of writer Tsubouchi Shōyō and had been renovated and expanded for students. It was operated by the Tokiwa Association, a foundation for talented students established by the former owners of the property, the Hisamatsu household, who sought to train students from their domain.

With the dorm as his basis, Shōda spent his student days with Shiki, with other pals from Ehime and with his new classmates. Serving as supervisor of the dorm was Naitō Motoyuki. Naitō managed the teenagers well. He himself hailed from the Matsuyama domain and had studied at the Shōheizaka Academy. After serving as a minor deputy counsellor (*han gon-no-shō-sanji*) in his domain, he transferred to the Ministry of Education as a counsellor and became an educator. The students often gathered around Naitō after dinner and opened talk circles, carrying out meaningful conversations about literature, politics and a range of other fields.

With a recommendation from Shiki, Shōda won an academic sponsorship from the Tokiwa Association. The foundation covered his lodging fees and gave him 7 yen a month for his living expenses; after he entered law school, the stipend was raised to 10 yen a month. He then received another 2 yen a month from his brother living in Gifu. It was an age in which a man could buy 10 kilograms of white rice for about 70 sen. With some 9 yen a month to spare, Shōda lived a cushy student life. But he carefully calculated and recorded all his income and expenditures. It was not for nothing that he ended up in the treasury ministry.

Even with so much spare change, Shōda did not splurge his time and money on the vaudeville theatre and variety shows (*yose, gidayū*) to which his peers regularly flocked. And when his peers went on meandering strolls around town to let off their pent-up energies, Shōda declined and stayed home. He said he 'had his reasons'.

He expended his energies on sports. He obsessed over boating and baseball in his early years of high school. His athletic compulsions might have been to compensate for his frail constitution: he wrote in his journal on the first day of 1890, 'I've been training hard at baseball this winter break. My skills have improved a lot, and at the same time my body has gotten stronger.' Even after he moved on to university, he insisted on practising swordsmanship whenever he returned home. It was not just his body he was training. It was his mind.

Shōda played baseball with Shiki and his hometown buddies. As they played baseball, they played a messenger role, too. Whenever they returned to Matsuyama for winter break, they headed down to the military training grounds to swing a bat or to the harbour to dabble in beach activities. Folks around town saw them and learned about the new, strange things they were doing. They had objectives beyond sports, too. Shōda, Shiki, Akiyama and their gang banded together to form the so-called 'Hometown Crew' (*dōkyōkai*), and whenever they returned home they gave speeches and held panels to inspire younger students.

Fervour for literary and social studies engulfed dorm life back in Tokyo. The Matsuyama kids partook in this new culture. They read everything, from Chinese classics to English literary history. They came and went and talked about books with Onozuka, Tawara and other classmates from high school. They had a political bent, too. Like many of their classmates, they subscribed to the Min'yūsha publications *Kokumin no tomo* and *Kokumin shinbun*, and they frequented lectures and speeches at the Imperial University.

The 1890 general elections for the brand new Imperial Diet sealed their interest in politics. Shōda went to the Diet himself with Suzuki Shigetō, a Diet member and fellow Matsuyama man, as his guide. He observed the Diet in session and was fascinated especially by the ferocious debates that unfolded over budgetary allotment. He became engrossed in thinking about the relationships among the regime, the Diet, citizens and tax collection. He even decided in the last year of secondary school that he wanted to dedicate himself to studying taxation. His passions fanned into flame, he started attending new kinds of lectures, including those by treasury bureaucrats such as Tajiri Inajirō and Soeda Juichi and such heavyweights of the financial world as Shibusawa Eiichi.

Shōda's fascination with taxation became the basis for a more sweeping interest in economics. Almost every month, he went down to Kanda to visit the *kankōba*, a sort of forerunner to department stores in which a range of shops came together to form a collective commercial centre.[44] He would walk around the facility and stop to drink wine or coffee on his way back to his dorm. This was his pleasure in life. He witnessed the scores of people buzzing around Tokyo's shops after the Sino-Japanese-War and gained a visceral sense of the booming economy around him. He combined this first-hand experience with scholarly study of texts, and from there his vision of state finances and political economy expanded. He had found a form of fun even better than the lectures and theatre his friends enjoyed.

College in Tokyo: From the provinces to the capital

Reforms of every part of the national education system, from the lowest levels all the way to university, began with the 1886 Edict on Schools (*gakkōrei*). Primary and secondary schools opened across the country. With the formalization of a clear flow from elementary to middle to high school and then to university, young men across the provinces began to cultivate dreams of studying in Tokyo and of rising autonomously through the world (*risshin shusse*) by learning.

Village leaders fuelled the academic fire of ambitious boys. Erstwhile domainal heavyweights across the country began sponsoring scholarly associations, such as the Tokiwa Association of Matsuyama. These new groups gave ambitious youth the chance to pursue learning at university regardless of whether they were samurai or commoners.

Such developments were especially visible in Yamaguchi prefecture, which had invested in building its own secondary school early on. Yamaguchi native Kamiyama, of the Twenty-Eight Group, graduated top of the first graduating class of the prefectural school. But his family fell on hard times. He wrote, 'My family finances are dwindling quickly, and we've now reached a point where it looks as if achieving my goals will be very difficult.'[45] Just as he tumbled into despair, he was scooped up by the Suō-Nagato Educational Society (*Bōchō kyōikukai*), an association of townsmen founded in time for the graduation of the first class of secondary schoolers. With a fellowship from the Educational Society, Kamiyama was able to move on to the First High School in Tokyo.

As fervour for higher levels of education spread, magazines began printing admissions advice aimed at boys seeking to enrol in high school or military school. By 1888, *Sample Questions and Answers for Secondary School Exams* (*Kōtō chū gakkō nyūgaku shigyō reidai kaitō*), a reference book for secondary school tests, had already been put out by the publisher Keigyōsha. The book covered a sweep of subjects including Japanese, world and United States history; world geography; physics; chemistry; natural history; botany; and zoology. It was marketed as a reliable reference work edited by actual university graduates.

Publications continued to proliferate. From 1890, Shōnen'en publishers printed the *Guide to Studying in Tokyo* (*Tōkyō yūgaku annai*) annually, and from 1901, Sekibundō began printing yearly editions of *The Girls' Guide to Studying in Tokyo* (*Joshi Tōkyō yūgaku annai*), a publication for female students. Diary books assigned to middle schoolers, such as those printed by Kinkōdō and Tokyo Book Publishers (*Tōkyō shoseki shuppan*), regularly included a 'Guide to Schools in Tokyo' as an appendix. The supplement included not only details of curricula and examples of exam questions at various schools but also concrete tips on practical matters such as degree qualifications, guarantors, dealing with illness and political activism. Youth in the provinces read these books and began developing dreams of a capital they had never seen in person.

What drove these students to study? They almost universally cited the opportunity to rise autonomously in the world (*risshin shusse*) that was opened up by academic pursuit. An 1892 text written by Jōnan Isshi and published by Shōbidō, *The Ambitious Youth's Companion* (*Shōnen rishi no tomo*), celebrated tributary students such as Hatoyama Kazuo and Isawa Shūji alongside such founding fathers as Kido Kōin and Saigō Takamori to impress upon youths the necessity of studying hard. Tributary students were indeed the cynosure of youths in the provinces, who sought to ascend to Tokyo, dedicate themselves to learning and make a life for themselves, just as the tributary students did. Another youth publication, *Youth Rising in the World* (*Seinen to risshin shusse*), provided these young men with descriptions of the life courses of the tributary students. The text was written by Watanabe Shūji and published by Daigakukan-kan in 1900.

The concept of 'studying' (*benkyō*) itself, one that persists to this day, took root by the mid-1880s. The lyrics of songs appearing in 'Aogeba tōtoshi', a compilation of elementary school tunes, exhorted children to 'earn a reputation through autonomous will and to work hard'.[46] Dreams of further education merged with passions for rising through the world by autonomous will into a single universe of thought.

Learning and marriage: In pursuit of distinguished progeny

The path of learning led to other destinations, too. In a new age in which people were judged not only by their lineage but by the schools they attended, talented students received frequent offers of adoption or marriage. Distinguished men in the provinces without distinguished progeny began scavenging through the school system to find promising men to adopt or men to whom they could give their daughters. They could spot these young upstarts quite easily in middle school. Then they would throw money at them, enable their further study and fold them into the family after they entered high school or university.

To take two teenagers who had never known or seen each other and clunk them together in a marriage might strike us as rather rash. But to students eager to rise in

Figure 4.7 Hamaguchi Osachi (right) and his family, *c.* 1905. *Source:* Amago Todomu, *Heimin saishō Hamaguchi Osachi,* Hōbunkan, 1930, front page.

the world, it was hardly a bad idea. In the Edo era, it was often second- or third-born sons who dedicated themselves to academic pursuits. These men were not direct heirs to their fathers. Study replaced inheritance as their means to a good future. Because academic success thus led young men out of their lineages, often households were left without successive generations of academic achievement. Folding a talented young man into a family became an easy, instant way of resolving this problem.

A case in point was Hamaguchi Osachi. He was born the third son of the Mizuguchi household in Godaisan, an outskirt of Kōchi. After his father left to work as a forester, his eldest brother, fourteen years his senior, took the helm of the household and entered into the service of the Kōchi prefectural government. His second brother, six years older than he, then became principal of the Kōchi Third Middle School (*Kōchi daisan chūgakkō*) and gained renown as one of the most outstanding educators in the prefecture. Raised in a privileged environment where Chinese studies reigned, Osachi himself earned stellar grades and entered middle school in Kōchi.

A rather subdued, understated child, Osachi went largely unnoticed during his earliest days of middle school. But he gradually distinguished himself. He commuted the 6 kilometres between Godaisan and his middle school tirelessly. In his third year, he earned full marks in ethics, English, history, botany, calligraphy and physical education and over 90 points in all subjects except for physics. He skipped to the fifth year. It did not take long for his neighbours to hear word of an exceptional kid who had just jumped a year.

Osachi caught the eye of Hamaguchi Yoshinari, a man of samurai heritage in Tamura town, Aki district (*gun*), some 50 kilometres north-east of Godaisan. Yoshinari descended from a long lineage of some eighteen known generations, but his own two sons died young. He was left without an heir. His one daughter performed prodigiously in elementary school and proceeded to the Kōchi Girls' Normal School (*Kōchi joshi shihan*). She bore exceptional talent, and Yoshinari wanted to find her a similarly exceptional husband.

Unconstrained by Tamura town lines, Yoshinari extended his search for a good son all the way into the city of Kōchi. He heard of a certain young Osachi, a boy who had stood out from the pack of kids at his middle school, who carried a gentlemanly comportment and who excelled in both physical and artistic pursuits. Yoshinari made his advances. Persuaded, Osachi married into the Hamaguchi family after graduating from middle school.

Newly wed, Osachi went on to the Third High School in Osaka and the College of Law in Tokyo on funds he acquired from the Hamaguchi household. He then entered the Ministry of Finance, passed the higher-level entrance exams and took up posts in Yamagata and Matsue. By the time he returned to the treasury in Tokyo as a secretarial officer in 1897, Yoshinari had passed on. No doubt he departed in peace.

University students and high school students: Interactions through magazines

High schoolers in the provinces saw their own ideal future selves in the image of university students standing at the entryway to new learning and new careers. Like Shōda, university students returned home in the summers and spread baseball, lecture gatherings and other fads they picked up in Tokyo. They regaled high schoolers with tales of college. High schoolers listened, mesmerized. The two groups developed deep bonds. When middle and high schoolers went on strike, for instance, solicitous college students would even return home to help mediate.

Magazines functioned as an important link between university students and youths back home. Not simply generic journals, the magazines were specialized publications for students and alumni of specific middle or high schools. An example is the aforementioned *Seinen shisō* of the Third High School. University students packed such publications with new information, whetting the imaginations of those following in their footsteps.

Magazines provided forums in which high schoolers could ask questions and receive answers about their academic trajectories. In the thirteenth edition of *Shōshikai Magazine*, for instance, which was the publication for the alumni association of the Sendai Second High School, a student asked whether he should major in law or in politics to secure a good future.[47] A reply came from Inoue Junnosuke, a graduate of the same school, then a student in English law at the Imperial University Law School and later president of the Bank of Japan and treasury minister.

Inoue sent back two letters. In the first, while denying that he was trying to win talent over to his own preferred discipline, he argued that politics and economics, both subsumed at the time under political science, were disperse, inchoate fields compared to law. He recommended that the inquiring student pursue legal studies. In his second letter, he provided concrete scenarios. Becoming a professional scholar was difficult regardless of whether one studied law or politics. If students wanted to become bureaucrats, they needed knowledge of law, and if they aimed at a rank of bureau head or higher, they needed knowledge of politics and economics as well. If they wanted to enter the private sector, they could attain posts of considerable distinction regardless of which field they studied.

Kyoto Imperial University was established in Meiji 32 (= 1899). Just a year after its founding, the pages of the *Shōshikai Magazine* turned into a battleground between students at Kyoto Imperial University and those at Tokyo Imperial University, now renamed from just 'Imperial University'. The two camps vied to recruit talent to their respective schools. Kyoto students in particular, relative latecomers, pitched hard. They boasted, 'because [our] professors are by and large rising stars who have just circled through the West, they can more than hold their ground against Tokyo professors'; they flaunted the fact that their 'professors work exclusively at the university, and so they are particularly solicitous and kind toward students'.

But Kyoto students could not but acknowledge that they were at a marked disadvantage on the higher-level exams. They lacked the connections of their Tokyo rivals with examiners and with regnant academic theories. They wrote, 'In short, on the written portion, and especially on subjects like constitutional law, it is particularly difficult to pass the exams for higher-level officers. Our theories are vastly different from theirs. If your only goal is just to pass the exams, then indeed we think that going to Tokyo University is the safe choice.'

High schoolers in every age watch and mimic university students. This age was no different. The fad in this day was oratory. After the inauguration of the Diet, 'mock

Diets' spread across schools. The Second High School, for instance, held its first mock Diet session in 1893. Later, after a three-year interruption, it began holding mock sessions every year. The mock Diet became an arena for students to try out their skills. Students would send in their own mock bills for deliberation and review. At first the bills reflected the immediate concerns of students: 'Proposed legislation for exemptions from conscription for graduates of the Imperial University'; 'Proposal for the establishment of Tōhoku University'. But as time passed, they increasingly reflected the actual political world: 'Bill on religion'; 'Electoral reform for the House of Representatives'; 'Proposal to adopt the Roman alphabet as the national script'. Students were becoming more sophisticated.

Roles in the mock Diet evolved, too. At first there were only a chairman, ministers and representatives. But soon political camps began to appear: government committee members, secretarial officers and officers of the Freedom, Progressive and Imperial parties (*Jiyūtō, Shinpotō, Teikokutō*), including chief party minister (*innai sōri*) and general affairs committee members (*sōmu iin*). The boys were punctilious in their mimicry. Students in English law acted as Freedom Party officials; those in German law worked as Imperial Party strongmen. It was this era that reared the young men who went on to uphold Taishō democracy.

--

Thus it was that professional education took shape at Japan's universities, that the regime installed an exam employment system for its bureaucrats and that across the provinces of the nation young men rose up, striving to make a life for themselves through learning and government employment. If Ōkuma's was the generation to build the structures of the bureaucracy, then this was a new generation, one that put those structures to work, one that applied human talent within newly installed government systems.

Japan, the nation-state, suddenly became something much bigger after the First Sino-Japanese and Russo-Japanese wars. The roles and responsibilities of the government expanded accordingly. New men emerged: a generation of exceptional talent participating in state politics, a generation of human resources upholding the executive government, a generation that most of all embodied the spiritual mandate of the Charter Oath that all citizens pursue their calling. These men seized on the chance to exercise the fullness of their talents at the very heart of the state.

The Age of Constitutional Government: From Oligarch-Bureaucrats to Scholar-Bureaucrats, 1890s–1910s

The inauguration of the Meiji Constitution in 1889 and the opening of the Imperial Diet in 1890 culminated the era of constitutional striving, an era that had sought to lay down the foundational designs of Japanese governance. Now began a new era, an age of constitutional government, a time to set new systems of politics to work. About a quarter of a century had elapsed since the Meiji Restoration. Japanese politics began anew. Achievement followed achievement, as if the vigour of the Restoration era had been regained. These accomplishments gave rise to the Seiyūkai cabinet of Hara Kei in 1918, the first genuine party cabinet, as it is known.

Even as politicians from the oligarchy continued to wield influence during the run-up to party rule and responsible cabinets, genuine party politicians, too, gained power. The division of authority ordained by the Meiji Constitution yielded still other kinds of politicians, such as those from the military and those from the bureaucracy. From this perspective, Japanese party politics arose from the creativity of and from competition among politicians from the parties, politicians from the bureaucracy and bureaucrats already serving in official posts.

In this competition lay ferocious desire for and shattered dreams of political power. As a result of both, new alliances formed between politicians and bureaucrats seeking the mantle of authority. In this chapter, let us examine, against the backdrop of evolving political contingencies, the processes that led from the early days of the constitutional polity to the rise of party politics.

The Waihan administration of Ōkuma and Itagaki: Bureaucracy and the first party cabinet

The limits of oligarchic rule: A structure for passing the buck

The approach of the opening of the Imperial Diet dramatically transformed the cabinet system, which had emerged at the centre of the constitutional system as an organ with both responsibilities and powers. The system began as one described with the term 'powers of the cabinet' (*naikaku shokken*), in which state ministers were subject to the overbearing power of the prime minister, or to what we might call 'grand chancellorism' (*dai saishō shugi*). The system changed into one of 'officers of the cabinet' (*naikaku kansei*) who operated on the principle of equality among the various government ministers (*kakuryō byōdō shugi*).[1]

The change originated in the collapse of the Cabinet of Kuroda Kiyotaka in 1889, which had followed that of Itō Hirobumi in 1888 and then disintegrated because of deep disputes over the question of treaty revision. Since the Restoration, domainal-factionalist oligarchs had ruled alongside a powerful prime minister in a coherent system, but cracks appeared between the two sides under Kuroda. Voices calling for a re-evaluation of the powers of the prime minister began to swell.[2]

Another factor contributed to the change. The original system of Cabinet powers (*naikaku shokken*) had placed Cabinet ministers under the authority of the prime minister. But this system existed in potential contradiction with Article 55 of the Meiji Constitution, which held that government ministers must serve autonomously as aides to the Emperor (*tandoku hohitsu*).[3] Faced with this problem, the Cabinet seized on the opportunity presented by the collapse of the Kuroda administration to diminish the overriding powers of the prime minister, to make all state ministers equal in rank and to transform the Cabinet into a deliberative council made up of the head officers of the executive state.

The prime minister was designated the chair of this new council of equals, but even so, the Cabinet lacked a necessary authority who could unify it. It faced another complication, too. In the proposal papers (*sōgi*) they had each submitted with the inauguration of the new system of cabinet officers (*naikaku kansei*), the state ministers had called for a principle of unanimity to guide the internal functioning of the Cabinet. The Cabinet somehow had to ensure both the independence of each ministry of the executive state and the unanimity of the members of the Cabinet. The two goals contradicted each other, and this contradiction generated a structural flaw wherein obstacles to reform easily led to mass resignations. The prime ministership thus became a cumbersome post with paltry powers and ponderous responsibilities. Every time another Cabinet dissolved, cabinet ministers tried to dump the post on one another. The problem became not who would become the prime minister but who had the capacity to take on the role.

For the first seven cabinets until the third administration of Itō Hirobumi in 1898, the Satsuma and Chōshū factions alternated in posting one of their men as prime minister. It was a system premised on the equilibrium of power at which factionalist oligarchic forces in the regime had arrived. This arrangement succeeded in sustaining harmony among the powers behind the Meiji Restoration, and it indeed resulted from the reality that the prime ministership continued to be a profoundly undesirable position until after the dissolution of the oligarchic balance of power. There had emerged here a structure of governance in which men in the administration monopolized power but continually shifted responsibilities onto one another.

As long as the opposition popular parties and their demands for tax reduction acted as a common cabinet enemy, the system worked. Forces within the Cabinet managed to maintain a united front. But circumstances changed when the oligarchs and the popular parties began to link arms after the outbreak of the First Sino-Japanese War in 1894. Their increased collaboration succeeded in smoothing the functioning of the Diet, but as members of the parties began to enter the Cabinet, the fate of a given administration began to fall under partisan sway.

January 1898 was a case in point. The second Cabinet of Matsukata Masayoshi was ruling in alliance with the Progressive Party, or Shinpotō, of Ōkuma Shigenobu. As soon as the Matsukata Cabinet tried to raise land taxes to finance mounting costs after the Sino-Japanese War, the Shinpotō responded with fierce resistance.[4] Forced into mass resignation, the Cabinet collapsed. Itō Hirobumi was entrusted with forming a successor cabinet. He sought to break through the impasse by appointing cabinet ministers from both the Freedom Party, or Jiyūtō, and the Shinpotō. But with elections coming up soon, the two parties decided not to cooperate. Itō dissolved the House of Representatives (*Shūgiin*). The parties responded by forming a grand alliance in opposition to tax increases, and they merged to form a new party, the Constitutional Government Party, or the Kenseitō. Ōkuma and Itagaki took the presidency (*sōsai*) of the new party.

Calls mounted among oligarchic elements to suspend the Constitution and push through with tax increases independent of the Diet, but Itō had his eyes further down the horizon.[5] If the state and the parties did not cooperate, the entire system of constitutional government would cease to function. With this concern in mind, Itō broke the precedent of alternating between Satsuma and Chōshū prime ministers. He called for the Emperor to ordain that Ōkuma and Itagaki, heads of the new Kenseitō, form a new cabinet.

The first party cabinet in Japanese history, the first Ōkuma administration, was thus formed on 30 June 1898. Ōkuma held a dual post as prime minister and foreign minister, and Itagaki served as home minister. The Cabinet is commonly known as the Waihan Cabinet, a name formed by combining characters from the names of Ōkuma and Itagaki.

Bureaucrats and the first party cabinet

The formation of a party cabinet rattled the world of bureaucracy, which had spent long years under the influence of oligarchs. Yamagata Aritomo quipped, 'at long last, the edifice of the Meiji regime has fallen and been replaced with a party cabinet', but the words might as well have been those of any of the oligarch-bureaucrats, who had spent the years since the rise of the Popular Rights Movement butting heads with popular parties across the country. To the oligarchs, the change in power represented ignominious defeat.

Many state officials quit the government rather than sully themselves with service under a vile party regime. The higher the rank of the official, the more sharply he felt disinclined against partisan politics. Resignations swept widely from deputy ministers (*jikan*) all the way to the governors of the prefectures. The renegade officials did not expect the new cabinet to last long. Imagining a future when they would regain the posts they surrendered, they thought that they could wait it out until the oligarchs returned to power.

But then there were other bureaucrats, men who interpreted things differently, who saw in the rise of a party cabinet the dawn of a new form of rule. These were the scholar-bureaucrats who had graduated from the newly formed national university.

One such scholar-bureaucrat was Mizuno Rentarō. He had held posts in the First Bank (*Dai'ichi ginkō*) and the Ministry of Commercial and Agricultural Affairs before entering the Home Ministry and becoming one of its central members. Unlike the oligarch-bureaucrats, who were transfixed on the radicalist image of the popular parties that had emerged during the Popular Rights Movement, Mizuno had gained a new impression of the parties. That impression came from his association with leaders of the Jiyūtō, the Freedom Party, when he served as a secretary for Home Minster Itagaki in the Second Cabinet of Itō Hirobumi.[6] Mizuno realized that bureaucrats could never hope to build a constitutional polity supported by the citizenry without any contact or common ground with the masses at large.

Behind this thinking was what Mizuno had learned at university. He had studied British law, and he took the two-party British system as a model for constitutional states. He had grown fed up with the endless stand-offs between the state and the Diet during the earliest years of the Japanese parliamentary system. Could they not learn to get along? In the emergence of the first party cabinet, he found reason to believe that rancour could finally yield to collaboration.

Other bureaucrats even entered the political parties while still occupying their official governmental posts. One such official was Soeda Juichi, a Fukuoka man who graduated from Tokyo University in 1884 and became head of the Budget Bureau (*shukeikyoku*) of the Ministry of the Treasury. After the resignation of Tajiri Inajirō, deputy treasury minister, Soeda was sought out as the new treasury deputy in the Waihan administration. Soeda had the option of declining the post and falling on the same sword on which his oligarchic seniors had fallen. But Soeda seized on the promotion. And not only that, he decided to enter the Constitutional Government Party (*Kenseitō*) himself while serving as deputy minister. The act of entering a political party while still in bureaucratic service sent shockwaves across the regime, not least among the oligarchs. Vitriol was heaped on Soeda. He was accused of being dazzled by the glitz of a position as a deputy.

The employment of Soeda arose less from his individual will than from negotiations between the Constitutional Government Party and the Ministry of the Treasury.[7] The entirety of the upper echelons of the treasury ministry had signalled that it would resign once the Waihan Cabinet came to power. But Matsuda Masahisa, a former member of the Freedom Party who became the Waihan treasury minister, realized he could not overcome the revenue deficit facing the ministry without support from treasury bureaucrats. He tried to persuade the men not to resign.[8] Receiving a Matsuda olive branch, the treasury executives gathered together to plan their response. They decided to call for the promotion of Soeda, head of the leading division of the ministry, to deputy minister. Their demand was accepted. Now in cooperation with the party cabinet, the Ministry of the Treasury succeeded in implementing large-scale increases in indirect taxes.

Why, then, did Soeda take the plunge into party politics? He did so because of the demands of Ōkuma and his band, who viewed the post of deputy minister as part of the central administration. Other deputies in other ministries, men such as Tajiri, had rebuffed Ōkuma and resigned. But Soeda decided to play along. No doubt he calculated that joining the Constitutional Government Party himself would help the interests of the ministry as a whole.

And Soeda saw the rise of the Waihan Cabinet as an opportunity to transform national politics in general, not just a chance to further the interests of the treasury ministry. If the parties gained experience in actually governing, they would evolve away from their irresponsible position of relentless criticism and would develop into subjects of serious policy debates geared to reality. Soeda believed that if this maturation occurred, then the regime could avoid conflicts between the executive and legislative branches and finally break through the endless changes of administrative control and the political and administrative stagnation that those changes wrought.[9]

At first, scholar-bureaucrats such as Soeda had been deemed rich in practical skills but lacking in drive and spirit, for they had emerged onto the political scene after the rise of the constitutional order; they did not have the experience of upheaval and change that the Restoration bureaucrats did. But unlike the oligarchic bureaucrats, who viewed constitutionalism as just a means of rule, the scholar-bureaucrats viewed it as a principle of the modern nation-state. They sought to transcend the binary model of oligarchs or party politicians, and, envisioning a future of collaboration between the executive and legislative branches, they set about building a foundation for a new order. To the scholar-bureaucrats, the rise of the party cabinet signalled the first steps towards a new form of governance.

Itō Hirobumi directed the transition to this new mode of rule. After Itō recommended Ōkuma and Itagaki to the Emperor as his successors in the Cabinet, he summoned the two politicians and carefully explained to them the necessity of cooperating with the bureaucracy.[10] Having now seized the helm of power, the parties needed to reach over to and make compromises with the bureaucracy. They needed to increase understanding and appreciation in the bureaucracy of the nature of party rule. The transition to party cabinets followed the formation of a professional bureaucracy as a means of establishing the legitimacy of the new constitutional system, he explained.

To scholar-bureaucrats envisioning cooperation between the executive and legislative branches, the greatest enemy of the day was the old regime, the oligarchic forces that sought to thwart the professionalization of the executive branch. Ten years had elapsed since the inauguration of the probationary employment system, and state posts all the way up to heads of ministry bureaux (*kyokuchō*) had now been populated with scholar-bureaucrats. But posts from deputy minister (*jikan*) up remained monopolized by oligarch-bureaucrats from the domainal factions. Many among the oligarch-bureaucrats resented the specialized skills of the scholar-bureaucrats.

Suspicions lurked, too, that men with relations with the domainal-factionalist oligarchs had an advantage in getting promotions. Scholar-bureaucrats came from all across the nation, but some claimed that there were discrepancies based on place of origin in how bureaucrats climbed the state ladder.

Mori Masataka, for instance, a bureaucrat in the Home Ministry who hailed from Yamagata prefecture, had grievances. Born in 1866, he graduated in French law and was hired through the Probationary Employment system. In a letter to Mizuno Rentarō, a fellow Tōhoku man, he vented his concerns: 'Men like us from Mutsu and Dewa domains, men who have no domainal-oligarchic ties – no matter how hard we work, other folks end up stealing credit for our exertions, and [the blame for] errors then gets thrown on our shoulders, and then there's more. The employment of personnel really is nothing more than a form of cruelty towards the weak.'[11] To men like him from origins outside the oligarchy, the rise of party cabinets and the elimination of the oligarchic bureaucracy provided an opportunity to escape perennial mistreatment.

Ten years had come and gone since the rise of the government examination system and the founding of the Imperial University. The state bureaucracy had been revamped and readied for further change. In their young, susceptible days, scholar-bureaucrats had encountered the Popular Rights Movement and pursued legal or political studies with dreams of parliamentary politics. Once the road to government was opened to them, they brought about a sea change in the mentality of the regime and consolidated the foundations of rule by party politics.

Spoils or talent?

Unlike the oligarchic forces in the state, popular opinion welcomed the rise of the party cabinet. Moderate newspapers joined the papers of the political parties in hailing the change as a sign of progress in constitutional government. Now curiosity came to focus on how the party cabinet would actually run the government. Would the popular parties, until now mere broken records demanding tax reduction and opposing the regime, be able to run a state over which they had taken control? People had both expectations and anxieties.

The oligarch-bureaucrats, not least of them Yamagata Aritomo, feared that the new government would revise the constitution and formally recognize a parliamentary cabinet system (*giin naikaku sei*), creating a structure wherein the regime would be dominated by the Diet. The oligarchy foreboded that, if such a Belgian-style constitutional parliamentary system were to be inaugurated, then the sort of populism overrunning Spain or Greece at the time would overcome Japan, policy would become subject to the whims of a mercurial public and the entire state would deteriorate irrevocably.[12]

But the Meiji Constitution was a document bestowed by the Emperor onto his subjects (*kintei kenpō*), and it was the Emperor who reserved the right to propose amendments to it. He had heeded a recommendation from Itō Hirobumi and called on Ōkuma and his band to form a cabinet, but it is not as if he trusted these new rulers. He viewed them with suspicion. To persuade an unsympathetic Emperor to support amendments to the Constitution posed a formidable challenge for Ōkuma and his team. It was more practical to try to engage with the executive state directly and pursue reform in that way. They calculated that they could make party politics a reality in the process of running the government even without making systemic or structural changes to the state.

The ultimate sovereign of the state was the Emperor, and it was through his bidding that cabinets could be formed – this basic premise of government did not change, regardless of whether the oligarchs or the parties held control of the Cabinet. What Ōkuma and his band could do in these circumstances was to stress that, unlike the oligarchs, who formed 'irresponsible cabinets' that splintered easily and ended frequently in mass resignation, the parties could form responsible cabinets held together by unity of political opinion.

In their first step towards party politics, members of the Waihan administration took their ministerial posts without vacating their party affiliations, flaunting the fact that theirs was a party cabinet. Protocol up to this point had dictated that official state posts be filled by impartial, non-partisan men. The Waihan Cabinet disavowed this system. All new ministers who entered the Cabinet or the state bureaucracy from the Constitutional Government Party retained their party affiliations. They thus tacitly declared the advent of a cabinet by party rule.

The regime next reconfigured its relations with the bureaucracy. Prime Minister Ōkuma announced a clear distinction between political officers (*seimukan*) and administrative officers (*jimukan*). He committed to ensuring that administrative officers retained their posts under a new regime as long as they did not oppose the efforts of a new cabinet. The designation 'political officer' descended from the 'partisan officers' (*seitōkan*) Ōkuma proposed during the 1881 political crisis and whom he tasked with political roles; that of "administrative officer" (*jimukan*) descended from the 'permanent officers' (*eikyūkan*), who were intended to ensure continuity in the executive state. By thus distinguishing between political and administrative officers, the Waihan administration signalled that decision-making on matters of policy remained in the hands of the political leadership, even as it made clear its intent to cooperate with the administrative and executive officers under its helm.

The question here lay in the permissible scope of political appointments. According to the proposal of 1881, deputy ministers as well as heads of principal ministerial bureaux would be political officers. As explained previously, most bureau heads had been elevated to the rank of *chokunin* officer. The change was intended to provide better benefits for and to secure more posts for a burgeoning number of bureaucrats. Because there were no qualification-based restrictions for the hiring of *chokuninkan*, there was flexibility in their appointment; the Cabinet could select personnel as it pleased.

This freedom to make appointments was supposed to allow for an effective hiring system. But in fact it was this very freedom that posed problems. It permitted party members with no previous connections to officialdom to lead personal appointment campaigns and lobby to get themselves hired. The Waihan administration filled the posts of minister and deputy minister, the latter of which connected ministers to their ministries, with party men. But to the extent possible it sought to keep the men already sitting in bureau-head posts (*kyokuchō*) in their seats without replacing them with party men. The foremost piece of advice Itō had lent to the Waihan leaders was to cooperate with the executive state and, indeed, that was the principle on which the Cabinet was operating.

But in direct opposition to the expectations of the ruling administration, the rank and file of the party ramped up their post-hunting campaigns. Hordes of lobbyists began descending on Tokyo and swarming party headquarters while members of the Diet campaigned hard to land appointed posts. Supporters from their hometowns sought to help them snag new jobs, and Diet members scurried about to help land bankrupt relatives cushy posts in the officialdom. The party membership, meanwhile, swelled with new entrants hungry for a piece of the new bureaucratic pie. Shirase Nobu, for instance, later known for his exploration of Antarctica but at the time a second lieutenant (*shōi*) in the army reserves, sent Ōkuma a résumé with the words

'MEMBER OF THE KENSEITŌ' scrawled in huge letters on the front. He wanted a post at the helm of a prefectural subdivision of Hokkaido.

The Constitutional Government Party, still a hodgepodge, failed as an organization to manage the frenetic post-hunting that followed the first real administrative change of power in Japanese history. This organizational failure allowed members of the party to begin directly lobbying state ministers. Ministers became overwhelmed by the situation. At this critical juncture immediately after the formation of a new cabinet, the administration came to a standstill.

The Waihan Cabinet ended up populating close to sixty posts, including those of the deputy ministers, with party men. Even while promulgating the ideal of a responsible cabinet, the regime filled state ranks with men of vested interests who had lobbied for their posts. The popular-opinion honeymoon ended. The masses hurled vituperation at the regime. And bureaucrats themselves, expecting a total revamping of the government after the fall of the oligarchic regime, let out a long sigh as they witnessed how the oligarchs were simply replaced by other men with vested interests.

Constructive personnel employment, vested personnel employment

But the Cabinet was not so unprincipled as popular opinion made it out to be. Two processes were unfolding simultaneously. Feeding the vested interests of party officials occurred together with the positive construction of a system of responsible cabinets. Let us embark from the latter development.

The Waihan Cabinet regarded the deputy ministers as central figures in the construction of a responsible cabinet. Hoping to inculcate in them consciousness as party members but seeking also to have them retain their posts in the bureaucracy, the Cabinet sought to persuade sitting deputy ministers to join the ruling party. But the deputies were already powerful oligarchic bureaucrats. Suspicious of the rising influence of partisan politics, the deputies flocked out of the government.

Faced with these resignations, Ōkuma and his band filled all minister and deputy minister posts with party members and placed a deliberative council made up of these men at the centre of a new model of administrative rule. By establishing this new policy-making body, they hoped to cut across the various ministries and break through government sectionalism. Now all minister and deputy minister positions in all departments, except for those of the army and navy, were populated by men from the Constitutional Government Party. The deputy treasury minister was a former bureau head who was promoted and then joined the party.

Party men acceded to *chokunin* counsellor (*sanjikan*) posts in the foreign, treasury, education, agricultural-commercial and communications ministries, too. The counsellors (*sanjikan*) were the brains of the ministries, responsible for matters relating to laws and ordinances (*hōrei jikō*). Many were outstanding scholars of notable talent. Unlike intra-ministerial conference bodies (*shōgi*) today, the deliberative bodies made up by the counsellors, known as the Conferences of Counsellors (*sanjikan kaigi*), were not formal institutions, but they nonetheless took up substantive policy- and decision-making tasks in each ministry. The *chokuninkan* posts marked the summit of the hierarchy of counsellors. By filling these positions with partisan talent, the Ōkuma regime could build close links between the party and the executives ministries and work through these personnel to instil in the ministries a deeper understanding of and a cooperative outlook towards the party cabinet. The counsellors thus functioned as crucial human resources who could help the party regime gain command over the executive ministries. Through the Conference of Ministers and Deputies at the level of the Cabinet and the Conferences of Counsellors within executive ministries, Ōkuma and his regime set up structures for decision-making indispensable to the development of a responsible cabinet.

The regime most glaringly betrayed its vested interests in the appointment of bureau heads and local and provincial officers. The party government seized control over a range of posts that had once functioned as bulwarks against partisan activity, including that of the head of the Prefectural Governance Bureau (*kenchikyoku*) in the Home Ministry, later renamed the Provincial Affairs Bureau (*chihōkyoku*); that of the head of the Public Security Bureau (*keihokyoku*); the police superintendence (*keishi sōtoku*); and the posts of the governors (*kenchiji*) and heads of police (*keibuchō*) in the provinces. In the increasing latitude for partisanship it gave itself, we can discern a regime scheming to expand its party base. Many erstwhile members of the Freedom Party who had controlled the Home Ministry gained appointments. A range of other official positions with powers of authorization (*kyoninka kengen*) were filled with members of the Constitutional Government Party, including the positions of the head of the Supervisory Bureau of the Ministry of the Treasury (*kantokukyoku*); the Hokkaido and public works (*dobokukyoku*) bureaux of the Home Ministry; the bureaux of agricultural affairs, of fisheries and of forestry in the Ministry of Agricultural and Commercial Affairs; and the Railway Bureau of the Ministry of Communications.

This was an era in which Hokkaido marked the frontier of national development. Ever since Kuroda Kiyotaka served as head of the Hokkaido Development Commission, Kagoshima men like him had dominated development posts on the island and held a firm grip on concessions and rights there. The Waihan Cabinet came in and swept their oligarchic interests away. It appointed Sugita Teiichi, a leading figure in the erstwhile Freedom Party, as head of the Hokkaido governorship, and it ejected all those with oligarchic connections from positions of prefectural and subprefectural authority. It filled their vacated seats with members of the Freedom Party.

From here, members of the Constitutional Government Party, whether of Freedom Party or Progressive Party (*Shinpotō*) provenance, flocked to Hokkaido to swarm over concessions in the development projects or railroads. Party politics had felled the oligarchic government, but now it was the members of the parties who seized the chance to plunder interests in Hokkaido. They did not stop to look over their shoulders at the path that had led them there.

Reforming structures of rule: Strengthening the functioning of the Cabinet

The image of party members racing about to seize political posts and win economic concessions punctured the aura of anticipation around the rise of party cabinets. The regime could find no other means of repairing its damaged reputation other than by producing real results.

Reforming structures of rule became the primary means by which the regime could prove itself. Ōkuma and his team set up an ad hoc committee in the Cabinet for research on political affairs. Made up of the deputy ministers, the committee called for ministers themselves to attend its meetings, indicating an intent to carry out sweeping reform. All members of the committee, with the exception of members from the army and navy, came from the parties. The new organization piqued the interest of public opinion and helped the Waihan Cabinet enter a stage of visible reform, overcoming the convulsions of its earliest days.

Founded on 13 July 1898, the investigating committee had deliberated on no fewer than sixty bills by 4 September.[13] Proposals ranged from general measures for managing the government to specific ideas such as the simplification of administrative procedures for state documents, the elimination and merging of ministry bureaux and divisions and the dissolution of the District System (*gunsei*). Some proposals called for the eradication of political appointments to the state and even of the police department (*keishichō*) and the Ministry of Justice, which had butted heads with the popular parties. Still other proposals demanded total reform of the appointment of civil officers in the bureaucracy. The bills swept broadly in range and delved deep in their intended reforms.

The deliberations of the committee centred primarily on how to build a structure of rule that would enable standardized policy-making across the regime. The discussions aimed at overcoming two problems: first, the principle of dividing spheres of government authority (*buntan kanri gensoku*), which enabled sectionalism, and second, the principle ordained in clause 55 of the Constitution stating that each cabinet minister had to operate independently (*tandoku hohitsu*), a system that impeded Cabinet unity.

The committee proposed that individual ministries retain their administrative capabilities and specializations, but that power to make decisions and call for systematic adjustments to the government as a whole be concentrated in the Cabinet. To make the plan work, first the Cabinet itself had to function more effectively. The Waihan administration placed Taketomi Tokitoshi, a man of outstanding personal and intellectual qualities, formerly of the Progressive Party, who was close to Ōkuma, as head of the cabinet secretariat (*naikaku shokikan chō*), and it established the office of the prime minister (*shushō kantei*) as a space for carrying out the general coordination of the state. Up to this point, decision-making had largely occurred in the personal domiciles or official residences of influential ministers. Moving these processes to the office of the prime minister strengthened the centripetal forces of the Cabinet. The regime further placed former Progressive Party (*Shinpotō*) man Kōmuchi Tomotsune at the head of the Legislation Bureau (*hōseikyoku*), where he had already accumulated rich executive experience, and it added more counsellors (*sanjikan*) under his helm. Together, Kōmuchi and his underlings engaged in general management of the regime through their work screening laws and ordinances (*hōrei shinsa*). They functioned as the brains of the Cabinet.

If these auxiliary institutions were thus shored up, all the regime had to do was to solidify a space for general coordination of the government. The prime minister had no substantive powers to coordinate the state, and the Constitution decreed that all state ministers function independently and separately, as we have seen. Under these circumstances, it made sense for any necessary adjustments in coordinating the state to be made at the level of administration, before the Cabinet undertook its deliberations.

The committee therefore called for the establishment of a Conference of Cabinet Counsellors (*naikaku sanjikan kaigi*), which would function as a consultative organ that would deliberate on affairs before they reached the Cabinet. The deputy ministers and *chokunin* counsellors (*chokunin sanjikan*) of each ministry were appointed as cabinet counsellors. The conference they formed met the day before the Cabinet itself met. They gathered in the Cabinet Chamber, carried out whatever coordination measures were necessary and submitted what they had accomplished to the Cabinet the following day. Deputy ministers and *chokunin* counsellors thus continued to hold specialized knowledge of their own particular ministries, but their new affiliation with the Cabinet helped bring them together and break through sectionalism. And in the event that the Conference of Cabinet Counsellors failed to take adequate measures to ensure the unity of the state, cabinet ministers were prepared to take steps in their stead. It was a carefully thought-out blueprint that enabled a range of styles of reform, whether they emerged from gradual adjustments, vague strategies or decisions from influential political leaders.

With the rise of the Conference of Cabinet Counsellors, the erstwhile Conference of Counsellors (*sanjikan kaigi*) of each ministry was dissolved. Apart from one *chokunin* counselor who held a political post, all its members were redeployed as administrative officers (*jimukan*). By restricting all decision-making functions to the cabinet ministers, their deputies and *chokunin* counsellors, the regime clearly distinguished between 'political affairs' (*seimu*), the realm of politics, and 'administrative affairs' (*jimu*), the realm of practical executive administration.

The political upheaval of 1881 had indicated a need for a division between party officials (*seitōkan*) and permanent officials (*eikyūkan*) based on how members of the government were appointed, either by political favour or by qualifications. The new emerging arrangement reconfigured this division along a distinction between administrative and political affairs. The reforms aimed at a division of government functions: professional bureaucrats would make proposals, and the Cabinet would be entrusted with making decisions and amending those proposals.

The proactive structural reform measures advanced by the ad hoc investigating committee were in fact the same proposals once put forth by former members of the Progressive Party (*Shinpotō*). Chased out of the regime after the schism of 1881, these men, the 'original bureaucrats' from before the inauguration of the constitutional system, regarded themselves as experts in their areas of policy and fought doggedly for regime reform.

But Itagaki and his band of former Freedom Party members at the helm of the regime were aiming not for the realization of party politics or the reform of structures of rule, but for the expansion of their party base through local officials and the police. These Jiyūtō partisans vehemently opposed reform proposals once designed and trumpeted by their Progressive Party rivals. Expecting that their Cabinet would be short-lived, Itagaki and his associates embraced the oligarchs and began preparing for what would come next.

The increasing estrangement of these two political camps within the Constitutional Government Party degenerated into a decisive stand-off during the general elections of the House of Representatives in August. The Freedom and Progressive parties had merged to form the Constitutional Government Party only two months before the general election. The merger discombobulated local political organizations, and candidates faced extraordinary difficulty adjusting to the new state of affairs. Across the nation, candidates from the two sides butted heads. Potential common ground for cooperation crumbled under their feet. In November, the Cabinet resigned en masse. Just five months after the rise of the first party cabinet, the Cabinet collapsed onto and obstructed the newly developing road to party politics. New life was breathed into oligarchic cabinets.

A change in power and the partisan polticization of the bureaucracy

The oligarch-bureaucrats return to power: The second Cabinet of Yamagata Aritomo and the Kenseitō

It was Yamagata Aritomo who came to power after the Waihan Cabinet came crashing down in November 1898, the thirty-first year of the Meiji era. Unlike Itō, who assembled a different staff for each new venture he was undertaking, Yamagata had surrounded himself with bureaucrats and military men who pledged ongoing fealty to him and who formed a political bloc known as the Yamagata faction. Now building a national administration for the second time, Yamagata assembled an oligarchy wherein the fulcrum of power lay, as in oligarchic cabinets before, in the Satsuma political clan: besides Katsura Tarō, army minister; Aoki Shūzō, foreign minister; Kiyoura Keigo, justice minister; and other such men from his own Yamagata faction, men from Satsuma-dominated ministries such as Matsukata Masayoshi, treasury minister, rounded out the Cabinet.

But not even Yamagata could not make an administration function without cooperation from forces in the Diet. Yamagata won over the support of the Freedom Party strand of the Constitutional Government Party, which was hankering for tangible gains in the regime, and pulled off a hike on land taxes, a measure long sought but not yet achieved. The Constitutional Government Party, in turn, won its share of benefits: looking ahead towards general prefectural elections the following year, it succeeded in keeping Ogura Hisashi, a party member and the man responsible for electoral supervision (*senkyo torshimiari*), in his office as head of the Public Security Bureau (*keihokyoku*). As a result, the Kenseitō managed to trounce its rival, the Kenseihontō, in elections in over half of the prefectures, thereby winning a majority of seats.

In shoring up rule, the Yamagata Cabinet chased out party members whom the Ōkuma-Itagaki Cabinet had employed into the bureaucracy, and it thereby regained territory the oligarchy had lost. Not only did the Cabinet restore such oligarchic bureaucrats as finance deputy Tajiri Inajirō, but it revised the Edict for the Employment of Civil Officer altogether so that all men in official posts from the level of deputy minister and below be hired by their qualifications rather than by politics (*shikaku nin'yō*). It further claimed that, per the will of the Emperor, any reforms relating to power over the system of government officials, such as reforms of the cabinet officer system, of the system of officials within individual ministries and of the employment of civil officials, had to pass through inspection and deliberation by the Privy Council before being effected. The regime set up precautionary bulwarks against easy interference in the bureaucratic system.

Because these changes allowed reform to proceed without party input, members of the Constitutional Government Party cried foul. In response to their resistance, the Yamagata Cabinet split the responsibilities of the deputy ministers, who had to this point been involved in both political and administrative affairs (*seimu, jimu*). It delegated political affairs to the chief ministry secretary (*kanbōchō*) and administrative affairs to the head of general affairs (*sōmu chōkan*), a position equivalent to the administrative deputy minister (*jimu jikan*) of later years. By allowing the possibility of hiring party men into the role of chief ministry secretary through a political-hire rather than merit-hire system, the Yamagata Cabinet managed to mollify the Constitutional Government Party.

The role of chief ministry secretary at this time differed vastly from that today. The post involved little actual involvement in processes of decision-making, and it mainly entailed tasks that bureaucrats found cumbersome, such as dealing with the Diet. It was a job for people desperately seeking positions in the regime. Yamagata himself described it as 'a rank just a bit better than that of private secretary'.[14]

The rise of cross-sectional parties (*ōdangata seitō*): The Seiyūkai as a composite structure of politicians and state officers

As it grew accustomed to being the party in power through its close relationship with the ruling administration, the Constitutional Government Party relinquished its ideal of placing the parliament at the centre of the government and turned towards enthusiastic participation in the programmes of the oligarchic regime. It responded zealously when in 1900, Itō Hirobumi, who had been toying with the formation of a new political party, called for the assemblage of a new cross-sectional or big-tent partisan organization that would encompass party politics, bureaucracy and the financial world. The party supplied Itō with a foundation for the new organization.

A new party, the Rikken Seiyūkai, was founded on 15 September 1900. Itō summoned men from a wide cross-section of society under his fold. He of course pursued unaffiliated members of the parliament, but he went further: to members of prefectural assemblies, to mayors, to members of municipal councils and to other such local and provincial political figures; to officials of the council for merchants and artisans (*shōkō kaigi*); to heads of companies; to big taxpayers; to bankers and lawyers; and to important mainstays in prefectures across the country. But it ended up being the Constitutional Government Party that most enthusiastically welcomed Itō and the bureaucrats around him.

Let us take a look at the faces that made up the Seiyūkai. The men who listed themselves as its founding members were Watanabe Kunitake, governor of Kōchi and minister of finance; Saionji Kinmochi, ambassador to Austria-Hungary, foreign minister and marquis; Kaneko Kentarō, commissioner for the Bureau for Investigation of State Systems (*seido torishirabe goyōgakari*), minister of agricultural and commercial affairs and baron; Suematsu Kenchō, head of the Prefectural Governance Bureau and minister of communications; Watanabe Kōki, chancellor of the Imperial University; and Tsuruhara Sadakichi, consul general in Shanghai and trustee of the Bank of Japan; and others. Ad hoc general committee members (*ka sōmu iin*) were Tsuzuki Keiroku, deputy foreign minister; and Hara Takashi or Kei, deputy foreign minister and secretary-general (*kanjichō*). Joining them as party members were Sameshima Takenosuke, head of the cabinet secretariat, and Den Kenjirō, deputy minister of communications. Thus amassed at the party camp were bureaucrat-politicians known as the Itō faction. And when Itō formed his own Cabinet in October 1900 for the fourth Itō administration, it was these men who stood at the centre of the ruling Seiyūkai and of the administration under its helm.

But few of these men remained in the party for long. When Itō was appointed as head of the Privy Council and left his post at the helm of the party, many of these faces, too, disappeared from the Seiyūkai. Most already had stable positions as ministers and imperially appointed members of the House of Peers (*kizokuin chokusen giin*), whereas the parties had their own separate internal histories and an internal hierarchy based on a record of party contributions. For men already secure in their political posts, there was no reason or benefit in remaining in and fighting for the parties.

Among a younger generation in the early Seiyūkai clan were Tsuzuki, Tsuruhara, Den and Hara, the last of whom went on to inaugurate the era of party cabinets. After Itō entered the Privy Council, Tsuzuki became head of the cabinet secretariat (*naikaku shoki kanchō*), Tsuruhara transferred to mayor of Osaka and Den launched an attack on the party leadership and withdrew from the party. Only Hara remained.

Hara had been discovered by Inoue and Mutsu in the agricultural-commercial and foreign ministries, and had displayed extraordinary talent. But his road in the world of government had not been easy. His relations with Inoue were dubious. Mutsu, the man on whom he had counted for support, died early. After Mutsu passed on, Hara quit his post as a state official and went down to Osaka in search of new opportunities. But then the Seiyūkai formed, and he decided to put his political life on the line and take his chances with the new party.

Hara at first imagined himself proceeding down a path as a bureaucrat-politician like Kaneko Kentarō or Itō Miyoji. He sought a post as a cabinet minister when the Fourth Itō Cabinet was being installed. His wish went unfulfilled. He then pursued a seat in the House of Peers. It was this same Hara who went on to become the first commoner prime minister, but at this point, as a bureaucrat, he fixated on gaining an appointment by the Emperor to a stable position in the peerage. He was not selected.

To say that this was when Hara took his first steps as a party man would not be an exaggeration. He had started out as a Johnny-come-lately bureaucrat-politician in the Itō faction. After he failed to make the cut for imperial selection to the House of Peers, he was given the seat that Hoshi Tōru had vacated as minister of communications. But then the Cabinet collapsed within just half a year of its formation, sending Hara tumbling from the stable ground on which he sat. Determined to remain on the political road, in August 1902 Hara ran in the seventh general elections for the House of Representatives as a candidate in the first ward of Iwate Prefecture, or Morioka city. He prevailed in a ferocious electoral battle against the former mayor of Morioka and embarked on a career as a full-blown party politician.

An alternation of generations and a 'cabinet of deputies'

Let us return to the question of what happened to the ruling administration. It had seemed that the fourth Itō administration, a new cabinet formed in 1900 from the now-ruling Seiyūkai, was sturdy. But it was beset by deadlocks in the still hodgepodge cabinet system. Calling for fiscal austerity, Finance Minister Watanabe Kunitake stood off against members of the erstwhile Constitutional Government Party, who demanded an expansionary fiscal policy. In June 1901, just nine months after they acceded to power, members of the Cabinet were forced to resign en masse.

Rising to the vacated helm was Katsura Tarō, a man belonging to a generation younger than that of Itō and Yamagata. The Seiyūkai had found their hopes of sustaining administrative power dashed, but the successor Cabinet still could not do without cooperation from the Seiyūkai. The regime needed someone who could manage that cooperative relationship, and there was no one suited to the role besides Katsura. As deputy minister of the army, he had gained connections with the Diet, which he used as political capital. And it was he who served as a link between Yamagata Aritomo and the Kenseitō. The two forged deep bonds as Japan moved towards signing an alliance with Britain and waging war against Russia.

The formation of the First Katsura Cabinet constituted a landmark in the historical trajectory of the bureaucracy. The faces at the helm of the state ministries suddenly became younger. Katsura populated ministerial posts with talented men belonging to his own generation. It was a deliberate effort to replace the genrō with a new generation.

Komura Jutarō became foreign minister. 'Perennial underling Komura', who had striven for the foreign minister post ever since his days as a tributary student, finally made it after thirty years of trying. Posted as home minister was Utsumi Tadakatsu, a man of exceptional talent who had spent his own thirty years as a local official.

Young talent filled other cabinet posts, too. Kiyoura Keigo rose to minister of justice. Like the justice ministry, the education ministry promoted homegrown talent, bringing back Kikuchi Dairoku, who had served as deputy minister of education but had then been transferred to the chancellorship of the Imperial University. Up to this point, the minister of education had long been a purely nominal post held by a man with no connections to education administration. As calls for school reform swelled, the ministry now sought someone with a higher degree of specialized knowledge.

The man who became minister of finance, Sone Arasuke, attended the Army Academy (*rikugun heigaku ryō*) in Osaka with Katsura. Unlike Katsura, who continued down the road of military bureaucracy, Sone headed to France for five years to study legislation. From there he entered the Legislation Bureau as a counsellor (*hōseikyoku sanjikan*) and became the first-ever chief of the secretariat of the House of Representatives (*shūgiin giin shoki kan chō*). Then he won a seat in the House of Representatives and rose all the way to deputy chair of the House. He was a Renaissance man, a product of the systems for training human resources that arose in the Meiji era. That the regime placed Sone, a man with intimate connections with the Diet, at the centre of the Ministry of Finance just as the Russo-Japanese War intensified was seen as an indicator that the Cabinet would approach the Diet with a willingness to engage in dialogue.

In the shadow of cabinets gone before it, a young new cabinet filled with such first-timers appeared as a lightweight. It was pilloried as a 'cabinet of deputies'. But as bureaucrats intimately familiar with executive government filled ministerial posts, the fact was that the Cabinet had now gained extraordinarily high functional capacity. To the deputy posts within their own ministries, the cabinet members now promoted homegrown bureaucrats.

Some fretted that staffing a cabinet with men of such extraordinary practical abilities would exacerbate sectionalism. Their fears played out in reality. Inter-ministerial bickering regularly rocked the First Katsura Cabinet. A case in point was the pay-hike movement for judicial officers that unfolded under the watch of Kiyoura, minister of justice. Kiyoura did nothing as members of the judiciary turned up pressure on the Ministry of the Treasury to receive pay increases. His inaction was taken as speaking volumes. In a new cabinet system now modelled on 'little-chancellorism' (*shō saishō shugi*), or the diminished role of the prime minister, such deep sectionalism could easily lead to instability. Ministers could not readily resolve problems that arose among them, for unlike the relationship between Katsura and Yamagata, one between a minister and a *genrō*, the relationship between Prime Minister Katsura and Justice Minister Kiyoura was one of equals. Katsura could conceivably have relied on Yamagata to help resolve Cabinet conflicts, but to do so would have been to surrender his objective of empowering a new generation of men.

Katsura managed to pull his Cabinet out of the crisis by emphasizing fiscal discipline in the management of the Cabinet. Finance was something at which Katsura, who had gained his initial foothold in the bureaucracy by managing military affairs, was adept. He had built relations with the Diet by demonstrating his skill in financial matters. Now he applied that same expertise to help weld together his executive government.[15]

This problem-solving strategy had positive implications for the relationship between Katsura and the *genrō*. By placing particular emphasis on state finance, Katsura endeared himself not only to Yamagata but also to Inoue Kaoru, who had a penchant for financial matters. He thus won the support of both Yamagata and Inoue, and his Cabinet could operate with two regime heavyweights behind it who were ready to bring the government into balance if ever it fell out of equilibrium. For the duration of the Russo-Japanese War, which lasted for a year and a half from February 1904, the Cabinet, propped up by the favour of two *genrō* and the Seiyūkai, managed to keep the nation unified and committed.

The Keien era of Katsura and Saionji: Signs of stability and change

Once he was finished attending to the aftermath of the Russo-Japanese War, Katsura fulfilled his long-standing promise to abdicate power to Saionji Kinmochi and the Seiyūkai, which had cooperated with the wartime regime. January 1906 marked the inauguration of the first Cabinet of Saionji Kinmochi. Formed by collaboration between Katsura and Saionji, the Cabinet was not monopolized by the Seiyūkai. Rather, it was inaugurated as a coalition government that included bureaucrats from the Yamagata-Katsura faction.

This First Saionji Cabinet held power for two-and-a-half years before it handed the helm back over to Katsura in July 1908. Katsura then formed his second Cabinet and established what is known as the 'reciprocal goodwill' (*jōi tōgō*) between the Katsura Cabinet and the Seiyūkai. When the second Katsura administration then handed power smoothly back over, once again, to Saionji for his second Cabinet, it became clear that an era of political stability had at last arrived.[16] This was the Keien era, the name Keien functioning as a portmanteau of characters for Katsura and Saionji, much as the title Waihan did for Itagaki and Ōkuma.

Despite its political stability, the Keien era marked a time of radical upheaval for members of the bureaucracy. Because administrative power flowed so smoothly back and forth between two different political forces, bureaucrats faced a clear choice, a choice whose starkness had no precedent: did they choose the Katsura camp or the Seiyūkai camp?

When it acceded to power in July 1908, the Second Katsura Cabinet carried out a sweeping dismissal of deputy-level bureaucrats. Only two men, both close associates of Yamagata, kept their jobs: Kawamura Jōzaburō, deputy minister of justice, and Nakashōji Ren, deputy minister of communications. Amid the long two-and-a-half years during which the Saionji Cabinet ruled, deputy-level bureaucrats had developed intimate connections with the Seiyūkai. Their presence in the state would have been profoundly inconvenient for Katsura as he formed a new cabinet.

Every one of the bureaucrats dumped under Katsura was a scholar-bureaucrat who had received specialized education in law at the Imperial University. Did the regime really need to jettison these valuable human resources, men with specialized talents, for purely political and partisan reasons? Why?

The problem extended back to the First Katsura Cabinet. In December 1903, Katsura dissolved the system of separating the posts of chief ministry secretary (*kanbōchō*) and of head of general affairs (*sōmu chōkan*), a separation that had been set up by Yamagata. The chief ministry secretary had served as a political deputy minister, and the general affairs head as an administrative deputy minister. With the disbanding of these posts, the deputy roles merged again into one. The chief secretary post had, in any case, been disparaged as a useless appendix of the state, a post set up only to satiate the demands of Kenseitō post-hunters.

Disparagement notwithstanding, there had been a purpose to this system. In order to divide politics from administration, or to clearly demarcate the realm of politicians from that of administrative bureaucrats, the system had separated the administrative line of 'minister–head of general affairs (*sōmu chō kan*)–bureau chief (*kyokuchō*)' from the political line of 'minister–chief ministry secretary (*kanbōchō*)–ministerial secretary (*daijin kanbō*)'. It was based on this understanding that the Fourth Itō Cabinet had appointed a Seiyūkai member as chief ministry secretary in each ministry and carried forward with the operation of the ministries by separating political and administrative affairs. Katsura saw no need for this system. Just three years after the executive reforms were put into place, he bulldozed them.

The logic behind the decision to excise the 'appendix' that was the chief ministry secretary post made its own sort of sense. Katsura and his team of men were themselves bureaucrats, and the professional bureaucrats in the ministries were their underlings. Bringing in a political appointee from outside the bureaucracy and placing him in the post of chief ministry secretary would only make a mess of administrative affairs, the Katsura administration thought. But evidently the members of the regime had not realized that this sort of logic only applied when they themselves were in power.

Dissolving the separate posts of chief ministry secretary and head of general affairs meant that the new single deputy minister who replaced them had to wear both political and administrative masks. The deputy would therefore have to operate on political premises. If there were no changes in government power, then there would be no major problems. But if political power transferred from one party to another, then the deputy serving under one administration would not be able to continue under the next. The mass dismissal of deputy-level bureaucrats every time power changed hands became a new normal state of affairs. It was a phenomenon unseen under the oligarchic cabinets.

Partisanship thus infiltrated the bureaucracy. Bureaucrats became coloured as either Katsura- or Seiyūkai-faction men. When Saionji came to power, bureaucrats serving under Katsura were all tossed out. And then when Katsura came back to power, those same men were lugged back into the government, and Saionji bureaucratic heavyweights were then ejected. And then the whole process was repeated when Saionji once again seized power. Personnel became partisan. Bureaucrats had no choice but to move under the sway of their political affiliation.

This partisan tendency was especially pronounced in appointments to the head of the Public Security Bureau and the superintendence of the national police force, posts that operated in secrecy. When Katsura came to power, Arimatsu Hideyoshi rose to the helm of the Public Security Bureau and Ōura Kanetake to the police superintendence; when Saionji came to power, he swapped them out with Koga Renzō and Anraku Kanemichi, respectively. Cabinet bureaucrats, too, were appointed along partisan lines. Under the Katsura Cabinet, Shibata Kamon, a probationary-system hire from Yamaguchi born in 1863, was appointed head of the secretariat (*shoki kan chō*), and Ikki Kitokurō was placed as head of the Legislation Bureau; under Saionji, Minami Hiroshi and Okano Keijirō were appointed to those respective positions. Minami, who was born in Toyama prefecture in 1869, had passed the higher-level exams; Okano was a university professor junior to Ikki. The administrative bureaucracy below these men in the secretariat was largely swept clean with each change in power. As an organ meant to coordinate and manage the entire state, the Cabinet had transformed into a deeply political institution. These personnel changes manifested that transformation clearly.

Bureaucratic partisanship deepens

Katsura and the Seiyūkai enjoyed cordial relations. The Seiyūkai propped Katsura up when he teetered, and Katsura served the demands of the Seiyūkai. The two sides got along because they existed symbiotically. In August 1911, once Katsura had finally sorted through long-standing diplomatic problems, he transferred power once again to Saionji, giving rise to the Second Saionji Cabinet.

The Cabinet this time found itself in circumstances vastly different from those of the First Saionji Cabinet. The first time Saionji acceded to power, the Seiyūkai lacked the power to stand alone at the helm of the regime. It needed the support of Katsura. But after five years of successfully navigating the wake of the Russo-Japanese War, the Seiyūkai found the political set-up flipped: now the Seiyūkai, backed up by political power-holders, was buttressing the Katsura Cabinet. It was less that Katsura yielded power to Saionji than that he entrusted it with him.

After consulting with political heavyweights such as Hara Kei and Matsuda Masahisa, Saionji rejected recommendations Katsura had made to him for the Cabinet and the bureaucracy and instead formed a responsible cabinet dominated by the Seiyūkai. Hara and Matsuda retook their respective posts as home and justice ministers. Seiyūkai leaders and other personnel close to Saionji populated other ministerial posts. To fill the critical role of minister of finance, the regime needed a man with influence and financial expertise that could rival those of Katsura. Lacking such a man within the Seiyūkai, the regime poached Yamamoto Tatsuo, the president (*sōsai*) of Kangyō Bank, for the post. Popular opinion hailed the new cabinet as the party government the public had long anticipated.

This inclination to self-sufficiency in the Katsura Cabinet was manifest no less in appointments to the bureaucracy. To avenge for the actions of the Second Katsura Cabinet, Saionji swept the deputy level of every ministry clean and restored the upper-level bureaucrats serving under his first Cabinet back to their posts. The partisanship of the bureaucracy, which had begun with the reshuffling of the bureaucracy under the Second Katsura Cabinet, thus became a fixed practice as changes in administration continued. To become a deputy minister now signified affiliation with one or another strand of political power.

How did the bureaucrats themselves interpret this move towards partisanship? We have already seen how some resented the infiltration of oligarchic power into their ranks and hoped to entrust the government to party politicians. But it did not necessarily follow that bureaucrats who wanted party politics found themselves embraced by the more partisan Saionji Cabinet and shrugged off by the more oligarchic Katsura regime. A different configuration arose as a result of the systematization of the professional bureaucracy.

Twenty years had passed since the introduction of the probationary employment system. The upper-level officialdom was now almost exclusively filled with scholar-bureaucrats who had received university educations. The bureaucracy had become increasingly homogeneous. And as the personnel of the bureaucracy became more uniform, so too did it become more systematized.

In the early years of the Meiji era, only those rare bureaucrats who had journeyed to the West bore specialized professional knowledge. As the bureaucracy developed, these scarce bureaucrats found demands for their skills pulling them in every direction. Responding to endless solicitations, they jumped from ministry to ministry. Some, meanwhile, stayed in the same post for ten years until the structures for which they were responsible came into being. Personnel hiring at this point proceeded according not to any system but to the schemes of the regime and suitability to those schemes.

Once a system for supplying human resources from universities fell into place, a steady stream of some thirty to fifty young scholars began entering the state ministries every year. And as the supply of professional bureaucrats grew, the personnel system became more systematized. A standardized organization of personnel seniority was established as men hopped around various posts for two to three years and made their way up the ranks of the officialdom. They rode the system and escalated through its ranks semi-automatically, each ultimately promised a future as a deputy minister, a bureau head or another such upper-level bureaucratic role.

The trouble was that political and administrative affairs were muddled. To win a post as a deputy minister or bureau head, a man had to develop a close relationship with the ruling powers and proceed with executive functions in conformity with their political will. And then when the ruling administration changed, a bureaucrat would become marked with the political affiliation he had carried. The changes of a new age and the modernization of the bureaucracy submitted professional bureaucrats to the rising tide of partisanship.

Once a bureaucrat was thus marked with a certain political hue, he could not escape ouster when a new regime of a different hue came to power. During the age of the oligarchy, a booted bureaucrat could win the solicitude of an oligarch-politician and gain an imperial appointment to the House of Peers (*Kizokuin giin*). But by the Katsura-Saionji era the House of Peers had been saturated with men, and private-sector industry still lacked the vitality to sustain defectors from the government. To engage the parties as a means of preserving their posts and sustaining their political lives became an important decision bureaucrats faced.

In policy affairs, too, the distance between bureaucracy and partisan politics shrank markedly. By actively drawing men from the bureaucracy into the parties, the Seiyūkai, which had pursued reform of the political parties, established a pipeline between the two sides. Seiyūkai members acted as agents through whom bureaucrats engaged with members of the political research committees (*seimu chōsakai*) of the various parties, tipping them off to budgetary information or giving them advance briefings on policy. Thus the bureaucracy and political parties gradually grew closer.

Party politicians and scholar-bureaucrats: Hara Kei and the Home Ministry

The Katsura-Saionji era brought about dramatic changes in the relationship between the parties and the bureaucracy. Various factors undergirded those changes: scholar-bureaucrats came to fill the majority of bureaucratic posts; the bureaucracy and its personnel hiring system became highly systematized; bureaucrats themselves acutely discerned the turning tides towards partisan politics. Still, despite the rise of party politics, so-called Yamagata-faction oligarchs retained substantial power, especially over the Home Ministry, the Ministry of Agricultural and Commercial Affairs and the Ministry of Communications. At times, ministers found themselves mere pawns of the dictates of such men as Kiyoura Keigo and Ōura Kanetake.[17]

Amid these changes, Hara Kei and Matsuda Masuhisa were reappointed by the Seiyūkai, and each set about building bridges between the bureaucracy and the party. Let us set the clock back slightly and trace the case of Hara and the bureaucrats of the Home Ministry.

Hara Kei, or Hara Takashi, became home minister in the First Saionji Cabinet in January 1906. His tenure as communications minister in the Fourth Itō Cabinet marked his first stint as a cabinet minister. He gained renown by acting as a thorn in the side of Watanabe Kunitake, the minister of finance, and obstructing Watanabe's go-it-alone designs, even as a cabinet rookie. But the communications ministry was a lightweight compared to the juggernaut Home Ministry, a stronghold of the oligarchic faction over which Yamagata reigned. Anxieties spread: could Hara handle his new role as home minister?

Preceding Hara as home minister was Kiyoura. Having long served as head of the Public Security Bureau (*keihokyoku*), Kiyoura, together with former police superintendent Ōura, wielded formidable influence over the world of police. Hara took over to find deep divides between the Provincial Affairs Bureau (*chihōkyoku*), filled predominantly with scholar-bureaucrats, and the public security bureau, filled predominantly with men from the police force or the military. He began his reform of the home ministry by shrewdly manipulating relations between the two factions.

In April, with sessions of the Imperial Diet now behind him, Hara convened the first conference of head provincial officials (*chihō chōkan kaigi*) since rising to his new post. The conference brought prefectural governors (*chiji*) from across the country to a central location both to instil in them a sense of government policy and to hear out their opinions and incorporate those opinions in policy. The conference ordinarily proceeded with the regime setting forth topics of consultation and governors then expressing their perspectives on those topics. A hundred schools of thought would contend, and the conference would devolve into a place for governors to excoriate the regime. The governors, who largely belonged to the oligarchic faction, now rubbed their hands in anticipation of a chance to face off against Hara, a man of partisan origins.

Hara showed his true worth. Rather than present topics of discussion ordained by the regime, he forewent precedent and demanded that governors themselves submit opinion papers on which the conference would consult. The governors seized on the chance, and papers flooded in from across the realm.

The conference began. Hara took up the towering piles of paper that had accumulated under his watch and threw them right back at the governors, assailing them with questions about their ideas instead of answering their proposals himself. Governor after governor stood nonplussed. It turned out that it was not they but their underlings who had written the papers. The governors had turned documents in without even understanding their content. Hara swiftly booted out all governors of this kind, sweeping his government clean of dead-weight personnel he deemed 'decrepit'.

Even as he jettisoned bogus proposals, Hara took up ideas he deemed useful and transformed them into law. This approach gave him the chance not only to make government policy more effective but also to excavate men of particular talent. Hara exploited the conference to do out with the old and in with the new, to scope out new government policies and to employ new human resources.

Dumped from their posts were men such as Higaki Naosuke, the Okayama governor born in Yamaguchi in 1851, who had risen to their posts long ago after working their way up through the system. They were replaced by such scholar-bureaucrats as Mabuchi Eitarō, a Gifu man born in 1867 who had passed the higher-level official exams and had served as one of the ghost writers of the governor proposal papers. Hara exploited the opposition between oligarchic bureaucrats and scholar-bureaucrats that had been lurking since the days of the Ōkuma-Itagaki Cabinet. By showering the scholar-bureaucrats with favour, he built a new foundation for his ministry. The Home Ministry was no doubt the home turf of Yamagata factionalism, but new scholar-bureaucrats with no direct connections to Yamagata had entered the ministry after Yamagata had left his ministerial post. The dumping of oligarchic mainstays in favour of young scholars constituted not only a departure from oligarchic factionalism but also a break from Yamagata himself.

This new direction for the ministry appeared in personnel. A scholar-bureaucrat rose to the post of deputy minister for the first time ever: Yoshihara Saburō, a Chiba man born in 1854 originally hired through the probationary employment system. He was promoted to deputy minister from his role as head of the bureau of provincial affairs. Replacing him in provincial affairs was Tokonami Takejirō, a Kagoshima man who, despite his provenance, lacked close relations to the oligarchic potentates and who had not found success in the ministry after his probationary-employment hiring.[18] The Saionji Cabinet had developed close ties with the Satsuma faction through Makino, the minister of education, and through Haseba Sumitaka, a Seiyūkai man; Hara won support from the Satsuma clan by placing Tokonami in a position of importance and thereby managed to proceed with reform of provincial government.

Reform proceeded on multiple fronts. Mizuno Rentarō, who had long set his hopes on the rise of party politics, applied his long years of experience and knowledge as ministerial secretary (*daijin hishokan*) to hiring new personnel. In legislative matters, scholar-bureaucrats who had graduated at the top of their classes at university wielded their expertise as counsellors (*sanjikan*). These counsellors included Inoue Tomokazu, an Ishikawa man born in 1871 who was hired through the probationary employment system and later became governor of Tokyo prefecture; and Ariyoshi Chūichi, a Kyoto man born in 1873 who passed the higher-level official exams and later became governor of Hyōgo prefecture. Revamping personnel and reconfiguring policy proceeded together and advanced reform.

Hara extended his hand into the administration of the police, too. The national police force, a bastion of oligarchism and a tool for the suppression of the Popular Rights Movement, was abhorred by the political parties. Hara came to the ministry just as the police, which had used brute force to crush the Hibiya Riots following the Russo-Japanese War, faced mounting popular opprobrium. Calls for the total dissolution of the police department were circling through the public. Hara seized on the turn in popular opinion to launch reforms of the police department. Up to this point, the superintendent of the police had reported both to the prime minister and to the home minister because he commanded the entirety of the upper-level police. Hara moved the superintendent under the sole authority of the Home Ministry, where the superintendent became equal in rank to prefectural governors. The change meant that the administration of the police force fell under the jurisdiction of the Home Ministry just as other domestic executive organizations did.

In May, Hara proceeded with reshuffling personnel in the police department. After attenuating the influence of the Ōura faction there, he himself made his first presentation to the police force as home minister. Before him stood young rising scholar-bureaucrats now serving as head officials in the police, men such as Inoue Kōsai, born in Gifu in 1871, who passed the higher-level exams and later became deputy home minister; Isawa Takio, whom we have already encountered; and Okada Bunji, born in Yamagata in 1874, also a higher-level exam man, and later superintendent of the police. Hara overhauled the structures, personnel and policies of police administration. Across his field of authority, he actively hired scholar-bureaucrats, and by flaunting an employment system based on meritocracy and combining it with changes in policy, he seized control of the Home Ministry.

The technique of pushing reform forward by applying new policies was something particularly Hara, a man who had accumulated experience as a professional bureaucrat, could do. To him, the changes in policy symbolized a move to party politics itself.

The re-emergence of powerful prime ministers: The inauguration of the Edict on Public Forms

Itō Hirobumi had moved up to the Privy Council and withdrawn to the background of party politics, but even so, he continued to offer structural support for the emergence of party-based responsible cabinets. That support came through the revision of the cabinet officer system (*naikaku kansei*) and the promulgation of the Edict on Public Forms (*Kōshikirei*), both of 1907.

The original cabinet officer system limited the number of ordinances that required a countersignature from the prime minister and allowed ordinances related to the administrative functions of an individual ministry to pass with just the countersignature of the head of the relevant ministry. Even though clause 2 of the cabinet officer ordinance demanded that the system 'preserve the unity of the divisions of executive government', no adequate powers existed to coordinate the ministries, which were headed by strong-willed, independently minded men. The state had no recourse but to rely on the abilities of the prime minister himself and on the *genrō* in each of the executive fields of specialization to coordinate the regime.

But with the rise of a new generation, the *genrō* retreated from the front line of government, and as the executive government became increasingly specialized, the clashing interests of individual ministries became starker. It became clear that a means of coordinating the ministries had to be developed in the structure of the government, not in the men who operated within it. To build such a structure, Itō used his dual role as head of the Privy Council and as president of the Research Bureau for Institutions of the Imperial Chamber (*Teishitsu seido chōsa kyoku*) to embark on revision of the cabinet officer system.

On 10 October 1906, as the First Saionji Cabinet steadily held the helm of the state, Itō revised the Public Documents System (*Kōbunshiki*), which had determined the format of all laws and ordinances, and presented the new Edict on Public Forms

(*Kōshikirei*) to the Meiji Emperor. The commentary appended to the 'Proposal for the Edict on Public Forms' made clear that all edicts and ordinances had to carry the countersignature of the prime minister by the time they were publicly proclaimed 'because [the prime minister] has the responsibility to supervise each of the divisions of the executive state'. The requirement of a countersignature endowed the prime minister with the authority to preside over and coordinate the general affairs of the state. The regime foresaw resistance from the individual ministries.

The Saionji administration, which had been in search of ways to strengthen the uniformity of the Cabinet, consented to this change. With this approval from the Cabinet, the Edict on Public Forms proceeded, according to state regulations, to undergo inspection by the Privy Council. The Privy Council set up an investigation committee to consider the document, and it populated that committee mostly with advisers (*komonkan*) close to Itō Hirobumi. Tanaka Fujimaro, a former bureaucrat in the education ministry, chaired the committee and was joined by other such Itō associates as Hachisuka Mochiaki, former daimyo of Tokushima and education minister, Itō Miyoji, Nomura Yasushi, Okano Keijirō, Suematsu Kenchō and Kiyoura Keigo. Okano held a dual role as head of the Legislation Bureau. On 21 December, the committee approved the proposal without any major objections.

The trouble lay in the next step. The Privy Council itself, which was made up primarily by advisers (*komonkan*) of the Yamagata faction, now had to consider the proposal. Deliberations occurred on 26 December. They began with Tanaka Fujimaro, the head of the investigative committee, reporting on the results of its discussions. Then Okano explained the content of the ordinance itself. Okano said nothing of the significance of the countersignature. Stressing the parts of the document that touched on the Constitution and on the regulations of the imperial chamber, he deflected the attention of the Privy Council advisers to these matters. Thus the Edict on Public Forms was inaugurated after thorough deliberations, and the powers of the prime minister to manage the regime, powers that had been rolled back with the fall of the system of cabinet powers (*naikaku shokken*), were once again clearly articulated.

From here, the ministries began to function according to the new regulations, with the exception of the army and the navy, which won an exemption for matters pertaining to the military once they figured out the true intent of the reforms. Under a prime minister endowed with broad-ranging coordinative powers, the Cabinet began to function as a unified whole.

The rise of a two-party system

The Rikken Dōshikai, the second cross-sectional party

The political stability of the Keien era had created what was known as 'an era of calm' (*nagi no jidai*), but, amid this ostensible tranquillity, the Seiyūkai had been gaining greater self-sufficiency and the bureaucracy had been growing increasingly partisan. These structural shifts beneath the surface erupted in a political upheaval that shattered the era of stability. The impetus for the upheaval lay in the First Movement to Protect Constitutional Governance, or the Taishō Political Crisis, as it is known.

Having been welcomed by popular opinion as a genuine party cabinet, the second Cabinet of Saionji exploited its support to launch large-scale administrative reform. But it crashed into opposition from the army, which demanded that the regime expand the size of the army by two divisions (*niko shidan zōsetsu*). Uehara Yūsaku, the army minister, resigned in protest when his demands were not met, and no successor could be appointed. The Cabinet teetered on the edge of mass resignation.

Popular opinion bore down on the army. The public claimed that a cabinet that had drawn from mass support to move vigorously ahead with executive reform was being undermined by a barefaced army craving greater size. Attempts to form a successor cabinet floundered. The *genrō* gathered no fewer than eleven times to consult on the situation. They finally settled on Katsura as the man to succeed Saionji, and Katsura became prime minister yet again. He was their sixth candidate.

Throughout the Keien era, Katsura had gained greater independence both from the influence of Yamagata and from reliance on the Seiyūkai. He now formed his own Cabinet made of Katsura-faction bureaucrats. He reappointed Gotō Shinpei as communications minister; promoted Wakatsuki Reijirō, who had served as deputy minister of the treasury when Kastura held a dual post as treasury minister and prime minister, to the helm of the treasury ministry; placed Nakashōji Ren, a former communications deputy, as agricultural and commercial affairs minister; and installed Shibata Kamon, former head of the cabinet secretariat, as education minister. He even left his mark on the army. Kigoshi Yasutsuna, head of the first division of the army, had been seen as a member of the Katsura faction, but Katsura ejected him from his post to make a point of asserting his independence from Yamagata. Katsura aimed to build a cabinet that rebuffed behind-the-scenes manipulation from the *genrō*, that stood on its own and that bore a high degree of unity. He was bent on forming a government dominated by his own faction.

But popular opinion turned sharply against the new government and challenged the manoeuvres of Katsura. The returnee prime minister's background as a Chōshū army man became a source of scepticism among the public. And his appointments to his Cabinet generated an image of a reactionary, oppressive regime. He selected the man who had presided over the upper-level police force, Ōura Kanetake, as home minister. And he chose the man who had crushed the Hibiya Riots in his capacity as head of the police department secretariat (*keishichō kanbō shuji*), Kawakami Chikaharu, as general superintendent of the police. Denunciation of the oligarchy amplified. It merged into the Movement to Protect Constitutional Governance and rippled across the entire nation.

In January 1913, with a new session of the Imperial Diet impending, the Seiyūkai opened a general party conference and made plain its intention to take a hostile stance towards the new Cabinet of Katsura. After twelve years of cordial relations, the Seiyūkai slammed the door on Katsura and raised a battle cry to win back political power.

The rival Rikken Kokumintō, a refurbished version of the Kenseihontō, held its own conference at the same time. It was an imbroglio. Fifteen years of struggling out of power since the fall of the Waihan Cabinet had enervated the party. The party could hardly hope to regain political power. Its very survival was on the brink. To break through the stagnation, party officials including Taketomi Tokitoshi and Ōishi Masami darted. They sought to join a brand new organization, a second grand cross-sectional big-tent party, one in which they could be the ones to hold power. It turned out that the new face at the head of this party would be none other than Katsura himself.

Having discerned during the Keien era the limits of reliance on the Seiyūkai, Katsura set about forming a party with himself at its centre. He felt he needed a new party, one that would surpass the Seiyūkai to become the leading political organization of the nation. He calculated that marshalling the forces of the Kokumintō would help provide him with substantial activation energy. His interests aligned conveniently with those of the Kokumintō.

On 20 January, Katsura called for the formation of a brand new party with Gotō Shinpei, communications minister, as chief of staff. He planned a broad organization that would include a range of actors: the political faction known as the Central Club (*Chūō kurabu*), made up of such men as Ōura Kanetake; members of the House of Representatives who had defected from the Kokumintō; members of the House of Peers belonging to such factions as the Research Group (*Kenkyūkai*) and the Tea Party (*Sawakai*); and, of course, bureaucrats belonging to the Katsura faction. The party name, at first the Unified Party of Constitutionalism, or Rikken Tōitsutō, and later the Party of Common Constitutional Will, or Rikken Dōshikai, advertised the cross-sectional model of its new organization.

On 7 February, Katsura publicly proclaimed the founding of this new party, the Rikken Dōshikai. Now two cross-sectional parties, the Seiyūkai and the Dōshikai, shared the political stage. The stability and the changes of the Keien era recast the opposition between the oligarchy and the popular parties into a competition between two major cross-sectional parties.

Katsura schemed to use the Dōshikai to crush the Seiyūkai and establish single-party supremacy. But he stumbled out of the gate. He had counted on members of the House of Peers to support him. They applauded the birth of the new party but declined to participate in it themselves. Only a handful of figures joined the new party: Katō Kōmei, Wakatsuki Reijirō, Hamaguchi Osachi, Gotō Shinpei and Nakashōji Ren, as well as Egi Tasuku, who became head of the cabinet secretariat; Nagashima Ryūji, son-in-law of Katsura and acting head of the Finance Bureau (*rizaikyoku*) of the treasury ministry; and other such men.

As the Movement to Protect Constitutional Governance whirled about them, members of the government had no need to put all of their hopes in a single Katsura basket. They could still count on Yamagata, the father of political forces. In any case, the vision of a mass Katsura political party stumbled, but a second political party to oppose the Seiyūkai had indeed been born.

Political ripples turn to waves: The Seiyūkai and the first Cabinet of Yamamoto Gonbée

The formation of a new party intensified political opposition and vastly expanded the Movement to Protect Constitutional Governance. Hemmed in by the vociferations of the movement and haunted by the memories of the Hibiya Riots, on 10 February the Imperial Diet called for the mass resignation of the Katsura Cabinet. Just three days had elapsed since the formation of the Dōshikai.

Rising to replace Katsura was navy admiral (*taishō*) Yamamoto Gonbée, a Kagoshima native known also as Yamamoto Gonnohyōe. Propped up by both the navy and the Satsuma faction, Yamamoto won the favour of the Seiyūkai and succeeded in forming a new cabinet. For two days from the formation of the Cabinet to 22 February, the new prime minister participated in the general conference for Seiyūkai members of parliament and pledged to bring the party platform into the policies of his administration. Thus was born a Satsuma-Seiyūkai coalition government that carried on the legacy of the Second Saionji Cabinet.

But the Satsuma clan, unlike the Chōshū faction, lacked men suited to positions in the Cabinet or bureaucracy, to the extent that it had to nominate Makino Nobuaki as foreign minister. To be sure, there was talent in the farm system: besides Tokonami Takejirō, there was Ōkubo Toshitake, the 1865-born younger brother of Makino, a doctorate holder from the Martin-Luther-Universität Halle-Wittenberg and the governor of Osaka; and Yamanouchi Kazuji, born in 1866, a political-science graduate and Probationary Employment hire who was head official in the Hokkaido prefectural governorship. But none had quite enough experience to justify appointment to the Cabinet. These young upstarts were given subsidiary roles beneath the Cabinet, roles intended to prop the Cabinet up. Tokonami became president of the Railway Institute (*tetsudōin sōsai*) and Yamanouchi was placed as head of the cabinet secretariat.

Yamamoto Gonbée confronted the dire personnel shortage head-on. To help fill the especially important post of finance minister, he turned for help to Matsukata Masayoshi, Satsuma-clan *genrō* and former finance minister. Matsukata recommended Takahashi Korekiyo, president of the Bank of Japan. To the helm of agricultural and commercial affairs, a ministry that held power over the development of the provinces, was chosen Yamamoto Tatsuo, a former president of Kangyō Bank who had served in the Saionji Cabinet. Okuda Yoshito, who had served as an Itō-faction deputy minister of education, was promoted to education minister. As part of an arrangement between the Seiyūkai and Yamamoto Gonbée, all three ministers became party members of the Seiyūkai.

Ministers came directly from the Seiyūkai, too. Hara was posted to the Home Ministry and Matsuda to the Ministry of Justice, each for the third time. Motoda Hajime, who had served as deputy chair of the House of Representatives, entered the Cabinet for the first time, as communications minister. Kuratomi Yūzaburō, head of the judicial division of the governorship general of Korea, was initially considered for the head of the Legislation Bureau, but due to strong legislative demands in Korea the appointment ended up going for the third time to Okano Keijirō, a man close to the Seiyūkai. It was supposed to be a coalition government, but the balance of power leaned heavily towards the Seiyūkai.

The individual ministries were well prepared for the rise of a new cabinet. The Third Katsura Cabinet had restocked the deputy-level posts with men of the scholar-bureaucrat generation. A new generation of professional bureaucrats filled the ministerial roles just as the regime plunged into the Taishō crisis.

At the centre of the new generation stood an increasingly formalized group of bureaucrats affiliated with the Seiyūkai faction. Mizuno Rentarō, head of the Provincial Affairs Bureau under the Second Saionji Cabinet, became deputy home minister. Hashimoto Keisaburō, treasury deputy during that same era, moved to occupy the deputy post in the agricultural and commercial ministry. And Inuzuka Katsutarō, governor of Osaka at the time, became communications deputy. All were men who had risen to posts of prominence under Seiyūkai administrations but who were dumped by the Katsura Cabinet. Now they returned to the government. Mizuno had earlier lost the deputy post to Tokonami, a man senior to him in age. The chance to regain his post had arrived.

As new Seiyūkai men filled some posts, Katsura-era holdouts held their roles as deputies in the ministries of finance, justice and education. Shōda Kazue, of the Twenty-Eight Group, held on to his appointment as treasury deputy. Both the treasury and the justice ministry had managed to establish an independent system of personnel. All administrations, regardless of partisan affiliation, had come to recognize the exceptional specialization required of bureaucrats in the treasury and justice ministries, and they afforded the two departments political leeway.

The Budget Bureau (*shukeikyoku*) of the treasury ministry, its leading subsidiary organ, found a new leader in Kagoshima-born Ichiki Otohiko. Ichiki had made substantial contributions to administrative reform under the Second Saionji Cabinet. There was ample justification for the new Cabinet to knock Shōda off his perch and promote Ichiki to the deputy post. But it had been just three months since Shōda had taken his post. The government decided to give Shōda a pass, and from here Shōda became a rare member of the Twenty-Eight Group affiliated with the Seiyūkai.

In the justice ministry, Oyama Atsushi managed to retain his post as deputy minister because of the exceptional nature of his ministry. He grew increasingly close to the Seiyūkai and, before long, joined the party and became a member of the House of Representatives. The rise of party cabinets dramatically altered the image bureaucrats had of their future careers.

Yamamoto Gonbée explodes onto the scene: Two bureaucratic reform measures

The Movement to Protect Constitutional Governance did not die down. Yamamoto Gonbée unleashed aggressive reform measures to quell it. He well understood that the reason for his Cabinet's existence lay in expectations of reform. It just so happened, too, that reform created a means to resist the preponderant influence of the Seiyūkai, which now held more than half of the posts in the Cabinet.

Two reform measures became emblems of the Yamamoto administration. The first involved a relaxation of requisite qualifications for the employment of the army minister. The second entailed a similar relaxation for the hiring of deputy ministers and bureau heads.

Up to this point, the appointment of the army minister had occurred according to an active-duty officer system: to prevent the parties from meddling in military affairs, only active generals or active lieutenants could be appointed as army minister. This requirement became the direct reason for the collapse of the Second Saionji Cabinet.[19] Popular opinion demanded the dissolution of the system and the further consolidation of the Cabinet.

The posts of deputy minister and bureau head were once filled in a free-hire system, but, to prevent post-hunters in the parties from gaining power by purely political means, the regime had installed a qualification-based hiring system for those positions, as we have seen. Now, under the banner of opening up the government and liberalizing employment, the political parties sought to revert to a more relaxed system that would allow their party officials to attain state posts. The government, too, wanted to exploit political hires to make each government ministry align more closely with the will of the Cabinet. By these two reform measures, the regime intended to reform the state in anticipation of the inauguration of genuine party cabinets.

In March 1913, Prime Minister Yamamoto announced the two reform measures to the plenary session of the Imperial Diet in the form of an answer to a question posed by a lawyer from the Seiyūkai. From here, Yamamoto ploughed ahead vigorously, sometimes forcefully, to make his proposals a reality.

On 13 June, reform of the army and naval ministries was formally proclaimed, and the requirement that the army minister and his deputy be active-duty officers was revoked. Momentum now on its side, the regime flung itself into reforming the employment system for deputy ministers and bureau heads. It proposed an open-style system that would not stipulate any qualification-based restrictions on hiring. The reform intended to clear the path to political hires, and towards that end, it had three other aims.

The first objective was to allow the political parties to win control over bureaucratic institutions. The parties were no longer so naive as to allow post-hunters to run wild once the deputy minister and bureau-head posts became political ones. Knowing they had to avoid becoming the object of popular opprobrium, they planned to fill the deputy and bureau-head posts with professional bureaucrats. At the same time, if they managed to expand the scope of acceptable political appointees all the way down to the level of bureau head, they would help advance the partisanship of the bureaucracy even past the levels it had attained in the Keien era. And if they managed then to institutionalize these designs, they could scoop not only such readily politicized ministries as the Home Ministry but also the highly specialized and autonomous treasury and justice ministries into the partisan fold. They could exploit bureaucrats sympathetic to the Seiyūkai and make a more consolidated political administration possible.

To realize these plans, the regime needed to win over the deputy ministers. To hold a conference of deputy ministers the day before the Cabinet met had become a standard practice by the late Meiji era. Bills and proposals passed through this ministry conference before they reached the Cabinet. The system of general government coordination the Waihan administration had imagined in its Conference of Cabinet Counsellors was realized here, in the Conference of Deputies (*jikan kaigi*).

The second objective of the Yamamoto reform proposal was to siphon personnel with expertise in executive government over to the political parties. In anticipation of party rule, the political factions needed to nurture prospective candidates for cabinet posts and steep them in policy matters. And in cases when a heavyweight with thin specialized knowledge ascended to the helm of a given ministry, he would need savvy auxiliaries to help him.

Faced with the mass entry of bureaucrats into the new party of Katsura Tarō, Hara called for Seiyūkai-leaning bureaucrats to side formally with his party. They accepted. The ideals of party politics and indeed their own political survival were at stake. And thus, under the banner of 'repairing the political parties' unfurled by Itō, human resources with expertise in policy began to gather under the helm of either the Seiyūkai or the Dōshikai.

The third objective was to loosen the stranglehold that legal studies had on the bureaucracy. A new sense was beginning to emerge both within and beyond the government that the time was ripe for a reappraisal of the professional bureaucracy. Most scholar-bureaucrats hailed from law school, and their expertise did not go beyond the fields they studied at university: law, politics and economics.

As executive government became increasingly specialized, problems that well surpassed the capabilities of law trainees had begun to overcome the state. Professional bureaucrats with training in medicine and engineering would have been best suited to address these problems, but they occupied lowly positions as technical bureaucrats. The pervading belief in the supremacy of legal studies was resulting in the stagnation of the executive branch.

Hara Kei, home minister, banded with Okuda of the education ministry and Okano of the Legislation Bureau to draft a revised version of the Edict on the Employment of Civil Officers (*bunkan nin'yō rei*) that would incorporate these three objectives.

To pass, the edict had to overcome the hurdle that was Yamagata Aritomo, head of the Privy Council. Unlike in the days of the Edict on Public Forms, Hara and his men had no phalanx led by Itō Hirobumi to back them up. The Privy Council, considering itself the guardsman of the institutions of the state, set up an investigative committee made up of political bureaucrats close to Yamagata to look into the proposed revision.

Even with all his gumption, Yamamoto Gonbée could only manage to win a compromise: free employment with no regard to qualifications would be allowed for deputy ministers, but the line was drawn there. Bureau heads could not be political appointees. The first and the second objectives of the reform were thus to some extent achieved. But the third objective, which bore directly on the modernization of executive institutions, perennially remained a point for further discussion. With political considerations given priority over more logistical matters of executive functioning, the problem of practical administration stayed unresolved.

From here, technical experts from engineering backgrounds joined together to form the Technical Governance Association (*kōseikai*) and other such hybrid government-civilian political organizations to call for reforms to a tendentiously legalist executive state.[20] Reforms of the examination system for higher-level bureaucrats did proceed, resulting in the expansion of the subjects tested. But the expansion never went past fields in the humanities and social sciences, and solutions to the problem of specializing the bureaucracy went nowhere further.

From the bureaucracy to the parties: Mizuno Rentarō, 'minister of personnel'

The revised Edict on the Employment of Civil Officers was publicly proclaimed in August 1913, the second year of the Taishō era. With the proclamation, a host of officials marched into the Seiyūkai: Tokonami, president of the Railway Institute; Mizuno Rentarō, deputy home minister; Oka Kishichirō, head of the Public Security Bureau; Hashimoto Keizaburō, deputy minister of agricultural and commercial affairs; Inuzuka Katsutarō, deputy minister of communications; and Koyama, deputy minister

Figure 5.1 Mizuno Rentarō at the official residence of the Minister of Home Affairs, 1918. *Source:* Matsunami Jin'ichirō, ed., *Mizuno Hakushi koki kinnen ronsaku to zuihitsu*, Mizuno Rentarō sensei koki shukugakai jimusho, 1937, p. 818.

of justice. All had held posts of responsibility under Saionji during the Keien era and had coalesced as a Seiyūkai-faction group.

The mass entry of deputy-level bureaucrats into the political parties shook the world of officialdom. It was not just that the men had joined politics. They had done so while still holding their government posts. Newspapers critical of the Yamamoto Cabinet derogated the revised employment edict as an Edict on the Entry of Deputy Ministers into the Political Parties. They suspected that deputies had no choice but to join the party if they wanted to retain their executive posts.

Was that really the case? If it was true that partisan affiliation had become a requisite for holding a deputy post, then we would expect that deputies in the finance and education ministries would have followed their peers into the Seiyūkai. But they did not. No doubt there were forces, both visible and not, that sent men in the direction of the parties. But individual inclination mattered greatly, too.

If personal will formed a major reason for entering party politics, then we must delve more deeply into the thoughts and actions of those individuals who indeed made the move. Both Mizuno and Tokonami have left remarks on the participation of bureaucrats in partisan politics.

Let us begin with Mizuno Rentarō, an Akita man born in 1868 who studied English law, graduated in 1892 and was hired through the probationary employment system. The Home Ministry usually demanded that its officers shuttle back and forth between

Figure 5.2 Tokonami Takejirō (centre), Minister for Home Affairs, with Prime Minister Hara Takashi (right), 1921. *Source:* Maeda Renzan, *Tokonami Takejirō den*, Tokonami Takejirō denki kankōkai, 1939, p. 553.

the national centre and the provinces, but Mizuno was an unusual case who managed to remain in the national centre throughout his ministry career. Over his long years as a secretary to the home minister, he gained intimate knowledge of the men staffing the ministry and earned the nickname 'minister of personnel'. He became a major power-holder in the ministry.

Mizuno enjoyed friendly relations with the Freedom Party of Itagaki Taisuke, and, as an admirer of the British parliamentary cabinet system, he demonstrated a particular understanding of and sympathy towards the political parties. A turning point came for him when he encountered Hara Kei, then home minister in the First Saionji Cabinet. As explained above, Hara had set about winnowing prefectural governors, ruthlessly tossing out men he deemed effete. Aiding Hara in this decision-making was none other than the minister of personnel, Mizuno Rentarō, who wielded his thoroughgoing familiarity with the Home Ministry for the benefit of Hara.

The importance with which Hara, a party man, viewed Mizuno transformed Mizuno's life as a bureaucrat. When the Second Katsura Cabinet replaced the Saionji Cabinet, Hirata Tōsuke took the helm of the Home Ministry and populated its major posts with oligarchic henchmen: Ikki became deputy; Arimatsu Hideyoshi, head of public security; and Kamei Eizaburō, superintendent of the police. Mizuno was removed from the mainstream of power and sent on official business to Europe and America. The move was clearly a demotion, simply painted over with face-saving veneer. Even after Mizuno returned home, he was kept waiting for a reappointment as bureau head. When he was finally rehired, he was dumped into the Public Works Bureau, a nexus of technical bureaucrats from which civil officials usually steered clear.

Despite these clear signs, Mizuno could not quite fathom the shrinking distance between politics and bureaucracy. In an essay he published in 1909, just after he returned from the West, Mizuno maintained that a clear distinction had to exist between the role of politicians and that of bureaucrats, and he insisted that that distinction had to be elucidated in the regime. 'If a [bureaucrat] wishes to be a politician, he has no other choice but to vacate the post he is in,' Mizuno averred.[21]

Mizuno weathered three years of poor treatment before being selected to lead the Provincial Affairs Bureau, the main bureau of the Home Ministry, for a revenant Seiyūkai-Saionji Cabinet. Under Hara, he set about reforming bureau administration. When the army expansion problem drove the Cabinet to mass resignation, Mizuno joined his superiors in leaving the regime, and with a recommendation from Hara he received an imperial appointment to the House of Peers. It was abundantly clear, if anyone bothered to notice, that Mizuno had transformed into a Seiyūkai-faction bureaucrat.

Mizuno at last ascended to the position of deputy minister under Home Minister Hara with the rise of the first Cabinet of Yamamoto Gonbée. Witnessing how Mizuno lent himself to political affairs well outside the scope of his administrative duties, Hara persuaded Mizuno to join the Seiyūkai, telling him, 'You're quickly reaching a point where it doesn't even make sense for you to hold an administrative position.' Hara was shrewd. There was no better means of maintaining ascendancy over the Home Ministry than through its so-called Minister of Personnel. Dangling before Mizuno such projects as the reform of the oligarchy and the development of the provinces, especially the Tōhoku region, Hara persuaded Mizuno to join him.

Hara valued Mizuno greatly. In 1907, the Akita branch of the Seiyūkai tried to put Mizuno forward as a candidate for the House of Representatives. Mizuno showed interest. But Hara did not grant his blessing. He came up with excuses: Mizuno is an amateur, just an administrative bureaucrat; the masses will not take a man like that; since Akita is a ferocious political battleground, he might very well end up tasting defeat. Hara insisted that Mizuno would be better off in the House of Peers, where he could set his highly professionalized skills to work in favour of the party.

In later years, Mizuno recollected, 'A deputy minister or other such bureaucrat with particular connections could not go against the opinions of the minister, and he had little choice but to enter the parties and lead a political life.' A human resource of his exceptional talent could probably have become a minister even without joining a party.

But Mizuno had spent his youthful years dreaming of the day of party rule, and now, in the prime of his life, he determined to take a gamble on a life in politics.

And indeed, from hereon, Mizuno exerted himself in pursuit of party rule. He became a bond linking the bureaucrats of the Home Ministry together, whether in his own party or as a member of the political affairs research team (*seimu chōsa kai*). And in the House of Peers he served a similar function as a supporting pillar of the Kōyū Club, the Seiyūkai faction within the house.

From the bureaucracy to the parties: Tokonami Takejirō, black sheep of the oligarchy

Tokonami Takejirō graduated with a degree in politics in 1890, entered the government through the probationary employment system, became president of the Railway Institute and from there entered the Seiyūkai. But his life deviated from the standard road to power from Kagoshima, the oligarchic bastion where he was born in 1866. It is said that his father, Masayoshi, an officer in the judiciary, did not get along with others in his hometown. Takejirō operated under the influence of these unfavourable circumstances. (Masayoshi was an extraordinary artist, and some of his oil paintings survive today, including a portrait of General Ulysees S. Grant and a depiction of the ceremony for the inauguration of the Meiji Constitution.) In any case, that the younger Tokonami was transferred to a post as Akita governor and then was selected to head the bureau of provincial affairs only after a direct appeal to Hara testifies to his identity as a black sheep of oligarchic origins.

Tokonami worked towards the abolition of the national district system (*gunsei seido*) under Home Minister Hara Kei during the first Cabinet of Saionji. The district offices (*gunyakusho*) were strongholds of Yamagata factionalism. Tokonami set about destroying them. Unsurprisingly, then, the Second Katsura Cabinet was hostile to Tokonami. He was not dismissed from his post, but he was removed from the new chain of decision-making that ran from Ikki, deputy minister, to Arimatsu, head of the Public Security Bureau, down to Kamei, superintendent of the police. Tokonami remained head of the Provincial Affairs Bureau, but he was blocked from involvement in affairs pertaining to local and provincial personnel and forced to taste the bitterness of this deprivation of power. So Tokonami called it quits himself. He left his post and headed to Europe and America, waiting for the arrival of a new day.

Despite this fall from grace, power-wielders in the Satsuma clan had begun pinning their hopes on Tokonami ever since he began to distinguish himself under Hara. Once Tokonami rose to deputy home minister under the Second Cabinet of Saionji, influential Kagoshima bureaucrats including Yamanouchi Kazuji and Ōkubo Toshitake began to establish furtive lines of communication with him. Their bonds became even tighter when fellow Kagoshima man Yamamoto Gonbée established a new cabinet dominated by the Seiyūkai. Tokonami's political value rose. But his increasing prominence meant that he had to navigate a volatile area between the Satsuma clan and the Seiyūkai.

A decisive moment came at the end of 1913, when Prime Minister Yamamoto paid a visit to Tokonami to sound him out before his imperial selection to the House of Peers. Imperial appointees enjoyed substantial remuneration and lifetime tenure in the House. They held a sinecure after which everyone in the bureaucracy yearned, just as Hara himself once had.

Already part of the Seiyūkai, Tokonami paid a visit to his personal guarantor, Hara, and asked about what he should do about the offer from Yamamoto. Hara urged him to forgo his seat in the House of Peers and instead pursue one in the House of Representatives. Hara indicated to Tokonami the path that he himself had taken and persuaded him that pursuing the political mainstream as a politician in his own right would take him to a better future.

Tokonami conveyed his decision to Yamamoto: they lived in a world now revolving around parliamentary politics, and in such circumstances, he could not turn his back on the political parties. The parties had problems, no doubt, but hurling invectives at them from the outside would do no good. As long as things were this way, he might as well dive right into the centre of politics, sully himself in its muddiness and, by working hard from the inside to make improvements, push both politics and the nation as a whole forward. Such was Tokonami's reasoning.

Tokonami had himself been a scholar-bureaucrat who had yearned for the realization of party rule. He had spent his younger days contributing to the nation by serving in financial affairs, and as he grew older he moved to improving local and provincial administration. After navigating the Taishō Political Crisis, he encountered the greatest problem of the day: the inauguration of party rule. He decided that he himself should be one to lead the way to party politics.

At this juncture, Tokonami bluntly confessed the challenges he had faced in his own life as a scholar-bureaucrat. The generation of Yamamoto Gonbée, he claimed, had achieved a shining record of service after the Meiji Restoration and had attracted the admiration of the masses. But the generation of Tokonami was different. Even if they hailed from the same oligarchic origins as their forebears, men of this generation had come to the political game later, and they had to play under different rules. They had no way of gaining influence and power other than by joining the political parties and working with their peers as a concerted group. Such bitter reflections acted as mordant criticism of Yamamoto and his band of oligarchic politicians, who had gained influence during the most prosperous era of the political past.

As the dawn of a party cabinet drew nearer, no one could rely any longer on the oligarchy to prop them up in the world of politics. The universities, the government ministries and the army had all opened their doors wide to human talent. Young men from across the nation were entering them. Tokonami had made it far along this road, but to go further he needed organizational support. The oligarchy, enervated, would not do. It was the parties who could make his ambitions a reality. Party politics stood at the crossroads of the past dreams, the present reality and the future strivings of scholar-bureaucrats.

It was not as if the scholar-bureaucrats had no fears. They could easily have chosen to remain safely in bureaucratic officialdom. But the sea before them changed, and, as Katsura appeared on the opposite side with a new political party, they decided to take the plunge into politics. Katsura had long submitted to the oligarchic factions of the bureaucracy, but now that he had broken free and launched a new party the contrast between Katsura- and Seiyūkai-faction politics had deepened. Men urgently felt that now was the time to pick their side.

The logic of political participation: Oligarchic politics and the limits of old-style Diet members

Why did scholar-bureaucrats participate in party politics? Let us consider the question from the perspective of the new Katsura party, just as we have from that of the Seiyūkai. Wakatsuki Reijirō has left an account of the processes that led Katsura to form his party. Originally from Shimane prefecture, where he was born in 1866, Wakatsuki obtained a degree in French law in 1892 and was hired through the probationary employment system before entering the Ministry of the Treasury.

Figure 5.3 Wakatsuki Reijirō (left) in London, as the special financial delegate of the Empire of Japan, 1907. *Source:* Wakatsuki Reijirō, *Kofūan kaikoroku*, Yomiuri shinbunsha, 1950, front page.

According to Wakatsuki, Katsura conveyed his desire to form a new political party to the Meiji Emperor after the mass resignation of the Second Katsura Cabinet. He argued that the Emperor would need the support of the entire populace now that the *genrō* were ageing, and he claimed that the popular parties would act as necessary channels for that support. Wakatsuki recalled why he himself had followed Katsura into the new party: 'I will join together with part of the citizenry and take up political authority; let us go and fight hard in the Diet.'[22]

Fellow treasury bureaucrat Hamaguchi Osachi has recorded even more concrete thoughts on the rise of party politics. Hamaguchi was a Kōchi man born in 1870. After graduating with a degree in politics in 1895, he entered the bureaucracy by passing the higher-level officer examinations.

Hamaguchi faced a decision with the rise of the third Cabinet of Katsura. Gotō Shinpei, the minister of communications, had heard of the talents of Hamaguchi and invited him to enter his ministry as deputy. Hamaguchi joined the Katsura faction of bureaucrats and accepted the offer from Gotō, fully aware it would lead to his membership in the new party.

Hamaguchi disapproved of the politics of compromise that had emerged from the stability of the Keien era. He maintained that the political parties had to become the driving force of constitutional government themselves and put an end to rule by bureaucracy. He called for the inauguration of responsible party rule in a two-party system. Hamaguchi believed that the British-style parliamentary system, about which he had written his graduation thesis, had now come within reach in Japan.[23]

The Diet, not the bureaucracy, was the greater obstacle to parliamentary government. During its earliest days, the Diet had become a scene of sharp clashes between the government, which advocated a principle of transcendental cabinets, and the parties, which called for parliamentarianism. But the fervour of parliamentary politics gradually died down under the banner of national unity as constitutionalism was put more thoroughly into effect and as the nation moved towards wars with China and Russia, wars that put the fate of the entire country at stake. In the airs of high politics, far from the sight of everyday citizens, the passion for parliamentarianism was largely snuffed out.

Parliamentary politics had been hollowed out. Members of the Diet often served honorary posts that did not last beyond a single term. Many were provincial power-holders who knew nothing about policy matters. They wielded their veto power whenever matters seemed to encroach on their private interests, but they did little more than this; they lacked the mettle to engage proactively in national political affairs. Even as the Diet evolved over time, its representatives remained little more than an assembly of tax collectors. They could not keep up with the increasing specialization of policy matters, to the extent that the chair of the Diet began to lament the vacuity of their endless, repetitive debates. The spirit of public debate proclaimed by the Charter Oath was fading fast.

More than the Seiyūkai, it was the Katsura faction that recognized that the regime had exhausted the utility of the politics of compromise. Members of the Katsura band set about assembling human resources who had genuine policy understanding. They sought to use popular elections to gain legitimacy. And they resolved to use the Diet as a genuine place for politics. The party politics of which they had dreamed in their younger years could never come about in the mouldering Diet before them, a Diet that did little more than run after concessions in development projects across the country.

The times provided a tail wind to these reforms. With the national crisis presented by the Russo-Japanese War over, the straitened finances of the post-war era made prudence in policy crucial. Spaces for public debate had expanded, too, after the Russo-Japanese War, and as a result a parliamentary politics that had once been in retreat gave signs of recrudescence.

Amid these changes, the stand-off between two great parties, the Seiyūkai and the new party of Katsura, endowed citizens with the possibility of a real choice between two different government administrations, signalling the origins of party politics in the truest sense. It was for this reason that bureaucrats chose to participate in the parties. They had an impulse, a restless urge, to themselves be the ones to finally make constitutional government a reality.

The rise of scholar-bureaucrats and the birth of a two-party system

The Taishō Political Crisis brought about two major structural changes in modern Japanese politics. The first was the rise of a new generation. Tokonami, Mizuno, Wakatsuki and others of the probationary employment system climbed from deputy posts to cabinet ministerial posts. Members of the Twenty-Eight Group such as Hamaguchi, who had passed the higher-level officer exams and entered the government by its means, now ascended from bureau head posts to deputy posts. The second change involved the birth of broad-ranging, cross-sectional political parties and a genuine movement towards party rule. These two transformations fatefully arrived together during the political crisis. As human resources arose to carry the government forward, history turned a new page.

Scholar-bureaucrats themselves had seen this vision of the future from early on. Hata Toyosuke was one such scholar-bureaucrat. Born in Tokyo in 1872, he graduated from the Imperial University in 1896 with a degree in politics and, after passing the higher-level officer exams, he entered the Home Ministry. In his student days, he had mapped out this trajectory in his diary: he would enter the Home Ministry, rise to the level of prefectural governor and then switch over to the House of Representatives, where he would then aim for a ministerial post.[24] Even as their ideals were obstructed by oligarchic barriers, scholar-bureaucrats who had studied the ideals of constitutional politics nurtured growing expectations of party politics.

The generation preceding that of these young scholar-bureaucrats could not accept the ideals of party politics. The aftermath of the death of Katsura Tarō at the end of 1913 manifested their aversion to politics. In the process of weathering his passing and holding the inauguration ceremony of the Dōshikai afterward, Katō Kōmei, Watasuki, Hamaguchi and other such scholar-bureaucrat party members came together and vowed to carry out the dying wishes of Katsura. But men of the generation before them such as Gotō Shinpei and Nakashōji Ren quit the party. They had been motivated by gaining political power through a grand political party under the helm of Katsura, not by the ideals of party politics themselves, as Hamaguchi had been.[25] Gotō and his band could still rely on Yamagata and the *genrō*, with whom they enjoyed deep relations, to win them back their posts as bureaucrat-politicians.

But in such circumstances, not even Yamagata, the father of bureaucratic factionalism, could prevent scholar-bureaucrats from participating in politics. 'How regrettable that such good men as Hamaguchi and Hashimoto have suddenly become party men and defiled themselves with the depravity of partisanship,' Yamagata lamented, revealing the unbridgeable gap between his view of constitutional governance and that of the scholar-bureaucrats.[26] Indeed, at last, the bureaucracy came to lose its function as a bulwark against the political parties and embraced partisanship intimately.

Why did the parties welcome bureaucrats?

The nature of the political parties transformed with the entry of scholar-bureaucrats. Most striking was how the bureaucrats enhanced the policy-proposal capabilities of the parties.

Until this point, even though they received advance briefings on policy affairs, the parties had only limited access to policy materials, restricting their ability to conduct policy research. But once men from the bureaucracy began linking the parties to the government ministries, the asymmetry of policy information began to be resolved. Not only did the new bureaucrat-politicians participate in the policy research committees of the parties, but they also actively wrote policy papers in party publications and deepened the understanding of the political rank and file in such matters. Men who had no experience in elections or in other political affairs managed to make their presence valuable.

The pipelines the scholar-bureaucrats built between the executive ministries and the parties benefited the ministries no less than the parties. It was cumbersome for the bureaucrats to go repeatedly to policy research committee gatherings, but as the understanding and knowledge of men in the parties deepened, the substantial long-term pay-off of their links became clear.

To the parties, the scholar-bureaucrats represented future candidates for cabinet ministerial posts. We might think, looking from the vantage point of today, that the parties were brimming with men intent on joining the Cabinet, whether by their own self-promotion or by nomination from others. But party heavyweights at the time feared being barraged by questions in the Diet and tended to avoid the Cabinet. And it was sometimes the case that those who did pursue ministerial posts lacked adequate capabilities. To post a party official with inadequate policy knowledge to a ministerial post in the Cabinet could have eroded trust in party politics. Even if there were party leaders with sophisticated policy knowledge, to place them in ministerial posts while others remained stuck in the party would be to sow seeds of conflict. This complex configuration of problems and interests gave rise to a division of labour wherein up-and-coming party men attended to party affairs (*tōmu*) and men coming from the bureaucracy attended to matters of political governance (*seimu*).

Putting men who originated in the bureaucracy forth as cabinet ministers would engender smooth relations with the executive ministries. The party bureaucrats could win support, too, from other party men seeking to expand their partisan influence. They could put forward cogent policy proposals that would win the sympathy of the *genrō*. And if they managed to be elected, then popular opinion would rally behind them. To gather men from the bureaucracy into the party fold and to make them cabinet ministers constituted a significant strategy whereby a party not only maintained internal and external stability but also moved towards rule by party cabinets.

The Keien era marked the apex of the politics of compromise, but it was also a time when the limits of government sectionalism, a sectionalism that arose from the principle of divided management responsibilities, were badly exposed, especially in the railway expansion problem that engulfed the state. The birth of party cabinets, of responsible cabinets, resulted from both the trends and the demands of the era. Two major cross-sectional parties had worked out a relationship between partisan politics and the bureaucracy. Now the problem lay in reconstructing the relationship between the Cabinet and the ministries and in ensuring the internal consistency of government policies.

Towards the era of party cabinets

The demise of the oligarchic bureaucracy: The failure of Kiyoura to form a cabinet

The extraordinary success of the first Cabinet of Yamamoto Gonbée in carrying out large-scale reform created expectations for long-lasting government stability. Things did not go that way. In 1914, suspicions over a corruption scandal involving the German company Siemens and the Japanese Navy, the latter of which propped up Yamamoto, erupted into the open and drove the Yamamoto Cabinet to mass resignation.

Forming a successor cabinet proved difficult beyond precedent. The division of powers ordained by the Meiji Constitution was now taking root in the government. There was no shortage of men to represent the interests of the parties, of the officialdom or of the *genrō*, but few could be found who could win support from all three of those factions. The *genrō* appointed Tokugawa Iesato, sixteenth in the Tokugawa lineage, as head of the House of Peers to help manage the post-Yamamoto crisis. But Iesato resigned immediately.

The *genrō* next chose Kiyoura Keigo to lead the House of Peers. He hesitated, but Kiyoura set his hopes on cooperation from the Seiyūkai and acceded. There was no reason for someone who had long served as a Yamagata-faction bureaucrat to reject the *genrō*.

The expectations of men from his hometown also contributed to the decision. Kiyoura was born in Kumamoto, a region that had produced Yokoi Shōnan, Inoue Kowashi and other talented men who contributed to the Meiji Restoration. But no Kumamoto man had made it to the seat of the prime minister. Kumamoto power-holders were desperate to put someone there. They gathered daily at the estates of Tokutomi Sohō or Kiyoura in the Ōmori area of Tokyo prefecture and plotted the inauguration of a Kiyoura Cabinet. With Katsura now gone, they calculated that the Seiyūkai would rally behind Kiyoura.

Assigned to negotiations with the Seiyūkai were Munakata Tadasu and Kobashi Ichita. Both were bureaucrats in the Home Ministry who hailed from Kumamoto and enjoyed close ties with Hara Kei. On the Seiyūkai side, Matsuda Masahisa had fallen gravely ill, and there were few chances of forging an alliance except through Hara. But Hara balked at the negotiations. The Seiyūkai was in the throes of crisis. Saionji had taken responsibility for the Taishō Political Crisis and resigned as party president, and Matsuda had been stricken by illness. Hara feared that cosying up to Yamagata-faction bureaucrats in these circumstances would splinter the party. The Seiyūkai did not offer support. No Kiyoura Cabinet was formed at this point.

Kiyoura wrote in his recollections that he had benefited neither from exceptional treatment from his fellow Kumamoto men nor from the political protection afforded by marital ties. He had studied hard and built his life by dint of his own efforts. It seems that he just happened to have been born too early and wound up in the era of oligarchism. He had won a foothold in oligarchic government by dedicating himself to the design of state institutions. But regardless of how he himself thought of things, he came to stand as a representative of a bureaucracy by domainal factionalists. His failure to form a cabinet symbolized the end of the era of oligarchic bureaucracy.

Towards a two-party era: Bureaucrats and the Second Ōkuma Cabinet

The failure to form a Kiyoura Cabinet pushed the *genrō* to the brink. As the state elite faced confusion, Ōkuma Shigenobu swept in.

On 16 April 1914, Ōkuma assembled anti-Seiyūkai forces around a Dōshikai core and formed a new cabinet. Public opinion hailed the formation of a new administration around a man who had won public admiration through his contributions to constitutional governance. Ōkuma had fought resistance and gained support in over thirty-two turbulent years since the political crisis of 1881. He well knew that he could not simultaneously appease both the scheming *genrō* and an expectant public. He decided to set about reforming both, saying, 'Our nation today suffers from the baneful influence of both the bureaucracy and the political parties. I have determined to set myself to cementing the foundations of constitutional governance.'[27]

The core of the Second Ōkuma Cabinet was the Dōshikai. Katō Kōmei, president of the party, was appointed foreign minister, and Wakatsuki Reijirō became treasury minister; Dōshikai men originating in the bureaucracy populated the most important ministries. From party origins, Ozaki Yukio and Taketomi Tokitoshi entered the Cabinet. Ozaki, seen as a scrupulous man who would fare well in elections, was placed in the justice ministry, a stronghold of party men. Taketomi, well trusted by Ōkuma, went to the communications ministry, which held concessions for development projects across the country. With snap elections planned in the near future, the regime placed Ōura Kanetake in the agricultural and commercial ministry, a department with strong influence in the provinces. Men from the ruling Dōshikai were appointed to all other cabinet posts, except those of the two military ministries and the education ministry, rounding out an Ōkuma Cabinet that won recognition for its stable internal coherency.

This Dōshikai inclination was apparent in appointments to deputy posts, too. The Twenty-Eight Group dominated deputy minister positions. Hamaguchi went to the treasury, Kamiyama Mitsunoshin to agriculture and commerce and Shimo'oka Chūji to the Home Ministry. Isawa Takio became superintendent of the police. Thrilled, the Twenty-Eight Group held a celebration. Hamaguchi and Shimo'oka then ran in the general elections for the House of Representatives a year later, and Kamiyama and Isawa began to lay the groundwork for a Dōshikai faction in the House of Peers. The same division of labour that had arisen between Mizuno and Tokonami in the Seiyūkai, that between men originating from the parties and those from the bureaucracy, took hold in the Dōshikai.

But the justice and communications ministries, to whose helms party men Ozaki and Taketomi had risen, did not make partisan appointments. They went ahead with conventional hiring practices on an annual basis. From this point until the rise of the Hara Kei Cabinet in 1918, the Ministry of Communications proceeded with a customary practice of staggering the terms of service and times of replacement for the head of the ministry and his deputy.

In the Ministry of Justice, the head of the legal affairs bureau (*hōmukyoku*), Suzuki Kisaburō, was promoted to deputy minister. Suzuki was the son-in law of Hatoyama Kazuo, who had switched over from the Kenseihontō to the Seiyūkai. He could have been ejected as part of a partisan reshuffling of executive posts, but here the Ōkuma Cabinet decided to wait and abide by the regular schedule of personnel appointment. The Ministry of Justice was an unusual place.

Dividing political (*seimu*) and administrative (*jimu*) affairs

The new Ōkuma Cabinet carefully scrutinized the policies its predecessors in the Seiyūkai had made, and it then moved towards change, not least in the bureaucracy. The Seiyūkai had transformed the deputy minister post, the position that stood at the helm of both political and administrative affairs, into a partisan one. By doing so, it had subordinated the government ministries under the political will of the ruling administration. Ōkuma now sought to undo this system and to move forward with his long-held commitment to a system that distinguished between political and administrative affairs.

The ruling Dōshikai supported this plan. Party members hailing from the bureaucracy, from Katō Kōmei down, agreed that they needed to secure the autonomy of government ministries by distinguishing between politics and administration. They had their own motives deep down. Bureaucrat-politicians had flimsy track records within their own party, and their control over internal party affairs was at best tenuous. Even though they had the support of their party, they wanted to ensure that they could run the administration without allowing influence from party men to become too strong.

Entry into the First World War increased the bureaucratic workload, but the Ōkuma Cabinet took determined strides towards reform. In October, it pushed a revised version of the Edict on the Employment of Civil Officers through the Privy Council and announced it publicly. Once again, hiring for the post of deputy minister became based on qualifications, and the position came under the control of professional bureaucrats. A new road was opened for party men to take other posts charged with political affairs: those of the *sanseikan*, or undersecretary, and the *fuku sanseikan*, or vice-undersecretary.

At the centre of this new system stood the undersecretary, who was tasked with political affairs. His role differed substantially from that of the cabinet counsellors (*naikaku sanjikan*) of the Waihan administration or the chief ministry secretaries (*kanbōchō*) of the Fourth Itō Cabinet. He acted as an auxiliary to the cabinet minister and as a liaison to and negotiator with the Diet, but his role ended here. The collective assembly of the undersecretaries of each ministry, though it existed, had no continuity with the Cabinet itself.

From the Keien era onward, the Conference of Deputy Ministers had regularly met prior to cabinet meetings and engaged in preliminary research, as explained earlier. It was for this reason that the Seiyūkai had removed qualification restrictions from the employment of deputies and subordinated them under their influence. Coordinating government affairs now fell on the deputy ministers charged with administrative duties, and the undersecretaries were removed from that domain of responsibility.

The difference between the new undersecretaries and the erstwhile chief ministry secretaries was stark. Unlike the chief ministry secretaries, who exercised authority over the cabinet secretaries (*daijin kanbō*), the undersecretaries and vice-undersecretaries were not granted staffs of their own. They were removed from decision-making within their respective ministries and entrusted with negotiating with the political parties and the Diet, tasks professional bureaucrats avoided. They enjoyed relatively comfortable positions. The reform proposal sailed through the approval process of the Privy Council, raising no particular objections among the executive government or the bureaucracy.

The Seiyūkai and the Dōshikai had drawn up strikingly contrasting models of the legislative and executive arms of the political parties and the state ministries, of politicians and bureaucrats. From here on, the two pre-war political parties continued to clash along these fault-lines until the era of party cabinets came to an end.

Deputy minister or member of parliament? The decisions of Hamaguchi and Shimo'oka

The twelfth general elections of the House of Representatives in March 1915 marked the first real showdown between the Seiyūkai and the Dōshikai. Hara Kei had risen to the presidency of the Seiyūkai and Katō Kōmei to that of the Dōshikai. Now came the first elections with this new configuration.

That so many men from the bureaucracy ran in this election distinguished it from prior ones. The Seiyūkai put up twenty-eight men originally from the bureaucracy for election, of whom twenty won after fighting as members of a party out of power. Among the bureaucrat-candidates were Inuzuka Katsutarō, former deputy minister of communications, who ran in Yamagata; Hata Toyosuke, former governor of Tokushima prefecture, who ran in Saitama; Sugiyama Shigorō, former head of the Home Ministry Bureau of Public Health (*eiseikyoku*), who ran in Kanagawa; and Munakata Tadasu, former governor of Tokyo prefecture, who ran in Kumamoto.

The public lauded the election of more members of parliament with origins in the bureaucracy. It especially welcomed what it viewed as the transformation of the Seiyūkai from a conglomeration of activists holding out from the defunct Freedom Party to a genuine policy-making organization that recruited members of the bureaucracy. Prospects looked favourable for the Seiyūkai, which had been embattled since the heyday of Itō Hirobumi.

The Dōshikai, now competing for the first time as a ruling party, ran twenty-two former bureaucrats in the election, of whom seventeen were elected. The candidates included Hamaguchi, deputy minister of the treasury, who ran in Kōchi city, and Shimo'oka, deputy home minister, who ran in Hyōgo prefecture. But in its quest to separate political and administrative affairs, the ruling Ōkuma Cabinet had refused to allow sitting members of the bureaucracy to hold dual posts as members of the House of Representatives. Hamaguchi and Shimo'oka were criticized for running for political office while serving in bureaucratic posts. Just four months later, they were removed from their posts as deputy ministers and reassigned as undersecretaries.

Hamaguchi and Shimo'oka thus both chose to renounce their roles as deputy ministers and aim for the House of Representatives. That choice meant that they forwent imperial appointment to the House for Peers and instead opted to be voted into the House of Representatives by the popular electorate. They well understood that Diet members without support from the electorate would not survive as party politicians once the era of party rule arrived. Their own hometowns welcomed the candidacy of men who could become fit for cabinet minister positions.

Shimo'oka had a particularly strong urge to run. He had been prepared to lead a life as a political nomad after the Third Katsura Cabinet resigned en masse and he was chased out of his role as deputy minister of agriculture and commerce. But Yamagata, chair of the Privy Council, rescued him, unwilling to let his talents go to waste. He placed him in the important position of head of the Privy Council secretariat. In that capacity, Shimo'oka composed a long opinion paper to obstruct the reform blitz of the Yamamoto Cabinet. Things were complicated. Shimo'oka was a Katsura-faction man who benefited from the solicitude of Yamagata.

Because of his particular positioning, Shimo'oka felt compelled to seek the blessing of Yamagata when the Ōkuma Cabinet tried to recruit him as deputy home minister. Yamagata offered his approval on the condition that Shimo'oka refuse party affiliation. Shimo'oka ran in the general elections and was voted into the House of Representatives even without affiliating with the Dōshikai, and he looked forward to participation in the Diet by forming the Kōyū Club, an assembly of non-Seiyūkai, politically unaffiliated men. Ironically, these non-partisan manoeuvres only went to expose to Shimo'oka the limits of operating outside the parties.

As speculation over the mass resignation of the Ōkuma Cabinet mounted in 1916, Shimo'oka tried to work through the offices of Ōkuma and Yamagata to persuade Yamagata to make Katō Kōmei of the Dōshikai the next prime minister. Katō, a politician originating in the bureaucracy, largely fell in line with the Yamagata ideology, and, if guided by Yamagata, he would proceed faithfully. So Shimo'oka made his case.

But Shimo'oka was rebuffed. In October 1916, Terauchi Masatake formed a new cabinet with the support of the Seiyūkai. Shimo'oka fulminated. He ripped into Yamagata; this choice would tarnish his legacy, he warned.

Shimo'oka protested that, in an age in which the citizenry had awakened and public opinion had been roused, to appoint a transcendental non-party cabinet was to deviate from the proper course of constitutional governance. Even if leaders had qualms about party cabinets, building a cabinet without negotiating with the political parties was out of touch with the times.

Shimo'oka sought to realize a model of party-bureaucracy collaboration originally set forth by Ōkuma. But his negotiations with the regime broke down and he defected from the Yamagata faction, signalling a new determination to lead the charge towards party rule. 'I implore your excellency', he said, 'to allow the world of politics to stand unrestrained and independent and to allow men the freedom to open up new worlds of their own.'[28] There was no stopping the rush to party rule.

As the advent of party politics drew near, scholar-bureaucrats broke free from the oligarchs and chose to enter political parties. Nothing would become of them, they realized, if they remained politically neutral subordinates of Yamagata Aritomo. In January of the following year, Shimo'oka renounced his neutrality, threw his weight behind the founding of the Kenseikai and took his first official steps as a party man.

The word of Yamagata had lost import even for those closest to him. Into the Terauchi Cabinet, the last transcendental cabinet, had filed Gotō Shinpei, Nakashōji Ren, Den Kenjirō and others of this final generation of oligarch-bureaucrats, men who had disavowed party politics. By forming this transcendental cabinet, they rang the death knell of their age of oligarchism.

The collaboration of politicians and bureaucrats: The rise of the Hara Cabinet

The era of the oligarchy ended. Party politics arrived. In September 1918 (= Taishō 7), the Terauchi Cabinet signalled that it would resign and take responsibility for the havoc wreaked by the Rice Riots. The resignation signalled the fecklessness of an oligarchic cabinet with no common ground with the citizenry in the post-First World War era. The prognostications of Shimo'oka had come true.

Power passed not to the Kenseikai but to the Seiyūkai. The Cabinet of Hara Kei, known as the 'first genuine party cabinet' in Japanese history, was inaugurated on 29 September. A new era dawned.

Celebrated as it rose to power, the Hara Cabinet was laden with heavy expectations. Those expectations came not only from the long-awaited appearance of party rule but also from the leadership prowess of Hara himself. Surely there was no need to worry about the relationship with the bureaucracy, people thought, now that Hara had risen to the helm. For it was Hara who, for no fewer than three terms, had used his stable leadership powers to direct the course of the Home Ministry, that organ that flattered itself as the 'authority among the authorities'. And it was he who had, as president of the Seiyūkai, harmonized a discordant party. No doubt the party would function well under his helm. Even when faced with critical problems in diplomacy and finance, Hara had been sure not to charge ahead on his own; he had built a constructive relationship with the *genrō*, ensuring that no attacks on his policies would blindside him. There was ample reason for optimism among the public. Hara was the rare man who could find coherency in the structure of divided rule ordained by the Meiji Constitution.

Hara's governing philosophy had been informed by wide-ranging study and experience. He originated from Mutsu, a rebel army stronghold. He studied English and French from a young age and then enrolled in the law academy of the Ministry of Justice, where he pursued legal studies. From there he became a newspaper journalist, carefully observing both politics and the reality of provincial life. He then turned to the bureaucracy and set his sights on administrative structures, seeking reform of the bureaucracy in the agricultural-commercial and foreign ministries. It was Hara, for instance, who set up an independent exam system for diplomatic and consular officers, folding the once-haphazard system of consular appointments into the pattern of state exams.

Hara then found his interests expand from administrative rule to constitutional politics. These new interests drove him to contribute to founding the Seiyūkai. But Hara lacked a record that would demonstrate to his peers the kind of man he was. The posts he had held, whether in newspaper journalism or in finance, had been stopgaps. He recognized this problem after he joined the Seiyūkai: even though he had made it as a cabinet minister, he was not selected to the House of Peers. He could align with Itō, he could join the Seiyūkai, but somehow he could never compete with other Itō-faction bureaucrats. He could not overcome this inferiority. And so he decided to run for the House of Representatives and transform into a political man.

Then came his breakthrough. Hara understood political administration, and he had professionalized skills in executive governance. The parties and their members lacked such expertise. After the Fourth Itō Cabinet fell and Itō-faction bureaucrats began exiting the Seiyūkai, Hara, with his knowledge in both executive and legislative governance, won attention. No one else in the Seiyūkai could counter Katsura by speaking to him in his own language. Hara could. By exploiting his skills in shrewd negotiations with Katsura, he raised his standing in the party. He matured into a leader who could stand on an equal footing with old-timer Matsuda Masahisa.

The relationship with Katsura turned increasingly contentious once Saionji formed his Cabinet and the Seiyūkai took control of the government. Hara prized bureaucrats hostile to the oligarchic establishment and began gathering them by his side. He established a common vision with them of overcoming the ageing structure of oligarchic rule and of creating a new system of governance. He folded both them and their policies into the Seiyūkai by working to turn their ideas into practical reform. One by one, talented men from the bureaucracy began filing under Hara and into the Seiyūkai.

Members of the Hara Cabinet: An administration of bureaucrats

Stars of the Seiyūkai gathered in the Cabinet of Hara Kei. Takahashi Korekiyo took the helm of the treasury and Yamamoto Tatsuo that of agricultural and commercial affairs again. Having won a seat in the House of Representatives and having become a major force in the Kyushu arm of the Seiyūkai, Tokonami was promoted to home minister. All three had participated in the Seiyūkai under the Yamamoto Cabinet.

Nakahashi Tokugorō became minister of education. Hailing from Ishikawa prefecture, where he was born in 1861, and holding a degree in law, Nakahashi had made major contributions to the Seiyūkai during its days out of power. He was a politician of bureaucratic origins who had served in the Legislation Bureau and the Administrative Bureau of the House of Representatives (*Shūgiin jimukyoku*), where he worked on the structures of the Diet. He then rose to head of the Merchant Marine Bureau (*kansenkyoku*) of the communications ministry before transferring out of the government and serving as head of Ōsaka Shōsen, a merchant marine company, in which capacity he became a major financial backer of the Seiyūkai.

Even though he originated from the bureaucracy, Nakahashi lacked intimate knowledge of education administration. And he took his post just as the education ministry was struggling with a major new policy of increasing schoolteachers. To help rectify this lack of expertise, Hara appointed Minami Hiroshi, head of the Saionji Cabinet secretariat, as deputy minister of education. He made such strategic appointments in the communications ministry, too. Under Noda Utarō, communications minister and the only cabinet official with no executive experience, he placed Hata Toyosuke as a defence against possible contingencies. Noda entrusted most ministerial work to Hata and dedicated himself to coordination endeavours with other ministries and the ruling Seiyūkai.

In the Ministry of Justice, the toughest corner of the government, first the regime considered promoting Suzuki Kisaburō, the deputy minister, to minister. But Suzuki reviled the Seiyūkai partisanship of the new Cabinet. He declined. Hara decided to take a simultaneous appointment as minister of justice himself, but to treat Suzuki as the minister for all practical purposes. Later on, when collaboration between the Seiyūkai and the Research Group of the House of Peers deepened, the head of the Research Group, Ōki Enkichi, took on an exclusive role as minister of justice. But even this appointment did not imply a violation of the independence of the Ministry of Justice from partisanship. It hinted, rather, at the furtherance of the relationship between the parties and the justice ministry as one of mutual autonomy.

The ministries themselves welcomed the bureaucrat-politicians who came to their helm. They had feared that the establishment of party cabinets would allow ruling parties to make reckless, foolhardy demands of them. The appointment of ministers with whom they could engage in genuine dialogue became a source of relief. Members of the Home Ministry in particular found reassurance in the selection of one of their own as head of their ministry.

As fears of government sectionalism arose again, efforts at general coordination in the Cabinet to avoid executive splintering gained unprecedented importance. In this connection, Hara gave particular attention to the auxiliary organs of the Cabinet. He appointed not men from the bureaucracy but party leaders to take charge of those organs. To the chair of the cabinet secretariat, the organ that controlled administrative affairs, Hara selected Takahashi Mitsutake, who had served as a secretary when Hara worked as home minister. Takahashi was tasked with establishing coherency and coordinating communication in the Cabinet.

At the head of the Legislation Bureau (*hōseikyoku*) was placed Yokota Sennosuke. A student of Hoshi Tōru, Yokota emerged in the professional world as a lawyer and, since he belonged to an electoral district in Ibaraki, became affiliated with the Kantō faction. Hara, an organizer of the faction, discovered Yokota. When Hara sensed as president of the Seiyūkai that control of the Cabinet was starting to come within his grasp, he came to rely on the political judgement of Yokota and called on him to help maintain a favourable balance of power with Yamagata and the other *genrō*.

Up to this point, the head of the Legislation Bureau had been seen as a post fit for such men as Ikki Kitokurō and Okuno Keijirō, who had served as legislative bureaucrats or as professors at the law school of the Imperial University. Perhaps it was thought that a certain line had to be drawn between practical politics and research on bills and laws. And, indeed, the head of the Legislation Bureau in the First Yamamoto Cabinet, Okuno, had been dismissed by Yamamoto for associating too closely with the Seiyūkai. Despite this history, Hara chose Yokota, a party man, to serve as head of the bureau, even as he appointed bureaucrats and not long-time partisan leaders to every cabinet post. This selection displayed the canny understanding Hara had of administrative institutions.

The Cabinet could not take up a legislative bill unless the bill went through review by the Legislation Bureau. Because the counsellors (*sanjikan*) who made up the bureau rarely changed posts, they had amassed specialized knowledge and experience whose depth surpassed that of the bureaucrats in the ministries, who changed their posts every two years. The ministries regarded the Legislation Bureau as the guard-tower of policy-making: if someone seized control of it, he could, through policy work, survey and control the entirety of every government ministry. And that is precisely what Hara, in his shrewdness in appointing Yokota, did.

A Yokota-strain pro-Seiyūkai faction emerged in the bureaucracy of the Legislation Bureau after Yokota took over, and the bureau became an instrument for the political authority of the Seiyūkai. The waves of partisanship released by the emergence of the first genuine party cabinet overcame even the Legislation Bureau.

Towards the era of genuine party cabinets

The new relationship established between the political parties and the bureaucracy changed the structure of the parties. Communications with the central government coalesced around the chief party secretary (*kanjichō*), Hiro'oka Uichirō. The members of the General Affairs Committee (*sōmu iin*) took on the role of conveying the will of the central regime to members of the party.

With this new structure in place, the state began providing elaborate advance briefings to the ruling party. The Political Affairs Research Committee (*seimu chōsakai*) of the party had been disparaged as not a research organization so much as a game centre with no real theory of government policy. Hara appointed men originating from the bureaucracy as heads of the committee and of its subdivisions, and he worked to invigorate the deliberations of the organ. He built a new research facility for it and set scholars to work on policy research as its members. The character of the committee transformed.

The relationship between the Seiyūkai and Yamagata Aritomo improved, and as the House of Peers began to look more favourably on the party, one of its major barriers was removed. The party tapped into the channel of power linking Yamagata and Kiyoura to win backing from the Research Group, the largest faction of the House of Peers. This new support had positive implications for the ability of the party to lead the constitutional state.

By these means, Hara succeeded in establishing a stable administration. The founding of the 'first genuine party cabinet', a cabinet that disempowered long-standing state leaders and empowered party men, especially those originating in the bureaucracy, consummated some twenty years of gradual adjustments to the system of Japanese party politics. A political party indeed served as the foundation of the new Cabinet, but men who originated in the bureaucracy firmly held decision-making power. The core of the Seiyūkai had to grapple with this delicate internal structure of power, one that seemed to hearken back to the relationship between the Katsura-faction bureaucracy and the Seiyūkai under Saionji. Even while maintaining the trappings of a party cabinet, then, the party and the executive ministries secured a stable relationship by a dual structure of power made up of both the bureaucracy and the parties. What had emerged, then, was a pseudo-party cabinet, a composite structure of both the ideals and the on-the-ground reality of constitutional governance. This was nothing short of a grand design of modern Japanese politics hammered out by Hara, a man with intimate expertise in government institutions.

It might have been that Hara saw no meaningful distinction between bureaucrats and party men in the first place. Both were politicians. They differed only in their fields of specialization. Men from the bureaucracy, who had sophisticated knowledge of executive government, needed to run for office, to make their rounds around the electoral districts and to gain leadership experience over party men within the organization. The partisan politicians, who had familiarity with party affairs, were expected to accumulate executive experience, to deepen their knowledge of policy matters and to prepare to became candidates for cabinet ministerial posts. Thus it was hoped that both could be potential candidates for ministerial posts. After all, Kobashi, who became deputy home minister; Inuzuka, who became deputy minister of agricultural and commercial affairs; and Hata, who became deputy of communications, had all run for and obtained a seat in the House of Representatives. And Oka Kishichirō, superintendent of the police, and Minami, deputy minister of education, held posts in the House of Peers even as they participated in Diet politics.

Hara designated the most promising young party men as *chokunin* counsellors (*chokunin sanjikan*) and dispatched them to the executive ministries. By folding them among the counsellors of the ministries, who were charged with drafting laws and ordinances, Hara hoped that young party men would associate closely with their deputy ministers and deepen their own understanding of executive affairs. Hara's expectations were met. Matsuda Genji of the Home Ministry, Mitsuchi Chūzō of the treasury and Mochizuki Keisuke of agricultural and commercial affairs all eventually went on to become cabinet ministers. Such talented, capable young men were trained without any distinction between partisan politics and official bureaucracy.

At the same time, the professionalized expertise of the bureaucracy became a source of concern. As the specialized division of the executive state proceeded further, the era of the legislative polymath well versed in all legislative affairs reached an end. The social transformations of the aftermath of the First World War gave rise to new fields of executive affairs, such as labour administration and social policy. The ministries responded to these transformations by sending their young bureaucrats on study-abroad endeavours to America and Europe once again. As these men increased their specialized knowledge, they approached the political parties to help them implement policies they envisioned. But other bureaucrats emerged who viewed the pork-barrel politics and vested partisanship of party rule with hostility. Oligarchy had yielded to rule by party politics, and now a new underground of opposition began to form based not on visceral aversion to the oligarchy but on a rational critique of partisanship.

--

The twin births of the Imperial Diet and of a system of professional bureaucracy produced a history in which the two together worked as the drivers of constitutional government. Ten years after they emerged, they yielded the Seiyūkai, the first cross-sectional political party. The two forces then became further entangled during the Keien era. As they came to support and sustain one another, they created an increasingly factionalized, partisan bureaucracy.

After twenty-two years, these processes led to the formation of the Dōshikai, the second major cross-sectional party. Bureaucrats began participating unabashedly in party politics. The once-separate threads of party politics and the bureaucracy were woven together and recombined into two new threads: the Seiyūkai and the Dōshikai, which stood for two different conceptions of how to link party politics and the bureaucracy. Party rule in Japan was brought about by young, ambitious men from the provinces who pursued their own will into the parties, into the bureaucracy and into a modern nation-state. The stability they produced created a new era of rule.

6

Developing Human Resources under
Taishō Democracy

The centre of modern Japanese politics transformed over time. It began with oligarchic despotism. The oligarchy evolved into a government by collaboration between the oligarchs and political parties. This collaborative structure yielded to a party-cabinet state that ruled through cooperation between the parties and the bureaucracy. Along the way, the institutions of the executive government expanded to meet growing demands. Young men across the country, awakened to the ideal of rising through the world by their own will, became bureaucrats and partook in governance. Through the upheavals of the Russo-Japanese War, the Taishō Political Crisis and the First World War, and amid a rising tide towards democracy, bureaucrats became the supporting foundation of rule by party politics.

Bureaucrats entering this stage of history walked into a framework of constitutional government that was already hammered out and into organs for training human resources that were already established. They came of age and took action under conditions entirely different from those of the Restoration bureaucrats, the oligarch-bureaucrats or even the early scholar-bureaucrats. What meaning did the young men of this generation find in becoming bureaucrats under a system already preordained for them?

The era of exam supremacy

The system of using examinations to hire bureaucrats faced no major hiccups from its inauguration in 1893. It is true that the rise of the Waihan Cabinet in 1898 spawned rumours among university students that wide-scale administrative reforms would include a halt to hiring new graduates. Students exerted immense pressure on the government in response, stoking tensions. But the exams still proceeded that year as planned. That students reacted with such vehemence reveals how fixed the exam-hire system had become in their minds.

The number of successful examinees on the higher-level civil officer exams increased steadily every year from a measly six people in the first year of exams to thirty-seven, then to fifty, then to fifty-four. By the Russo-Japanese War, the figure had plateaued at around fifty people per year. The stabilized flow of new university graduates into the government acted as proof of the heady progress Japan was making towards a nation-state of executive dominance. After long years of trial and error from the beginning of the Meiji period, the institutional structure of the executive ministries had more or less taken shape with the reforms of the Waihan administration. The end of the seemingly endless reconfiguration of executive departments and the calcification of administrative structures allowed the government to begin planning its personnel hiring practices more systematically.

The executive government burgeoned. Victories in the Sino- and Russo-Japanese wars gave greater voice to the general citizenry, and, as the public made increasingly diverse policy demands of the government, the scope of the state widened. The formal colonization of Taiwan in 1895 and of Korea in 1910 presented more unprecedented administrative demands of executive officers. Old-style oligarchic-bureaucrats retreated, knocked off their posts by young upstarts. The number of university graduates hired into the government steadily increased to 106 in 1909 and to 148 in 1912. Competition on exams turned cut-throat as companies in the non-state sector cut back on employment amid the economic downturn after the Russo-Japanese War.

Between 1899 and 1918, Tokyo Imperial University implemented a commendation system in which the Emperor bestowed silver watches on students of exceptional academic achievement. The paths these silver-watch luminaries took after graduation suggest how strongly the inclination towards the bureaucracy had taken hold in their minds. Eighty-eight men from the law school received silver watches over the twenty years of the programme. Of them, fifty-four entered the bureaucracy. Of the remaining students, the vast majority either became university professors or entered business. Twelve men became professors, including Uesugi Shinkichi, Yoshino Sakuzō, Hatoyama Hideo, Hozumi Shigetō and Suehiro Izutarō. Ten entered business, going mainly to zaibatsu such as Mitsui, Mitsubishi and Sumitomo.

These students welcomed the government policy that all higher-level civil officials be hired through qualification-based rather than politically motivated appointments, a policy designed to prevent spoils-hunting by the parties. As long as they made no catastrophic mistakes along the way, men entering the bureaucracy after passing exams could reliably count on eventual promotion to division head, bureau head or deputy minister. Regulations safeguarding the status of government officials (*bungen seido*) kept their places in the government secure. For all practical purposes, bureaucracy was a lifetime career, even at a time when lifetime employment had yet to be introduced in the non-state sector. Students were drawn into officialdom by this promise of stability, a promise they could find nowhere else.

Of the fifty-four bureaucrats belonging to the Imperial University silver-watch coterie, nineteen entered the treasury; fifteen, the Home Ministry; thirteen, commercial and agricultural affairs; and four, communications. Three went to other ministries. The treasury and home ministries secured the most talented personnel; the agricultural-commercial and communications ministries drew men in with their reputation for encouraging study-abroad among employees. Once the Taishō era dawned, students began to steer clear of the Home Ministry because of its reputation for politicization. The treasury became the prime destination for the best students.

The men who entered the bureaucracy during this era constituted a generation born around 1890. The Cabinet, the Constitution and the Imperial Diet all already existed at the time of their birth. The era of constitutional striving had closed. Now, in the era of the Sino- and Russo-Japanese wars, men of this 'constitutional generation' invested their energies in their own individual selves and strove to make a name for themselves in life.

Imperial University students and the woes of a preordained path

Young men in the throes of their youth often found that trudging along a preordained path from high school through the Imperial University to the bureaucracy could be depressing. Should they proceed down this paved road and make lives for themselves that way, or should they try to blaze another trail and then end up meandering through life? Such were the anxieties of the young men of the constitutional generation.

One agonized youth was Kawai Yoshinari. He entered the Ministry of Agricultural and Commercial Affairs in 1910, made it as deputy minister of agriculture and forestry, and eventually became welfare minister after the Second World War. He bore witness to the anguish of his younger years in his autobiography, *Portrait of a Meiji Youth.*[1]

Kawai was born in May 1886 to a businessman's family in Fukumitsu, Toyama prefecture, not long after the establishment of the cabinet system. He was in his final

Figure 6.1 Kawai Yoshinari (left), commemorative pictures of passing the entrance exam for the Imperial University, 1907. *Source:* Kawai Yoshinari, *Meiji no ichi seinen zō*, Kōdansha, 1969, p. 149.

spurt towards entering the Fourth High School in neighbouring Kanazawa prefecture when, one day in February 1904, the sound of a bell announced the arrival of a special edition of the newspaper. Hostilities had opened in the Russo-Japanese War. Distracted by daily updates on the war, Kawai found he could not devote himself to his studies. He decided to muster his will, move to Kanazawa and cut off the outside world to toil and toil for twelve hours a day, for days on end. In June, Kawai made it. He entered the Fourth High School at the very top of his entering class.

A vibrant spiritual culture buzzed about the Fourth High School. At its centre stood Nishida Kitarō, who was in the midst of honing his ideas for his book *An Inquiry into the Good* (*Zen no kenkyū*). Under Nishida, Kawai developed a profound interest in democracy. He engaged in a deep exploration of democratic ideas with the *Journal of the North Star Association* (*Hokushinkai zasshi*), his school alumni publication, as his platform.

An underdog rebel spirit fuelled the academic fire of Kawai and his classmates. They resented their foes at the First High School. Students of the First High School reigned comfortably at the summit of the high school pecking order, donning school hats with two white stripes that had become an object of yearning for middle schoolers across the nation. Crawling with white-stripe rejects, the Fourth School became a hotbed of uneasy admiration and seething jaundice.

Kawai finished his studies at the Fourth High School in September 1907, three years after he started, and proceeded to the law school of Tokyo Imperial University, a centre for men trying to rise through the world and make a name for themselves. Kawai cradled excitement but also a nagging obsessiveness that spurred him to try harder. Standing side by side with the prodigies of the First High School, he jittered. He could not let his inadequacies be exposed. Among his new classmates from the First High School were such talented men as Ishizaka Taizō and Yoshida Shigeru, not the well-known future prime minister but a different man of the same name who became a bureaucrat in the Home Ministry. Other classmates included Ogasawara Sankurō, of the Third High School; Shigemitsu Mamoru, of the Fifth High School; Matsumoto Gaku, of the Sixth High School; and Makino Ryōzō, of Yamaguchi High School.

Kawai spewed venom to demobilize his own fears. The First High clique often set up camp in the front row of the lecture hall, and whenever they got up to go somewhere, they held their seats by leaving their notebooks behind. Kawai raged at their seat occupation tactics. He took notes furiously during lectures and hit the library with steely discipline, fighting to outstudy his rivals.

But the more Kawai studied, the more his studies seemed to open up a gaping hole somewhere in his being. Lectures were not so interesting as he had expected. No instructor lit a fire in his heart the way Nishida did. Class was insipid. Most courses involved just an annual rehashing of the same set of notes.

Listless lectures quickly snuffed out the flames once kindled in Kawai. From the second half of his first year of college, he gave up on going to lectures. He copied notes off his friends, and, as so many of his peers did, he made it through his exams by studying from lecture records he bought from a store near the university. He spent his free time playing tennis at the dorm for Kanazawa boys. Forlorn now of any sense of purpose, Kawai tumbled into neurosis. He was stricken by blood congestion in his brain no fewer than three times. He continually missed the year-end exams required to advance to the next year of college, and he was forced to take make-ups. He led a rough life.

It was not just Kawai who groused about the cookie-cutter humdrum class had become. Other students testified to the same problem. The only things that captured their attention were the constitutional debates between Minobe Tatsukichi and Uesugi Shinkichi and a newly inaugurated class on colonial policy. Learning had lost the youthful allure of its earliest days at university. And instructors did nothing to reverse the problem.

Kawai finally began to overcome his afflictions in the second half of his third year, the first time he managed to avoid missing his year-end exams. Seemingly out of nowhere, he dedicated himself to a new ambition: passing the higher-level civil officer exams while still a university student. The typical path to officialdom at this time was to graduate in June, to enter an executive ministry as an affiliated officer in July, to take a long summer break and then to sit for the exams in November. Once they passed the exams, men would be appointed as a *sōninkan*-level officer and be formally employed by the government. Kawai decided he wanted to accelerate the process by a year.

Any high school graduate could take the preliminary officer exams as graduates of private law academies did. Since graduates of the Imperial University were exempted from preliminary examinations altogether, few of them went out of their way to take the civil-officer exams before receiving their degrees, a process that would have required them to sit the preliminary round. But because Kawai thought his grades were not good enough to get him the job he wanted, he sought to hedge his bets and try to pass the exams early on.

His efforts paid off. In 1910, Kawai passed the higher-level officer exams, placing in the top 10 per cent of test-takers. He placed second among all test-takers who were still at university, outperformed only by Ishii Sōkichi, then a student at Chūō University and later a professor at Meiji University. Kawai pulled off a major turnaround.

As graduation approached, Kawai found himself summoned by an old acquaintance, Yahagi Eizō, a professor of agricultural policy. Yahagi wanted to talk about employment. He encouraged Kawai to join Sumitomo. Because Yahagi's responsibilities for economics studies at university had given him connections to the world of enterprise, Sumitomo had called on Yahagi to recommend bright students to the company. But Kawai turned Yahagi down, telling him that he had already passed the higher-level officer exams the previous year.

Yahagi changed tune and now suggested that Kawai join the Ministry of the Treasury. Kawai was aiming to join the newly formed Development Bureau (*takushoku kyoku*) in the Cabinet, but Yahagi tried to nudge him away, warning him that he would have no way of understanding the latest colonial policy without speaking French. Yahagi believed that men with exams score as good as Kawai's should enter the treasury. But Kawai refused, saying that tax work simply did not jibe with his personality.

Yahagi then tried another option. He told Kawai that the Ministry of Agricultural and Commercial Affairs had afforded the university one spot for one graduate. He encouraged Kawai to go meet a liaison for that post, Matsumoto Jōji, a professor of commercial law. After graduating from university, Matsumoto had served as a *chokuninkan*-rank counsellor for the agricultural-commercial ministry. He had then returned to the Imperial University and served as a pipeline between the two. Kawai agreed. He obtained a recommendation from Matsumoto and set out for the agricultural-commercial ministry.

Awaiting Kawai at the ministry, located in Tsukiji, was Ōkubo Toshitake, the third son of Ōkubo Toshimichi. Unlike his older brothers, Toshinaka and Nobuaki, who accompanied the Iwakura Embassy abroad, Toshitake was a scholar who attended the First High School, went on to study in America and Germany and earned a doctorate in Japanese constitutional politics. He served as a governor under the Home Ministry before being summoned to the agricultural-commercial ministry, where he took the helm of the bureau of commerce and industry (*shōkōkyoku*) and took on the task of revamping bureau administration. Under Toshitake, Kawai applied himself to the administration of bonds and securities and to problems relating to the price of rice and of other goods.

Professors as mediators and coordinators

Students at the Imperial University at this time generally gained employment through the mediation of their professors. Once the spring of their fourth year of college arrived, students went to professors to whom they were particularly close and asked them for job help.

Professors worked not only to mediate between employers and employees but to coordinate employment from the Imperial University. Sometimes students had their own ties with alumni in desirable government ministries, but even in such instances they ultimately entered those ministries by recommendation of their professors. Professors listened to the desires of their students, judged their suitability for a given post and made recommendations in accordance with the demands of the executive ministries.

Because they had this central role in the process, professors sometimes succeeded in persuading students to change their minds about their preferred career paths. An exemplary case was that of Gotō Fumio, who entered the Home Ministry in 1908, served as head of the Public Security Bureau and eventually rose all the way to home minister. Gotō at first wanted to be employed in the colonies.[2] Amid the dull routinization of courses across the university, colonial policy had emerged as one of the few popular classes. The imaginations of young men ran after what appeared in their classes as a new world with infinite possibilities for development. Scores of students hoped to apply their skills in the colonies, and one of them was Gotō Fumio.

Gotō was a prodigy who graduated sixth out of the sixty-nine students in the politics division of the law school. He had full confidence that he would gain employment in the field he desired. When spring arrived, he paid a visit to Professor Hozumi Nobushige and communicated his wish to work in the colonies. Hozumi promised to convey the message to Kodama Gentarō, governor general of Taiwan and a relative of Hozumi. But when Gotō returned to Hozumi a few days later, Hozumi told him that the governorship general only employed men who had already gained executive experience in the metropole. He suggested that Gotō first spend some time in the

Home Ministry. Left with little choice, Gotō then made his way to Mizuno Rentarō, of the Home Ministry, and ended up being employed there. On the higher-level exams in November, he placed at the very top of the exam pool.

What Hozumi said was not true. As we have already seen, the colonies had been employing men straight out of university from around the time of the Russo-Japanese War. In 1908, when Gotō finished university, new university graduates were being employed in the governorships general of both Korea and Taiwan.

Then why was Gotō rebuffed? He was not rejected from the colonies so much as shepherded towards the Home Ministry. If we consult rankings of university graduates, which were made public until 1918, we find that not a single man who placed in the top ten of his class was employed in the colonies. The highest achievers were funnelled into the most important executive ministries. The mediating and coordinating roles of professors, then, involved not only heeding the hopes and dreams of their students but also administering to them a strong dose of reality.

Prying open a narrow door: the case of private universities

Whereas students at the Imperial University anguished as they trudged down a preordained path, students at private law academies strained to prise open a narrow door that would put them on that path in the first place. They struggled to find ways to make it in life. The process by which Satō Kōzaburō made it into the Home Ministry is instructive. Satō graduated from the Tokyo Professional School (*Tōkyō senmon gakkō*), today's Waseda University, in 1900, and entered the Home Ministry that year. He was born in Fukuoka in 1868 and later went on to become governor of Fukui prefecture.

To overcome the disadvantage of attending a private law academy, Satō began trying the higher-level civil officer exams from his second year at university. The strategy paid off. He passed the oral component of the exam with little trouble in his third year. Bristling with excitement, he paid a visit to Kuratomi Yūzaburō, a prior student from his hometown of Kurume. Kuratomi held an exceptional record as head of the Civil Punishments (*minkei*) Bureau of the Ministry of Justice. A man like Kuratomi would surely lend a hand to one following him from home, Satō thought. He appealed to him for help. But Kuratomi brusquely turned him away. His prospects suddenly looked bleak.

Satō decided to confront the problem head-on. He paid a visit to Ikki Kitokurō, head of the committee on higher-level exams. For Satō, who was striving for the Home Ministry, visiting Ikki had exceptional meaning. Ikki had been the very first Probationary Employment hire into the ministry. Satō had high expectations of their meeting.

The very first question that came out of Ikki's mouth was which class Satō belonged to, implying, of course, which year Satō had graduated from the Imperial University. Satō replied that he came from the Tokyo Professional School (*Tōkyō senmon gakkō*), to which Ikki, his attitude clouding over, muttered, 'Oh, a private academy.' Satō's spirits were shattered. As we saw in the case of Okada in Chapter 4, it was not as if the executive ministries did not seek out graduates of private law academies. They only wanted those who did exceptionally well on the exams. Satō had placed twenty-fifth out of the thirty-one men who passed the exam. He could not count on exceptional treatment.

Figure 6.2 Satō Kōzaburō in the Tokyo Professional School, *c.* 1899. *Source:* Satō Kōzaburō, *Kōgaku Jijoden*, Satō Tatsuo, 1963, p. 42.

Satō grew desperate. Now he went after Kamiyama Junji, an old acquaintance working as a bureaucrat in the Home Ministry. Born in 1870, Kamiyama hailed from Kumamoto and graduated with a degree in German law in 1895. He was a stand-out of the Twenty-Eight Group who rose to the crucial post of head of the texts division of the Public Security Bureau (*keihokyoku toshoka chō*) in just his fourth year in the Home Ministry. Beyond his official work, Kamiyama offered university students study circles to prepare them for the higher-level officer exams. Satō was a member of these study circles from early on. Kamiyama made efforts on behalf of Satō, but perhaps because Satō came from a private academy, or perhaps because his grades were not good enough, they led nowhere.

Satō had declined an offer from the Ministry of Agricultural and Commercial Affairs the previous year. Oda Hajime, a counsellor (*sanjikan*) in the ministry and a lecturer in administrative law at the Tokyo Professional School, had set his sights on Satō. Oda was serving as a ministerial secretary (*daijin hishokan*) and gathering young new graduates for employment in the government. He sought to collect talent from the private academies, too, and so he summoned Satō. But Satō wanted to join the Home Ministry. He yielded his spot to a friend.

The private law academies had brought in bureaucrats to teach legal subjects even while they held posts in the regime. Many of their lecture notes remain today in the National Diet Library. As they worked part-time teaching statutory interpretation for the national exams, these bureaucrats formed links between the private law academies and the executive ministries of the state.

By this point, Satō had figured it was about time to give up on his dreams of joining the Home Ministry. He called on support from those who had graduated from private law academies and now served as bureaucrats. The law academies had an alumni association called the Dōshikai, or Association of Common Will, which was headed by Miwa Kazuo, a drop-out from Meiji Law School. Miwa worked for the Audit Board (*kaisei kensa in*). Satō decided to join him there.

Kamiyama unleashed his wrath on Satō after hearing of the decision. He had put his own job on the line trying to procure Satō a place in the Home Ministry. When a spot opened up in the Home Ministry the following May, Satō finally entered the Ministry without any major difficulties and was allotted to the texts division, where Kamiyama worked. When Kamiyama later became governor of Gunma prefecture, Satō rose to the head of the division of internal affairs.

The story of Satō appears to reveal a wide gulf between graduates of the Imperial University and those of private law academies, but in fact there was little distinction between them when they entered the executive ministries. Indeed, virtually all students who passed the exams managed to find employment in the government. Of the eight private law academy graduates who passed the exams in 1899, Satō's year, six were employed as *sōninkan*, and they secured posts in the ever-popular home, treasury, and agricultural-commercial ministries.

The gap between private and Imperial graduates opened up once promotions began. Only three men from private law academies made it to the post of deputy minister: Takeuchi Tomojirō, Hanihara Masanao and Yamamoto Kumaichi.[3] Among graduates from 1899, there were some who went to the colonies or who were hired as mainline state officials, but their promotions came at a plodding pace. Only two had steady, smooth promotions: Satō and Hattori Jinzō, who became governor of Shinchiku, Taiwan.

A Tokyo Imperial University academic faction had emerged, a faction that simply displaced that of the oligarchs, we might rightly say. We must wonder if, more than any structural factors, it was the feelings of superiority and inferiority among students themselves that influenced how they were sorted in the bureaucracy. These were men who had climbed the educational ladder after the national school system had already been established and the edict on the Imperial University promulgated. Ambition had been institutionalized in a sort of 'academization of desire' (*yokubō no gakkōka*). They knew that they would need to take exams to enter the bureaucracy and eventually seek employment. The differences in the rank of their universities thus left their mark on personnel employment.

Ideas of exam supremacy and obsessions with grades worked in conjunction with the stabilization of executive administration to give rise to a systematized form of personnel hiring. These developments swept away arbitrary hiring through favouritism and connections. But the system itself was quickly becoming rigid and intractable.

New stratification, new factionalization

The virtues and sins of score supremacism

Score supremacism, the belief that grades were of the utmost importance, reared its head not only in the bureaucracy but in the Imperial University itself. As soon as they stepped foot on campus, students were engulfed in competition for the best grades. Word had it that graduation exam scores had an outsized effect on prospects after university. The Home Ministry only takes students with exceptional graduation scores; even in other ministries, grades at university and rankings on the higher-level officer exams continue to influence promotion after entry – as such rumours flew, young men fixated on and obsessed over grades.

Testimony to this fiery determination to outscore rivals appears in the diary of none other than Ashida Hitoshi, prime minister in 1948. Born in Kyoto in 1887, Ashida aimed to become a foreign affairs officer. He graduated from the First High School, entered the Tokyo Imperial University Law School, and graduated in 1912 with a degree in French law, after which he eventually became a member of the House of Representatives and, of course, prime minister. As his end-of-year exams approached in his first year, he wrote in his diary, 'You make it in the world by dint of your grades. They determine the ground on which you take your first step. Three-quarters of your university grades are predicted just by your performance in your first year. I've got to try exceptionally hard during this, the first year.'[4] The days when tributary students vied with one another to vindicate the honour of their domains had long passed. In the score supremacism of the late Meiji era, men ran after individual success.

But we have already witnessed the case of Kawai Yoshinari, whose academic passion burned to nothing at university. College classes were a snoozefest. Professors who just read straight off the book for the entire class; tests where students just had to write stuff for the full time – the systematization of learning had turned university courses into hollow formalities. Nothing stimulated students as the courses of Kaneko Kentarō, who reflected the verve and thrill of a nation-state just entering into being, once did. Ōmachi Keigetsu, an author who studied at the college of humanities (*bunka daigaku*) at Tokyo Imperial University, trenchantly reflected, 'College students would say: don't read that many of the reference texts; just keep your notebook by your side and get good grades on your tests, pass the higher-level civil officer exams, campaign well to get a higher-level official post, get a private car, and find a beautiful woman and make her your wife.'

College students would get hold of a notebook, memorize its content in preparation for their exams and then get scintillating grades. As they repeated this rote process over and over again, their intellect and abilities atrophied. Such were the concerns of

Yoshino Sakuzō, a graduate student at the law school of Tokyo Imperial University. Yoshino wrote a series in a newspaper called 'How to succeed on exams' under the penname 'Student △△' in which he offered strategies for getting good grades.[5] But even as he offered advice, he expressed deep unease that students were so fixated on exams that they had lost all wherewithal and spirit.

Yoshino diagnosed the situation. The general public thought that exams at the Imperial University Law School were so hard that students often failed, he said, but in reality the exam questions were so ignominiously easy that there was shame in sharing them with the wider public. Men failed so often only because they were lazy and sclerotic. He concluded his series of articles by writing, 'Unless students at the law school have more liberal, more vibrant minds, in the end I do not think they will have any way of repudiating the criticisms of the general public.'

As the national education system took root and as the nation-state itself took form, score supremacy took reign and turned education and employment into mere formalities. Graduation theses, once required of the generation of Hamaguchi Osachi, became a thing of the past. This was an era in which a man could secure his future by assembling notes, studying mindlessly and mechanically, and then getting good grades by this rote memorization. The benefits of score supremacy were clear, but now too were its perils.

First class, second class

It was indeed true that university grades mattered, at least in student employment. Grades played a paramount role in determining when a man was hired into the bureaucracy.

Students with good grades at the Imperial University won recommendations from their professors; were hired in June, immediately after they graduated; and were given a chance to begin preparation for the higher-level officer exams in November. Those without recommendations from professors were left preparing for the exams on their own after they graduated. They were hired if they passed the exams. Students who were otherwise blasé about their soporific classes therefore competed fiercely and collected notes in anticipation of final exams from the moment they stepped on campus.

With mordant self-deprecation, Matsumoto Gaku described those who were hired right after graduation and had the chance to prepare for exams during employment as 'first class', and those who had to pass the exams before entering the state ministries as 'second class'. Matsumoto himself was a second-class man. Born in Okayama in 1886, he graduated with a degree in politics in 1911. He eventually became head of the Public Security Bureau and entered the House of Peers.[6]

The emergence of this first-class, second-class distinction among graduates gave rise to complicated states of mind. One would think that being a member of the first class would allow a smooth-sailing ride and plenty of leeway. But once a man entered the first class, the higher-level officer exams ceased to be mere tests he had to pass. They became formidable hurdles. A first-class man would not be forgiven for failing. To men who had coasted comfortably through college, excelling at everything they did and never tasting the agony of failure, entry into the first class came with insurmountably great pressure. To these men, the exams became 'the foremost task after employment'.[7] Failure in the exams essentially meant losing their qualifications for the job.

To first-class men who prided themselves as being the very best of the best, the higher-level exams thus appeared as the first major barrier they had to overpass as bureaucrats. The exams echoed in their ears as shots in the dark. Even exceptionally talented men in the first class could unexpectedly fail. Kamino Katsunosuke, a future deputy treasury minister, failed in 1896, as did Egi Tasuku, later head of the cabinet secretariat and minister of justice, in 1897.

How did men who had just been employed by the executive ministries find time to study for exams? The ministries well understood their conundrum. They employed them as affiliated officers (*zokkan*) in July and then gave them no substantial work until they completed the exams in November. Newly appointed men would finish their hellos and introductions in the ministry quickly and get down to business studying for their exams – in effect, it was the first job they were assigned.

Study intensified during the summer. The new employees took long summer breaks, headed somewhere cool and camped out to study. The Komeya Inn at Chūzenji Lake in Nikkō, which no longer operates; the Tsuruya Inn in Karuizawa, which does; and Gōra Hakone were their havens. Second-class men as well as graduates from private academies no less went on study camp.

The reality of exams: The case of Ishii Mitsujirō

The recollections of Ishii Mitsujirō capture the nature of exams during this era. Ishii graduated from the Tokyo Higher Academy for Studies in Commerce (*Tōkyō kōtō shōgyō gakkō*, or *Tōkyō kōshō* for short), today's Hitotsubashi University, and entered the Home Ministry in the third year of the Taishō era (= 1914). Born in Fukuoka in 1889, he went on to become a counsellor (*sanjikan*) in the governorship general of Taiwan, a member of the House of Representatives and minister of trade and industry (*tsūsan shō*) in the post-war era.

Ishii began taking the foreign officer exams from his second year of university both to see if he could pass and to practice. When school went on break, he headed with his friends to Mount Haruma in Gunma to prepare for the exams. He failed the foreign officer exams in September 1913. He figured he would take the civil officer exams in November, too, just to practice.

Ishii was stunned on the higher-level civil officer exams by the question on constitutional law: 'Discuss the theory that the emperorship is an organ of the state' (*tennō kikan setsu*). Ishii was taking the exam at precisely the same time Minobe Tatsukichi and Uesugi Shinkichi were engaged in a furious debate over this very question of constitutional theory. He belonged to the Minobe camp. But on the exam committee sat none other than Uesugi. He dithered, refusing to sell himself out just to propitiate an examiner but knowing full well that revealing his Minobe inclinations would jeopardize his prospects of passing. He decided just to summarize the main arguments of each camp. The strategy pulled him through. He passed the written portion of the exams without significant difficulty.

Figure 6.3 Ishii Mitsujirō, on the last day of the civil officer exams, 1913. *Source:* Ishii Mitsujirō, *Kaisō hachijū hachinen*, Karuchā Shuppan, 1976, p. 99.

Next came the oral exams. Ishii shaved his head and grew out his beard to prepare. A firm believer in the training methods of Zen, he convinced himself that since he carried a steely constitution, much stronger than that of others, he should attack the exams as if he himself were examining the exam committee, not the other way around. But he was racked by nerves when the exams came. The civil law portion included the notion of 'disappearance' in law (*shissō*), and he did not know what to make of it. Taking advantage of hearing trouble among the examiners, he got them to repeat the question over and over, and as they did so, he figured out what they were trying to get at. Sly techniques notwithstanding, he was anxious over the results of his test. He used Zen to mollify his nerves.

Ishii passed. The imperial certificate of exam success he received from the Legislation Bureau had the words 'number three' marked on it. He had placed third on the exam. A friend approached him, told him that those kinds of grades would easily place him in the Home Ministry, and encouraged him to forgo his inclination towards the foreign service. Ishii's interest was piqued. Through an old acquaintance, he went to meet with Shimo'oka Chūji, deputy home minister. He was about to be employed.

Soon enough, Ishii found himself in employment interviews at the Home Ministry, the pinnacle of the executive state. Fourteen candidates were up for interviews: ten from Tokyo Imperial University, three from Kyoto Imperial University, and Ishii, from the Tokyo Higher Academy for Studies in Commerce. Each was summoned individually into the interview chamber, where he spoke for thirty minutes with the deputy minister, bureau heads, the police superintendent and the head of the secretarial division.

Ishii's long-standing desire to enter the foreign service came up during his interview. Seeing that Ishii had majored in consular studies at university, the head of districts (*gunchō*) asked him if he were not better off at a consulate somewhere. Kouchi Asakichi, head of the Public Security Bureau and a Fukuoka man like Ishii, followed up, telling him to join the foreign service since Fukuoka had produced no talented foreign officers yet. Miffed, Ishii retorted that he had not come for career advice. The interview taxed the grit and determination of applicants.

Just as the meeting was coming to a close, a peculiar man sitting on the sidelines suddenly piped up and asked, 'Yo, you drink?' 'I drink folks under the table,' Ishii shot back. He was hired on the spot. The strange man was Isawa Takio, superintendent of the police. With Isawa as his personal guarantor, Ishii embarked on a career as a police bureaucrat.

The value of the higher-level civil officer exams

The trend of passing the higher-level civil officer exams while still at university, a trend we witnessed in the cases of Kawai Yoshinari and Satō Kōzaburō, emerged around the time of the Russo-Japanese War. In 1907, three men, Hozumi Shigetō, Kawada Isao and Nagaoka Ryūichirō, all took the exams while still at university, and they placed first, fourteenth and twentieth respectively from among seventy-seven successful exam-takers. They attracted widespread praise.[8] Having lost his scholarship during his third year due to poor academic performance, Nagaoka had plotted to take the exams as part of a comeback. Hozumi and Kawada then rode on his coat-tails.

With this case as a precedent, students from the late Meiji era to the early Taishō era who sought to assert themselves and elbow ahead of their classmates began to take this new route.

Even those students who wanted to enter the non-state sector rather that gain bureaucratic employment took the higher-level officer exams. They did so just to see how they would fare, of course. But there was utilitarian value, too: success on the exams acted as testimony of exceptional abilities. And, of course, you could always lord it over your classmates if you passed.

As the number of graduates from the Imperial University steadily increased, graduation in itself ceased to bear sufficient witness to talent. Exam success and grades became ways to prove oneself.

Fascinating historical sources not just on how the exams were taken but on how they were graded remain to this day. In the papers of Kanai Noboru, the Tokyo Imperial University professor whom we encountered in Chapter 4 as a young political science major brooding over his prospects, we find records of the oral exams he administered in 1901, 1902 and 1905.[9]

Kanai was responsible for scoring the economics portion of the exam. His grades ranged widely, from as low as 30 to as high as 80 out of 100. In the remarks margin of his score sheet, he provided comments and wrote 'yes', 'no' or 'maybe' for each examinee.

It seems that some students tried to squirm out of tough questions: 'Blathering about American magazines and whatnot' (55 points), Kanai jotted; 'Keeps yakking about supply and demand' (48 points); 'Is obfuscating a bit' (55 points). Students then were hardly different from those today. But the exams were not just exercises in pressure-cooking students, it seems. Some of Kanai's comments reveal real humour: 'Tosa drawl' (40 points); 'Looks like Tanaka Ryūzō' (50 points). On the score sheet for the winner of 80 points, the highest score, appeared one simple word: *Kotobuki. Mazel tov.*

Comments most often touched on the character of the applicant: 'obdurate' (40 points), 'daft, underling-ish' (42 points). It is often said that oral exams reveal the character of the interviewee. The comments above were, of course, the subjective opinions of Kanai, but it seems that that was indeed the case.

Marriage in the eyes of scholar-bureaucrats: The case of Ashida Hitoshi

Young students were propelled up the academic ladder by a nagging urge not to lose out to the men around them and by the promise of self-realization embodied in the ideal of rising though the world. But things did not always go the way they wanted. They slipped along the trajectories they charted towards their futures. And sometimes they tumbled off into an abyss of depression. We have already seen how the diary of young Ashida Hitoshi was shot through with undulations of joy and depression, each wave following the tides of his grades. But something else distressed young Ashida even more than his grades did.

Ashida's father, Ashida Shikanosuke, was a prominent figure who rose from village head to member of his prefectural council to member of the House of Representatives. Buoyed by the influence of his father, Hitoshi and his brother, two years his senior, coasted into the law school of Tokyo Imperial University. Ashida Hitoshi was in awe of Mutsu Munemitsu and wanted to trace his footsteps into the foreign service. His prospects glittered.

But the future clouded over when Ashida entered the Imperial University. The family business crashed. Financing for Ashida's education became uncertain. His grades foundered. Motivation evanescing, he turned to heaving broadsides at the university. Exams castrated students, he said. They were a tactic to subordinate men to society. University did nothing to inculcate culture in men and just sold them bits and pieces of academic knowledge, slapping value on humans after unleashing them to brawl over grades without any ideals or principles or genuine passions. Ashida severed ties with his peers at the law school and wallowed in book klatches at cafes.

Figure 6.4 Ashida Hitoshi (centre) and his father and brother, 1909. *Source:* Miyano Chō, *Saigo no riberarisuto Ashida Hitoshi*, Bungeishunjū, 1987, front page.

Then came the problem of marriage, adding to the woes of the young Ashida. Men from the First High School and the law school of the Imperial University came with promises of solid futures. They were highly desirable marriage partners. Ashida's desirability was compounded because he was the second-born in his family. He did not succeed his father in lineage, opening a chance for other households to take him into their line. Men like him were barraged with marriage proposals. People even went to the administrative offices of the university to approach Ashida, asking, 'Would you like to be adopted into our family?'

One day a marriage proposal of particular salience came Ashida's way. It was a proposition to marry a granddaughter of Inoue Kaoru, the man who had served for so many years as foreign minister. The proposition came from Shibusawa Eiichi, who mediated between Ashida and the family of the marquis Inoue. Ashida had caught the eye of Shibusawa by serving as a private tutor in the Shibusawa household dormitory. He was already seeing someone at the time, but he found this new proposition attractive. He wanted, after all, to become a foreign officer.

But the proposal went up in smoke. Ashida's brother, an officer in the treasury, was stricken with tuberculosis after he was conscripted into the army. He died. Then Hitoshi himself was admitted long-term to hospital with his own illness. As the Inoue marriage prospects slipped away, the bitter aftertaste of what could have been lingered long with Ashida.

Determined to recover, Ashida began going out with numbers of different women. And as he did so, he came to a stark realization about himself. Whenever the possibility of marriage approached, he found himself thinking foremost about the power and influence of his potential wife's parents or of their financial advantages. He began agonizing over himself, a self that saw marriage as nothing more than a means of rising in the world.

Ashida finally managed to shake out of his funk when he passed the foreign officer exams in the fall of 1911. It was not a wife with connections who pulled him out of the doldrums. It was, of all things, an obituary for Komura Jutarō acclaiming Komura's dedication and contributions to his country. 'My hankering to marry into money or prestige has disappeared now,' Ashida wrote. 'I'm going to throw my bags on my back and take off for some distant land and go out wandering there on my own. To hell with social status. I have my own lot in life.' Ashida read his own future in Komura's.

Freed from the shackles of depression, Ashida finally married in 1918, after a long romance and just after he returned from his first foreign assignment, in Russia. His wife hailed from not a political but a trading family. Some around Ashida opposed the marriage, warning him that it would do nothing to promote his prospects in life. Ashida ignored them.

Power marriages

Marriage became a means for scholar-bureaucrats to gain power and partake in nepotism and family politics. Among the men who passed the officer exams in 1907 while still at university, for instance, Nagaoka married the daughter of Hirata Tōsuke; Hozumi, the daughter of Kodama Gentarō; and Kawada, the daughter of Tsukuda Kazumasa, vice-president of the Industrial Bank of Japan (*Kōgyō ginkō*). Many bureaucrats married into the families of longstanding politicians from the early Meiji era or especially those of veteran bureaucrats. Mizuno Rentarō, the 'Minister of Personnel' in the Home Ministry we encountered in Chapter 5, acted as the middleman in an astonishing number of marriages, most often between the daughters of bureaucrats senior to him and young upstart bureaucrats. It seems that we need to tack the phrase 'of distinguished pedigree' after the word 'woman' in the satirical command from Ōmachi Keigetsu we encountered earlier to 'find a beautiful woman and make her your wife'.

Fathers believed that marrying their daughters off to talented rising bureaucrats would secure stable futures for those daughters. The practice benefited sons-in-law, too, who could inherit the bureaucratic experience and human networks of their fathers-in-law and who felt that family discord would arise less easily if they married into households of a familiar occupation. The families taking in the sons-in-law likewise found this common ground appealing.

Some men took their bureaucratic dynasties to redoubtable extents. Ōmori Shōichi, who worked as the head of general affairs in the Home Ministry and then as governor of Kyoto prefecture for fifteen years, virtually made the Home Ministry his family business. His eldest son, Kaichi, worked as a Home Ministry bureaucrat, as did four of his sons-in-law: Nakagawa Nozomu, Ikeda Hiroshi, Kodama Kuichi and Shigenari Kaku.[10]

The development of such family dynasties in the bureaucracy might seem to throw back to the ways of the Edo era and to fly in the face of the principles of the Charter Oath. Members of the dynasties themselves, of course, did not see things that way. They were simply sliding into the profession most familiar to them, that of their parents. They wanted to carry down the capital their parents had accumulated, just as the children of merchant families did. That schools, exams and other such bottlenecks blocked their paths only compounded their resolve to capitalize fully on the family business.

Cordoned off by high barriers of deep specialization and personal connections, officialdom developed into a densely cohesive network in part because households turned the bureaucracy into a family business, continually generating new men from within the system. This tendency for self-regeneration became particularly entrenched among members of the foreign service because of the unusual circumstances in which they raised their families abroad.

The calcification of officialdom notwithstanding, new systems to send talented men to the national centre did emerge with the strengthening of the Japanese economy over the Sino- and Russo-Japanese wars. New scholarship organizations as well as wealthy men willing to fund young prodigies proliferated across the nation. Ishii Mitsujirō, for instance, received about 12 yen a month from the Arima household, the household of his former samurai lord. Nagaoka Ryūichirō, the precocious student who passed his exams in his third year, received funds from his former lord in addition to the regular support the university provided to scholarship students.

Money came from other sources, too. Some men received financial aid while in high school from the head priests of their village shrines, the financial officers of their town halls or even from the saké-producing households of Nada, today a district of Kobe. Such was the case of Kawanishi Jitsuzō, who was born in Hyōgo in 1889, graduated with a degree in German law in 1914, entered the Home Ministry and eventually became governor of Tokyo prefecture.[11] His was an era in which regions of particular economic strength made an effort to promote their young men in the national centre.

The rise of regional factions

Once employment through exams took root as a standard practice, officialdom was wrested away from domination by the oligarchy and reconfigured into ministerial units and family dynasties, two new forms of factionalism. Another form of factionalism emerged, too: that of common birthplace, as we saw in the case of Kumamoto prefecture. The oligarchic influence of such Meiji strongholds as Satsuma and Chōshū had attenuated, opening up opportunities for other regions to establish their own cliques.

Let us take up the case of Nagano prefecture and consider how hometown factions formed as young men gained education and employment.

The earliest years of Nagano as a modern prefecture involved continual geographic change. The prefecture was formed by merging several mid- to small-sized domains, including the Matsushiro domain, which was of 100,000 *koku*; the Matsumoto domain, of 60,000 *koku*; and the Ueda domain, of 50,000 *koku*. After the dissolution

Figure 6.5 Students in Nagano Middle School, *c.* 1910. *Source:* Kondō Jōtarō tsuisōshū henshū iinkai, ed., *Tsuisō Kondō Jōtarō*, 1980, p. 24.

of domains and installation of prefectures, the middle and southern sections of present-day Nagano, including the region of Hida, formed the prefecture of Chikuma. Chikuma was then merged with a smaller version of Nagano prefecture to form a larger Nagano. It took until August 1876 for Nagano prefecture to cover the entire area of historical Shinano province. This early splintering of what is today Nagano allowed the area to send out no fewer than twelve tributary students from twelve domains, including Isawa Shūji of Takatō domain, during the days of the tributary-student system.

Middle schools were established in Matsumoto, Nagano, Ueda and Iida. Education took off across Nagano prefecture – was it because it snowed heavily and people had developed a predilection for passing time by arguing? – and the prefecture produced a multitude of future education ministry bureaucrats, including Isawa, Tsuji Shinji and Sawayanagi Masatarō. Intent on establishing high school education in their home region, men campaigned hard to have the Seventh High School built in Nagano, despite initial plans to have it built in Shikoku. Kagoshima obstructed the campaign, but no matter: the men fought hard to bring the Eighth and Ninth High Schools to Nagano. The Eighth ended up in Nagoya, but the Nagano men finally succeeded with the Ninth in 1910. The construction of the school was suspended after the Second Saionji Cabinet fell, but nine years later, the Matsumoto High School opened at long last. It was clear that people across Nagano were profoundly conscious of educational matters.

The greater fervour for higher levels of education after the Russo-Japanese War appears strikingly in alumni magazines published by prefectural middle schools. The fourteenth edition of Nagano Middle School's *Alumni Association Magazine*, published in 1909, includes contributions from graduates who had gone on to the Tokyo Normal High School (*Tōkyō kōtō shihan gakkō*) and the Yamaguchi Commercial High School (*Yamaguchi kōtō shōgyō gakkō*). Just as alumni once wrote glowingly about their university experiences in the alumni magazines of high schools, now that same custom appeared among middle school alumni in high school who wrote in the magazines of their middle schools.

Middle school alumni regaled readers with stories of new trends and academic ambitions at their new high schools, fuelling the intellectual fires of a new generation of middle schoolers. Letters from alumni became a regular magazine feature from the sixteenth edition of the *Alumni Association Magazine*, published in 1911. Every edition featured stories from three different graduates. Those graduates had gone on to such schools as the Second, Seventh and Eighth High Schools, Waseda University, Tokyo Imperial University and the Army Officer Academy (*rikugun shikan gakkō*).

Because the attempt to bring the Seventh High School to Nagano was foiled, the young men of Nagano ended up going mainly to the First High School or alternatively to the more proximate Fourth High School in Kanazawa or Second High School in Sendai. It was not as if the Second High School was particularly close to Nagano. But the principal of the school, Nakagawa Hajime, had Nagano roots: he left Iida domain as a tributary student to the University-South College before entering the education ministry as a bureaucrat. He then worked as a secretary for Mori Arinori, the first-ever education minister. It was he who struck down Mori Arinori's assassin on the day of the inauguration of the Meiji Constitution. Nakagawa served as principal of the Fourth and Fifth High Schools before going to the Second High School in Sendai. He had amassed deep experience as both an educator and an executive bureaucrat. He recruited Miyoshi Aikichi, among the first generation of middle school principals in Nagano, to serve as head of teachers at Second High, providing further impetus for Nagano men to go to Sendai.

After high school came the Imperial University and the higher-level officer exams. Nagano men climbed this ladder programmatically. The number of Nagano men in the law school of the Imperial University swelled steadily, allowing the prefecture to produce scores of scholar-bureaucrats. Over the twenty-one years between 1897 and 1917 during which the official publication of the bureaucracy (*Kanpō*) revealed the origins of successful exam-takers, Nagano ranked fifth nationally in the number of scholar-bureaucrats it produced. It counted 71 men from its climes, trailing only Tokyo, with 223; Yamaguchi, with 84; Fukuoka, with 79; and Okayama, with 73. It was a sterling record for a prefecture made from no major domains and with no major oligarchic connections.

Isawa Takio and the rise of regional factions

With so many men marching from Nagano into the executive ministries, it was only natural that hometown bonds would begin to link Nagano bureaucrats into a prefectural clique. These bonds, manifest both in abstract interpersonal influence and in concrete moves men made to liaise for their hometown buddies, influenced the specific ministries that students joined when they entered officialdom.

Sharp trends indeed emerge when we sort bureaucrats of Nagano origin by the ministries they entered. It is little surprise that many went to the executive behemoths of the home and treasury ministries. But it is striking how regularly Nagano executive officers joined two other ministries that generally did not take new graduates: the justice and education ministries. The justice ministry was home to Yokota Kuniomi, and the education ministry was the domain of Tsuji, Isawa, Sawayanagi and other such Nagano leaders. Young men were ushered into the two departments by these elders.

As they filled the ranks of the bureaucracy, Nagano executives formed their own bureaucratic association and gathered as a team whenever the opportunity allowed. They called their group the Association of Equine Airs (*Bafūkai*), skewering the Nagano custom of eating horse meat. At the centre of the Airs stood a handful of men who had entered the Home Ministry just as the Meiji era turned to the Taishō.[12] Each of them had found his way there through Isawa Takio, that peculiar man whose official interview question to Ishii Mitsujirō was, 'Yo, you drink?'

Isawa Takio was born in 1869, the second year of the Meiji era, in Takatō.[13] His elder brother was Isawa Shūji, a tributary student from the same domain who became a bureaucrat in the education ministry. Under the austere tutelage of Shūji, Takio made his way through Keiō Gijuku, the Third High School, and the law school of the Imperial University before entering the Home Ministry in 1895 and passing the higher-level exams. He gained a strong track record mainly as a provincial official and was then hired as a scholar-bureaucrat, first as the superintendent of police under the second cabinet of Ōkuma Shigenobu. From there he transformed into a Kenseikai-Minseitō bureaucrat-politician and began channelling forces from the House of Peers to build his own power. As chief of the Twenty-Eight Group, he gathered a multitude of bureaucrats under his helm.[14]

It does not seem that Isawa intended to be identified primarily with his political hue. It is true that he was dismissed by the Seiyūkai when he was serving as governor of Wakayama prefecture, but he maintained close, cordial relations with Hara Kei, Tokonami Takejirō, Mizuno Rentarō and other Seiyūkai stalwarts.

Isawa sought to assert himself less as a politician than as the head of the 'Isawa faction', a coalition that centred on the Home Ministry and that called for a neutral bureaucratic way between the parties. Members of his faction included primarily Equine Airs bureaucrats from Nagano whom he had nurtured during his years as superintendent of the police, men such as Gotō Fumio and Maruyama Tsurukichi. Other members included Kinoshita, Shinohara, Kodaira and Karasawa, whom we have already encountered, as well as Aoki Kazuo, Kobayashi Jirō, Kondō Jōtarō, Masuda Kaneshichi and Akabane Minoru.[15]

Isawa guided members of his faction at critical moments, and when he himself acceded to such significant posts as mayor of Tokyo and superintendent general of Taiwan, he assembled these men in a core group of specialized administrators who helped him amass a considerable executive record. The political powers and human networks generated by Isawa became the central force in state administration from

1932, the start of the so-called 'era of bureaucratic cabinets' (*kanryō naikaku ki*), and endowed government functioning with a degree of stability. The prefecture, as a group knit together by modernity, thus became a unit of collective action. The Isawa faction from Nagano functioned much as did the Kumamoto faction, which included Munakata Tadasu and Kobashi Ichita and had worked to place Kiyoura Keigo as prime minister, and the Okayama faction, which included Akagi Tomoharu and Tsugita Daizaburō and had formed the core of a new generation of bureaucrats.

Bureaucrats and the era of democracy

Shifting views on governance

The conclusion of the Russo-Japanese War and the attainment of the autonomy and independence envisioned in the Meiji Restoration revolutionized Japanese government. The *genrō* slipped from positions of state leadership to ones of mere coordination. The political helm fell into the hands of a line of bureaucrats guided by Katsura Tarō and of a faction of Rikken Seiyūkai politicians guided by Saionji Kinmochi. Rule by party politics came within reach.

These transformations brought about four major changes for young men who entered the bureaucracy in pursuit of individual achievement and success: changes occurred in their views on governance; in the paths they took in life; in their educational environments; and in their policy goals. Let us begin with changes in their views on governance.

We have already seen how students, regarding rule by party politics as simply the way things were supposed to be, reviled Katsura and his band, seeing them as an oligarchic outgrowth. The Tasihō Political Crisis instilled in them an expectation that the era of party politics was nigh. Hoshino Naoki, for instance, was a third-year student in the First High School at the time. Born in Kanagawa in 1892, he graduated university with a degree in politics in 1917, entered the treasury ministry, and went on to become president of the Cabinet Planning Institute. Witnessing how the headquarters of such pro-Katsura newspapers as the *Niroku shinpō*, the *Kokumin shinbun* and the *Yamato shinbun* were all torched during the Taishō Political Crisis, and how the police did nothing to stop the violence, he came to the realization that times had fundamentally changed.

The relationship between the military and the bureaucracy had changed, too. Before the Russo-Japanese War, young men striving to rise in the world faced a stark binary choice between becoming a bureaucrat or becoming a military man. Aspiring military officers entered the Army Officer Academy (*Rikugun shikan gakkō*) or the Naval Academy (*kaigun hei gakkō*) after middle school, whereas those aiming for the bureaucracy went to high schools. Each went his own way.

The Russo-Japanese overturned this state of affairs. With major military threats neutralized, the government made cuts to the army and navy. The prestige of the military fell accordingly. Its reputation was then further tarnished as the public heaped vitriol on it during the Taishō Political Crisis and as the Siemens Incident spread suspicions of systematic corruption in the navy.

Yet the number of men seeking to join the army and navy did not decline. The outbreak of the First World War in 1914 fanned the popularity of the military. The Army Academy fielded 4,328 applicants in 1916. Each spot in the school had twenty men competing for it.[16] Applicants found appeal, no doubt, in the fact that the army academy did not charge tuition.

These numbers belied indicators pointing to new trends. The case of Kogane Yoshiteru, born in 1898, was one such indicator. In 1915, Kogane, who ranked third in his graduating class at the Odawara Middle School, took the entrance exams for the Army Academy. He went on not to enrol in the army but to graduate with a degree in French law in 1922, enter the Agricultural and Commercial Affairs Ministry, become head of the Bureau of Energy (*nenryōkyoku*) and rise to postal minister in the post-war era. Kogane did pass the army exams, just one of seven men that year to do so out of over one hundred exam-takers. But right before entering the academy, he changed his mind. The entrance exams for the Army Academy were a five-day, stay-overnight affair in which students took tests on no fewer than eighteen different subjects. Kogane made it through the entire event and yet still chose not to enrol. It is said that a lieutenant in the artillery corps (*hōhei tai'i*) had told him to steer clear of the army regardless of the results of the exams; he was better off applying his talents not in the army but somewhere they would find use. Kogane was persuaded.

We of course cannot know the true intentions of the defeatist lieutenant. But Kogane took the advice, stopped just before entering the army and swerved to the First High School. He became friends at First High with such luminaries as Kawabata Yasunari and Serizawa Kōjirō. Kogane passed his days of youth in a world of fecund education and training.

Numbers soon caught up to anecdotal indicators. Rumours proliferated after the end of the First World War that the army was overpopulated and that promotion through its ranks was no longer possible. The state, too, indicated an inclination towards military retrenchment. Men began to worry about their prospects in the military. The number of applicants to the Army Academy plummeted from 3,926 in 1917, to 2,971 in 1918, to just 1,109 in 1921. Tides began to turn as men approached the age of party rule.

The diversification of life courses

The boom and bustle brought about by the First World War reconfigured the perceived hierarchy of prestige among executive ministries. The two ministries charged with economic and financial matters, the Ministry of the Treasury and the Ministry of Agricultural and Commercial Affairs, gained in popularity, while the Home Ministry, that 'authority among the authorities' standing atop the hierarchy, found its appeal blunted. One sign of these changes lay in the ministries chosen by silver-watch recipients we encountered earlier. Another appears in Tokyo Imperial University, which split its economics programme (*gakka*) from its politics programme in 1902 and established a new programme in commerce (*shōgyō*) the following year. The two new programmes merged in 1919 to form the Department of Economics.

Transformations in social circumstances made employment in non-state businesses an increasingly viable and appealing option for university students. For all practical purposes, students at the law school had long had only two choices after they graduated: to become bureaucrats or to become lawyers. Backed by favourable economic conditions, private businesses began actively offering a third path, tempting talented men with promises of high remuneration.

The number of men who passed the higher-level civil officer exams and then chose to enter the non-state sector climbed continuously. Only one or two a year had chosen to take this alternative route at first. Then the number suddenly jumped to ten in 1912. New corporate hires went to Mitsui, Mitsubishi, the merchant marine company Ōsaka Shōsen and the Osaka Asahi News paper. Mitsui & Co. hired five men in 1914, signalling that the non-state sector was willing to put up a fight to win over university talent. Most of the men Mitsui hired had passed the civil officer exams while still at university.

Among these defectors to the non-state sector, Nagano Mamoru attracted exceptional attention. He graduated fifth in German law in 1915, and then ranked third on the higher-level exams before darting from officialdom and becoming the secretary of Shibusawa Eiichi. In Chapter 4, we encountered the case of Mizuno Rentarō, who grew disgruntled during his foray into the First Bank and returned to government officialdom. Now, a quarter-century later, the reverse trend appeared. Young men found greater appeal in the private sphere, which afforded them ample room for growth and development, than in the stultified structures of executive government.

The number of men who quit the bureaucracy and transferred to the private sector steadily increased. Behind the defections lay an ever-bloating executive branch hosting ever-greater numbers of bureaucrats. This bureaucratic corpulence was evident just in the number of men passing the higher-level officer exams. In the second year of the tests, 1895, thirty-seven men passed. Twenty years later, in 1915, 136 did. The figure had quadrupled. But the number of executive posts above the level of bureau head did not increase, apart from in the colonies. Bottlenecks began to strangle prospects for bureaucratic promotion.

Even if a student managed to climb to the upper echelons of officialdom, the partisan politicization of the bureaucracy left no guarantee that he could retain his job for the long term. Every student had to consider the possibility that he would be knocked off somewhere in the process of climbing. That so many chose to enter the treasury or the agricultural-commercial ministry was because work in those ministries lent itself easily to transfer to the private sector.

The case of the Home Ministry in this respect was complicated. Students regarded the colonies, like private enterprise, as an exciting new frontier. Many aimed to enter the governorships general of Korea and Taiwan or the ruling authority of the Kwantung region (*J*. Kantō, *Ch*. Guandong), in present-day north-east China.[17] But the executive offices in the colonies rarely took men straight out of university. Men chose to enter the Home Ministry tentatively and take stock of prospects of transferring to the colonies later, as Gotō Fumio did.

But many tried to steer clear of the Home Ministry because it often sent new hires into police administration. People reviled the police as oppressors of the masses, a perception owing most notably to the brutal suppression of protestors during the Hibiya Riots. And because of confidentiality problems, men often found they could not leave police administration once they entered. The appeal of the Home Ministry to young bureaucrats was the chance to gain diverse executive experience under its wide umbrella. Being cordoned off in the police department undermined the point of joining the ministry. The high barriers that separated the police from other members of the ministry contributed to the development of two separate Home Ministry factions, that of the police and that of the provinces.

An example in the development of the police faction was the experience of Maruyama Tsurukichi, who joined the Home Ministry in 1909 and rose to superintendent of the police.[18] Maruyama at first wanted to enter the education ministry, but it only accepted a few men. Maruyama then signed up for the Home Ministry, where he found in the local improvement campaigns (*chihō kairyō undō*) and agrarian moralist campaigns (*hōtokushugi undō*) elements of an education wider in scope than he originally envisioned. Setting his sights on executive work in localities, he began ferociously studying for the higher-level exams. He passed.

But then came job interviews. The applicants waiting alongside Maruyama ranked second, sixth, eleventh, fifteen, eighteenth and twentieth among the 130 men who had passed the exams. Maruyama ranked 105th. He was hired into the ministry but not as a provincial official. He was sent off to the police department, where he was assigned as head of the public security division in Kagawa prefecture. No opportunity to flee from the police appeared thereafter. Before he knew it, he had become known as 'Maryuama, the police guy.'

Maruyama became a poster-child of the police faction in a Home Ministry bifurcated by the police and the provinces. He lost any chance of switching over to the other side. Once again, the specialized demands of different executive roles had engendered bureaucratic sectionalism. Maruyama often used his story to caution students of a younger generation to beware if they wanted to find careers beyond the police department.

The popularity of the Home Ministry further declined once the colonies themselves began actively seeking out new graduates, rendering moot an original impetus to enter the ministry. The changes wrought by the Russo-Japanese War thus transformed the nature of government in Japan. The state moved from managing the nation primarily through the Home Ministry to fostering growth primarily through the Ministry of the Treasury and the Ministry of Agricultural and Commercial Affairs. And with this transformation, the life courses of students, too, began to swerve in different directions.

Changes in the educational environment

The educational environment of Japan changed dramatically, just as life courses did. Fervour for education and for rising in the world swelled the number of student applicants to middle and high schools, but the number of high schools remained stagnant across the nation. Between 1909, when the Eighth High School was established in Nagoya, and 1919, when the Second Edict on High Schools called for the construction of new schools, the total number of high schools across the nation remained restricted to the so-called 'number schools', from First High to Eighth High.

Admissions rates to high schools plummeted accordingly. Competition turned fierce. In the 1900s, one-in-two applicants made it into high school. That ratio fell to below one-in-four a decade later.

The Ministry of Education did not sit by idly. In response to intensifying exam competition, it established common nationwide entrance exams in 1902 and allowed students the possibility of entering their second-choice schools if they were not admitted at their first choice. It was as a result of this policy that the Fourth High School in the days of Kawai Yoshinari teemed with First High rejects.

The case of Fourth High sheds light on how common nationwide exams created a clear hierarchy of high schools and in fact exacerbated the problem of student competition. To mitigate rivalry, schools reverted in 1908 to administering their own exams and selecting their own students. Boys generally began to choose schools not by ranking but by geographic location: those in Tōhoku went to the Second High School; those in Kansai, to the Third; Hokuriku, the Fourth; Kyushu, the Fifth and Seventh; Chūgoku and Shikoku, the Sixth; and Tōkai, the Eighth.

But the First High School remained in a class of its own. It did not budge from the pinnacle of high school prestige and continued to be the object of dreams for the best and brightest across the nation. That the top student at the Imperial University would be a graduate of the First High School was seen as just a matter of course. It is said that when Aoki Kazuo placed first on his freshman-year exams after graduating from First High and entering the Imperial University in 1912, he was thanked for 'being the one to uphold the honor of First High'.[19] Aoki won a silver watch when he graduated four years later.

The exceptional prestige of First High turned students into little megalomaniacs at times. The boys of First High won a reputation as brutes deficient in basic human cultivation. Privilege came with disadvantages for the students themselves, too. As boys who had trounced the competition, they had never had the chance to taste defeat in their younger days. Even the slightest headwinds could knock them into an abyss of despair as they grew older. Life was not all silver watches.

New life was breathed into these young men by Nitobe Inazō, a young rising educator. Born to samurai in Morioka domain, he was a bright prodigy who went to the Agricultural Academy of Sapporo (*Sapporo nōgakkō*), studied abroad in America and Germany, and then applied what he had learned in Taiwan. His deep experience won him a post as principal of the First High School in 1906. Nitobe stepped into an environment where admission into First High in itself guaranteed a spot at a university and success thereafter. With little to worry about, young men squandered their time by indulging in sports.

Nitobe spurred students to seek out opportunities to build character. He assembled them outside of class hours and spoke to them about current affairs, expanding the scope of their conversations to touch even on Goethe and Carlyle. Students began frequenting the Nitobe home, which was close to school.

An opulent global consciousness, first-hand experience in the colonies, an understanding of humanity rooted in Christian faith – Nitobe had everything young men of the day were looking for. To boys who had spent their middle school years amid the frenzy of the Russo-Japanese War, the post-war represented a time of prosperity, but a time in which the future seemed vexingly uncertain. The breadth and depth of the cultivation Nitobe offered appeared as a sort of salvation to anguished youths searching for purpose in life. Nitobe transformed the atmosphere of First High. But then, in 1913, Nitobe was appointed as a professor in the law school of Tokyo Imperial University and was tasked with teaching courses on colonial policy. He left, having spent just six years at First High. Yet the window he opened to new currents of culture let his influence pass beyond just his school and to high schools across the nation.

The year after Nitobe left First High, a young scholar of politics returned from Europe to the Tokyo Imperial University law school. He was Yoshino Sakuzō, the man who had once written a column called 'How to succeed on exams' under the penname 'Student △△.' After a stint in the Qing Empire serving as a private tutor in the household of Yuan Shikai, Yoshino became an assistant professor under Onozuka Kiheiji. He then spent three years from 1910 studying in Europe.

Yoshino returned to give bracing courses on political history. Rather than deadpan political theory and knowledge, Yoshino sought to explore the political movements to which modern European political theory had given rise. He then related this history to the political reality of Europe at the time. His classes vibrated with energy.

Yoshino lectured at a time when the tensions that eventually led to the First World War were enveloping Europe. Students, concerned with forces emanating from a continent away, found themselves magnetized by these novel classes and felt premonitions of upheavals that would soon seize their own nation. Yoshino and his courses, together with Nitobe and his classes on colonial policy, opened the eyes of students to the world beyond the seas.

Transformations in policy goals

As Japan was left rummaging for new national goals in the wake of the Russo-Japanese War, young men who had come of age in an era that extolled personal cultivation (*kyōyō shugi*) and who had learned of the shifting winds and political effervescence of Europe began to think and speak about democracy. In 1919, the Association of New Men at Tokyo Imperial University (*Tōdai shinjinkai*), or the Shinjinkai, formed around Yoshino Sakuzō, and as other 'New Dawn Societies' (*Reimeikai*) promoting democratic principles sprang up among intellectuals across the nation, so too did socialist movements sweep across the country.

It was not students who had entered the bureaucracy who actively promoted these various movements. Steering the new trends were students who forewent officialdom and campaigned for new causes beyond the confines of government. But it was not as if the bureaucrats were apathetic about reform. They showed new policy inclinations, unlike those of their forebears.

Experience travelling in the West widened the worldviews of these students-turned-bureaucrats. During his tenure as home minister, Gotō Shinpei proposed a system wherein bureaucrats in their mid-thirties and ranked at the level of division-head (*bu ka chō*) could be selected for study abroad. The sixth year of the Taishō era (= 1916), saw the first contingent of men go abroad on the Gotō scheme. Maruyama Tsurukichi, then head of the securities division of the Public Security Bureau (*keiho kyoku hoan bu*), and Hotta Mitsugu, head of the internal affairs division in Kyoto (*Kyōto fu naimu bu*), were selected.[20] The second contingent was made of Gotō Fumio and Yamada Junjirō, officers in the home ministry secretariat.[21] The third contingent was made of Tago Ichimin, head of the aid and relief division of the provinces bureau (*chihō kyoku kyūgo ka*), and Nagaoka Ryūichirō, head of the police affairs division of the Public Security Bureau (*keiho kyoku keimu ka*).[22]

From the third contingent on, voyagers to the West were given specific research tasks. Tago, for instance, was enjoined to look into social projects, and Nagaoka into policing during times of war. But Gotō quietly told them to drop their research straitjackets and look broadly into every dimension of European society. He wanted his men to break free from their isolated reading rooms and to go and see and hear for themselves *in situ*, exploring everything from theatre and film, and speech rallies and churches, to slums.

But some men could not wait for government funds to come their way. Antsy, they quit the bureaucracy and set sail themselves. Karasawa Tochiki, the silver watch prodigy of 1915 who entered the Imperial University Law School from the Second High School, was one such man.[23]

In the fall of 1917, when the study-abroad scheme was first implemented, Karasawa was working in the Public Security Bureau of the Home Ministry. He left his post and went to America and Europe, self-funded. The men who were selected for official trips abroad were all division heads some six to ten years older than he was. By the time his turn would come, the World War and the Russian Revolution would have been over. Determined to see the transformations of the world with his own eyes, Karasawa chose retirement and supported his own study abroad.

The Home Ministry study-abroad programme placed its participants on leaves of absence (*kyūshoku seido*), and since the limit on a leave of absence was two years, no man could be abroad for longer than that term. But Karasawa, not bound by such restrictions, spent over three years touring Europe. It is true that he was left without an official post for a year after he returned home. But then an older alumnus from Second High serving as governor of Ibaraki welcomed him as head of the accounting division of the prefecture. Karasawa was ushered back into the world of bureaucracy.

During their sojourns in Europe, the Home Ministry pioneers found their interests drawn to a range of problems at the time, including state control of people during times of war, maintenance of public security, the status of the war-wounded, social movements and the evolution of the Russian Revolution. From their experience, they painfully felt the need for social policy in Japan. Hotta, Gotō, Tago and Karasawa placed particular emphasis on this problem as they proceeded with their research programmes.

These men foresaw an eruption of movements in Japan calling for wide-ranging political participation. They thought deeply about Japanese society after the First World War and predicted that universal suffrage was only a matter of time in Japan. To prepare for its advent, they carried out painstaking research on such matters as speech rallies, posters and pamphlets, the benefits and harms of small electoral units, and women's suffrage units. And they brought their newfound knowledge back with them to Japan. Following these early pioneers, a host of other men who entered the Home Ministry in 1909 followed one another abroad.[24]

These investigations culminated in the founding of the Social Bureau (*shakaikyoku*) of the Home Ministry. Charged with overseeing social policy, the new bureau became popular among bureaucrats and attracted not only applicants from beyond the Home Ministry but even men hoping to transfer to the bureau from within. Because the bureau became so desirable, men had to strike out on their own and gain specializations still not available through university education in order to perform outstanding work the bureau would notice. The bureaucrats who returned from their voyages to the West engaged in such work, exerting themselves to publish their findings and conduct further research. They turned the Chamber of Counsellors (*sanjikan shitsu*) in which they laboured into a bristling scholarly hub. And then yet another object of study-abroad desire emerged with the founding of the International Labour Organization in Geneva.

The homogenization of the Home Ministry had created a government ministry with a stuffy, stagnant atmosphere. But once the local improvement campaigns spearheaded by Tokonami and Inoue in the late Meiji era were folded into the new policy fields opened up by study-abroad bureaucrats, new winds blew.

The duty of bureaucrats

Just as the Home Ministry did, the Ministry of the Treasury struck out on new policy paths. A younger generation of bureaucrats proposed revisions to existing income tax laws, which had been devised to benefit large corporations and their associates. They called for a fairer distribution of the burden of general taxes. These were policy changes born of the same social-policy consciousness that emerged in the Home Ministry.

The Seiyūkai cabinet of Hara Kei adopted these reform proposals in 1920. From the perspective of party cabinets, these were crucial plans that shored up national revenue, which had fallen short during war, and responded to the demands of citizens, expressed most strikingly in the Rice Riots, to ameliorate economic divisions among people. The reforms primarily involved imposing dividend taxes, implementing a more thoroughgoing progressive tax on labour salaries, and providing more favourable treatment to earners of low incomes. They benefited the parties, the bureaucracy and the citizenry alike.

The shifting currents towards new forms of policy led to the rise of a moderate faction of policy-making that transcended the divide between bureaucracy and politics. Most notable among these moderates was the New Japan Alliance (*Shin Nihon dōmei*) formed in 1925 by Home Ministry bureaucrats close to Isawa Takio and by young men in the House of Peers such as Konoe Fumimaro.[25] Konoe graduated from First High in 1912 and entered the humanities division of Tokyo Imperial University, but then transferred to the law school of Kyoto Imperial University. He belonged to the same generation as Karasawa and his cohort.

Three years younger than Konoe was Yasui Seiichirō, a man who entered the Home Ministry in 1917 but chose to study abroad on his own. He was born in Okayama in

1891 and graduated in 1917 with a degree in German law. Yasui had already spent some eight months in Berlin when, in October 1922, he wrote these words:

> The baleful effects of formalized legal studies and formalized executive government have already been amply exposed in the Home Ministry, but I have sensed those effects especially clearly after having come to Germany. The era of exerting all of our energy to put up but hollow appearances with no spirit and with no originality has passed. So long as Japan fails to extricate itself from these evils, whether in learning or in government administration, it will not become something with real life.
>
> I think that a Japan that fails to understand how it is orienting its internal elements, a Japan that lets its eyes be vainly dazzled by any newfangled thing, finds itself in genuine danger. That politician who grasps what the life that inheres in Japan really is and then thinks about how to bring that inherent life into reality through new words and new organizations – he is a wise politician and a loyal citizen.[26]

Yasui spent his days abroad studying the local institutions of Germany, France and Britain. He wanted to understand the foundations on which these local structures were established. The days of importing foreign institutions into Japan had passed. A new era of reconfiguring those structures according to indigenous customs and history had arrived. Yasui believed that, to engage in this renovation project, his fellow builders needed to understand the original foundations on which their prefabricated structures had been built. He engaged in thoroughgoing research based on these thoughts.

Upon his return to Japan, Yasui rejected voices of dissent and ran for office in the first-ever universal elections, held in the third year of the Shōwa era (= 1928). He was defeated. But his research did not go in vain. His studies and impressions in Germany went on to find application in the post-war regeneration of Tokyo, where he served as head officer in the prefectural government and governor of the prefecture.

As the era of party rule took form in Japan, men such as Yasui took a neutral, middle road in the political world and acted as force of restraint on the problems arising from partisanship. They reclaimed the specialized skills and professionalization required of policy work. In a government by party politics, this neutral road was their calling. It was their path, their pursuit of their very duty as bureaucrats.

Conclusion: The Making of Government and Bureaucracy

The birth of the bureaucracy, the birth of modern Japan

Did men make the times, or did the times make men?

To strive for autonomy in the face of encroaching Western imperialists, to struggle through the process of learning, to build up the structures of a nation-state – these trails that made modern Japan were carved out by bureaucrats, by men born in the throes of upheaval, by men who plunged into a pursuit of unknown knowledge, by men who each became an autonomous living resource for a new nation.

The times and the men, bound together in an inextricable double helix, each made the other as generation followed generation. The cataclysms of the bakumatsu era gave rise to 'men of spirit' (*shishi*) who, desperate to resolve a crisis of government overcoming them, dove into Western learning. Spurred by new knowledge, these men became the motive force behind the Meiji Restoration. They transformed into Restoration bureaucrats and built up a new government. And to secure the human resources to succeed them, they nurtured new men of talent by sending young men to learn in the West.

As they exerted themselves to rear a fledgling nation, the Restoration bureaucrats dreamed of a future constitutional state. To the task of building that state they summoned the young men they had sent abroad. They ushered youth from across the country onto the road to the bureaucracy in order to build a government by executive supremacy and to keep it functioning. Universities arose to provide these young men with a professional education and to supply the government with human resources trained especially in law.

Once the Meiji Constitution was inaugurated, the Restoration bureaucrats, now standing at the summit of the executive state, developed into oligarchic politicians. Sometimes jostling with the political parties, sometimes cooperating with them, these oligarch-politicians carried the burden of governance. Young scholar-bureaucrats with university degrees wielded their specialized knowledge in support of these leaders. But these young officials did not remain satisfied with their subordinate roles for long.

They kindled dreams of rule by party politics, a form of government in which the citizens at large could participate.

On the heels of the First Sino- and the Russo-Japanese wars, Japan entered the Taishō era with its goal of national autonomy fulfilled. Scholar-bureaucrats then achieved their own autonomy, developing into politicians of bureaucratic origin. They became the stalwarts of the Rikken Seiyūkai and the Kenseikai, the organizations that enabled rule by party politics. As scholar-bureaucrats who had graduated from university, they took charge of state policy. They then evolved into politicians and established a recurring cycle that powered Japan into the future: a cycle of talent progressing from academy to bureaucracy to politics. It was here, in this pattern, that the dynamics between the times and the men, each making the other, played out.

Bearers of democracy: Government and participation

Three structures undergirded these dynamics: democracy as an institution, bureaucracy as a collective body and the individual self in pursuit of self-fulfilment. The interaction of the forces in these three structures propelled the greater structure they together composed – modern Japan itself – forward. The Charter Oath had heralded these three forces: it promulgated public debate, a way to expand participation in politics; it championed the unity and progress of the collective nation, for which both collaboration and competition were required; and it extolled the ideal of individual self-fulfilment, which could be achieved by both public and private will. Among the three, realizing of the principle of public debate played an indispensable role in securing legitimacy for the Meiji government. This ideal of public debate found its epitome in the opening of the national Diet and the rise of democratic government.

The Restoration bureaucrats embraced constitutional government as an ideal, but in practice they built a system of collaboration and competition firmly within the confines of the oligarchic regime. To allow for the stable growth of the nation while preserving their own posts of power, the oligarchs predicated constitutional government on the supremacy of the executive branch and restrained party politics. It is for this reason that the democracy of modern Japan has often been described as something limited, something incomplete.

But the oligarchy did not maintain exclusive control of the executive state. It allowed men from across the nation onto the road to the bureaucracy, the central organ of a nation of executive supremacy. And it thus cleared the path to participation not just in legislative government, through the Diet and the popular parties, but in executive government, in the state itself and in its ministries. The chance to partake in executive government galvanized youth across the archipelago and unleashed their energy as they vied to learn. After thirty years, the expansion of this system led to the collapse of the oligarchic government from within and reconfigured the political world into two large-tent cross-sectional parties. The emergence of a structure for competition dismantled oligarchic exclusivity, opened up new domains for popular participation and overturned the world of government.

Collectives of men: Collaboration and competition

The competition that animated modern Japan involved a battle not only among individuals but among collectives. The domainal or regional unit served as the most important locus of collective consciousness. Boys of common provenance developed a sense of cohesion as they tried to one-up one another within their domains. And as soon as they left their home regions, the domainal identities they cultivated spurred them to a broader struggle for dominance among the domains of the nation. The rivalry among tributary students was this kind of inter-domainal competition, a battle in which boys acted as if placards announcing their domainal affiliations were pinned to their backs. And the activity of young scholar-bureaucrats from Kumamoto, Nagano and Okayama reflected the structures that emerged from regional ideologies and interests and from regionally based feuds and alliances. Western learning and Chinese learning; official public schools and private schools; the so-called 'number schools' and the Imperial University – each, in its own ways, produced other kinds of collective identities. Rivalries raged among men within each group, but those same men presented a united front of cooperation as soon as they faced the outside world. And thus developed a pattern of collaboration and competition.

Vertical links between middle schools and high schools and between high schools and universities bore particular significance in fostering collective identity. The bonds among men of common academic provenance yielded a hankering among younger boys for the new knowledge their elders were acquiring. Alumni magazines, which mediated alumni-student interactions, revealed the depth of this desire. This incessant urge to know stood as a sign that regional identity overlapped with school identity to give shape to a particular kind of collective consciousness that stirred up a greater competitive spirit. Alumni presented schoolboys with adumbrations of who they would become, fanning their ill-defined but ebullient ambition.

The art of self-fulfilment: Public will and private will

The motive force in the making of modern Japan emerged from the assertion of the Five-Point Charter Oath that the very essence of the nation lay in the individual self pursuing his calling. Now that effort and ability could open roads once blocked by status affiliation, men spared no effort in pursuing their own life-trails. To make one's own path in life – it was an ideal befitting a nation-state built by those dubbed 'men of spirit'.

Men did not kindle ambition and strive after it only for the sake of public benefit. They were spurred by private interest, by a desire to break through the barriers of status affiliation and seize positions of influence, by a will to move their nation in the direction they themselves deemed best. No man could extricate public will from his own private will. And it was because the two were inseparable that the single force they constituted exerted such formidable power.

To build a bureaucracy in a land fuelled by this energy made scintillating sense. The bureaucracy let men seize positions of power by dint of their own effort and then use their posts to work for public good. Government policy was thus born as the ideal of government by public will jostled with yearnings for personal power whetted by private will. The spirit of competition that began in schools climbed with boys up into the bureaucracy, and as their ambition to fulfil their private interests before an ever-broader public increased, they evolved from bureaucrats into politicians. The bureaucracy folded a system of self-fulfilment, a system for men driven to action by their own autonomous will and ambition, into the structure of modern Japan itself.

The bureaucracy thus served as a medium to piece three structures of rule together: governance and participation in the institution of democracy; competition and collaboration in collective identities; and public will and private will in the individual self. And by bringing these structures together, the bureaucracy set into motion the larger composite structure that was modern Japan itself. Such was the duty of the bureaucracy. The birth of the bureaucracy was the birth of modern Japan. The making of the bureaucracy was the making of modern Japan.

The birth of the bureaucracy: Beyond the product of the times

If modern Japan succeeded in gaining independence and developing rapidly because of the bureaucracy, then so, too, did the bureaucracy matter in the isolation and defeat Japan faced in war. We must, then, consider one more dimension of the bureaucracy besides the three structures that undergirded it.

Born to a household of shogunal retainers and renowned for his work as a local official, Ōmori Shōichi wrote a twenty-point admonition to his eldest son after that son became a bureaucrat. He first delineated eighteen rather predictable points enjoining his son to be upright, to exercise justice, to work hard and to adhere to other principles of conduct befitting public responsibilities. He then appended two rather different clauses. 'Exert yourself in your occupation and strive after learning,' he wrote. 'Beware of the evils of partisanship.'

Ōmori underscored the idea that bureaucrats, in their capacity as public officials, had to engage in sustained learning and not be carried away by their quotidian occupational tasks. Only by studying not just from ancient classics but also from agrarian villages, from nature and from the sentiment of the people, and only by opening their eyes to the trends of the world, could bureaucrats begin to fulfil their duties. The era of legal studies had come and gone. If bureaucrats wanted to keep up with the times, they could not afford to settle for the rote desk-learning by which they had coasted through university.

The public relied on officials who gained mastery over the fundamentals of knowledge and then sustained their learning and applied it to actual practice. But as the national system of executive government took root, and as factions began to form around segments of administration in the executive ministries, the scope of experience a bureaucrat could acquire narrowed dramatically. A bureaucrat could get by just by repeating precedent. Bureaucrats began to inhabit an increasingly parochial world. The systematization of the bureaucracy stifled creativity.

Ferocious power struggles between the political parties unleashed the scourge of partisanship, which further curtailed learning among bureaucrats. The more will and ambition a bureaucrat had, the more inclined he was to join the parties. But those parties were embroiled in endless brawls, and administrative power changed frequently. The whole point of the executive state was to enable stability and continuity, but the partisan political model that bureaucrats upheld repeatedly rent that stability and continuity apart. Bureaucrats had approached party politics with anticipation and expectation. But doubt began to pervade their minds.

Mistrust of party politics led again to the rise of a government dominated by men from the bureaucracy. These men carried their own bureaucratic beliefs into the state. Because the failures of party politics had been imprinted so deeply in their minds, these bureaucrats forgot that it had been collaboration between the parties and the bureaucrats that had enabled the development of modern Japan in the first place. The Meiji era had exposed the limits of rule without direct contact with citizens at large, and it had revealed the folly of a government in which the sentiments of the people were merely conjured up by men within the state. Bureaucrats lost sight of the lessons of Meiji Japan. And they themselves thus started the countdown to war and defeat.

After defeat, bureaucrats once again marshalled their will, their learning and their expectations behind the reconstruction of their nation. The General Headquarters (GHQ) of the Allied Occupation imposed aptitude exams on bureaucrats to test their fitness for government. The bureaucrats found the tests inane, passing without difficulty. They flaunted their executive skills and applied their renewed will to post-war reconstruction. They became politicians once again and resurrected collaboration between the parties and the bureaucracy. Young men afire with their own private will and with the will of the public once again filed into the bureaucracy. And they sustained the structures of the bureaucracy into the future.

Well more than half a century has now passed since the end of the war and the Occupation. Japan has changed. And so, too, have the circumstances surrounding the executive state. The human talent on which the nation-state depends exists not only in the bureaucracy. It is everywhere.

The mission of modern Japan was 'that all be allowed to pursue their own calling so that there may be no discontent'. Today, people everywhere are pursuing their callings in ways that the men of the Charter Oath could hardly have imagined.

Notes

Introduction

1   Chalmers A. Johnson, *MITI and the Japanese Miracle: The Growth of Industrial Policy, 1925–1975* (Stanford, CA: Stanford University Press, 1982); Bernard S. Silberman, *Cages of Reason: The Rise of the Rational State in France, Japan, the United States, and Great Britain* (Chicago: University of Chicago Press, 1993); Nihon Keizai Shinbunsha, ed., *Kanryō: Kishimu kyodai kenryoku* (Tokyo: Nihon Keizai shinbunsha, 1994).

2   Makihara Izuru, 'Jimintō seiken to seiken kōtai', in Iio Jun, ed., *Seiken kōtai to seitō seiji* (Tokyo: Chūō kōron shinsha, 2013); Kobayashi Yoshikai, *Seiken kōtai: Minshutō seiken to wa nan de atta no ka* (Tokyo: Chūō kōron shinsha, 2012).

3   Nihon saiken Inishiatibu, *Minshutō seiken shippai no kenshō: Nihon seiji wa nani o ikasu ka* (Tokyo: Chūō kōron shinsha, 2013).

4   Mikuriya Takashi, '*Seiji shudō*' *no kyōkun: Seiken kōtai wa nani o motarashita no ka* (Tokyo: Keisō shobō, 2012); Makihara Izuru, *Kuzureru seiji o tatenaosu* (Tokyo: Kōdansha, 2018).

5   See, for example, Kanai Toshiyuki, *Gyōseigaku kōgi* (Tokyo: Chikuma shobō, 2018).

6   'Shushō kantei 7 tai 300: Misshitsuka no kaihi o', *Nihon keizai shinbun*, 27 November 2018.

7   Takeuchi Yō, *Risshin shusse shugi: Kindai nihon no roman to yōbō* (Kyoto: Sekai shisōsha, 2005).

8   For example, Marius B. Jansen, *Sakamoto Ryoma and the Meiji Restoration* (Princeton, NJ: Princeton University Press, 1961) and Marius B. Jansen, *Sakamoto Ryōma to Meiji Ishin*, trans. Hirao Michio and Hamada Kamekichi (Tokyo: Jiji tsūshinsha, 1965); Banno Junji, *Mikan no Meiji Ishin* (Tokyo: Chikuma shobō, 2007).

9   For example, Mitani Taichirō, *Nihon seitō seiji no keisei*, rev. edn (Tokyo: Tōkyō daigaku shuppansha, 1995); Banno Junji, *Nihon kindai shi* (Tokyo: Chikuma shobō, 2012).

10 Shimizu Yuichirō, *Seitō no kanryō no kindai: Nihon ni okeru rikken tōchi kōzō no sōkoku* (Tokyo: Fujiwara shoten, 2007).

11 Silberman, *Cages of Reason*.

12 Machidori Satoshi, *Minshushugi ni totte seitō to wa nani ka* (Tokyo: Mineruva shobō, 2018).

13 Muramatsu Michio, *Seikan sukuramu gata rīdāshippu no hōkai* (Tokyo: Tōyō keizai shinpōsha, 2010).

14 Earl H. Kinmonth, *The Self-Made Man in Meiji Japanese Thought: From Samurai to Salary Man* (Berkeley: University of California Press, 1981); Earl H. Kinmonth, *Risshin shusse no shakaishi*, trans. Hirota Teruyuki, Katō Jun, Yoshida Aya, Itō Akihiro, Takahashi Ichirō (Tokyo: Tamagawa daigaku shuppanbu, 1995).

15 For example, Ide Yoshinori, *Nihon kanryōsei to gyōsei bunka* (Tokyo: Tōkyō daigaku shuppankai, 1982).

16 Hata Ikuhiko, *Kanryō no kenkyū* (Tokyo: Kōdansha, 1983); Nihon keizai shinbunsha, *Kanryō.*

17 Sone Kengo, *Gendai Nihon no kanryōsei* (Tokyo: Tōkyō daigaku shuppankai, 2016).

18 On historical institutionalism, see Paul Pierson, *Politics in Time: History, Institutions, and Social Analysis* (Princeton, NJ: Princeton University Press, 2004); Paul Pierson, *Poritikkusu in taimu,* trans. Kasuya Yūko and Imai Makoto (Tokyo: Keisō shobō, 2010).

19 Machidori Satoshi, *Daigisei minshushugi* (Tokyo: Chūō kōron shinsha, 2015).

20 'Asa made zangyō "nemuranai Kasumigaseki" no genkai', *Nihon keizai shinbun,* 3 January 2015.

21 Maeda Kentarō, *Shimin o yatowanai kokka* (Tōkyō daigaku shuppankai, 2014).

Chapter 1

1 Or sixteen years by *kazoedoshi,* wherein a child is born as a one-year-old and adds a year to his age with every new calendar year.

2 Takahashi Hidenao, *Bakumatsu ishin no seiji to tennō* (Tokyo: Yoshikawa kōbunkan, 2007), 360.

3 Tada Kōmon, ed., *Iwakura-kō jikki* (Kyoto: Iwakura-kō kyūseki hozonkai, 1927), vol. 2, 182–183.

4 Translator's note: Lee Butler calls *buke tensō* 'envoys to the bakufu'. Lee A. Butler, 'Tokugawa Ieyasu's Regulations for the Court', *Journal of Asian Studies* 54, no. 2 (December 1994): 511. This translation of *shoshidai* comes from Mary Elizabeth Berry, 'Restoring the Past: The Documents of Hideyoshi's Magistrate in Kyoto', *Journal of Asian Studies* 43, no. 1 (June 1983): 60.

5 Takahashi, *Bakumatsu ishin no seiji to tennō,* 401–406.

6 Mitani Hiroshi, *Meiji ishin to nashonarizumu* (Tokyo: Yamakawa shuppansha, 1997).

7 Ibid.

8 Translator's note: The translations of these offices and of the term *sanshoku kaigi* come from John Breen, 'The Imperial Oath of April 1868: Ritual, Politics, and Power in the Restoration', *Monumenta Nipponica* 51, no. 4 (Winter 1996): 409–410, 420.

9 Dajōkan, ed. *Fukkoki* (Naigai shoseki, 1930), Keiō 3/ 12/15jō, vol. 1, 290.

10 Ibid., 291.

11 Nakane Yukie, *Teibō nikki,* Keiō 3/13/9 jō, in Kokusho Kangyōkai, ed., *Shiseki zassan* (Tokyo: Kokusho kangyōkai, 1912), vol. 4, 252–255.

12 Matsuo Masahito, *Ishin seiken* (Tokyo: Yoshikawa kōbunkan, 1995).

13 'Sanshoku bunka', in *Hōrei zensho,* Meiji 1/1/17.

14 'Sanshoku hakkyoku', in *Hōrei zensho,* Meiji 1/2/3.

15 Takahashi, *Bakumatsu Ishin no seiji tennō,* 508.

16 For example, Iwakura sent multiple demands to the Kumamoto domain to dispatch Yokoi Shōnan to the capital. Each time, the domain deliberated and responded to the imperial court by declining its request. See Hosokawa-ke Hensanjo, ed., *Higo-han kokuji shiryō* (Kumamoto: Kokusho kangyōkai, 1973), Keiō 4/3/8 jō, vol. 8, 266–268.

17 Sasaki Suguru, *Shishi to kanryō* (Kyoto: Mineruva shobō, 1984), 93.

18 In the requests they submitted to the imperial court to return to their domains, Kido and Hirosawa indicated that, even though they had ascended to the capital under the orders of their domains, they feared that continuing work for the new state would constitute betrayal of their command of their domainal lords. See Baba Yoshihiro, 'Meiji shoki no chōshisei ni tsuite', *Dōshisha hōgaku* 38, no. 5 (1987): 146–174.

19 *Hōrei zensho*, Meiji 1/2/21. It appears that this derived from a recommendation from *benji* Hiramatsu in the first month. See 'Benji Hiramatsu kenpaku', in Iwakura-kō kyūseki Hozonkai Taigaku Bunko Zō, ed., *Iwakura Tomomi kankei monjo*, 17:26 (Tokyo: Hokusensha, 1992–1994).

20 The appointments, places of origins and numbers of chōshi outlined below are based on Nihon shiseki Kyōkai, ed., *Meiji shiryō ken'yō shokumu buninroku* (Tokyo: Tōkyō daigaku shuppankai, 1981), vols 1–4.

21 Iwakura Tomomi ate Mutsu Munemitsu shokan, Keiō 4/8, in Sasaki Suguru, Fujii Jōji, Misawa Jun and Tanigawa Yutaka hen, eds, *Iwakura Tomomi kankei shiryō* (Kyoto: Shibunkaku shuppan, 2012), vols 1, 162–163.

22 Translator's note: Following Breen, 'The Imperial Oath of April 1868', 428, for this translation of *hanseki hōkan*.

23 Unless otherwise noted, the account of Yuri below derives from Yuri Masamichi, *Shishaku Yuri Kimimasa den* (Tokyo: Iwanami shoten, 1940).

24 Dajōkan, ed., *Fukkoki*, Keiō 3/12/18, p. 316.

25 Translator's note: translation taken from Wm. Theodore de Bary, Carol Gluck and Arthur E. Tiedmann, eds, *Sources of Japanese Tradition: Volume Two: 1600 to 2000, abridged*, 2nd edn (New York: Columbia University Press, 2006), 8.

26 Unless otherwise noted, the account below of the life of Itō derives from Shunpo-kō Tsuishōkai, ed., *Itō Hirobumi den* (Tokyo: Tōseisha, 1940), vol. 1.

27 Matsuo, *Ishin seiken*, 89.

28 Unless otherwise noted, the account of the life of Ōkuma below derives from Waseda Daigakushi Hensanjo, ed., *Ōkuma-haku sekijitsu tan* (Tokyo: Waseda daigaku shuppanbu, 1969) and Ōkuma-kō hachijūgo-nen shi hensankai, ed., *Ōkuma-kō hachijūgo-nen shi* (Ōkuma-kō hachijūgo-nen shi hensankai, 1926).

29 Umetani Noboru, 'Oyatoi gaikokujin', (Tokyo: Nihon keizai shinbunsha, 1965). pp.73-74.

30 Kunaichō rinji teishitsu Henshūkyoku, ed., *Meiji tennō ki* (Tokyo: Yoshikawa kōbunkan, 2000), Meiji 1/ 4/22jō, vol. 1, 681.

31 On this incident, see Kataoka Yakichi, *Urakami yonban kuzure: Meiji seifu no Kirishitan dan'atsu* (Tokyo: Chikuma shobō, 1991).

32 Waseda Daigakushi Hensanjo, ed., *Ōkuma-kō sekijitsu tan*, 123.

33 Ibid., 202.

34 For example, Ernest Satow decried the devolution of practical administration to lower-level bureaucrats, expressing his belief that nobles and daimyo in posts simply because of their lineage should be removed immediately. Itō Kenji, 'Meiji shonen ni okeru Ōkurashō kindai kanryō no keisei', *Keizaigaku zasshi* 67, no. 4 (1972): 68–92.

35 Nakaoka Tetsurō, *Kindai gijutsu no Nihonteki tenkai* (Tokyo: Asahi shinbun shuppan, 2013) p. 9.

36 'Seitai o sadamu', in *Dajō ruiten*, Meiji 1/intercalary-4/21. Housed in the Japan National Archives.

37 Elijah Coleman Bridgman, *Renpō shiryaku* (Yorozu heishirō, 1864).

38 Translator's note: translation based on but modified from that in de Bary, Gluck and Tiedmann, eds, *Sources of Japanese Tradition*, 9.

39 For a specific example, see Arakawa Shō, 'Boshin sensō ki no chihō tōchi to Shijō Takatoshi', in Shōyū kurabu and Kazoku shiryō Kenkyūkai, eds, *Shijō-danshaku ke no Ishin to kindai* (Tokyo: Dōseisha, 2012).

40 See *Dajō ruiten*, Yoshinaga no ikensho, Meiji 1/4/29.

41 *Hōrei zensho*, Meiji 1/2/10.

Chapter 2

1 Asai Kiyoshi, 'Meiji ninen no kanri senkyo', *Jinji gyōsei* 6, no. 4 (1955).

2 On the public elections described here and below, see 'Kōsen hō no shōsho', in *Ōkubo Toshimichi monjo*, vol. 3 (Tokyo: Matsuno shoten, 2004), 182–186.

3 See Asakura Haruhiko, ed., *Dajōkan nisshi*, vol. 4 (Tokyo: Tōkyōdō shuppan, 1985).

4 Rikō Mitsuo, Mori Sei'ichi, Sone Yasunori, *Manjō itchi to tasūketsu* (Tokyo: Nihon keizai shinbunsha, 1980).

5 *Hōrei zensho*, Meiji 2/5/21.

6 See the *Dajōkan nisshi*.

7 Maejima Hisoka, *Maejima Hisoka: Maejima Hisoka jijoden* (Tokyo: Nihon tosho sentā, 1997), 76–77.

8 See the *Dajōkan nisshi*.

9 'Kōgisho nisshi', in Asakura Haruhiko, ed., *Dajōkan nisshi*, vol. 4 (Tokyo: Tōkyōdō shuppan, 1985).

10 Yamazaki Yūkō, 'Meiji shonen no kōgisho, shūgiin', in Toriumi Yasushi, Mitani Hiroshi, Nishikawa Makoto, Yano Nobuyuki, eds, *Nihon rikken seiji no keisei to henshitsu* (Tokyo: Yoshikawa kōbunkan, 2005).

11 On the life of Kanda, see Kanda Naibu, ed., *Kanda Takahira ryakuden* (Tokyo: Kanda Naibu, 1910).

12 'Daigaku Nankō ni kōshinsei o oku', in *Dajō ruiten*, ser. 1, vol. 19, kansei, monkansei 5. Housed in the National Archives of Japan (*Kokuritsu kōbunshokan*).

13 Translator's note: This translation of *Kaiseijo* follows Marius B. Jansen, 'New Materials for the Intellectual History of Nineteenth-Century Japan', *Harvard Journal of Asiatic Studies* 20, no. 3–4 (December 1957): 580.

14 Ōkubo Toshiaki, *Nihon no daigaku* (Tokyo: Tamagawa daigaku shuppanbu, 1997).

15 The life of Ogura Shohei as outlined here is based on Matsumoto Uhei, *Shizen no hito Komura Jutarō* (Tokyo: Rakuyōdō, 1914). As explained below, Ogura was a relative of Komura who always served as his guide and leader.

16 Karasawa Tomitarō, *Kōshinsei: Bakumatsu Ishin ki no erīto* (Tokyo: Gyōsei, 1974). Oddly, this part of Hirata's life is not described in the standard chronicle of his life, Katō Fusazō, ed., *Hakushaku Hirata Tōsuke den* (Tokyo: Hirata-haku denki hensan jimusho, 1927). The rest of the following account of his life relies on this text.

17 National Archives of Japan, 'Kōshinsei kisoku'.

18 Katō, *Hakushaku Hirata Tōsuke den*.

19 Unless otherwise indicated, the following account of the life of Komura derives from Komura Shōji, *Kotsuniku* (Miyazaki: Kōmyakusha, 2005).

20 The following account of the life of Hatoyama derives from Hatoyama Haruko, *Hatoyama no isshō* (Tokyo: Hatoyama Haruko, 1929).

21 Meiji kyōikushi kenkyūkai, ed., *Sugiura Jūgō zenshū*, vol. 6 (Ōtsu: Sugiura Jūgō zenshū kankōkai, 1983).

22 The following account of the life of Isawa derives from Ko Isawa Shūji sensei kinen jigyōkai hensan iinkai, ed., *Rakuseki Isawa Shūji sensei* (Tokyo: Ko Isawa sensei kinen jigyōkai, 1919).

23 Unless otherwise indicated, the following account of the life of Hozumi derives from Hozumi Shigeyuki, *Meiji ichi hōgakusha no shuppatsu* (Tokyo: Iwanami shoten, 1988).

24 Sakuma Shōzan, 'Seikenroku', in Matsuura Rei, ed., *Nihon no meicho 30: Sakuma Shozō, Yokoi Shōnan* (Tokyo: Chūō kōronsha, 1970).

25 Karasawa, *Kōshinsei.*
26 Hashinami Gyorō, *Daigaku gakusei sogen*, vol. 1 (Tokyo: Ōzorasha, 1912).
27 Ibid.
28 Karasawa, *Kōshinsei.*
29 Hozumi, *Meiji ichi hōgakusha no shuppatsu.*
30 Ōkubo, *Nihon no daigaku.*
31 'Daigaku Nankō kisoku o sadamu', in *Dajō ruiten*, ser. 1, vol. 16. Housed in the National Archives of Japan (*Kokuritsu kōbunshokan*).
32 Komura, *Kotsuniku*, 42.
33 Unless otherwise indicated, the following account of the lives of the tributary students derives from Hashinami, *Daigaku gakusei sogen*, vol. 1.
34 Karasawa, *Kōshinsei.*
35 Saitō Shūichirō, *Kaikyūdan* (San Francisco, CA: Aoki taiseidō, 1908).
36 Hashinami, *Daigaku gakusei sogen*, vol. 1.
37 Hatoyama, *Hatoyama no isshō.*
38 Tōkyō daigaku hyakunenshi henshū iinkai, ed., *Tōkyō daigaku hyakunenshi, tsūshi 1* (Tokyo: Tōkyō daigaku, 1984).
39 Komura Jutarō, 'Makoto no ichiji', in Komura, *Kotsuniku*, 411.
40 Tsuji Naoto, *Kindai Nihon kaigai ryūgaku no mokuteki hen'yō* (Tokyo: Tōshindō, 2010).
41 Ibid.
42 Saitō, *Kaikyūdan.*
43 Hatoyama, *Hatoyama no isshō.*
44 Doboku gakkai, ed., *Furuichi Kōi to sono jidai* (Tokyo: Doboku gakkai, 2004).

Chapter 3

1 What is referred to here as 'department' is equivalent to a 'ministry' in the Japanese government today; the terms are both *shō* in Japanese. To avoid confusion with the contemporaneous 'Ministry of the Left' and 'Ministry of the Right', the term 'department' is used here. Once the ministries of the right and of the left are dissolved in the historical chronology of the chapter, the term 'ministry' is employed. The Japanese terms do not change.

2 The term 'minister' (*daijin*) here is not to be confused with the term as it is used today, as heads of the departments of the executive state such as the Ministry of the Treasury.

3 Unless otherwise indicated, information on the so-called 'coup d'etat of *haihan chiken*' comes from Matsuo Masahito, *Haihan chiken no kenkyū* (Tokyo: Yoshikawa kōbunkan, 2001).

4 Matsuo, *Haihan chiken*, and Matsuo Masahito, *Ishin seiken* (Tokyo: Yoshikawa kōbunkan, 1995), 210.

5 'Kenchi jōrei', *Dajōkan fukoku* 623 gō (1870/11/27).

6 Translator's note: The somewhat clunky term 'prefectural head' is used here for *kenrei* to distinguish it from the appellation *kenchiji*, or 'governor', which comes later.

7 A case in point is Satsuma-born Nagayama Moriteru, head of Chikuma prefecture, today the central part of Nagano prefecture. Nagayama himself travelled about the prefecture giving speeches to promote the proliferation of education. Chikuma attained the highest rate of elementary school enrolment in the country. See Shimizu

Yuichirō, "'Kyōikuken" no ima made to kore kara', in Toda Tadao, ed., *Gakkō o kaereba shakai ga kawaru* (Tokyo: Tōkyō shoseki, 2014).

8   'Jinmin yūdō no gi chihōkan e chokuyu', in *Chokugo rui, Meiji shōchoku, Ji Meiji gannen shi dō 29-nen 12-gatsu*, held in the National Archives of Japan (1873/5/20).

9   Shimizu Yuichirō, 'Waihan naikaku ni okeru ryōkan no jissō', *Nihon rekishi* 674 (2004): 52–70.

10 'Dajōkan shokusei narabini jimu shōtei o sadamu', in the 15th *maki* of the 1st *hen* of the *Dajō ruiten*, held in the National Archives of Japan.

11 'Sho shō kyō kaitaku chōkan ni inin no jōken o shimesu', in the 15th *maki* of the 1st *hen* of the *Dajō ruiten*, held in the National Archives of Japan.

12 Kasahara Hidehiko, *Meiji rusu seifu* (Tokyo: Keiō gijuku daigaku shuppankai, 2010), 65.

13 Shihōshō, ed., *Shihō enkaku shi* (Tokyo: Hara shobō, 1979).

14 Torio Koyata, 'Jijidan – san', in Torio Tokuan, ed., *Tokuan zensho* (Torio Mitsu, 1911), 564–566.

15 Ōkubo Toshiaki, *Iwakura shisetsu no kenkyū* (Tokyo: Munetaka shobō, 1976), 27–52.

16 Sugawara Morikuni, 'Iwakura shisetsudan no hensei', *Hōgaku shinpō* 109, no. 1–2 (2002).

17 See Pär Cassel, *Grounds of Judgment* (Oxford: Oxford University Press, 2012), 112, for this translation of *rijikan*.

18 Nishio Toyosaku, *Shishaku Tanaka Fujimaro den* (Nagoya: Kōsaijuku, 1934).

19 Nagayo Sensai, 'Shōkō shi shi', in Ogawa Teizō, Sakai Shizu, Matsumotot Jun and Nagayo Sensai, eds, *Matsumoto Jun jiden, Nagayo Sensai jiden* (Tokyo: Heibonsha, 1980), pp. 128–136.

20 Ibid.

21 Sugawara Morikuni, 'Iwakura shisetsudan no jūsha to dōkō ryūgakusei ni kansuru tsuikō', *Hōgaku shinpō* 104, no. 1 (1997): 51–78.

22 Tanaka Akira, *Iwakura shisetsudan no rekishiteki kenkyū* (Tokyo: Iwanami shoten, 2002), 33–38.

23 Ogawara Masamichi, 'Meiji shoki ni okeru kazoku no kaigai ryūgaku', *Nichi-Ō hikaku bunka kenkyū* 2 (2004), pp. 19–30.

24 Wada Eita, *Sake to kujira no Nihonjin: Sekizawa Meisei no shōgai* (Tokyo: Seizandō shoten, 1994).

25 Okada Yoshiharu and Hatsuda Tōru, 'Matsugasaki Tsumunaga no shoki no keireki to Aoki Shūzō Nasu bettei', *Nihon kenchiku gakkai keikaku kei ronbun shū* 63, no. 514 (1998), pp. 233–240.

26 'Shimizudani Kinnaru rireki shiryō', in *Shimizudani Kinnaru kankei monjo*, held by the Kensei shiryō shitsu of the National Diet Library.

27 'O kaibun tome', in *Shimizudani Kinnaru kankei monjo*, held by the Kensei shiryō shitsu of the National Diet Library.

28 Fusazō, *Hakushaku Hirata Tōsuke den*.

29 Kikuyama Masaaki, *Meiji kokka no keisei to shihō seido* (Tokyo: Ochanomizu shobō, 1993).

30 Sekiguchi Eiichi, 'Meiji rokunen teigaku mondai', *Hōgaku* 44, no. 4 (1980), pp. 464–505.

31 Hidehiko, *Meiji rusu seifu*, 103.

32 'Dajōkan shokusei shōtei', in the 14th *maki* of the 2nd *hen* of *Dajō ruiten*, held in the National Archives of Japan (1873/5/2). Kashihara Hiroki, 'Dajōkan-sei junshoku no jissō', *Nihon rekishi* 750 (2010), pp. 58–75.

33 Translator's note: For the sake of familiarity, we will refer to the Home Ministry as such here (and not as the 'Department of the Interior', which might be a better translation), but it is important to bear in mind that the Home Ministry (*naimushō*) was a *shō* like the Treasury (*ōkurashō*) or other executive departments, not an *in* like the Ministry of the Right. This terminological confusion in English becomes moot once the Three Ministries are dissolved.

34 Tanaka, *Iwakura shisetsudan no rekishiteki kenkyū*, 234.

35 Politicians at the centre of the government took heed of the reaction from popular opinion and were cautious in recommending men from their own domains. Ochi Noboru, 'Meiji shoki gyōsei kanryō no seikaku', *Shisō* 487 (1965).

36 Nakagawa Toshiyuki, 'Dajōkan naikaku sōsetsu ni kansuru ichikōsatsu', in Meiji Ishin shi gakkai, ed., *Bakuhan kenryoku to Meiji Ishin* (Tokyo: Yoshikawa kōbunkan, 1992).

37 Mikuriya Takashi, 'Kokkairon to zaiseiron', in Banno Junji and Miyachi Masato, eds, *Nihon kindai shi ni okeru tenkanki no kenkyū* (Tokyo: Yamakawa shuppansha, 1985).

38 Obinata Sumio, 'Jiyū minken undō to Meiji 14-nen no seihen', in Meiji Ishin shi gakkai, ed., *Kindai kokka no keisei* (Tokyo: Yūshisha, 2012), p. 128.

39 Mikuriya, 'Kokkairon to zaiseiron'.

40 Yazo was born in 1851 in what became Ōita prefecture and later became a secretary of the Council of State (*Dajōkan daishokikan*) and an official in the statistics division (*tōkei'in kanji*). Ozaki Yukio, born in 1858 in what became Kanagawa prefecture, became a lower-level secretary in the statistics division (*tōkei'in gonshō shokikan*).

41 Shimizu Yuichirō, *Seitō to kanryō no kindai* (Tokyo: Fujiawara shoten, 2007), ch. 1.

42 Banno Junji, *Nihon kensei shi* (Tokyo: Tōkyō daigaku shuppankai, 2008), 72.

43 Shimizu, *Seitō to kanryō no kindai*, ch. 2.

44 Ozaki Saburō, from Kyoto, was born in 1842 and was later head officer of the Legislative Bureau (*hōseikyoku chōkan*); Yasuba Yasukazu was from Kumamoto; Itō Miyoji, from Nagasaki, was born in 1857 and was later head officer in the cabinet secretariat (*naikaku shoki chōkan*) and minister of agricultural and commercial affairs (*nōshōmushō*); Ōmori Shōichi, from Shizuoka, was born in 1856 and was later head officer in the general affairs division of the Home Ministry (*naimu sōmu chōkan*) and governor of Kyoto (*Kyōto fuchiji*); Kiyoura Keigo, from Kumamoto, was born in 1850 and was later justice minister, home minister and prime minister; and Sufu Kōhei, from Yamaguchi, was born in 1851 and was later governor of Kanagawa (*Kanagawa kenchiji*).

45 Kawashima Atsushi, from Satsuma domain, was born in 1847 and was a former study-abroad student in Germany, a secretary in the treasury (*ōkura gon-no-daishokikan*) and later a member of the House of Representatives (*shūgiin giin*) and head official in Hokkaido (*Hokkaidōchō chōkan*); Miyoshi Taizō, from Akizuki domain, was born in 1845 and was a member of the justice ministry secretariat (*shihō shokikan*) and later head of the Court of Cassation; Yamazaki Naotane, from Nakatsu domain, was born in 1852 and was a former study-abroad student in France, a senior secretary in of the Council of State (*Dajōkan daishokikan*) and later head of the Prefectural Governance Bureau in the Home Ministry (*Naimushō kenchikyoku chō*); and Yoshida Masaharu, from Tosa domain, was born in 1852 and was a junior-ranking secretary of the foreign affairs ministry (*gaimu shō-shokikan*).

46 Takii Kazuhiro, *Doitsu kokkagaku to Meiji kokusei: Shutain kokkagaku no kiseki* (Kyoto: Mineruva shobō, 1999).

47 For instance, Ōtsu Jun'ichirō, *Nihon kanri nin'yō ron* (Kinkōdō, 1880).

48 Arakawa Kunizō of Chōshū was born in 1852 and was later head of the Prefectural Governance Bureau of the Home Ministry (*kenchikyoku*); Watanabe Renkichi was born in 1852 in Nagaoka domain; Yamawaki Gen, born in 1849 in Kanazawa domain, was later head of the administrative court (*gyōsei saibansho chōkan*).

49 Translator's note: With the dissolution of the Dajōkan system, it is now possible to refer without confusion to the executive departments (*shō*) as 'ministries' and their heads as 'ministers', which is how they are conventionally known in English. The name of the ministries themselves remains *shō*, but their heads are now *daijin* rather than *kyō*.

50 Chokurei no. 2, Meiji 19.

Chapter 4

1 This translation, by Itō Miyoji, comes from http://www.ndl.go.jp/constitution/e/etc/c02.html.

2 Itō Hirobumi, *Kenpō gikai* (Tokyo: Iwanami shoten, 1940).

3 Itō Miyoji, *Dai Nihon teikoku kenpō engi* (Tokyo: Shinzansha, 1974).

4 They were Takata Sanae of Tokyo; Amano Tameyuki of Nagasaki; Yamada Ichirō of Hiroshima; Okayama Kenkichi of Tokyo; Sunagawa Katsutoshi of Hyōgo; and Yamada Kinosuke of Osaka.

5 Manabe Masayuki, *Tōkyō senmon gakkō no kenkyū* (Tokyo: Waseda daigaku shuppanbu, 2010). The drop-out was Ichishima Kenkichi of Niigata.

6 Terasaki Masao, *Tōkyō daigaku no rekishi* (Tokyo: Kōdansha, 2007), 234.

7 Ibid., 235.

8 Takii Kazuhiro, 'Watanabe Hiromoto – Nihon no Arutohōfu', *Jinbun ronshū* 41, no. 2 (2006): 159–181.

9 Nakano Minoru, *Kindai Nihon daigaku seido no seiritsu* (Tokyo: Yoshikawa kōbunkan, 2003).

10 Nakayama Shigeru, *Teikoku daigaku no tanjō* (Tokyo: Chūō kōronsha, 1978).

11 Nakano Minoru, *Tōkyō daigaku monogatari* (Tokyo: Yoshikawa kōbunkan, 1999).

12 For example, see Nakagawa Kotomi, 'Bōchō kyōikukai ni yoru ikuei jigyō no tenkai', *Hiroshima daigaku kyōikubu kiyō* 41 (1992).

13 Chokurei no. 37, Meiji 20.

14 Kobayashi Kazuyuki, 'Kindai shoki no Nihon kanryōsei', in Hirata Masahiro and Ona Yasuyuki, eds, *Seikaishi no naka no teikoku to tanryō* (Tokyo: Yamakawa shuppansha, 2008).

15 'Bunkan shiken kyoku o naikaku ni oku', in the 4th *maki* of the 11th *hen* (Meiji 20) of the *Dajō ruiten*, held in the National Archives of Japan.

16 Translator's note: It is perhaps more idiomatic to translate *bunkan* as 'civil servant'; indeed, Richard Spaulding titles his book on the civil officer examinations, *Imperial Japan's Higher Civil Service Examinations* (Princeton, NJ: Princeton University Press, 2015). But the constellation of implications associated with 'service' is not necessarily present in the Japanese phrasing; 'civil officer' offers a more precise if less idiomatic rendering.

17 Shioiri Tasuke, *Kōtō futsū bunkan daigen shiken kyūdai hihō* (Tokyo: Nihon shoseki kaisha, 1889).

18 Sengaku koji, Shinshi no michi iyoiyo hirakete masumasu katashi, Hosei shisō, no. 112, 1890.

19 *Kanai Noboru kankei monjo*, held by the Tōkyō daigaku daigakuin hōgaku seijigaku kenkyūka fuzoku kindai Nihon hōsei shiryō sentā.

20 From *Kaneko Kentarō jishu den.*
21 Uchida Kōsai, from Kumamoto, entered the Foreign Ministry and later became foreign minister; Hayashi Gonsuke, from Fukushima, similarly entered the Foreign Ministry and became ambassador to Britain; and Hayashida Kametarō, also from Kumamoto, entered the Legislation Bureau and became head of the secretariat of the House of Representatives (*shūgi'in shoki kanchō*).
22 Kawai Yahachi, *Ikki sensei kaikoroku* (Tokyo: Ikki sensei tsuitōkai, 1954).
23 Wakatsuki Reijirō, *Kofūan kaikoroku* (Tokyo: Yomiuri shinbunsha, 1950), 42.
24 Matsunami Niichirō, ed., *Mizuno Hakushi koki kinnen ronsaku to zuihitsu* (Tokyo: Mizuno Rentarō sensei koki shukugakai jimusho, 1937).
25 Kanai, 'Seiji keizai gakusei no zento', in *Kanai Noboru kankei monjo.*
26 Shimura Gentarō, 'Meiji jidai kanri no kako oyobi shōrai', *Rikoku shin shi* 5 (1889).
27 Unless otherwise noted, all information about the life of Hara comes from Yamamoto Shirō, *Hara Takashi* (Tokyo: Tōkyō sōgensha, n.d.).
28 Tsurumi Yūsuke, *Seiden Gotō Shinpei*, vol. 1 (Tokyo: Fujiwara shoten, 2004).
29 Inoue Masaaki ed., *Hakushaku Kiyoura Keigo den*, vol. 1 (Tokyo: Hakushaku Kiyoura Keigo den kankōkai, 1935).
30 'Kiyoura bunko', held at Kagoshima kenritsu Kamoto shōgyō kōkō toshoshitsu.
31 Hata Ikuhito, *Kanryō no kenkyū*, 91.
32 Chokurei no. 183, Meiji 26.
33 Wada Ichirō, ed. *Kōkan Akimoto Toyonoshin kun* (Wada Ichirō, 1935). Akimoto passed the first year of the exams.
34 In *Okada Unosuke kankei monjo*, held by the Tōkyō daigaku daigakuin hōgaku seijigaku kenkyūka fuzoku kindai Nihon hōsei shiryō sentā.
35 Kamiyama kun kinen Jigyōkai, ed., *Kamiyama Mitsunoshin* (Kamiyama kun kinen jigyōkai, 1941).
36 *Kamiyama Mitsunoshin kankei monjo*, held by the Tōkyō daigaku daigakuin hōgaku seijigaku kenkyūka fuzoku kindai Nihon hōsei shiryō sentā.
37 Tanaka Yoshitsugu, ed., *Tanaka Jirō* (Tanaka Yoshitsugu, 1932), 95.
38 Nanbara Shigeru ed., Onozuka Keheiji (Tokyo: Iwanami Shoten, 1963), p. 32.
39 Amako Todomu, *Heimin saishō Wakatsuki Reijirō* (Tokyo: Hōbunkan, 1930).
40 Kyōto daigaku sōgō ningengakubu toshokan.
41 Sugawara, 'Saisho no kōbun shiken', in Sugawara Michimasa et al., eds, *Sugawara Michitaka den*, vol. 1 (n.p., 1993).
42 'Ni hachi kai kiji', held in the Shidehara heiwa bunko in the Kensei shiryō shitsu of the National Diet Library.
43 Held in Matsuyama shiritsu Shiki kinen hakubutsukan.
44 Suzuki Hideo, *Kankōba no kenkyū* (Tokyo: Sōeisha, 2001).
45 Kamiyama kun kinen jigyōkai, *Kamiyama Mitsunoshin*, 69.
46 Takeuchi Yō, *Risshin shusse shugii*, 26.
47 Held by the Tōhoku daigaku shiryōkan.

Chapter 5

1 Chokurei no. 135, Meiji 22.
2 Sakamoto Kazuto, 'Meiji nijūni nen no naikaku kansei ni tsuite no ichikōsatsu', in Inuzuka Takaaki, ed., *Meiji kokka no seisaku to shisō* (Tokyo: Yoshikawa kōbunkan, 2005).

3   Ōishi Makoto, *Kenpō chitsujo e no tenbō* (Tokyo: Yūhikaku, 2008), 189.

4   Sasaki Takashi, *Hanbatsu seifu to rikken seiji* (Tokyo: Yoshikawa kōbunkan, 1992).

5   Shimizu Yuichirō, *Seitō to kanryō no kindai: Nihon ni okeru rikken tōchi kōzō no sōkoku* (Tokyo: Fujiwara shoten, 2007), ch. 2.

6   Shōyū Kurabu and Nishio Rintarō, eds, *Mizuno Rentarō kaisōroku, kankei bunsho* (Tokyo: Yamakawa shuppansha, 1999).

7   Shimizu, *Seitō to kanryō no kindai*, 74.

8   Sasakawa Tamon, ed., *Matsuda Masahisa kō* (Tokyo: Kōsonkai, 1938), 182.

9   Soeda, 'Gōdō no seishin', *Kenseitō tōhō* 4 (1898).

10 'Itō Ōkuma Itagaki kaikenroku', *Itō Miyoji kankei monjo* 350, Kensei shiryō shitsu of the National Diet Library.

11 Matsunami Niichirō, ed., *Mizuno hakushi koki kinen ronsaku to zuihitsu* (Tokyo: Mizuno Rentarō sensei koki shukugakai jimusho, 1937).

12 Matsukata Masayoshi ate Yamagata Aritomo shokan, Meiji 31/6/18, from Matsukata Masayoshi kankei monjo 7.

13 'Gian tojikomi Meiji 31-nen bun', *Zatsu kōbunsho* 1819, in the National Archives of Japan.

14 *Tokudaiji Sanetsune nikki*, held by the Kunaichō shoryōbu.

15 Fushimi Taketo, 'Kokka zaisei tōgōsha to shite no naikaku sōri daijin', *Kokka gakkai zasshi* 120, no. 12 (2007), pp. 910–975.

16 Itō Yukio, *Rikken kokka no kakuritsu to Itō Hirobumi* (Tokyo: Yoshikawa kōbunkan, 1999).

17 Kagawa Etsuji, *Ōura Kanetake den* (Tokyo: Hakubunkan, 1921).

18 Unless otherwise noted, the account of Tokonami is based on Maeda Renzan, *Tokonami Takejirō den* (Tokyo: Tokonami Takejirō denki kankōkai, 1939).

19 Mori Yasuo, *Nihon rikugun to Nitchū sensō e no michi* (Kyoto: Mineruva shobō, 2010).

20 Wakatsuki Tsuyoshi, '"Hōka henchō" hihan no tenkai to seitō naikaku', *Shigaku zasshi* 114, no. 3 (2005), pp. 346–369.

21 Mizuno Rentarō, *Tazan no ishi* (Tokyo: Shimizu shoten, 1909).

22 Wakatsuki Reijirō, *Kofūan kaikoroku* (Tokyo: Yomiuri shinbunsha, 1950), 194.

23 Hamaguchi Fujiko, ed., *Zuisōroku* (Tokyo: Sanseidō, 1931), 16.

24 Hata Isoko, ed., *Hata Toyosuke* (Hata Isoko, 1935).

25 Hamaguchi, *Zuisōroku*, 19.

26 Itō Takashi, ed., *Taishō shoki Yamagata Aritomo danwa hikki: seihen omoidegusa* (Tokyo: Yamakawa shuppansha, 1981), 107.

27 Ōkuma, 'Shutsujin ni nozonde tenka ni sensu', *Shin Nihon*.

28 Yamagata ate Shimooka shokan, Taishō 5 (1916)/11, Shōyū Kurabu, ed., in *Yamagata Aritogmo kankei monjo*, vol. 2 (2006).

Chapter 6

1   Kawai Yoshinari, *Meiji no ichi seinen zō* (Tokyo: Kōdansha, 1969).

2   Mori Ariyoshi, *Seinen to ayumu Gotō Fumio* (Tokyo: Nihon seinenkan, 1979), 31.

3   Born in 1872, Takeuchi hailed from Yamanashi prefecture. He dropped out of the Tokyo Professional School and in 1898 entered the Ministry of Agricultural and Commercial Affairs, where he eventually became deputy minister. Hanihara, too, was a Yamanashi man, though he was born in 1876; he graduated from the Tokyo

Professional School in 1897 and entered the Foreign Ministry the following year, eventually becoming its deputy. Yamamoto, born in 1889, hailed from Yamaguchi, graduated from the East Asia Tung Wen College (J. *Tō-A dō bunsho in daigaku*; Ch. *Dongya tong wen shu yuan daxue*), entered the Foreign Ministry in 1919, and became deputy of the Ministry of Greater East Asia.

4   Fukunaga Fumio et al., eds, *Ashida Hitoshi nikki*, 2 vols (Tokyo: Kashiwa shobō, 2012).

5   Yoshino Sakuzō, *Shiken seikō hō* (Ibaraki: Seizansha, 2000).

6   Naiseishi Kenkyūkai, ed., *Matsumoto Manabu shi danwa sokkiroku* (Tokyo: Naiseishi kenkyūkai, 1967).

7   Aoki Tokuzō, *Omoide* (Tokyo: Ōkura zaimu kyōkai, 1966).

8   Hozumi was born in Tokyo in 1883, graduated with a degree in German law in 1908 and later became a professor at Tokyo Imperial University. Kawada, too, was born in Tokyo in 1883, graduated with a degree in politics in 1908 and later became deputy and head of the treasury. Nagaoka was born in Tokyo in 1884, graduated with a degree in German law in 1908 and became superintendent of the police.

9   *Kanai Noboru kankei monjo*, held by the Tōkyō daigaku daigakuin hōgaku seijigaku kenkyūka fuzoku kindai Nihon hōsei shiryō sentā.

10 Ōmori Kaichi was born in Tokyo in 1883, graduated with a degree in politics in 1909 and later became governor of Shimane prefecture. Nakagawa was born in Miyagi in 1875, graduated with a degree in English law in 1901 and became head of the Reconstruction Bureau (*fukkōkyoku*). Ikeda was born in Shizuoka in 1881, graduated from the law school of Kyoto Imperial University in 1905 and became governor of Kanagawa. Kodama was born in Yamaguchi in 1893, graduated with a degree in politics in 1919 and became deputy of welfare (*kōsei*) and general superintendent of the Chūgoku region. Shigenari was born in Okayama in 1901, graduated with a degree in English law in 1925 and became governor of Kagoshima.

11 Kawanishi Jitsuzō, *Kanmeiroku* (Tokyo: Shakai hoken shinpōsha, 1974).

12 These men were Kinoshita Makoto, born in 1884, a 1909 graduate in politics and later head of general affairs in the governorship general of Taiwan; Shinohara Eitarō, born in 1885, a 1911 graduate in German law and later deputy home minister; Kodaira Gon'ichi, born in 1884, a 1914 graduate in politics and later deputy of minister of agriculture and forestry; and Karasawa Toshiki, born in 1890, a 1915 graduate in politics and later head of the Public Security Ministery and deputy home minister.

13 Ōnishi Hiroshi, ed., *Isawa Takio to kindai Nihon* (Tokyo: Fuyō shobō shuppan, 2003).

14 Isawa Takio denki hensan iinkai, *Isawa Takio* (Tokyo: Haneda shoten, 1951).

15 Maruyama was born in Hiroshima in 1873, graduated with a degree in politics in 1909 and became superintendent of the police. Aoki was born in 1899, graduated with a degree in German law in 1916 and became president of the Cabinet Planning Institute (*Kikakuin*) and then treasury minister. Kobayashi was born in 1891, graduated with a degree in English law in 1917 and became head of the House of Peers secretariat. Kondō was born in 1894, graduated with a degree in English law in 1920 and became governor of Kanagawa. Masuda was born in 1898 graduated with a degree in law from Kyoto Imperial University in 1898 and became head officer in the Hokkaido governorship and head of the cabinet secretariat. Akabane was born in 1899, graduated from the research programme (*kenkyūka*) of the Tokyo Normal High School in 1927 and became deputy of the Information Bureau (*jōhōkyoku*).

16 Hirota Teruyuki, *Rikugun shōkō no kyōiku shakaishi* (Yokohama: Seori shobō, 1997).

17 Okamoto Makiko, *Shokuminchi kanryō no seijishi* (Tokyo: Sangensha, 2008).

18 Maruyama Tsurukichi, *Gojūnen tokoro dokoro* (Tokyo: Dai Nihon yūbenkai kōdansha, 1935).

19 Aoki Kazuo, *Waga kyūjūnen no shōgai o kaerimite* (Tokyo: Kōdansha, 1981), 18.

20 Hotta was born in Fukushima in 1876, graduated with a degree in German law in 1904 and later became deputy home minister.

21 Yamada was born in Aichi, graduated with a degree in German law in 1908 and became head of the Public Health Bureau.

22 Tago was born in Iwate in 1881, graduated with a degree in politics in 1908 and became head of the second division of the Social Bureau and later minister of agriculture and forestry.

23 Aritake Shūji, *Karasawa Toshiatsu* (Karasawa Toshiatsu denki kankōkai, 1975).

24 These men included Maeda Tamon, born in Osaka in 1884, a 1909 graduate in German law and later governor of Niigata and education minister; Tsugita Daizaburō, born in Okayama in 1883, a 1909 graduate in politics and later deputy home minister and head of the cabinet secretariat; Horikiri Zenjirō, born in Fukushima in 1884, a 1909 graduate in German law and later head of the cabinet secretariat and home minister; and Ōtsuka Isei, born in Kumamoto in 1884, a 1909 graduate in German law and later superintendent of the Chūgoku region.

25 Mori, *Seinen to ayumu Gotō Fumio*, 93.

26 Odaira Katsue, ed., *Daiichi taisen go no Doitsu – Yasui Seiichirō no Doitsu ryūgaku nikki yori* (Odaira Katsue, 1986), 196–197.

Bibliography

Introduction

'Asa made zangyō "nemuranai Kasumigaseki" no genkai'. *Nihon keizai shinbun*, 3 January 2015.

Banno Junji. *Mikan no Meiji Ishin*. Tokyo: Chikuma shobō, 2007.

Banno Junji. *Nihon kindai shi*. Tokyo: Chikuma shobō, 2012.

Hata Ikuhiko. *Kanryō no kenkyū*. Tokyo: Kōdansha, 1983.

Ide Yoshinori. *Nihon kanryōsei to gyōsei bunka*. Tokyo: Tōkyō daigaku shuppankai, 1982.

Jansen, Marius B. *Sakamoto Ryoma and the Meiji Restoration*. Princeton, NJ: Princeton University Press, 1961.

Jansen, Marius B. *Sakamoto Ryōma to Meiji Ishin*, translated by Hirao Michio and Hamada Kamekichi Jiji tsūshinsha, 1965.

Johnson, Chalmers A. *MITI and the Japanese Miracle: The Growth of Industrial Policy, 1925–1975*. Stanford, CA: Stanford University Press, 1982.

Kanai Toshiyuki. *Gyōseigaku kōgi*. Tokyo: Chikuma shobō, 2018.

Kinmonth, Earl H. *The Self-Made Man in Meiji Japanese Thought: From Samurai to Salary Man*. Berkeley: University of California Press, 1981.

Kinmonth, Earl H. *Risshin shusse no shakaishi*, translated by Hirota Teruyuki et al. Tokyo: Tamagawa daigaku shuppanbu, 1995.

Kobayashi Yoshikai. *Seiken kōtai: Minshutō seiken to wa nan de atta no ka*. Tokyo: Chūō kōron shinsha, 2012.

Machidori Satoshi. *Daigisei minshushugi*. Tokyo: Chūō kōron shinsha, 2015.

Machidori Satoshi. *Minshushugi ni totte seitō to wa nani ka*. Tokyo: Mineruva shobō, 2018.

Maeda Kentarō. *Shimin o yatowanai kokka*. Tōkyō daigaku shuppankai, 2014.

Makihara Izuru. 'Jimintō seiken to seiken kōtai'. In *Seiken kōtai to seitō seiji*, edited by Iio Jun. Tokyo: Chūō kōron shinsha, 2013.

Makihara Izuru. *Kuzureru seiji o tatenaosu*. Tokyo: Kōdansha, 2018.

Mikuriya Takashi. '*Seiji shudō*' no kyōkun: Seiken kōtai wa nani o motarashita no ka. Tokyo: Keisō shobō, 2012.

Mitani Taichirō. *Nihon seitō seiji no keisei*, rev. edn. Tokyo: Tōkyō daigaku shuppansha, 1995.

Muramatsu Michio. *Seikan sukuramu gata rīdāshippu no hōkai*. Tokyo: Tōyō keizai shinpōsha, 2010.

Nihon Keizai Shinbunsha, ed. *Kanryō: Kishimu kyodai kenryoku*. Tokyo: Nihon Keizai shinbunsha, 1994.

Nihon saiken Inishiatibu. *Minshutō seiken shippai no kenshō: Nihon seiji wa nani o ikasu ka*. Tokyo: Chūō kōron shinsha, 2013.

Pierson, Paul. *Politics in Time: History, Institutions, and Social Analysis*. Princeton, NJ: Princeton University Press, 2004.

Pierson, Paul. *Poritikkusu in taimu*, translated by Kasuya Yūko and Imai Makoto. Tokyo: Keisō shobō, 2010.

'Shushō kantei 7 tai 300: Misshitsuka no kaihi o'. *Nihon keizai shinbun*, 27 November 2018.

Shimizu Yuichirō. *Seitō no kanryō no kindai: Nihon ni okeru rikken tōchi kōzō no sōkoku*. Tokyo: Fujiwara shoten, 2007.

Silberman, Bernard S. *Cages of Reason: The Rise of the Rational State in France, Japan, the United States, and Great Britain*. Chicago: University of Chicago Press, 1993.

Sone Kengo. *Gendai Nihon no kanryōsei*. Tokyo: Tōkyō daigaku shuppankai, 2016.

Takeuchi Yō. *Risshin shusse shugi: Kindai nihon no roman to yōbō*. Kyōto: Sekai shisōsha, 2005.

Chapter 1

Archival sources

Dajō ruiten, held by the National Archives of Japan.
Kōbunroku, held by the National Archives of Japan.
Kiroku zairyō, held by the National Archives of Japan.
Minbukan, Minbushō, Jingishō kiroku, held by the National Archives of Japan.
Iwakura Tomomi kankei monjo, in Naikaku bunko.
Iwakura Tomomi kankei monjo, in Taigaku bunko.

Published sources

Aoyama Tadamasa. *Meiji Ishin to kokka keisei*. Tokyo: Yoshikawa kōbunkan, 2000.

Arakawa Shō. 'Boshin sensō ki no chihō tōchi to Shijō Takatoshi'. In *Shijō-danshaku ke no Ishin to kindai*, edited by Shōyū Kurabu and Kazoku Shiryō Kenkyūkai. Tokyo: Dōseisha, 2012.

Asakura Haruhiko, ed. *Dajōkan nisshi*. 4 vols. Tokyo: Tōkyōdō shuppan, 1985.

Baba Yoshihiro. 'Meiji shoki no chōshisei ni tsuite'. *Dōshisha hōgaku* 38, no. 5 (1987): 146–174.

Berry, Mary Elizabeth. 'Restoring the Past: The Documents of Hideyoshi's Magistrate in Kyoto'. *Journal of Asian Studies* 43, no. 1 (June 1983): 57–95.

Breen, John. 'The Imperial Oath of April 1868: Ritual, Politics, and Power in the Restoration'. *Monumenta Nipponica* 51, no. 4 (Winter 1996): 407–429.

Bridgman, Elijah Coleman. *Renpō shiryaku*. Yorozu heishirō, 1864.

Butler, Lee A. 'Tokugawa Ieyasu's Regulations for the Court'. *Journal of Asian Studies* 54, no. 2 (December 1994): 509–551.

de Bary, Wm. Theodore, Carol Gluck and Arthur E. Tiedmann, eds. *Sources of Japanese Tradition: Volume Two: 1600 to 2000, abridged*, 2nd edn. New York: Columbia University Press, 2006.

Enomoto Takamitsu, ed. *Enomoto Takeaki mikōkai shokan shū*. Tokyo: Shin jinbutsu ōraisha, 2003.

Hagihara Nobutoshi. *Mutsu Munemitsu*, vol. 1. Tokyo: Asahi shinbunsha, 2007.

Haraguchi Kiyoshi. *Boshin sensō*. Tokyo: Hanawa shobō, 1963.

Hosokawa-Ke hensanjo, ed. *Higo-han kokuji shiryō*. Kumamoto: Kōshaku Hosokawa-ke hensanjo, 1932.

Iechika Yoshiki. *Bakumatsu seiji to tōbaku undō*. Tokyo: Yoshikawa kōbunkan, 1995.

Inada Masatsugu. *Meiji kenpō seiritsu shi*. 2 vols. Tokyo: Nihon hyōronsha, 1938.

Inoue Isao. *Ōsei Fukko: Keiō 3-nen 12-gatsu 9-nichi no seihen*. Tokyo: Chūō kōronsha, 1991.

Inoue Kaoru Kō Denki Hensankai, ed. *Segai Inoue-kō den*, vol. 1. Tokyo: Naigai shoseki, 1933.

Inoue Katsuo. *Bakumatsu Ishin*. Tokyo: Iwanami shoten, 2006.

Inoue Mitsusada et al., eds. *Meiji kokka no seiritsu*. Tokyo: Yamakawa shuppansha, 1996.

Inuzuka Takaaki. *Terajima Munenori*. Tokyo: Yoshikawa kōbunkan, 1990.

Iokibe Kaoru. *Ōkuma Shigenobu to Seitō seiji*. Tokyo: Tōkyō daigaku shuppankai, 2003.

Ishizuka Hiromichi. *Nihon shihonshugi seiritsu shi kenkyū*. Tokyo: Yoshikawa kōbunkan, 1973.

Itō Kenji. 'Meiji shonen ni okeru Ōkurashō kindai kanryō no keisei'. *Keizaigaku zasshi* 67, no. 4 (1972): 68–92.

Itō Yukio. *Itō Hirobumi: Kindai Nihon o tsukutta otoko*. Tokyo: Kōdansha, 2009.

Kasahara Hidehiko. *Meiji kokka to kanryōsei*. Tokyo: Ashi shobō, 1991.

Kasahara Hidehiko. *Nihon gyōseishi josetsu*. Tokyo: Ashi shobō, 1998.

Kataoka Yakichi. *Urakami yonban kuzure: Meiji seifu no Kirishitan dan'atsu*. Tokyo: Chikuma shobō, 1991.

Katsuta Masaharu. '*Seijika' Ōkubo Toshimichi: Kindai Nihon no sekkeisha*. Tokyo: Kōdansha, 2003.

Kunaicho rinji teishitsu Henshūkyoku, ed. *Meiji Tennō ki*, vols. 1–2. Tokyo: Yoshikawa kōbunkan, 1969.

Makihara Norio. *Bunmeikoku o mezashite*. Tokyo: Shōgakkan, 2008.

Maruyama Kanji. *Soejima Taneomi haku*. Tokyo: Dainichisha, 1936.

Masumi Junnosuke. *Nihon seitōshi ron*, vol. 1. Tokyo: Tōkyō daigaku shuppankai, 1965.

Matsuda Kōichirō. *Edo no chishiki kara Meiji no seiji e*. Tokyo: Perikansha, 2008.

Matsueda Yasuji, ed. *Ōkuma-haku sekijitsu tan*. Tokyo: Waseda daigaku shuppanbu, 1969.

Matsumoto Sannosuke. *Nihon seiji shisōshi gairon*. Tokyo: Keisō shobō, 1967.

Matsuo Masahito. *Haihan chiken no kenkyū*. Tokyo: Yoshikawa kōbunkan, 2001.

Matsuo Masahito. *Ishin seiken*. Tokyo: Yoshikawa kōbunkan, 1995.

Mitani Hiroshi. *Meiji Ishin to nashonarizumu*. Tokyo: Yamakawa shuppansha, 1997.

Mōri Toshihiko. *Meiji Ishin seiji gaikōshi kenkyū*. Tokyo: Yoshikawa kōbunkan, 2002.

Mōri Toshihiko. *Bakumatsu Ishin to Saga han*. Tokyo: Chūō kōron shinsha, 2008.

Mutsu Munemitsu-haku ShichijisshūNen Kinenkai, ed. *Mutsu Munemitsu-haku: shōden, nenpu, furoku bunshū*. Mutsu Munemitsu-haku shichijisshūnen kinenkai, 1966.

Nagai Hideo. *Meiji kokka keiseiki no gaisei to naisei*. Sapporo: Hokkaidō daigaku tosho kankōkai, 1990.

Nakaoka Tetsurō. 'Kindai gijutsu no Nihonteki tenkai'. *Asahi shinbun shuppan*, 2013.

Nihon shiseki Kyōkai, ed. *Meiji shiryō ken'yō shokumu buninroku*, vols 1–4. Tokyo: Tōkyō daigaku shuppankai, 1981.

Nihon Shiseki Kyōkai, ed. *Nakayama Tadayasu rireki shiryō*, vol. 9. Tokyo: Nihon shiseki kyōkai, 1934.

Nihon Shiseki Kyōkai, ed. *Ōkubo Toshimichi nikki*, vol. 1. Tokyo: Hokusensha, 1997.

Nihon Shiseki Kyōkai, ed. *Saga Sanenaru nikki*, vol. 2. Tokyo: Nihon shiseki kyōkai, 1930.

Nihon Shiseki Kyōkai, ed. *Shiseki zassan*, vols 2 and 4. Tokyo: Tōkyō daigaku shuppankai, 1977.

Nihon Shiseki Kyōkai, ed. *Yamada hakushaku ke monjo*, vol. 5. Tokyo: Nihon daigaku, 1992.

Ogawara Masamichi. *Daikyōin no kenkyū*. Tokyo: Keiō gijuku daigaku shuppankai, 2004.

Ōkubo Toshiaki. *Iwakura Tomomi*, rev. edn. Tokyo: Chūō kōronsha, 1990.

Ōkubo Toshikazu, ed. *Ōkubo Toshimichi monjo*, vol. 3. Tokyo: Nihon shiseki kyōkai, 1929.

Ōkuma Shigenobu. *Ōkuma-haku sekijitsu tan*. Tokyo: Meiji bunken, 1972.

Ōkuma-kō hachijūgo-nen shi hensankai, ed. *Ōkuma-kō hachijūgo-nen shi*. Ōkuma-kō hachijūgo-nen shi hensankai, 1926.

Ōmura Masujirō sensei denki kankōkai, ed. *Ōmura Masujirō*. Tokyo: Hajime shobō, 1944.

Ōtsu Jun'ichirō. *Dai Nihon kenseishi*, vol. 1. Tokyo: Hōbunkan, 1927.

Ritsumeikan daigaku Saionji Kinmochi den hensan iinkai. *Saionji Kinmochi den*, vol. 1. Tokyo: Iwanami shoten, 1990.

Sasaki Suguru. *Bakumatsu seiji to Satsuma-han*. Tokyo: Yoshikawa kōbunkan, 2004.

Sasaki Suguru. *Shishi to kanryō: Meiji shonen no jōkei*. Kyoto: Mineruva shobō, 1984.

Satō Seizaburō. *'Shi no chōyaku' o koete: Seiyō no shōgeki to Nihon*. Tokyo: Toshi shuppan, 1992.

Satow, Ernest Mason. *Ichi gaikōkan no mita Meiji Ishin*, translated by Sakata Seiichi. 2 vols. Tokyo: Iwanami shoten, 1960.

Senda Minoru. *Ishin Seiken no chitsuroku shobun: tennōsei to haihan chiken*. Tokyo: Kaimei shoin, 1979.

Shibusawa Seien kinen Zaiden ryūmonsha, ed. *Sibusawa Eiichi denki shiryō*, vol. 2, Tokyo: Shibusawa Eiichi denki Shiryō Kankōkai, 1955.

Shōyū Kurabu, ed. *Yamagata Aritomo kankei monjo*, vol. 2. Tokyo: Yamakawa shuppansha, 2006.

Shunpo-kō Tsuishōkai, ed. *Itō Hirobumi den*, vol. 1. Tokyo: Tōseisha, 1940.

Sonoda Hidehiro, Atsushi Hamana and Teruyuki Hirota. *Shizoku no rekishi shakaigakuteki kenkyū: bushi no kindai*. Nagoya: Nagoya daigaku shuppankai, 1995.

Suzuki Jun. *Ishin no kōsō to tenkai*. Tokyo: Kōdansha, 2002.

Tada Kōmon, ed. *Iwakura-kō jikki*, vol. 2, Kyoto: Iwakura-kō kyūseki hozonkai, 1927.

Takahashi Hidenao. *Bakumatsu Ishin no seiji to tennō*. Tokyo: Yoshikawa kōbunkan, 2007.

Takemura Eiji. *Bakumatsuki bushi / shizoku no shisō to kōi*. Tokyo: Ochanomizu shobō, 2008.

Takii Kazuhiro. *Itō Hirobumi: chi no seijika*. Tokyo: Chūō kōron shinsha, 2010.

Tōkyō daigaku shiryō hensanjo, ed. *Hogohiroi: Sasaki Takayuki nikki*, vols. 2–3. Tokyo: Tōkyō daigaku shuppankai, 1972.

Toriumi Yashushi, Mitani Hiroshi, Nishikawa Makoto, Yano Nobuyuki, eds. *Nihon rikken seiji no keisei to henshitsu*. Tokyo: Yoshikawa kōbunkan, 2005.

Tōyama Shigeki. *Meiji Ishin*. Tokyo: Iwanami shoten, 1951.

Uchida Shūdō, ed. *Meiji kenpakusho shūsei*, vol. 1. Tokyo: Chikuma shobō, 2000.

Umetani Noboru. *Meiji zenki seiji shi no kenkyū*. Tokyo: Miraisha, 1963.

Waseda daigaku daigakushi shiryō sentā, ed. *Ōkuma Shigenobu kankei monjo*, vols. 5–6. Tokyo: Misuzu shobō, 2009–2010.

Waseda Daigakushi Hensanjo, ed. *Ōkuma-haku sekijitsu tan*. Tokyo: Waseda daigaku shuppanbu, 1969.

Yuri Masamichi. *Shishaku Yuri Kimimasa den*. Tokyo: Iwanami shoten, 1940.

Chapter 2

Amano Ikuo. *Daigaku no tanjō*. Tokyo: Chūō kōron shinsha, 2009.

Amano Ikuo. *Gakureki no shakaishi: kyōiku to Nihon no kindai*. Tokyo: Shinchōsha, 1992.

Asai Kiyoshi. 'Meiji ninen no kanri senkyo'. *Jinji gyōsei* 6, no. 4 (1955).
Asakura Haruhiko, ed. *Dajōkan nisshi*, 4 vols. Tokyo: Tōkyōdō shuppan, 1985.
Asō Makoto. *Nihon no gakureki erīto*. Tokyo: Tamagawa daigaku shuppanbu, 1991.
Bokutei Inshi. *Meiji jinbutsu no shōsō jidai*. Tokyo: Daigakukan, 1902.
Doboku Gakkai, ed. *Furuichi Kōi to sono jidai*. Tokyo: Doboku gakkai, 2004.
Hashinami Gyorō. *Daigaku gakusei sogen*, vol. 1. Tokyo: Ōzorasha, 1912.
Hatoyama Haruko. *Hatoyama no isshō*. Tokyo: Hatoyama Haruko, 1929.
Honda Kumatarō. *Jinbutsu to mondai*. Tokyo: Chikuma shobō, 1939.
Hozumi Shigeyuki. *Meiji ichi hōgakusha no shuppatsu*. Tokyo: Iwanami shoten, 1988.
Hozumi shōgaku zaidan shuppan, ed. *Hozumi Nobushige ibun shū*, vols 1 and 4. Tokyo: Iwanami shoten, 1934.
Inoue Kowashi denki hensan iinkai, ed. *Inoue Kowashi den shiryō hen*, vols 1–4. Tokyo: Kokugakuin daigaku toshokan, 1966.
Ishizuki Minoru. *Kindai Nihon no kaigai ryūgaku shi*. Kyoto: Mineruva shobō, 1972.
Itō Yukio. *Genrō Saionji Kinmochi: koki kara no chōsen*. Tokyo: Bungei shunjū, 2007
Jansen, Marius B. 'New Materials for the Intellectual History of Nineteenth-Century Japan'. *Harvard Journal of Asiatic Studies* 20, no. 3–4 (December 1957): 567–597.
Kaminuma Hachirō. *Isawa Shūji*. Tokyo: Yoshikawa kōbunkan, 1985.
Kanda Naibu, ed. *Kanda Takahira ryakuden*. Tokyo: Kanda Naibu, 1910.
Karasawa Tomitarō. *Kōshinsei: Bakumatsu Ishin ki no erīto*. Tokyo: Gyōsei, 1974.
Kasahara Hidehiko. *Meiji kokka to kanryōsei*. Tokyo: Ashi shobō, 1991.
Kashihara Hiroki. *Kōbushō no kenkyū*. Tokyo: Keiō gijuku daigaku shuppankai, 2009.
Katayama Yoshitaka. *Komura Jutarō*. Tokyo: Chūō kōron shinsha, 2012.
Katō Fusazō, ed. *Hakushaku Hirata Tōsuke den*. Tokyo: Hirata-haku denki hensan jimusho, 1927.
Ko Furuichi Danshaku kinen jigyōkai, Ko Furuichi Danshaku kinen jigyōkai, eds. *Furuichi Kōi*. Tokyo: Hakkō'nin Kitabayashi Katsuzō, Insatsujo Tōkyō Insatsu Kabushiki Kaisha, 1937.
Ko Isawa Shūji Sensei Kinen Jigyōkai Hensan Iinkai, ed. *Rakuseki Isawa Shūji sensei*. Tokyo: Ko Isawa sensei kinen jigyōkai, 1919.
Kokuritsu kyōiku kenkyūjo, ed. *Nihon kindai kyōiku hyakunenshi*, vol. 3. Tokyo: Kokuritsu kyōiku kenkyūjo, 1974.
Komura Shōji. *Kotsuniku*. Miyazaki: Kōmyakusha, 2005.
Kunaichō. *Meiji Tennō ki*, vol. 2. Tokyo: Yoshikawa kōbunkan, 1969.
Maejima Hisoka. *Maejima Hisoka: Maejima Hisoka jijoden*. Tokyo: Nihon tosho sentā, 1997.
Masumoto Uhei. *Shizen no hito Komura Jutarō*. Tokyo: Rakuyōdō, 1914.
Matsuo Masahito. *Haihan chiken no kenkyū*. Tokyo: Yoshikawa kōbunkan, 2001.
Matsuura Rei, ed. *Nihon no meicho. 30: Sakuma Shōzan, Yokoi Shōnan*. Tokyo: Chūō kōronsha, 1970.
Meiji Kyōikushi Kenkyūkai, ed. *Sugiura Jūgō zenshū*, vol. 6. Ōtsu: Sugiura Jūgō zenshū kankōkai, 1983.
Nagakubo Hen'un. *Sekaiteki shokubutsu gakusha Matsumura Jinzō no shōgai*. Tokyo: Akatsuki inshokan, 1997.
Naimushō. 'Saga zokuto Ogura Shokei kōjutsusho'. In *Ōkuma Shigenobu kankei monjo*, Waseda University Archives.
Ogawara Masamichi. *Seinan sensō: Saigō Takamori to Nihon saigo no naisen*. Tokyo: Chūō kōron shinsha, 2007.
Ōkubo Toshiaki. *Iwakura Tomomi*. Rev. edn. Tokyo: Chūō kōronsha, 1990.

Ōkubo Toshiaki. *Nihon no daigaku.* Tokyo: Tamagawa daigaku shuppanbu, 1997.

Ōtsu Jun'ichirō. *Nihon kanri nin'yōron.* Tokyo: Kinkōdō, 1881.

Rikō Mitsuo, Mori Seii'chi, Sone Yasunori, *Manjō itchi to tasūketsu.* Tokyo: Nihon keizai shinbunsha, 1980.

Saitō Shūichirō. *Kaikyūdan.* San Francisco, CA: Aoki taiseidō, 1908.

Shionoya Ryōkan. *Kaikoroku.* Tokyo: Shionoya Tsunetarō, 1918.

Tōkyō daigaku hyakunenshi henshū iinkai, ed. *Tōkyō daigaku hyakunenshi, tsūshi 1.* Tokyo: Tōkyō daigaku, 1984.

Tomita Hitoshi. *Umi o koeta Nihon jinmei jiten.* Tokyo: Nichigai asoshiētsu, 2005.

Tsuji Naoto. *Kindai Nihon kaigai ryūgaku no mokuteki hen'yō.* Tokyo: Tōshindō, 2010.

Yamazaki Yūkō. 'Meiji shonen no kōgisho, shūgiin'. In *Nihon rikken seiji no keisei to henshitsu,* edited by Toriumi Yasushi, Mitani Hiroshi, Nishikawa Makoto, Yano Nobuyuki, Tokyo: Yoshikawa kōbunkan, 2005.

Chapter 3

Akagi Suruki. '*Kanryō*' *no keisei.* Tokyo: Nihon hyōronsha, 1991.

Banno Junji. *Nihon kensei shi.* Tokyo: Tōkyō daigaku shuppankai, 2008.

Banno Junji and Miyachi Masato, eds. *Nihon kindai shi ni okeru tenkanki no kenkyū.* Tokyo: Yamakawa shuppansha, 1985.

Cassel, Pär. *Grounds of Judgment.* Oxford: Oxford University Press, 2012.

Iechika Yoshiki. *Saigō Takamori to Bakumatsu Ishin no seikyoku.* Kyotot: Mineruva shobō, 2011.

Inada Masatsugu. *Meiji kenpō seiritsu shi,* vol 1. Tokyo: Yūhikaku, 1960.

Iokibe Kaoru. *Ōkuma Shigenobu to seitō seiji.* Tokyo: Tōkyō daigaku shuppankai, 2003.

Iwatani Jurō. *Meiji Nihon no hō kaishaku to hōritsuka.* Tokyo: Keiō gijuku daigaku shuppankai, 2012.

Hiratsuka Atsushi, ed. *Zoku Itō Hirobumi hiroku.* Tokyo: Hara shobō, 1982.

Kasahara Hidehiko. *Meiji kokka to kanryōsei.* Tokyo: Ashi shobō, 1991.

Kasahara Hidehiko. *Meiji rusu seifu.* Tokyo: Keiō gijuku daigaku shuppankai, 2010.

Kashihara Hiroki. 'Dajōkan junshoku no jissō'. *Nihon rekishi* 750 (2010).

Kashihara Hiroki. 'Kaimei ha kanryō no tōjō to tenkai'. In *Ishin seiken no sōsetsu,* edited by Meiji Ishin shi gakkai. Yūshisha, 2011, pp. 173–204.

Kashihara Hiroki. *Kōbushō no kenkyū.* Tokyo: Keiō gijuku daigaku shuppankai, 2009.

Katō Fusazō, ed. *Hakushaku Hirata Tōsuke den.* Tokyo: Hirata-haku denki hensan jimusho, 1927.

Katsuta Masaharu. *Naimushō to Meiji kokka keisei.* Tokyo: Yoshikawa kōbunkan, 2002.

Kawaguchi Akihiro. *Meiji kenpō kintei shi.* Sapporo: Hokkaidō daigaku shuppankai, 2007.

Kikuyama Masaaki. *Meiji kokka no keisei to shihō seido.* Tokyo: Ochanomizu shobō, 1993.

Kobayashi Hiroshi, Shima Yoshita and Harada Kazuaki, eds. *Watanabe Renkichi nikki.* Tokyo: Kōjinsha, 2004.

Kobayashi Kazuyuki. 'Kindai shoki no Nihon kanryōsei'. In *Sekaishi no naka no teikoku to kanryō,* edited by Hirata Masahiro and Ona Yasuyuki. Tokyo: Yamakawa shuppansha, 2008, pp. 157–194.

Kunioka Keiko. 'Meiji shoki chihō chōkan jinji no hensen'. *Nihon rekishi* 521 (1991), pp. 66–83.

Matsudo Hiroshi. 'Seiteihō ni okeru jimu haibun tan'i no hen'yō to sono igi (2)'. *Hiroshima hōgaku* 31, no. 2 (2007), pp. 113–143.

Matsuo Masahito. *Haihan chiken no kenkyū*. Tokyo: Yoshikawa kōbunkan, 2001.

Matsuo Masahito. *Ishin seiken*. Tokyo: Yoshikawa kōbunkan, 1995.

Mikuriya Takashi. 'Kokkairon to zaiseiron'. In *Nihon kindai shi ni okeru tenkanki no kenkyū*, edited by Banno Junji and Miyachi Masato. Tokyo: Yamakawa shuppansha, 1985, pp. 119–140.

Matsuo Masahito. *Meiji kokka o tsukuru*. Tokyo: Fujiwara shoten, 2007.

Mōri Toshihiko. *Meiji rokunen seihen*. Tokyo: Chūō kōronsha, 1980.

Murase Shin'ichi. *Meiji rikken sei to naikaku*. Tokyo: Yoshikawa kōbunkan, 2011.

Nagai Kazu. *Kindai Nihon no gunbu to seiji*. Kyoto: Shibunkaku shuppan, 1993.

Nagayo Sensai. 'Shōkō shi shi'. In *Matsumoto Jun jiden, Nagayo Sensai jiden*, edited by Ogawa Teizō, Sakai Shizu, Matsumotot Jun and Nagayo Sensai. Tokyo: Heibonsha, 1980.

Nakagawa Toshiyuki. 'Dajōkan naikaku sōsetsu ni kansuru ichikōsatsu'. In *Bakuhan kenryoku to Meiji Ishin*, edited by Meiji Ishin Shi Gakkai. Tokyo: Yoshikawa kōbunkan, 1992, pp. 218–238.

Nakagawa Toshiyuki. 'Dajōkan San'in sei sōsetsu ki no U'in'. In *Kindai Nihon no seiji to shakai*, edited by Mikami Terumi sensei koki kinen ronbunshū kankōkai. Tokyo: Iwada shoten, 2001, pp. 161–187.

Nishio Toyosaku. *Shishaku Tanaka Fujimaro den*. Nagoya: Kōsaijuku, 1934.

Nihon shiseki kyōkai, ed. *Tani Kanjō ikō*, vol. 3. Tokyo: Tōkyō daigaku shuppankai, 1970.

Obinata Sumio. 'Jiyū minken undō to Meiji 14-nen no seihen'. In *Kindai kokka no keisei*, edited by Meiji Ishin Shi Gakkai. Tokyo: Yūshisha, 2012, pp. 123–158.

Ochi Noboru. 'Meiji shoki gyōsei kanryō no seikaku'. *Shisō* 487 (1965), pp. 151–165.

Ogawa Teizō, Sakai Shizu, Matsunoto Jun and Nagayo Sensai, eds. *Matsumoto Jun jiden, Nagayo Sensai jiden*. Tokyo: Heibonsha, 1980.

Ogawara Masamichi. 'Meiji shoki ni okeru kazoku no kaigai ryūgaku'. *Nichi-Ō hikaku bunka kenkyū* 2 (2004), pp. 19–30.

Ōishi Makoto. *Nihon kenpō shi*. 2nd edn. Tokyo: Yūhikaku, 2005.

Okada Yoshiharu and Hatsuda Tōru. 'Matsugasaki Tsumunaga no shoki no keireki to Aoki Shūzō Nasu bettei'. *Nihon kenchiku gakkai keikaku kei ronbun shū* 63, no. 514 (1998), pp. 233–240.

Ōkubo Takaki. *Yōkō no jidai*. Tokyo: Chūō kōron shinsha, 2008.

Ōkubo Toshiaki. *Iwakura shisetsu no kenkyū*. Tokyo: Munetaka shobō, 1976.

Ōshima Mitsuko. *Meiji kokka to chiiki shakai*. Tokyo: Iwanami shoten, 1994.

Ōtsu Jun'ichirō. *Nihon kanri nin'yō ron*. Kinkōdō, 1880.

Ōyama Shikitarō. *Wakayama Norikazu zenshū*. 2 vols. Tokyo: Tōkyō keizai shinpōsha, 1940.

Sakamoto Kazuto. 'Meiji nijūni nen no naikaku kansei ni tsuite no ichikōsatsu'. In *Meiji kokka no seisaku to shisō*, edited by Inuzuka Takaaki. Tokyo: Yoshikawa kōbunkan, 2005, pp. 141–171.

Sakamoto Kazuto. *Itō Hirobumi to Meiji kokka keisei*. Tokyo: Yoshikawa kōbunkan, 1991.

Sekiguchi Eiichi. 'Meiji rokunen teigaku mondai'. *Hōgaku* 44, no. 4 (1980), pp. 464–505.

Shihōshō, ed. *Shihō enkaku shi*. Tokyo: Hara shobō, 1979.

Shimizu Shin. *Meiji kenpō seitei shi*, vol. 2.Tokyo: Hara shobō, 1973.

Shimizu Yuichirō. '"Kyōikuken" no ima made to kore kara'. In *Gakkō o kaereba shakai ga kawaru*, edited by Toda Tadao. Tokyo: Tōkyō shoseki, 2014, pp. 195–244.

Shimizu Yuichirō. 'Waihan naikaku ni okeru ryōkan no jissō'. *Nihon rekishi* 674 (2004): 52–70.

Sugawara Morikuni. 'Iwakura shisetsudan no hensei'. *Hōgaku shinpō* 109, no. 1–2 (2002): 51–78.

Sugawara Morikuni. 'Iwakura shisetsudan no jūsha to dōkō ryūgakusei ni kansuru tsuikō'. *Hōgaku shinpō* 104, no. 1 (1997), pp. 51–78.

Sugawara Morikuni. 'Iwakura shisetsudan no menbā kōsei'. *Hōgaku shinpō* 91, no. 2 (1984), pp. 71–116.

Suzuki Jun. *Ishin no kōsō to tenkai*. Tokyo: Kōdansha, 2002.

Takahashi Hidenao. 'Haihan chiken ni okeru kenryoku to shakai'. In *Kindai Nihon no seitō to kanryō*, edited by Yamamoto Shirō Tokyo: Tōkyō sōgensha, 1991, pp. 5–92.

Takase Nobuhiko, ed. *Kaneko Kentarō chosaku shū*, vol. 4. Tokyo: Nihon daigaku seishin bunka kenkyūjo, 1996.

Takii Kazuhiro. *Doitsu kokkagaku to Meiji kokusei: Shutain kokkagaku no kiseki*. Kyoto: Mineruva shobō, 1999.

Tanaka Akira. *Iwakura shisetsudan 'Beiō kairan jikki.'* Tokyo: Iwanami shoten, 2002.

Tanaka Akira. *Iwakura shisetsudan no rekishiteki kenkyū*. Tokyo: Iwanami shoten, 2002.

Torio Koyata. 'Jijidan – san'. In *Tokuan zensho*, edited by Torio Tokuan, 564–566. Torio Mitsu, 1911.

Torio Tokuan. *Tokuan zensho*. Torio Mitsu, 1911.

Toriumi Yasushi. *Nihon kindaishi kōgi*. Tokyo: Tōkyō daigaku shuppankai, 1988.

Wada Eita. *Sake to kujira no Nihonjin: Sekizawa Akekiyo no shōgai*. Tokyo: Seizandō shoten, 1994.

Yamamuro Shin'ichi. *Hōsei kanryō no jidai*. Tokyo: Bokutakusha, 1999.

Meiji shiryō kenkyū renrakukai, ed. *Meiji seiken no kakuritsu katei*. Tokyo: Ochanomizu shobō, 1957.

Meiji Ishin shi gakkai, ed. *Kōza Meiji Ishin 3 – Ishin seiken no sōsetsu*. Tokyo: Yūshisha, 2011.

Maeda Mitsuo. *Puroisen kenpō sōgi kenkyū*. Tokyo: Kazama shobō, 1980.

Nishikawa Makoto. 'Haihan chiken go no Dajō kansei kaikaku'. In *Nihon rikken seiji no keisei to henshitsu*, edited by Toriumi Yasushi et al. Tokyo: Yoshikawa kōbunkan, 2005, pp. 36–57.

Nakanome Tōru. *Kindai shiryōgaku no shatei*. Tokyo: Kōbundō, 2000.

Okada Yoshiharu and Hatsuda Tōru. 'Matsugasaki Tsumunaga no shoki no keireki to Aoki Shūzō Nasu bettei'. *Nihon kenchiku gakkai keikaku kei ronbun shū* 63, no. 514 (1998), pp. 233–240.

Chapter 4

Amako Todomu. *Heimin saishō Wakatsuki Reijirō*. Tokyo: Hōbunkan, 1930.

Amano Ikuo. *Daigaku no tanjō*, vol. 1. Tokyo: Chūō kōron shinsha, 2009.

Asō Makoto. *Nihon no gakureki eriito*. Tokyo: Tamagawa daigaku shuppanbu, 1991.

Baba Tsunego. *Kiuchi Jūshirō den*. Tokyo: Herarudosha, 1937.

Banno Junji and Miyaji Masato, eds. *Nihon kindai shi ni okeru tenkanki no kenkyū*. Tokyo: Yamakawa shuppansha, 1985.

Banno Junji. *Nihon kensei shi*. Tokyo: Tōkyō daigaku shuppankai, 2008.

Chiba Isao. *Kyūgaikō no keisei*. Tokyo: Keisō shobō, 2008.

Fukaya Masashi. *Gakureki shugi no fūkei*. Nagoya: Reimei shobō, 1969.

Inada Masatsugu. *Meiji kenpō seiritsu shi*, vol 1. Tokyo: Yūhikaku, 1960.

Iokibe Kaoru. *Ōkuma Shigenobu to seitō seiji*. Tokyo: Tōkyō daigaku shuppankai, 2003.

Itō Hirobumi. *Kenpō gikai*. Tokyo: Iwanami shoten, 1940.

Itō Miyoji. *Dai Nihon teikoku kenpō engi*. Tokyo: Shinzansha, 1974.

Hara Yoshimichi. *Bengoshi seikatsu no kaiko*. Tokyo: Hōritsu shinpōsha, 1935.

Kanbayashi Keijirō. *Nihon gunsei chūkai*. Toyama: Keisetsukan, 1890.

Kamiyama kun kinen Jigyōkai, ed. *Kamiyama Mitsunoshin*. Kamiyama kun kinen jigyōkai, 1941.

Karasawa Tomitarō. *Gakusei no rekishi*. Tokyo: Sōbunsha, 1955.

Katō Fusazō, ed. *Hakushaku Hirata Tōsuke den*. Tokyo: Hirata-haku denki hensan jimusho, 1927.

Kawai Eijirō. *Kanai Noburu no shōgai to gakuseki*. Tokyo: Nihon hyōronsha, 1939.

Kawai Yahachi. *Ichiki sensei kaikoroku*. Tokyo: Ichiki sensei tsuitōkai, 1954.

Kikuyama Masaaki. *Meiji kokka no keisei to shihō seido*. Tokyo: Ochanomizu shobō, 1993.

Kitaoka Shin'ichi. *Gotō Shinpei*. Tokyo: Chūō kōronsha, 1988.

Kobayashi Kazuyuki. 'Kindai shoki no Nihon kanryōsei'. In *Sekaishi no naka no teikoku to kanryō*, edited by Hirata Masahiro and Ona Yasuyuki. Tokyo: Yamakawa shuppansha, 2008, pp. 157–194.

Manabe Masayuki. *Tōkyō senmon gakkō no kenkyū*. Tokyo: Waseda daigaku shuppanbu, 2010.

Matsudo Hiroshi. 'Seiteihō ni okeru jimu haibun tan'i no hen'yō to sono igi (2)'. *Hiroshima hōgaku* 31, no. 2 (2007), pp. 113–143.

Matsunami Niichirō, ed. *Mizuno hakushi koki kinen ronsaku to zuihitsu*. Tokyo: Mizuno Rentarō sensei koki shukugakai jimusho, 1937.

Miyake Setsurei. *Daigaku konjaku tan*. Tokyo: Ōzorasha, 1991.

Murase Shin'ichi. *Meiji rikken sei to naikaku*. Tokyo: Yoshikawa kōbunkan, 2011.

Nakagawa Kotomi. 'Bōchō kyōikukai ni yoru ikuei jigyō no tenkai'. *Hiroshima daigaku kyōikubu kiyō* 41 (1992).

Nakano Minoru. *Kindai Nihon daigaku seido no seiritsu*. Tokyo: Yoshikawa kōbunkan, 2003.

Nakano Minoru. *Tōkyō daigaku monogatari*. Tokyo: Yoshikawa kōbunkan, 1999.

Nakanome Tōru. *Seikyōsha no kenkyū*. Tokyo: Shibunkaku shuppan, 1993.

Nakayama Shigeru. *Teikoku daigaku no tanjō*. Tokyo: Chūō kōronsha, 1978.

Nanbara Shigeru et al. *Onozuki Kiheiji Hito to gyōseki*. Tokyo: Iwanami shoten, 1963.

Numata Satoshi. *Motoda Nagazane to Meiji kokka*. Tokyo: Yoshikawa kōbunkan, 2005.

Ōishi Makoto. *Nihon kenpō shi*. 2nd edn. Tokyo: Yūhikaku, 2005.

Ōkubo Takaki. *Yōkō no jidai*. Tokyo: Chūō kōron shisnsha, 2008.

Sakaguchi Jirō et al., eds. *Hakushaku Kiyoura Keigo den*, vol. 1. Tokyo: Hakushaku Kiyoura Keigo den kankōkai, 1935.

Sakamoto Kazuto. *Itō Hirobumi to Meiji kokka keisei*. Tokyo: Yoshikawa kōbunkan, 1991.

Shimura Gentarō. 'Meiji jidai kanri no kako oyobi shōrai'. *Rikoku shin shi* 5 (1889).

Shimizu Shin. *Meiji kenpō seitei shi*, vol. 2. Tokyo: Hara shobō, 1973.

Shioiri Tasuke. *Kōtō futsū bunkan daigen shiken kyūdai hihō*. Tokyo: Nihon shoseki kaisha, 1889.

Shōda Tatsuo. *'Shōwa' no rirekisho*. Tokyo: Bungei shunjū, 1991.

Spaulding, Richard. *Imperial Japan's Higher Civil Service Examinations*. Princeton, NJ: Princeton University Press, 2015.

Sugawara Michimasa et al., eds. *Sugawara Michiyoshi den*, vol. 1. n.p., 1993.

Suzuki Hideo. *Kankōba no kenkyū*. Tokyo: Sōeisha, 2001.

Takata Sanae. *Hanpō mukashibanashi*. Tokyo: Nihon tosho sentā, 1983.

Takeuchi Yō. *Gakureki kizoku no eikō to zasetsu*. Tokyo: Chūō kōron shinsha, 1999.

Takeuchi Yō. *Risshin shusse shugi*. Kyoto: Sekai shisōsha, 2005.

Takii Kazuhiro. *Doitsu kokkagaku to Meiji kokusei: Shutain kokkagaku no kiseki*. Kyoto: Mineruva shobō, 1999.

Takii Kazuhiro. 'Watanabe Hiromoto – Nihon no Arutohōfu'. *Jinbun ronshū* 41, no. 2 (2006): 159–181.

Takii Kazuhiro, ed. *Shutain kokkagaku nōto*. Tokyo: Shinzansha, 2005.

Tanaka Yoshitsugu, ed. *Tanaka Jirō*. Tanaka Yoshitsugu, 1932.

Terasaki Masao. *Tōkyō daigaku no rekishi*. Tokyo: Kōdansha, 2007.

Toriumi Yasushi. *Nihon kindaishi kōgi*. Tokyo: Tōkyō daigaku shuppankai, 1988.

Tsurumi Yūsuke. *Seiden Gotō Shinpei*, vol. 1. Tokyo: Fujiwara shoten, 2004.

Wada Ichirō, ed. *Kōkan Akimoto Toyonoshin kun*. Wada Ichirō, 1935.

Wakatsuki Reijirō *Kofūan kaikoroku*. Tokyo: Yomiuri shinbunsha, 1950.

Yamamuro Shin'ichi. *Hōsei kanryō no jidai*. Tokyo: Bokutakusha, 1999.

Yamamoto Shirō. *Hara Takashi*. Tokyo: Tōkyō sōgensha, n.d.

Yutaka Tezuka. *Meiji hōgaku kyōikushi no kenkyū*. Tokyo: Keiō tsūshin, 1988.

Chapter 5

Banno Junji. *Meiji kenpō taisei no kakuritsu*. Tokyo: Tōkyō daigaku shuppankai, 1971.

Banno Junji. *Taishō seihen*. Kyoto: Mineruva shobō, 1994.

Chiba Isao. 'Taishō seihen to Katsura shintō'. In *Nihon seiji shi no shin chihei*, edited by Sakamoto Kazuto and Iokibe Kaoru. Yoshida shoten, 2013, pp. 203–232.

Chiba Isao. *Katsura Tarō*. Tokyo: Chūkō shinsho. 2012.

Fushimi Taketo. 'Kokka zaisei tōgōsha to shite no naikaku sōri daijin'. *Kokka gakkai zasshi* 120, no. 12 (2007), pp. 910–975.

Hamaguchi Fujiko, ed. *Zuisōroku*. Tokyo: Sanseidō, 1931.

Hara Keiichirō, ed. *Hara Takashi nikki*. Tokyo: Fukumura shuppan, 1965.

Hata Isoko, ed. *Hata Toyosuke*. Hata Isoko, 1935.

Itō Takashi, ed. *Taishō shoki Yamagata Aritomo danwa hikki: seihen omoidegusa*. Tokyo: Yamakawa shuppansha, 1981.

Itō Yukio. *Rikken kokka no kakuritsu to Itō Hirobumi*. Tokyo: Yoshikawa kōbunkan, 1999.

Itō Yukio. *Rikken kokka to Nichiro sensō*. Tokyo: Bokutakusha, 2000.

Katsura Tarō. *Katsura Tarō jiden*. Tokyo: Heibonsha, 2008.

Kagawa Etsuji. *Ōura Kanetake den*. Tokyo: Hakubunkan, 1921.

Katō Masanosuke, ed. *Rikken minseitō shi*, 2 vols. n.p., 1935.

Kikuchi Gorō. *Rikken seiyūkai hōkoku shi*, 2 vols. Tokyo: Rikken seiyūkai hōkokushi hensanbu, 1931.

Kitaoka Shin'ichi. *Kanryōsei to shite no Nihon rikugun*. Tokyo: Chikuma shobō, 2012.

Maeda Renzan. *Tokonami Takejirō den*. Tokyo: Tokonami Takejirō denki kankōkai, 1939.

Matsunami Niichirō, ed. *Mizuno Hakushi koki kinnen ronsaku to zuihitsu*. Tokyo: Mizuno Rentarō sensei koki shukugakai jimusho, 1937.

Mikuriya Takashi. *Meiji kokka no kansei*. Tokyo: Chūō kōron shinsha, 2001.

Mitani Taichirō. *Nihon seitō seiji no keisei*. Tokyo: Tōkyō daigaku shuppankai, 1995.

Miyachi Masato. *Nichiro sengo seiji shi no kenkyū*. Tokyo: Tōkyō daigaku shuppankai, 1973.

Mizuno Rentarō. *Tazan no ishi*. Tokyo: Shimizu shoten, 1909.

Mori Yasuo. *Nihon rikugun to Nitchū sensō e no michi*. Kyoto: Mineruva shobō, 2010.

Nagai Kazu. *Kindai Nihon no gunbu to seiji*. Kyoto: Shibunkaku shuppan, 1993.

Ōishi Makoto. *Kenpō chitsujo e no tenbō*. Tokyo: Yūhikaku, 2008.

Sakamoto Kazuto. 'Meiji nijūni nen no naikaku kansei ni tsuite no ichikōsatsu'. In Inuzuka Takaaki, ed., *Meiji kokka no seisaku to shisō*. Tokyo: Yoshikawa kōbunkan, 2005, pp. 141–171.

Sanpōkai, ed. *Sanpō Shimooka chūji den*. Tokyo: Mitsuminekai, 1930.

Sasakawa Tamon, ed. *Matsuda Masahisa kō*. Tokyo: Kōsonkai, 1938.

Sasaki Takashi. *Hanbatsu seifu to rikken seiji*. Tokyo: Yoshikawa kōbunkan, 1992.

Shimizu Yuichirō. *Seitō to kanryō no kindai: Nihon ni okeru rikken tōchi kōzō no sōkoku*. Tokyo: Fujiwara shoten, 2007.

Shōyū Kurabu, ed. *Yamagata Aritomo kankei monjo*, vol. 2. Tokyo: Yamakawa shuppansha, 2006.

Shōyū Kurabu and Nishio Rintarō, eds. *Mizuno Rentarō kaisōroku, kankei bunsho*. Tokyo: Yamakawa shuppansha, 1999.

Soeda, 'Gōdō no seishin', *Kenseitō tōhō* 4 (1898).

Takii Kazuhiro. *Itō Hirobumi*. Tokyo: Chūkō shinsho, 2010.

Toriumi Yasushi, Mitani Hiroshi, Nishikawa Makoto, Yano Nobuyuki, eds. *Nihon rikken seiji no keisei to henshitsu*. Tokyo: Yoshikawa kōbunkan, 2005.

Wakatsuki Reijirō. *Kofūan kaikoroku*. Tokyo: Yomiuri shinbunsha, 1950.

Wakatsuki Tsuyoshi. '"Hōka henchō" hihan no tenkai to seitō naikaku'. *Shigaku zasshi* 114, no. 3 (2005), pp. 346–369.

Yamazaki Yūkō, Saionji Kinmochi kankei monjo kenkyukai, eds. *Saionji Kinmochi kankei monjo*. Tokyo: Shōkadō shoten, 2012.

Yokoyama Katsutarō, ed. *Kenseikai shi*. Hyōgo: Kenseikai shi hensanjo, 1926.

Chapter 6

Aoki Kazuo. *Waga kyūjūnen no shōgai o kaerimite*. Tokyo: Kōdansha, 1981.

Aoki Tokuzō. *Omoide*. Tokyo: Ōkura zaimu kyōkai, 1966.

Aritake Shūji. *Karasawa Toshiki*. Tokyo: Karasawa Toshiki denki kankōkai, 1975.

Fukunaga Fumio et al., eds. *Ashida Hitoshi nikki*, 2 vols. Tokyo: Kashiwa shobō, 2012.

Hara Yoshimichi. *Bengoshi seikatsu no kaiko*. Tokyo: Hōritsu shinpōsha, 1935.

Hirota Teruyuki. *Rikugun shōkō no kyōiku shakaishi*. Yokohama: Seori shobō, 1997.

Hosojima Yoshimi. *Ningen Yamaoka Mannosuke den*. Tokyo: Kōdansha, 1964.

Iwanaga Yūkichi kun denki hensan iinkai. *Iwanaga Yūkichi kun*. Iwanaga Yūkichi kun denki hensan iinkai, 1941.

Isawa Takio denki hensan iinkai. *Isawa Takio*. Tokyo: Haneda shoten, 1951.

Kawai Yoshinari. *Meiji no ichi seinen zō*. Tokyo: Kōdansha, 1969.

Kawanishi Jitsuzō. *Kanmeiroku*. Tokyo: Shakai hoken shinpōsha, 1974.

Kita Ikki. *Bunkan shigan yōran*. Tokyo: Kenshūkai, 1901.

Kondō Jōtarō tsuisō henshū iinkai, ed. *Tsuisō Kondō Jōtarō*. Kondō Jōtarō tsuisō henshū iinkai, 1980.

Maruyama Tsurukichi. *Gojūnen tokoro dokoro*. Tokyo: Dai Nihon yūbenkai kōdansha, 1935.

Masumi Junnosuke. *Nihon seitō shi ron*, vol. 4. Tokyo: Tōkyō daigaku shuppankai, 1968.

Mitani Taiichirō. *Taishō demokurashii ron*, new edn. Tokyo: Tōkyō daigaku shuppankai, 1995.

Mori Ariyoshi. *Seinen to ayumu Gotō Fumio*. Tokyo: Nihon seinenkan, 1979.

Naiseishi Kenkyūkai, ed. *Abe Genki shi danwa sokkiroku*. Tokyo: Naiseishi kenkyūkai, 1967.

Naiseishi Kenkyūkai, ed. *Aoki Tokuzō shi danwa sokkiroku*. Tokyo: Naiseishi kenkyūkai, 1964.

Naiseishi Kenkyūkai, ed. *Gotō Fumio shi danwa sokkiroku*. Tokyo: Naiseishi kenkyūkai, 1963.

Naiseishi Kenkyūkai, ed. *Hoshino Naoki shi danwa sokkiroku*. Tokyo: Naiseishi kenkyūkai, 1964.

Naiseishi Kenkyūkai, ed. *Iinuma Kazumi shi danwa sokkiroku*. Tokyo: Naiseishi kenkyūkai, 1969.

Naiseishi Kenkyūkai, ed. *Kawanishi Jitsuzō shi danwa sokkiroku*. Tokyo: Naiseishi kenkyūkai, 1964.

Naiseishi Kenkyūkai, ed. *Matsumoto Gaku shi danwa sokkiroku*. Tokyo: Naiseishi kenkyūkai, 1967.

Naiseishi Kenkyūkai, ed. *Matsumoto Manabu shi danwa sokkiroku*. Tokyo: Naiseishi kenkyūkai, 1967.

Naiseishi Kenkyūkai, ed. *Yasui Eiji shi danwa sokkiroku*. Tokyo: Naiseishi kenkyūkai, 1964.

Nakano Minoru. *Tōkyō daigaku monogatari*. Tokyo: Yoshikawa kōbunkan, 1999.

Nakasuji Naoya. *Gunshū no ibasho*. Tokyo: Shin'yōsha, 2005.

Odaira Katsue, ed. *Daiichiji taisen go no Doitsu – Yasui Seiichirō no Doitsu ryūgaku nikki yori*. Odaira Katsue, 1986.

Ogawa Heikichi kankei monjo kenkyūkai, ed. *Ogawa Heikichi kankei monjo*, vol. 1. Tokyo: Misuzu shobō, 1973.

Okamoto Makiko. *Shokuminchi kanryō no seijishi*. Tokyo: Sangensha, 2008.

Oku Kentarō. *Shōwa senzenki Rikken Seiyūkai no kenkyū*. Tokyo: Keiō gijuku daigaku shuppankai, 2004.

Ōnishi Hiroshi, ed. *Isawa Takio to kindai Nihon*. Tokyo: Fuyō shobō shuppan, 2003.

Shimizu Yuichirō. 'Kindai Nihon kanryōsei ni okeru kyōtō no keisei to tenkai'. In *Naganoken kindai minshūshi no shomondai*, edited by Nagano-ken kindaishi kenkyūkai. Nagano: Ryūhō shobō, 2008, pp. 121–154.

Takeuchi Yō. *Gakureki kizoku no eikō to zasetsu*. Tokyo: Chūō kōron shinsha, 1999.

Yoshino Sakuzō. *Shiken seikō hō*. Ibaraki: Seizansha, 2000.

Index